# THE EVERYDAY POLITICS OF RESOURCES

A volume in the series

## Cornell Series on Land: New Perspectives on Territory, Development, and Environment

*Edited by Wendy Wolford, Nancy Lee Peluso, and Michael Goldman*

A list of titles in this series is available at cornellpress.cornell.edu.

# THE EVERYDAY POLITICS OF RESOURCES

## LIVES AND LANDSCAPES IN NORTHWEST VIETNAM

### NGA DAO

CORNELL UNIVERSITY PRESS
*Ithaca and London*

First published 2025 by Cornell University Press

Library of Congress Cataloging-in-Publication Data

Names: Dao, Nga, author.
Title: The everyday politics of resources : lives and landscapes in northwest Vietnam / Nga Dao.
Description: Ithaca : Cornell University Press, 2025. | Series: Cornell series on land : new perspectives on territory, development, and environment | Includes bibliographical references and index.
Identifiers: LCCN 2024042490 (print) | LCCN 2024042491 (ebook) | ISBN 9781501780868 (hardcover) | ISBN 9781501780875 (paperback) | ISBN 9781501780882 (pdf) | ISBN 9781501780899 (epub)
Subjects: LCSH: Natural resources—Government policy—Vietnam, Northwestern. | Rural development—Vietnam, Northwestern. | Economic development projects—Social aspects—Vietnam, Northwestern. | Land use, Rural—Government policy—Vietnam, Northwestern. | Political ecology—Vietnam, Northwestern. | Rubber plantations—Government policy—Vietnam, Northwestern. | Water resources development—Government policy—Vietnam, Northwestern. | Mines and mineral resources—Government policy—Vietnam, Northwestern. | Forced migration—Social aspects—Vietnam, Northwestern. | Vietnam—Economic policy—1975-
Classification: LCC HC444.Z65 D36 2025 (print) | LCC HC444.Z65 (ebook) | DDC 333.709597/1—dc23/eng/20241121
LC record available at https://lccn.loc.gov/2024042490
LC ebook record available at https://lccn.loc.gov/2024042491

*To my parents and the northwesterners*

# CONTENTS

# PREFACE

When I first arrived as a researcher in the Northwest in 2004, Sơn La Dam and its associated resettlement was seemingly the only topic of conversation. However, the northwestern region of Vietnam had become not only the country's largest center of hydropower but had also seen the conversion of tens of thousands of hectares of farm and forestland into rubber plantations and hundreds of mines. Houses and farmland belonging to hundreds of thousands of people had been appropriated by both public and private investors to make way for dams, rubber plantations, and mining operations. While infrastructure had been improved with better roads, bridges, and schools, and some groups were economic beneficiaries of these territorial production projects, many more had experienced hardships and even become impoverished because of uneven development. I examine these processes in this book.

This book unpacks entanglements of various territorializations and their influence on everyday politics through three types of resource production/extraction—dams, plantations, and mines. These development processes have transformed agrarian landscapes and differentiated northwestern subjects. Drawing on my experience of more than twenty years working and researching in the Northwest, I trace how resource territorial subjects have emerged out of the politics over each sort of resource extraction and the ways the state has territorialized those sites in the course of development and modernization. I also show how processes of differentiation unfold among people who started from similar political and economic positions. For villagers in the Northwest affected by these types of development projects, changes in the nature and intensity of market integration as well as in production relations (changes in control of and access to labor and capital) are key driving forces for differentiation in these locales.

Based primarily on qualitative methods, this book offers a historical ethnography of a region where uneven development plays out along class, resource, and gender lines, and where ethnicity is shown in some cases to be malleable and in other cases to have hardened.[1] I show how ethnic difference is both reproduced and undermined through the centralizing and assimilatory processes of the Vietnamese Communist Party's nation-state-building projects, including development initiatives. This book also examines local responses among peasants and small farmers to uneven development and dispossession in rural areas, scrutinizing the agency they have and their decisions to compromise or resist.[2]

For my research in the Northwest, I use a political ecology lens to examine development and territorialization and to explore everyday dimensions of resource inequality produced by social and power relations, as well as critically assess dominant framings when decisions on resources are made.[3] Political ecology works across scale and recognizes multiple actors as having material impacts on landscape and livelihoods.[4] It helps me to understand how the lives of northwestern people have been shaped and reshaped by decision-makers in Hanoi, hundreds of kilometers away, regardless of whether they are Kinh or from other ethnic groups. My approach to political ecology draws together two processes: first, the production and transformation of landscapes, and second, subject formation of local people in contexts of increasing pressure on land, rural economic diversification, intensified migration flows, depeasantization, and environmental degradation.

Ethnographic analysis is a powerful tool that helps researchers make sense of realities and understand the production of place and its subjects as well as the state's power as experienced by local villagers. For me, ethnographic research changed my assumptions about development in the Northwest, opening up opportunities for generating new knowledge and connections. My interest in the Northwest grew out of the stories that my father told me of the region during my childhood. I did not have the opportunity to travel to the Northwest until 2004, when I began researching the displacement caused by the Sơn La Dam, the largest hydropower dam in Vietnam. Conducting research in upland regions of Vietnam, especially on topics like hydropower, rubber plantations, and mining, has been a challenging task, given the myriad rules at various levels of government, as well as the restrictions that come with researching sensitive industries.

A Vietnamese saying suggests "in a gourd (be) round, in a tube (be) long." In fact, every time we encounter a new subject, we reposition ourselves. Being Vietnamese, I encounter advantages and disadvantages when I conduct research in my own country. The advantages include a network of people and a language that I know, geographical locations that I am familiar with, and information to which I have access. However, the disadvantages are not negligible. I can be more vulnerable and exposed to higher risk than a foreigner when conducting research on so-called sensitive topics. For foreign researchers, if the government does not want them to conduct research on certain topics, it simply denies permission to access a site or related information. If the researcher does anything that displeases the government, that researcher may have to leave the country and may not receive a visa in the future. For domestic researchers, the risk level escalates. As most of my research topics in the Northwest concern controversial issues, I have always had a difficult time obtaining permission to conduct fieldwork and have had to take care with what questions I ask of whom.

Social power is not always visible and tangible, but the distinction between the uplands and the lowlands can make power appear more conspicuously, especially in the ways development processes work.[5] In general, lowland Vietnamese set the dominant narrative and see the uplands as poor and backward. Uplanders, while having never openly resisted the dominant narrative, remain proud of their land and traditions. Working within Vietnam's upland and lowland distinctions has helped me to understand both places better through my concern over lowland-upland power imbalances. I am Kinh Vietnamese, and in many ways I have gone through a process of transformation in conducting this research. Even though I cannot change certain things about myself, including the facts that I am a female, lowland Kinh Vietnamese, and a mother of two children, my life experience, and the relationships that I have built with people in the Northwest, have shifted my positionality over time. I first traveled to the Northwest with an interest in development and the aim of helping lift people out of poverty. In regard to my upbringing and education, my perspective on the Northwest, its land, and its people was in line with the dominant perspective in Vietnam. Gradually, though, I came to realize how the very development narrative driving my own interest was part of the hegemonic development project that was reproducing poverty, among other things. How could I reconcile the sense that many of the projects displacing the people in Sơn La, Lai Châu, and Điện Biên were devised and implemented by the Vietnamese developmentalist state with my own earlier-held beliefs that people in the Northwest needed more access to development?

In addition to an extensive use of secondary data, including newspapers and lived stories, academic research, and archival research, this book has relied on twenty years of research experience in the Northwest. I have traveled to the Northwest numerous times since the early 2000s, staying for varying lengths of time that total more than three years. Most of my time was spent with villagers who were displaced by the Sơn La hydropower dam, lost their land to make way for rubber plantations in Sơn La Province, or were affected by mining activities. Even though the Northwest became familiar to me in many ways, I am still an outsider to the northwesterners, just like everyone from outside the region. I can share and sympathize with their feelings, but their experience is not my own. Nevertheless, the boundaries between insider and outsider constantly shift. Given the large number of lowlanders migrating to the uplands, for example, the question of who is an insider and who is an outsider remains salient.

As someone coming from Hanoi—the same center of power that has for so long imposed its vision of development onto the Northwest—working to fit into the local environment was not easy. But it is precisely because it was so difficult that I have come to appreciate my various ethnographic experiences. Long-term, embedded methods of ethnography have offered insights into the effects of various projects on the agrarian landscape more broadly, as well as on food security in the villages. They helped me to understand connections between old and new villages and among villagers.

My focus when I began traveling to the Northwest as a researcher in April 2004 was how to build trust and maintain positive relationships with the ethnic minority people whom I met and who shared their stories with me.[6] Many of them became close friends whom I visit every time that I am in the region. During that first trip, I was affiliated with the Institute of Ecological Economy, a nongovernmental organization (NGO) that was conducting research on a pilot resettlement site for those displaced by the Sơn La hydropower dam in Muong Ta commune, Sơn La Province. This study was the first research conducted on the impacts of the Sơn La Dam on ethnic minority people in the Northwest. A year later, the headman who helped us with our research—and who remains a good friend today—lost his position after he became vocal about the hardships that his fellow villagers had suffered following resettlement. For the first time, I became deeply aware of the risks associated with conducting research, not just the potential risks for me but, more important, the risks for the people I encounter and who support me in my research. In 2005, I was among a group of researchers from the Vietnam Union of Science and Technology Associations (VUSTA) who conducted larger-scale research on displacement related to the Sơn La Dam. We traveled for two months and interviewed villagers in twenty-five locales across Sơn La, Lai Châu, and Điện Biên Provinces. This was when I first met my friends Khun, Hin, and E (all names of individuals and villages are pseudonyms, including in any references where the actual place is named). I have returned to the region to conduct follow-up research almost every year, embracing opportunities to learn more about their lives; I maintain good relationships with each of them. My position changed in 2008 when I returned as a graduate student associated with a Canadian university. After a few weeks of struggle, with support from a friend who worked for the Institute of Ethnology, a national research institute, I secured the necessary permission to conduct research. Since this experience, I learned to be careful in the research questions that I designed, and to carefully select who would accompany and assist me in the field. Even though I was no longer an NGO-affiliated researcher, I did not wish to damage the relationships I had built with Khun and other villagers during my previous trips.

Among my many trips, I stayed the longest at Khun's house. Although Khun is married, she spent most of her time at home by herself. Before retiring in 2019, her husband was an elementary school teacher who taught far from home at a school in a mountainous village of Hmông people. As a result, he was only home every other weekend when I was there. Her three sons, who were in high school at the time, were rarely home during the day. Her oldest child, a daughter, had married a man from a different commune and moved to his house three years previously in 2006. As a result, I could spend lot of time talking to Khun. She is my friend, an interpreter, and has been a wonderful guide for me in learning their culture. She taught me how to speak their language, Thái Đen (Black Thái/Tai). Unfortunately, I could manage only basic conversation, not enough for interviews. Nonetheless, this basic language skill helped me to understand the villagers' daily lives. Khun showed me around the village, took me to visit different homes, and even introduced me to families in the neighboring villages. During the fieldwork I tried to interview villagers in their language (with Khun's help) whenever possible, as I was aware that having people give their responses not in their languages also meant erasing their ability to express (and think of) themselves in their own languages. At the same time, I also understood the downside of using an interpreter, because content might vary with interpretation. I was grateful to have Khun as my gatekeeper in Muong Lanh and neighboring villages. According to Khun, the fact that I was married and had children made me mature and trustworthy, while being associated with a Canadian university earned me respect in her community.

Staying at Khun's house had its advantages and disadvantages. Since Khun was the village Women's Union representative, she knew many people.[7] She could connect me with women not just in her village but in the neighboring villages as well. In the meantime, I worried that other villagers might not be open about their concerns because of Khun's role. Luckily, villagers did not seem to care about any potential risk, and some even asked me to share their stories as widely as possible, hoping that their experiences might help to bring about policy change. Many showed me copies of letters that they had sent to the authorities and to Sơn La hydropower project's Resettlement Management Board complaining about unfair compensation that they received. When I came to stay in the region for four months in 2009, everyone in Muong Lanh village knew my name and why I was there; this made it so much easier for me in my daily work, as I could tag along to help in the field or drop by their houses when they had time to talk.

In villages like Khun's, I had the benefit of being able to connect with the women and had a greater chance to learn about their lives. Once the women knew that I had two children, they asked me many questions about my kids: How old are they? Which grade are they in? and so forth. These women spent a long time talking about their children, and they were very interested in how I raised and taught my children. From conversations about children, we could go on to talk about other things: their lives before the dam and the plantations, how things had changed without access to the river or land, and their concerns about land shortage and adaptation to a new life.

Staying in the village helped me to establish ongoing, mutual interaction with the villagers. As they were all curious about what I was doing and possibly hoping that I could somehow help them channel their concerns to higher levels of government, they were friendly and open to my questions. Many times people stopped by very early in the morning to say hello or talk to me before they went to the field; or I went over to their houses for a chat after their nap time in the afternoon. It was easy to interact with the women. I could help them with some of their work, like drying cassava or cleaning corn cobs, while chatting. They often told me about their lives on their old land, before the changes happened, about children, about other villagers, and about the difficulties they faced when they relocated or joined rubber plantations as paid workers.

Revisiting Muong Lanh and other neighboring villages of Muong Muon commune almost every year has offered insights unobtainable from a onetime visit. In revisiting sites, I have witnessed villagers' struggles and the ways they have coped with the changes in their lives. If I were not in Muong Lanh and Muong Muon in 2005 when the first ten families moved to their new village, had I not returned to visit almost every year since then, or had I not visited the rubber plantations in Muong Ma and Muong Che villages of the same commune for the first time in 2009, it would not have been possible for me to understand how much these resettlers/villagers have had to endure. Each visit brought out something new about people's lives. Sometimes there was good news, other times sad.

As my work first focused on dam-induced displacement, I spent more time with displaced communities, but a number of these villages were also affected by the establishment of rubber plantations. In such circumstances, I was able to conduct surveys and undertake hundreds of semistructured interviews with villagers over the years on both dam and rubber plantation issues. I also conducted surveys about lives before and after the resettlement with 123 dam-displaced households in Muong Lanh and Muong Nhuong villages in 2009. For households impacted by rubber plantations in Muong Tro, Muong Ma, and Muong Che villages, I surveyed seventy-five households a number of times (2009, 2014, 2016, 2017, and 2019). For these surveys and group discussions, I was joined by one of two research assistants—Lien or Thuy. When I was conducting research on resettlement, government officials tended to take me seriously during interviews, probably because they saw that I was affiliated with the Institute of Ethnology. I heard from acquaintances that local government officials also often equated my age to my trustworthiness, commenting, "Oh, she is a mature researcher, she won't cause any trouble." In the back of my mind, I have been attentive to the fact that writing about my research informants' concerns may cause controversy. For my research on rubber plantations, government officials' reactions have varied. Some officials were very open about their concerns and opposition to the project, while others were very reluctant and suspicious of my interviews. In general, officials at the lower levels—district and commune—tended to be more open and willing to share their thoughts and opinions compared to those who worked for the provinces. Because of the sensitive nature of extractive activities, I was granted only limited opportunities to conduct interviews with those who were impacted by mining. Reports and documents related to the issue have also been very difficult to obtain. Government officials at all levels often avoided my requests for interviews to discuss the impacts of mining on local people. As my interest in mining also developed later, I did not have the same length of stay with mining-affected communities as I did with villagers in Muong Lanh, Muong Nhuong, Muong Ma, or Muong Che. Because of travel restrictions due to COVID-19, fieldwork and in-person interviews in 2020 and 2021 were difficult. I had to rely on my research assistant Lien for updated information. This reality limited this book's section on mining. The Sin Quyen mining case addresses the labor situation prior to a mine collapse accident that happened in 2022. The accident led to a strong change in opinion of the local people about working in the mine, a shift that postdates the research for this book.

# ACKNOWLEDGMENTS

This book was almost two decades in the making. I owe a great debt to the many people who have shared their life stories with me—those I have spent much time beside or simply crossed paths with during my trips. They have made my research in the Northwest possible and continue to inspire me with their integrity and generosity. I dedicate this work to them.

I would like to share my deepest thanks to my advisory committee at York University, who guided and encouraged me and provided me intellectual support throughout my learning journey there. Peter Vandergeest was and is a model of scholarly research for me. Robin Roth and Libby Lunstrum provided encouragement and critical feedback. Special thanks to Jun Borras, Erik Harm, and Christian Lentz, who have spent much of their time reading and commenting on different chapters of my early drafts. They all have shaped my writing and thinking in significant ways. Since I joined the Department of Social Science at York University, I have found a very supportive intellectual community. I am grateful to Pablo Idahosa, Vanessa Lamb, Sonya Scott, and Salewa Olawoye, who have offered valuable feedback at different stages.

Vietnamese colleagues from the Vietnam Rivers Network, the Center for Water Resources Conservation and Development, the Institute of Ecological Economy, and the Institute of Ethnology have also shaped the research and manuscript in important ways. I thank Trần Văn Hà, Nguyễn Thị Ngọc Lan, Vũ Phương Anh, Nguyễn Vi Linh, Trần Đình Sính, Cao Việt Hưng, Phil Hirsch, Bruce Shoemaker, Ian Baird, Carl Middleton, Steve Coffin, Christie Coffin, Jun-Li Wang, David Davies, Đào Trọng Tứ, Đào Thanh Huyền, Nguyễn Mạnh Cường, Nguyễn Duy Chuyên, Đoàn Bổng, Đan Tiếp Phúc, Dương Anh Tuyên, Dương Thanh An, Tô Xuân Phúc, Lê Anh Tuấn, Lâm Thị Thu Sửu, Trịnh Lê Nguyên, Lê Sỹ Thắng, Lê Thị Vân Huệ, Nguyễn Quỳnh Anh, Bùi Hà Ly, Đặng Bảo Nguyệt, Nguy Thị Khanh, Nguyễn Thị Tú Oanh, Nguyễn Đức Anh, Nguyễn Lan Anh, Nguyễn Thị Hiếu, Bùi Liên Phương, Vũ

Hải Linh, Nguyễn Thị Hồng Vân, and Dương Thu Hằng for joining me in many fruitful conversations.

Thank you to Nancy Peluso, Wendy Wolford, and Michael Goldman for supporting this manuscript. I thank the anonymous reviewers for providing constructive comments and much-needed guidance. Their inputs have significantly improved the final shape of this book. I especially thank Alicia Filipowich and Matt Mullins for their meticulous attention to book details and its organization.

My research would not be possible without the generous support of various institutions. The Challenges of the Agrarian Transition in Southeast Asia (ChATSEA) award for dissertation fieldwork, York University's Faculty of Graduate Studies' fieldwork fund, the International Development Research Centre (IDRC) Doctoral Dissertation Fieldwork award, the Social Science and Humanities Research Council (SSHRC) Doctoral Research Fellowship, and an Ontario Graduate Scholarship provided crucial support. I also received a York University LA&PS minor research grant, York University's SSHRC explore grant, and a SSHRC Insight Development Grant.

Portions of chapters 2 and 3 were previously published as "Damming Rivers in Vietnam: A Lesson Learned in the Tây Bắc (Northwest) Region," *Journal for Vietnamese Studies* 6, no. 2 (2011); "Dam Development in Vietnam: The Evolution of Dam-Induced Resettlement Policy," *Water Alternatives* 3, no. 2 (2010); and "Political Responses to Dam-Induced Resettlement in Northern Uplands Vietnam," *Journal of Agrarian Change* 16, no. 2 (2016). Portions of chapter 5 were previously published as "Rubber Plantations in the Northwest: Rethinking the Concept of Land Grab in Vietnam," *Journal of Peasant Studies* 42, no. 2 (2015). Portions of chapter 6 were previously published as "Rubber Plantations and Their Implications on Gender Roles and Relations in Northern Uplands Vietnam," *Journal of Gender, Place & Culture* 25, no. 11 (2018).

Finally, I thank my family for their unconditional love and support throughout the years. Thanks to my father, who nurtured my love for the Northwest, and to my mother, who taught me to respect and appreciate diversity. I am grateful to Thanh for his love, humor, and patience, and for his willingness to take care of the kids when I was away for long periods of fieldwork every year, as well as to my daughter Linh San and my son Minh Khoa, who bring joy to my life and give me the energy to pursue my dreams.

# THE EVERYDAY POLITICS OF RESOURCES

# Introduction

*Resources, Territory, and Everyday Politics in Contemporary Vietnam*

On the bus back to Hanoi one day in June 2019, I was sitting next to a middle-aged woman from Sơn La. She was taking the long bus ride to visit her son and daughter-in-law who had left the village two years ago to work for a garment company in Bắc Ninh Province in the Red River delta, leaving their two children with the woman and her husband. During our four-hour shared ride, she told me about her life and her family. The son and his wife were only able to return to visit once every few weeks. This time she had to go to visit them because her daughter-in-law was sick. Before we said our goodbyes at the bus terminal in the capital, she told me, "I am hopeful that my son and his wife will save enough money to buy a piece of land to farm on one day in the near future. So they can go back to our village. I also hope our government will soon have good policies, either to give back the land to people or help us with more sustainable livelihoods so no young people, including my grandchildren, will be forced to leave their villages against their will."

Her family's story is like that of tens of thousands of other families in Vietnam's Northwest region. Because of land shortages caused by development projects such as large hydropower dams, rubber plantations, or mining, family members have had to out-migrate in search of employment. While these three different forms of resource extraction

1

for development in the Northwest have altered villagers' relationships with the land, forests, rivers, and one another, they have also created what can be called new "resource territorial subjects"—peasants without land and fishermen without access to rivers—who are in a constant mode of becoming rather than being. For northwestern peasants, becoming resource territorial subjects often means becoming landless or jobless, becoming migrant workers, marginal farmers, rubber workers, fighters, miners, store owners, debt owners, or, sometimes, alcoholics and drug users. My argument throughout this book is that materialities matter, the nature and institutional implementation of resource extraction matter, as do people's relationship with land and their everyday struggles for livelihoods. While the technologies of production dramatically affect the landscape and people of the Northwest, each distinct form of extraction nonetheless bears its unique set of impacts on local materialities, making territorialization on the ground different, depending on the industry. As upland farmers transform into landless laborers, northwesterners' agency, ethnicity, and differentiated experiences of development further complicate the process of territorial subject formation—an ongoing process that tightly links to everyday life and activities. This book centers these complexes within an analysis of state power, everyday politics of resource territories, narratives of development, and profound environmental change.

Situated along the Black River, the Northwest region (Tây Bắc) of Vietnam shares borders with the People's Republic of China and the Lao People's Democratic Republic (Lao PDR, or Laos). The region is characterized by ecological and cultural diversity and is home to approximately twenty ethnic groups, including Thái, Mường, Khmú, Dao, La Ha, and Hmông peoples. Because it is the homeland for many ethnic minority groups, the government has highlighted the Northwest in national policies as a strategic region for development, an approach that will be detailed in chapter 1. After the war with France ended in 1954, the government of North Vietnam chose the Northwest as the area to locate and develop the first state farms. In parallel with their establishment were state-led campaigns for socialist agricultural collectivization, fixed cultivation and sedentarization, and encouraging migration from the lowlands to the uplands. All these programs were entangled and reinforced processes of frontier expansion and landscape transformation. Northwest uplanders, while negotiating these policies, struggled to integrate into the new Democratic Republic of Vietnam.[1]

In 1986, the Communist Party of Vietnam's Sixth National Congress initiated the country's economic reforms—"Đổi Mới" in Vietnamese. These reforms both introduced a greater role for market forces for the coordination of economic activity between enterprises and government agencies, and allowed for private ownership of small enterprises and for the creation of a stock exchange for both state and nonstate enterprises. The reforms also include a reduction of government subsidies for social services and an ambitious public investment program aimed at improving productivity of "barren" land.[2] The introduction of a market economy with a socialist orientation sought to recognize the broad range of institutions and practices that have enabled varied forms of socialism, capitalism, and neoliberalism. Similar to reform efforts in China and other socialist countries in Eastern Europe, Đổi Mới reflects distinct continuities between past and present economic and cultural conditions that have stimulated "shifting and geographically variable recombinations of socialist and market initiatives."[3] These reforms have played a critical role in enabling the expansion of capitalism into frontier areas. In parallel with the expansion of capitalism to the northwestern frontiers, the reality for ethnic minorities has evolved into what I describe as a type of marginalizing integration, or exclusion through inclusion.

This book explores everyday politics that link to state territorialization via the natural resources development that has been taking place in the Northwest region of Vietnam from Đổi Mới in 1986 to the present. It is about the lives of people like the woman on the bus, her family, and their struggles to adapt to or resist changes imposed on them by the state and its elites. Each of the three key material transformations—hydropower, rubber plantations, and mining—reveals unequal power relations and complexity in everyday politics associated with state-building and the Northwest's development.

Tracing development policies and practices, state territorialization, and everyday politics in the Northwest leads me to pose the following key questions: How do different resource materialities contribute to different forms of state territorialization? How do the politics of everyday life associated with changes in resource extraction and access bring about differentiation within local communities? Why did villagers agree to give away their land for dams, rubber plantations, and mines, and how did they respond to the resulting changes? To answer these questions, I will explore territorialization as it is both imposed by various state agencies and actors and emergent through everyday politics;

the latter are enacted by the people subjected to different means and modes of territorialization for natural resource development.

This book examines the state through its different agencies and technologies of state resource control—dams, plantations, and mines—each with a distinctive relationship to or effect on the land in which massive resource extraction takes place. It reveals how political technologies and particular resource materialities produce territories, including territories with diverse material features and resource users whose agency becomes arrayed rather than shattered by government.[4] The stories about how these realities play out together in varied resource production and extraction areas are part and parcel of how state and other forms of territorialization emerge out of new relationships between the state, extractive processes and technologies, and people like Khun (see preface) and the woman on the bus who are affected by them. In short, I aim to explore how the creation of resource territories enables various forms of everyday politics and produces new territorial subjects and different beneficiaries. I also examine how new territorial subjects are produced through hydropower, rubber plantation, and mining, and how different actors—not just the state—take part in subject making. I reveal how ethnic minority people have actively engaged in everyday politics in their daily lives and activities through compromise, desire and aspiration, market engagement, and livelihood diversification as much as resistance.[5]

The book shows how the recent forced out-migration of many young ethnic minorities from the Northwest to different provinces in the Red River delta in search of employment reverses circumstances in earlier decades, and though not explored in most other research on territorialization and everyday politics in Vietnam, this reversal emphasizes the contradictory nature of development as a hegemonic project. Indeed, this new direction of labor mobility from upland to lowland plays a critical role in territorialization, further naturalizing the region's inclusion into the nation state. Similar to efforts in other Asian countries such as China or India, the Vietnamese government has been promoting temporary rural-to-urban migration as an important tool in alleviating poverty and enabling social mobility for the rural population.[6] Until recently, however, it was rare for people from upland ethnic minorities to migrate to the lowlands for temporary work. Most often, they did so only because they had no other options.

In the following sections, I will introduce three key processes that will be the core theoretical axes of the book—territorialization, development, and everyday politics—together with the important intersecting processes of landscape production, nation building, and subject formation and differentiation.

## Territorialization and the Production of Landscape

Territorialization, according to Vandergeest and Peluso, is a resource control strategy that involves the categorization of particular areas with the aim of regulating people and resources.[7] It is at the same time a process for coproducing resources and resource territories, such as political forests, while also contributing to the racialization of the population by differentiated resource access.[8] Emily Yeh explains how when territory and subjectivity are imposed by an authoritarian, socialist state, territorialization can be understood as a "deeply material and embodied process that involves the transformation of both subjectivities and landscapes."[9] Territorialization, in my view, is a process made visible in the creation of systems of resource control that are closely linked to the production of new frontiers when resources are discovered, invented, or claimed, often through the deployment of new extractive technologies.[10] Territorialization, however, is not just about resource control but also produces the resources—plantations, forests, etc. Territorialization involves remaking identities through formal classifications and transforming people's lives in ways that also change the practices through which they produce ethnic, gender, and other identities. The frontiers here, in the broad sense, represent the discovery or invention of new resources. Frontier spaces are closely connected to commodification of nature through multiple forms of dispossession, including land grabbing, water grabbing, and accumulations. A cycle of "frontier-territorialization-frontier-territorialization," as Rasmussen and Lund argue, reconfigures socioecological relations and challenges existing institutional arrangements in a nonlinear way.[11] In the creation of Northwest frontiers, this involves shifting dynamics of the intertwined relationships between natural resources including river, land, minerals, and institutional orders across space and time from household to village, from commune to regional and national levels over the last seventy years.

In my analysis, I argue that territorialization and everyday politics are two distinct but entangled processes. By territorialization in Vietnam's Northwest, I mean the state project of exclusion through inclusion of the Northwest's natural resources and its people into the

country's nation-building priorities. It is, in line with the abovementioned definitions, a process of making territory for making and controlling both resources and subjects. Once uplanders were included
in the nation-state-building process, they became citizens. As the government considered them to be "less developed" when compared to
lowland people, uplanders received government support for economic
development, education, health care, and other infrastructure through
special development programs. Such acts of inclusion, however, came
at a high cost—loss of access for uplanders to the resources that defined
their lives and livelihoods in the past. That very same inclusion has also
excluded them from decision-making related to resources that their
livelihoods have depended on, as well as cut their ties with their ancestors' land and their connection with the river and forest spirits that
northwesterners have lived with but also protected for many generations. I explore not just state territorialization but also how it changes
over time and crosses different activities. State territorialization as a
project of exclusion through inclusion may not be unique to Vietnam
or to the Northwest. I can see its footprints from Thailand to China to
India to Columbia, to Zimbabwe and other places where the cycle of
"frontier-territorialization-frontier-territorialization" has taken hold.[12]

Hydropower dams, rubber plantations, and mining all reflect the relationships between the center and frontiers in the process of making
territory in the Northwest. I see both territories and territorial subjects
as relational and continually produced rather than given.[13] Development planners justify these technologies of state resource control as
fuel for national economic development in general and the development of the upland areas where these new territories are discovered
in particular. The views of developers and investors, especially in the
post–Đổi Mới period, strongly reinforce development planners' justification for dam building. To turn water into electricity, dams displaced
hundreds of thousands of northwesterners—dam-induced territorial
subjects—whose communities were broken apart because of land shortages and were forced to leave their ancestors' home to learn new ways of
living in new places. When China created a new variety of rubber that
thrived on the other side of the border, the Vietnamese government
supported rubber companies to take thousands of hectares of forest
and farmland for rubber plantations to try their luck at home. This
process turned upland ethnic minority peasants into "modern rubber
workers" who struggled to survive without their own farming land.
When minerals were discovered and mined, northwestern territorial

subjects experienced land shortage problems similar to those brought on by dam-induced resettlement and rubber plantations, as they were displaced to make way for the mines. Many of them continue to encounter related challenges, such as air and water pollution. In all these processes, as I'll elaborate on in the following chapters, territorial subjects emerge as state territorialization intersects with everyday politics enacted in different resource sites, where different political ecologies and economies prevail. My study shows how the Vietnamese state's idea of development in place—in the Northwest—fails, as young people, like elsewhere in Southeast Asia, leave for work in cities. This then creates another site for the younger generation to enact new forms of everyday politics created by the land grabbing occurring in their home villages.

Several material landscape transformations have contributed to territorialization in the Northwest. Here I use Don Mitchell's concept of landscapes to refer to the land where people "are living in [it], working with it, and possessing it."[14] But, as Mitchell points out, this sort of landscape tends to get in the way of the dominant power. The question for the dominant power is "how to make the landscape reflect its interest rather than the interests of its inhabitants . . . how landscapes could effectively be taken from their 'owners,' be diverted to a different purpose."[15] Thus, to understand landscape production and transformation requires understanding the subject positions of support, resistance, or compromise of the people who live and work within these places, because not only their labor on the land but also their everyday experience of development plays a crucial role in producing the landscape. Landscapes might seem natural, but they are indeed social products. They contain both material realities and social relations. Investigating struggles in landscape production therefore not only helps to reveal unequal power relations among the actors involved but also unveils how these struggles are at the same time cultural, economic, and political.[16]

Ever since Vietnam's independence from France in 1954, state-led interventions have transformed the Northwest's landscape. First, state farms were formed in 1958 and continued operating through the 1960s and 1970s before their dissolution after market-led reforms in 1986. Meanwhile, collectivization and sedentarization programs in the 1960s, the government-promoted migration of lowland people to the uplands throughout the 1960s and up to the 1980s, and the project of development and economic reforms in the late 1980s have together driven hundreds of thousands of lowland Kinh people to settle in this mountainous region.[17] Second, after the institution of Đổi Mới in 1986, the project of development and market reforms shifted Vietnam from a centrally planned economy into a socialist-oriented market economy, where the socialist state creates partnerships with private companies to promote its market economy. In the Northwest, this process has been accompanied by the acceleration of dam development, rubber plantations, and mining.

In the 1990s and early 2000s, dams were developed at an unprecedented rate, with diversified investors, including public, private, and domestic funders as well as international donors. For development planners, building dams fits a broader strategy to provide energy for national growth and enables this ostensibly poor and backward region to keep pace with lowland industrialization and modernization. However, while hundreds of large and small dams built in the Northwest have largely created jobs for lowland workers and generate electricity to serve large cities in the deltas, the villagers who lost their land for the dams' construction have struggled for survival.[18] Perhaps more than ever, dams and their associated processes of displacement facilitate economic, cultural, and lifestyle changes for the Northwest's upland peoples. New roads and bridges are meant to provide easier access to the region and promote development. But the dams displaced hundreds of thousands of people like Khun's family, cutting their ties to their ancestors' land and eroding community cohesion.

In addition to the displacement caused by dams, the government has appropriated more than fifty thousand hectares of land from ethnic minority households since 2007 for rubber plantations and the construction of processing factories in three Northwest provinces—Sơn La, Lai Châu, and Điện Biên.[19] The provincial governments classified the large area used for rubber plantations as "barren" land. It did not matter that, in reality, fallow land is not empty land; rather, its users had cultivated it in the past and intentionally left it to rest. Land appropriated for rubber plantations in the Northwest included not only the so-called marginal or empty land, but also thousands of hectares of farmland that resettlers had received as compensation for their displacement from land flooded by dams.

Mining development came to the Northwest in a very different way. Unlike the hydropower and rubber plantation developments, where villagers were either induced to move with promises of better roads, schools, access to electricity, and compensation for land losses, or lured with the proposed economic benefits from becoming shareholders in a rubber company, mining arrived with few fancy promises. Villagers' adaptation has been unnecessarily difficult because of the authorities' and mining companies' lack of support. In these cases, the dispossession of collective rights and access to water and land has been equated with processes of privatization or marketization of these resources.

State territorialization via resource-related development projects, unfortunately, is not unique to the Northwest of Vietnam. Similar problems have occurred in many places in the Global South, such as in India's Narmada Valley, at the Bui Dam site in Ghana, on oil palm plantations in West Kalimantan, Indonesia, and at rare earth mining sites in Baotou in China's Inner Mongolia.[20] At all these sites, land conflicts, displacement, deforestation, water degradation, and biodiversity imbalances have occurred in tandem with the conversion of peasants into plantation workers, miners, and migrant laborers. Development-induced displacement, both ex situ displacement (being forced to move out of their homes) and in situ displacement (losing their previous entitlements without being relocated), sheds light on the processes of land dispossession and how development projects such as dams, rubber farming, and mining have reduced labor opportunities, increased indebtedness, and resulted in greater rates of out-migration in the Northwest.[21] In this process, many of the practices that express and actively form a people's ethnic identities are stopped, while new practices of landless laborers replace them.

## Development and Nation-Building

From a very young age, Vietnamese children are taught to see the territorial imaginary geobody of Vietnam as a nation formed in an S-shape, expanding from the northern mountainous region where it borders China to the southern tip of Ca Mau Province in the Mekong delta. Nation, according to Benedict Anderson's definition, is an "imagined political community" where members may have similar interests and "hold in their minds a mental image of their affinity."[22] By emphasizing the notion of nationhood for all Vietnamese people, regardless of their ethnicity, Vietnamese leaders have drawn on a sense of belonging to naturalize a form of postcolonial nationhood. As states make territories and subjects, they gradually turn a diverse group of individuals into a more homogeneous group of political subjects "owing their primary allegiance to the abstract notion of state."[23] Thus, building a nation also means building social subjects who belong to that nation. For the newly established Vietnamese nation in 1945, however, the challenge was that its geobody included many ethnic groups who had no common language and expressed all manner of cultural differences, including farming practices, dress, food, and art.[24] Among these many differences was a very clear divide between the uplands and the lowlands.[25] The Northwest region is named by the state after its location—to the northwest of Hanoi. The term itself implies that the perspective is already a Red River–centric perspective.[26]

While Thái people often refer to themselves as uplanders and to Kinh people as lowlanders, within the region itself many Thái people still consider themselves and are regarded by other ethnic groups, such as Hmông or Khmú, as lowlanders, because the word "lowland" has different meanings in Vietnamese. Lowland refers to a delta as a lower part of a river basin, as well as a valley or mountain foot.[27] Thái people, who reside primarily at the foot of the Northwest's mountains, are both lowlanders and uplanders. Thus, the upland-lowland distinction in the dominant discourse is essentially a political one that is being articulated in a national sense: the Northwest as a whole is the uplands, in contrast to the delta.

In Vietnam, Kinh (lowland people) account for 85.3 percent of the total population (more than eighty-two million people).[28] The other fifty-three ethnic groups are defined by the state as ethnic minorities. According to the Vietnamese nation-story, all ethnicities live in harmony and are united to form the larger Vietnamese family. Within the dominant discourse of unity and harmony, there is an unquestioned principle that lowland people are considered more advanced, even more civilized. This convention considers the upland region and its people backward, and has described uplanders as less developed.[29]

Despite this cultural chauvinism and sense of superiority, Vietnamese leaders of the Kinh ethnic group commonly asserted that they aimed to bring ethnic minorities into the nation and forge a sense of national unity. In a 1946 speech, for example, President Ho Chi Minh clearly highlighted his ideology of nationalism:

> Be they Kinh or Thổ, Mường or Mán, Gia-rai or Ê Đê, Xê Đăng or Ba Na and other ethnic minorities, fellow countrymen are all sons and daughters of Vietnam, blood brothers and sisters. Through thick and thin we share together joy and hardship, and help mutually in any circumstance. . . . The country and the Government are common to all of us. Therefore, our people of all nationalities must unite closely to defend our country and support our

Government. . . . Rivers may dry up and mountains may erode but our unity has never diminished.[30]

According to President Ho, regardless of their ethnicities, all sons and daughters of Vietnam were called to unite, defend the nation against foreign invaders, and build a strong country at all costs. Thus, with the formation of the nation-state and the invocation of landscape, definitions of ethnic minorities and majorities were used along with notions of development and progress. In this context, the concept of development gains its power because it is seen as a fundamental project that works to strengthen the state-led nation-building process.

Soon after the defeat and withdrawal of the French colonial power, President Ho repeated this sentiment in a 1955 speech: "The minorities are now our brothers, and if we want them to progress, want them to develop their culture, then we must wipe out prejudice between the nationalities; we must promote solidarity, and we must love one another like brothers under one roof."[31] In such speeches, Vietnamese leaders regularly asserted that minorities needed the help of lowland Kinh in order to progress and that they could do so by joining in solidarity with the nation. Similarly, documents of the Vietnamese Communist Party articulate a policy to "unify the ethnic groups [of Vietnam] on the foundation of equality and mutual assistance for independence, freedom, and common welfare."[32] However, over time, the political, intellectual, and moral leadership of the dominant, lowland group developed into a form of continuous domination of northwestern peoples and territories. It is worth noting that among fifty-three ethnic minority groups, there are only six groups with populations above one million. They are the Tày, Thái, Mường, Hmông, Khmer, and Nùng, who mostly reside in upland regions. While Thái people are a minority in the nation, in the Northwest they are the majority. However, as a Thái ethnic person joked to me one day in 2009 when I was conducting research on resettlement related to the Sơn La Dam, "Now it's easier to find lowland Kinh people here in Điện Biên than finding ethnic minority people." Laughing, he then recited a very popular phrase that I have heard many times in the region: "Thái Đen, Thái Trắng, Thái Bình—three Thái are in consensus to completely destroy Điện Biên," which, indeed, was modified from a popular slogan in the 1960s and 1970s to encourage lowland people to come to the Northwest: "Thái Đen, Thái Trắng, Thái Bình—three Thái are in consensus to construct Điện Biên."[33]

I argue that such displays of love and brotherhood by the government serve as a thin veil over a wish to incorporate the uplands into a Kinh-centric world. Even though this government's strategy to incorporate the frontiers was not unique to the Northwest—one can easily find similar stories elsewhere in Vietnam and indeed across the globe—the mottos of brotherhood and national interest have been effective ways to construct ethnicity in the service of land appropriation.[34] The seemingly fraternal relationship between the state and ethnic minorities nevertheless is founded on a subordination of the latter to the nation-state's developmental projects. In the Northwest, locals experience the state as a force in its own right, even when it is personalized in the form of cadres and local officials of Kinh or another ethnic background. In this mountainous region, while a small group of powerbrokers with ethnic minority backgrounds (mostly Thái) have been able to take advantage of the changing circumstances, the majority of northwesterners have struggled to cope with changes in the environment, in their access to resources, and in cultural transformations.[35]

Since its independence, the Vietnamese state has passed through multiple political phases, with different foci and priorities, but has portrayed itself throughout as the provider of public services and support to marginalized, ethnic minority groups in mountainous regions.[36] A key original principle of the Vietnamese state that remains unchanged since independence is that the people own the land, which the state manages on the people's behalf.[37] However, the state has created state land through dams, rubber plantations, and mines, expropriating lands once worked and occupied by smallholders who farmed for their own food. The state in this context functions in a similar way to what Antonio Gramsci described as a *sociopolitical order* constituted by a "combination of force and consent which are balanced in varying proportions, without force prevailing too greatly over consent."[38] To understand projects of rule in the Northwest, I draw on Gramsci's notions of state hegemony and the manufacture of consent as a crucial guide, which explains how state power informed consent and fostered conduct.[39] For Gramsci, a combination of these two overlapping spheres—rules through force and rules through consent—always characterizes the state and produces governable subjects in a continued tangling of territorialization and subject formation. He emphasizes that hegemony is both political and economic.[40] I employ two Gramscian insights critical for understanding territorialization and everyday politics in the Northwest: the power of dominant narratives for the interests of the state and its elites, and the constant struggles of subordinate subjects whose interests are politically and ideologically constructed.[41] In the Northwest, government officials and investors (public and private) allied themselves in promoting resource extraction for the "greater good of the nation," which led northwesterners to consent by associating their own interests with national interests, but not without struggles.

In controlling the Northwest, the Vietnamese state has combined both forms of rule—the coercive apparatus and the ideological apparatus. On one hand, overtly coercive institutions such as the police, army, and judiciary keep people in line by forcing them to conform to expected modes of conduct. On the other hand, the state has maintained its power through the use of a more diffuse and subtle, yet in my view more effective, ideological apparatus that largely prevents potential opposition and consolidates its territory.[42] The state service provisions, which all fall under the rubric of "development," significantly contribute to the state's ability to maintain political order and strengthen its presence in these regions through its cadres at all levels. From the perspective of government officials and most lowland people, the uplands would have remained backward until this very day had they not received Vietnamese government support. I have often heard this mantra over my twenty years of conducting fieldwork in the region: "Ethnic minority people are very lazy and backward. They don't like to work. They just wait for subsidies from the government. How can they ever get better?"[43] Indeed, this view has also been shared among certain groups of upland people who consider themselves to be more developed than others. Thus, it is not uncommon to find the adoption of government officials' ideas and stereotypes among members of stereotyped communities. Even though in contemporary Vietnam the elites in Hanoi imposed the idea of development, local elites, especially Thái elites, have benefited by pulling development into their own backyards, building connections, and networking to gain power and financial resources.[44] Stated differently, development works, in part, by co-opting local elites and is therefore not simply a top-down project.

Northwesterners embrace differing opinions about development. In mining-affected areas in Lào Cai, for example, while many villagers hate the mines because of the associated land losses due to pollution and displacement, working in the mine quickly became desirable for many young villagers who wanted to escape a farmer's life. For a few years, there was a constant struggle between locals and outsiders over employment in the mine. At the same time, in mining communities, grievances, resistance, and redress have occurred more frequently and more intensively than they have in the landscape of hydropower dams and rubber plantations. Development thus can be seen as both a desire and a threat for its recipients.[45] Individuals' value and labor are fundamental in understanding how development is experienced and negotiated in everyday politics.

In exploring landscape production and everyday politics in the Northwest, I focus on development as the government's hegemonic project. In doing so, I also draw on Michel Foucault's concept of governmentality as a crucial complement to Gramsci's notion of hegemony for understanding development and the Northwest's contentious landscape and subjects. Foucault's writings on biopolitics and governmentality have inspired many scholars working on power and subjects.[46] As subject formation is also a highly geographical process, a growing number of scholars are introducing spatial questions when studying power and subject.[47] The work of Donald Moore, for example, looks at tangled connections of power, subject, and territory while highlighting spatial sensitivity to cultural politics. When examining the play of subjection and agency as various forms of territorialization work in Tibetan landscapes, Emily Yeh underlines that agency or capacity to act also produces changing landscapes. In the Northwest, development as hegemonic project, on the one hand, transforms landscape, and on the other hand serves as means to discipline consent, influence conduct, fetishize culture, impose norms, differentiate, exclude, and include.

Government, as Foucault frames it, "did not refer only to political structures or to the management of states; rather it designated the way in which the conduct of individuals or groups might be directed. . . . To govern, in this sense, is to structure the possible field of action of others."[48] Foucault believed that government was in essence a way to influence the "conduct of conduct." The government is therefore not solely wielded by way of the state monopoly on violence, but is a productive domain of "strategies, techniques and procedures through which different forces seek to render programs operable, and by means of which a multitude of connections are established between the aspirations of authorities and the activities of individuals and groups."[49]

Development, as a field of actions, is a form of power concerning progress, and defines people as the object of improvement.[50] As Foucault highlights, governmentality entails different rationalities that "overlap, lean on each other, challenge each other, and struggle with each other: art of government according to Truth, art of government according to the sovereign state's rationality, art of government according to economic agent's rationality, and more generally according to the rationality of the governed themselves."[51] How do these arts of government play out and interweave in everyday subject-making in the Northwest through dams, rubber plantations, and mining? The *regime of Truth* uses the rationality of science to claim expertise and progressive development to justify improvements and interventions—that is, how development projects such as dams or mines lead to the greater good of society, in general, and individuals' lives, in particular. *Sovereign power* is about the state monopoly of the legitimate use of violence and invoking the rule of law, for example, in land acquisition and displacement for dams, rubber plantations, and mines. *Disciplinary power* relates to notions of progressive development to generate "subjectified subjects," in which governments and developers aim to induce in people norms and ethical behaviors based on the belief that hydropower dams, rubber, or mining means progress, and thus, antidam or antirubber is morally wrong.[52] Finally, *neoliberal power* prevails when the government conducts local villagers' behavior and acceptance by approaching them as rational agents who would benefit economically from joining a development project such as a rubber plantation or becoming miners.

Development as policy, a form of government that tries to accomplish rule, from Vietnamese leaders' perspectives entails intervention as trusteeship and, in Tania Li's words, "the will to improve."[53] In this mode of development, the Vietnamese state enacted or made itself the trustee of what it determines to be the best pathway for those it has deemed unable to find it themselves—those the ethnic Kinh majority describe as the "backward" northwesterners. As development is associated with contestation, negotiations, compromises, and even cooperation, understanding how development works and is perceived in the Northwest is the best way to explore the cultural politics of northwestern agency in the transformation of landscape.[54] In the literature on development, the word "development" itself is used, on the one hand, to refer to the process of transition or transformation toward a modern, capitalist, and industrial economy, a use that equates the term with modernization and capitalist development. On the other hand, it is also defined in terms of quality of life and standard of living and refers to the reduction or amelioration of poverty and material want.[55] Though the two differ—capitalist development often causes rather than cures poverty, and those who engage in it show little concern for the interests of the rural poor—the Vietnamese state regularly conflates the two meanings, implicitly equating modernization with the elimination or alleviation of poverty. More importantly, for Vietnam after the introduction of Đổi Mới in the late 1980s, the issue is not just capitalism but development driven by economistic visions, regardless of whether those visions are organized around capitalism, socialism, or other things. The capitalist development processes in this context intersect with socialist (or quasi-socialist) state structures to enable the broad range of institutions and practices in the creation of resource commodification and market economy expansion in frontier areas. Development experts and trustees associated with the government try to rule by creating governable subjects and governable spaces.[56] Thus, understanding the processes that produce development as a historically singular process requires a sensitivity to regions, political economy, and politics.

## Everyday Politics of Resource Territories

In his work on lowland peasant society in Vietnam, Benedict J. Kerkvliet highlights the notion of everyday politics, which "involves people embracing, complying with, adjusting, and contesting norms and rules regarding authority over, production of, or allocation of resources and doing so in quiet, mundane, and subtle expressions and acts that are rarely organized or direct."[57] Kerkvliet identifies three types of politics: official, advocacy, and everyday politics. The key to differentiating everyday politics from the other two types is that the former is not organized, and it occurs in people's daily life. Kerkvliet divides everyday politics into four different forms: support, compliance, modifications and evasions, and resistance.[58] Sarah Turner, when examining Hmông villagers' livelihoods in northern upland Vietnam, found that their everyday politics regarding livelihoods stretch across this entire spectrum.[59] It is worth noting that while considerable research has been conducted on everyday resistance, the same cannot be said for other forms of everyday politics.[60] Everyday forms of resistance "refer to what people do short of organized confrontation that reveals disgust, anger, indignation, or opposition to what they regard as unjust or unfair actions by others more wealthy or powerful than they."[61] Because of the state's strict surveillance over people's resistance since Vietnam's independence, opportunities to openly oppose the state's policies are scarce. In reality, however, people adversely affected by the state's development policies have their own tactics that can be effective and are not necessarily overt forms of resistance.[62] Such is the case when resettlers gathered money to invest in tree planting and house building on the original sites before resettlement, in order to obtain higher compensation; or when they delayed moving or giving up their land or quietly cleared common land for farming; or when local cadres took the side of ordinary people in their fight against the government and dam/rubber/mine investors. In other instances, everyday resistance can be more overt, as when dam resettlers held resettlement officers hostage to demand their compensation, or rubber resisters chopped down rubber trees, or mine-impacted villagers dug trenches to prevent mining trucks to pass, or sent petitions to the authorities to fight against mining companies, as I will illustrate later.

Support involves the deliberate "endorsement of the system," and compliance is more a matter of "going through the motions of support without much thought about it."[63] These two forms of everyday politics can include the daily practices of people not just in subordinate positions but also in superordinate roles (headmen, community representatives). One large area of everyday political support in the Northwest involves interactive relations within households, among neighbors, between villagers and village administration (headman, village party secretary, etc.) and investors. It was common to find headmen who worked hard to persuade villagers to move to resettlement sites or contribute land to rubber plantations. Families with more land were eager to join plantations, with a hope to gain better income in the future. They then created strong connection with rubber companies' field staff. Examples of compliance are when we see thousands of people who agreed to move to make way for dams, or who contributed their land to rubber plantations, or who just accepted the mines operating in their backyards. Without resisting, they worked out their own ways to adapt to change. Indeed, compliance rather than support encompasses daily activities that play a key role in sustaining authority and an existing power system. Between everyday compliance and resistance are the everyday modifications and evasions that often occur at the expense of neighbors and other people in similar conditions.[64] For instance, resettlers who relocated before their fellow villagers grabbed the best lots to build their houses, regardless of any pre-move agreement; or the headman who arranged for the most convenient plots in the plantations to go to his family. In my research, I see everyday politics embedded in the daily lives and experiences of resource-affected people in the Northwest who are bound not only to resource production and distribution practices but also to food production, livelihood maintenance, cultural and identity transformation, social interaction, and resistance—all of which closely link to subject formation. People's choices of action depend on a specific balance of opportunities that are embedded in historically shaped cultural and social relations and particular local materialities. Everyday life is, indeed, a contested site mediated by broader relations of powers—both external and internal—and local practices and interventions that are embedded in a territory.[65] In the Northwest, this territory is the hydropower dams, the rubber plantations, and the mines. Thus, a focus on the politics of everyday life reveals the mundane decision-making in livelihood maintenance, identity, and cultural transformation as well as in negotiation, compromise, and resistance.

Differentiation is a crucial aspect of the process in which resource territories produced new territorial subjects and different beneficiaries. With all the changes in terms of access to and control over land, water, and other resources, differentiation proceeded, both in the sociological sense, which refers to indicators of inequality in which social class is constituted in terms of privilege and deprivation, and in the materialist sense, which identifies class in terms of the social relations of production.[66] Gillian Hart and colleagues identify differentiation as a historical-geographical process that is profoundly influenced by economic, political, and cultural forces peculiar to a society, and which may thus evolve in ways that differ from those in other societies.[67] Geographical settings influence one's set of opportunities and outcomes. Families have different starting points, and processes of upward and downward social mobility are not linear.[68] Thus, local differentiation among resource users, which is mediated by class, gender, ethnicity, and other social relations, normally conditions the micropolitics of struggles over control of and access to resources.[69] Changes in land use, quality, quantity, species, water flow, etc., all actively participate in the ecology, but at the same time are all entangled in a social web.

The more development projects that break ground in the Northwest, the harder it will be for ethnic minority villagers in this region who already struggle with a range of different livelihood trajectories. Rural people are "combining livelihoods in new ways across sectors and developmental spaces, they embody new desires and aspirations, and their values are often different from those of past peasant generations."[70] For people in the Northwest, plural activity—a situation in which agricultural activities are combined within and outside the production unit or where there is a combination of agricultural activities carried out within the production unit and nonagricultural activities in industry, commerce, and/or services—best describes their livelihood trajectories, just as it does for Khun and her neighbors.[71]

As dams or mines displaced villagers and/or they became rubber workers, they lost their connection with the land. Once landless, they were forced into many different pathways, including becoming paid workers. "Plural activity" became not simply economic activity but also political. It contributes to the formation of the post-socialist subject in response to hegemonic development projects.[72] In these processes, those who are impacted must piece together their livelihoods because the position that the state forced them into does not actually make sense to them. Exploring struggles over the making and remaking of the Northwest landscape reveals that it is not only the state and its apparatuses that impose these processes, but also part of the local society, which embeds these processes through individual agency, subjection, and altered relationships to territory.

Examining everyday politics and differentiation helps to unfold processes of northwestern territorial subject formation, which I see as a dynamic and emergent construct that is embodied and relational, depending on subject interaction with materialities involved in extraction.[73] To understand political technologies produced in the Northwest, I rescale them to resettlement sites, rubber plantations, and mining areas that various actors—including government officials at all levels, and both private and state-owned companies—claim. I pay particular attention to the lives and work of people to understand how external material forces intertwine with individuals' agency in producing everyday politics and new territorial subjects. Resource extraction and commodification in Northwest Vietnam has intensified local villagers' struggles in negotiating their everyday realities as resource production and extraction transform the environments within which they live. Villagers' relations with the government and with the resources allegedly being developed for their benefit have manifested themselves in new survival strategies. Even though people experience change in diverse ways, there are some broad tendencies in place. For example, villagers moved from subsistence farming to engaging in various forms of wage labor. Their subjectivity is changing because of their relationship to land, time, and space, in terms of how they work, how they live and interact with one another, how they shape their livelihood strategies, and how they have to understand income and food. That subjectivity changes relationally in terms of the villagers being newcomers in the community, being outcast, part-time farmers, being migrant workers, as well as in shifts in gender roles and relations. For the three main forms of landscape transformations highlighted in the following chapters, subjectivity is changing—totally disrupting the sense of what is traditional and permanent—with the introduction of thinking in terms of modernity, being closer to the city, convenient to the market, and the new generations' desire for development. It also changes in one's relation to the state, to power, and in one's perception of authority. A careful look at this history reveals the complexities and contradictions of agency among people in the Northwest as they respond to state building and development processes.

## Plan of the Book

This book is structured around three key themes: territorialization, the process of exclusion through inclusion; development, a hegemonic project concerning progress; and everyday politics of resource materialities, an ongoing struggle coping with changes. These three themes closely link to the production and transformation of the Northwest and its people since Đổi Mới in 1986. The three main parts of the book correspond to the three major contemporary landscape transformations: dams, rubber plantations, and mining. Part 1, "Dams," examines the politics of dam development in Vietnam and the Northwest and how it produces frontier everyday politics. Part 2, "Rubber," explores how rubber plantations as a development project and a form of resource extraction have exacerbated landscape transformation and enabled subject-making in different ways compared to hydropower dams. Part 3, "Mines," traces territorialization that links to both state and private sector and how this creation of resource territories has enabled everyday politics associated with land/water pollution, land and livelihood losses, migration, and the industry's other impacts.

The book concludes that understanding how everyday politics unfolds helps us reject dominant ways of framing development as a "will to improve." As a discursive tool or practice, "development" hides histories of loss for the people who live in its shadow—these play out with the dam, the plantation, and the mine. These concealments attempt to maximize the value that can be produced from the land, a value built not just on the land's efficient use, but on the myriad losses borne by the people of this resource-rich region. Detailed empirical studies like this book, which engage in historical ethnography with particular attention paid to the everyday life and work of people affected by shifting access to resources, thus improve our understanding of how everyday politics and landscape transformation have occurred through multiple forms of territorializations.

# CHAPTER 1

# The Cultural Politics of Development

It was two days before a new moon and pitch-black outside. My colleagues and I were spending our first night at Khun's house in Muong Lanh in November 2005. After a long ride from Điện Biên—about three hundred kilometers of mountain road—we all just wanted a nice shower. We were quickly disappointed—she did not have a bathroom. Khun and her family had moved to this resettlement site only a month earlier. For Khun's family, like their neighbors, the house itself was the first priority—not a bathroom.[1] "You can bathe outdoors, or I can take you to Mr. E's house," Khun told us. It turned out that among the newly built homes in the village, the only house with a bathroom belonged to Mr. E, who lived a short walk from Khun's house. After a few minutes of reluctance, as it was late and very dark outside, I grabbed my flashlight and set off with two female colleagues.

"Ah, come on in. I am glad that at least my bathroom can be put to use." I was a bit puzzled by this remark but did not say anything. Mr. E made us tea. While waiting for my turn to shower, I tried to pay him a compliment: "Wow, your house is beautiful. You must be very proud that you are the first one to complete the house, including the bathroom." He looked at me and smiled sadly:

Nah, not quite. I don't want it; but we have to have it anyway. I want to be able to continue bathing in the river as I used to do my whole life before moving here. I miss the river. You don't know how it felt to swim in the river after a long working day. It was open and familiar. Here, everything is bound up. I don't like the bathroom, and I haven't used it at all. I bathe outdoors next to the water tank over there. I can't stand the walls. They make me feel confined, and I can't breathe. I want to be able to swing my arms and legs freely when I bathe. Can't do that in that tiny bathroom.

Mr. E continued: "Our life depends on the river, our culture is associated with the river, our memories are all with the river. Now we are displaced far from the river. How will our life be?"

I became motionless. I didn't feel like a shower anymore. My head was tangled with questions about the tangible and intangible values that were being lost because of the massive hydropower dam development project. I imagined the ways that this loss is affecting the displaced people, including their lifestyles, culture, community connections, emotional and spiritual attachments to land, river, and forest. I was shocked at realizing how mundane things in our everyday life such as a toilet space or a bathroom could have powerful impacts on shaping cultural identities and instigate struggles for subordinate people who were trying to affirm what they valued or what they believed they were entitled to.[2] Their subjectivity changes because of the changes they experienced in their relationship to the land, in their interaction with the river, and in the way they continue to live their everyday lives.

A few days later, I was able to schedule a meeting with a Kinh cadre who was the head of the Division of Culture in the Sơn La Department of Culture, Information, and Sport, to discuss these questions. While he talked with much regret about how his department lacked sufficient funding to collect ethnographic objects and relics before the flooding of the soon-to-be created Sơn La reservoir, he did not seem too worried about intangible losses. According to him, there would not be much change to people's cultural lives after their resettlement, except perhaps changes related to work habits, since the resettled families now had smaller plots to farm. When asked about the possibility of the erasure of ethnic minorities' cultural identities in the post-resettlement period, he said, "Well, they are losing their cultural identity anyway. Assimilation and Kinhnization have been happening over the last half century. Resettlement will only accelerate it. So you can't blame hydropower for everything." Perhaps he was right. Hydropower was not the first or the only culprit to have transformed this region's landscape and eaten away at its people's cultures. State farms, collectivization, migration, rubber plantations, and mining have also played a role, albeit on different scales.

Trying to discern what transformation has happened to Northwest Vietnam is no straightforward task. Have the people in the region benefited from development projects directed and sponsored by Vietnamese modernization efforts? Or have their lives been forever violated by forces of destruction? The answer depends on whom you ask, of course. If you ask a central planner, you will be answered with statistics and numbers praising electrification, poverty reduction, and increased production. But as you begin to talk to people in the area, the question becomes more complex. Of course, they may have a modern bathroom now, but they have lost much to gain something that they do not even care to use. Indeed, the everyday lived experience is a counterclaim to the government's rationality of progressive development.

Since the Thái ethnic group is in the majority in the Northwest, the Thái people that I worked most closely with have relationships to development different from those of the Hmông, La Ha, or Khmú. Among the Thái, there are factions and hierarchies, elites who have gained much, and marginalized individuals who have lost everything. Even among the Thái who seem to have gained the most, the question remains fraught, and the answer that one gives may depend on how the question is asked, or in what context. The same person may answer the same question in different ways. If those who are asked are thinking about material goods and income—how many Vietnamese dong (VNĐ) they have access to or how much rice their fields produce each season—some may say that their lives have developed or been improved. But the same people may go on to say, sometimes in the very same conversation, that their lives have been marked by loss—loss of access to a beloved river, loss of flavor and diversity in their food, loss of identity in their children, and loss of pride.

In the following sections, I will explore the embodied resource territorial subjects (again, peasants without land and fishermen without rivers) and the cultural transformations in every life that are associated with the advent of hydropower dams, rubber plantations, and mines. I reveal ambiguities of development and highlight how a long-term, fieldwork-based approach to understanding territorial subject making, everyday politics, and territorialization uncovers a complex set of transformations on both intangible and material levels. The intangible losses cannot be added up in a ledger book in the same way that hectares of land, kilowatt hours, tons of rice, or incomes and expenses in

VNĐ can be summed up. But they do add up—they add up to a story of profound social and cultural change that is hidden by the standard focus on the quantifiable improvements normally used as development indicators. In addition to this, I show that even positive quantifiable indicators, when surveyed properly, show real forms of material deprivation emerging in the wake of development. People have lost land and income, are incurring new expenses, and face added economic hardships even as they appear on paper to have gained in some development indicators.

## The Northwest

Originating in Yunnan Province, China, at an elevation of fifteen hundred meters, the Black River (Sông Đà) runs 1,183 kilometers, of which the final 495 kilometers fall within Vietnamese territory. In Vietnam, the river courses diagonally through the Northwest region, where the topography varies from high mountain ranges to plateaus and valleys, in different climate regimes. The rainy season lasts from May to October and provides 75-78 percent of the annual rainfall. The land area of the Northwest equals one-third of the total area of northern Vietnam, but its population density has been historically low compared to lowland provinces. For example, in 1958, the region's population density was estimated to be seven people per square kilometer, compared to forty-five hundred people per square kilometer in Thái Bình, a lowland province in the Red River delta.[3]

Since 1945, this region and its people have gone from being a battlefield in the Indochina War with the French (1945-1954), to enduring the American War (1955-1975) and surviving the Third Indochina War, or as Vietnamese call it, the Border War (1979-1980). More recently, in a time of peace, when the country opened its economy to global flows of trade and investment after economic reforms in the late 1980s, local people have had to cope with being a focal point for economic development, including an accelerated establishment of hydropower dams, rubber plantations, and mining, as well as all the displacements these entailed.

The region's distinct topography and cultural and ethnic diversity have given it a special political position. During the Lý dynasty, and consistent with policies inherited from previous dynasties based in remote mountainous areas, Lý Thái Tổ applied the *cơ mi* (loose binding) policy after he became king in 1010. In addition to giving titles and

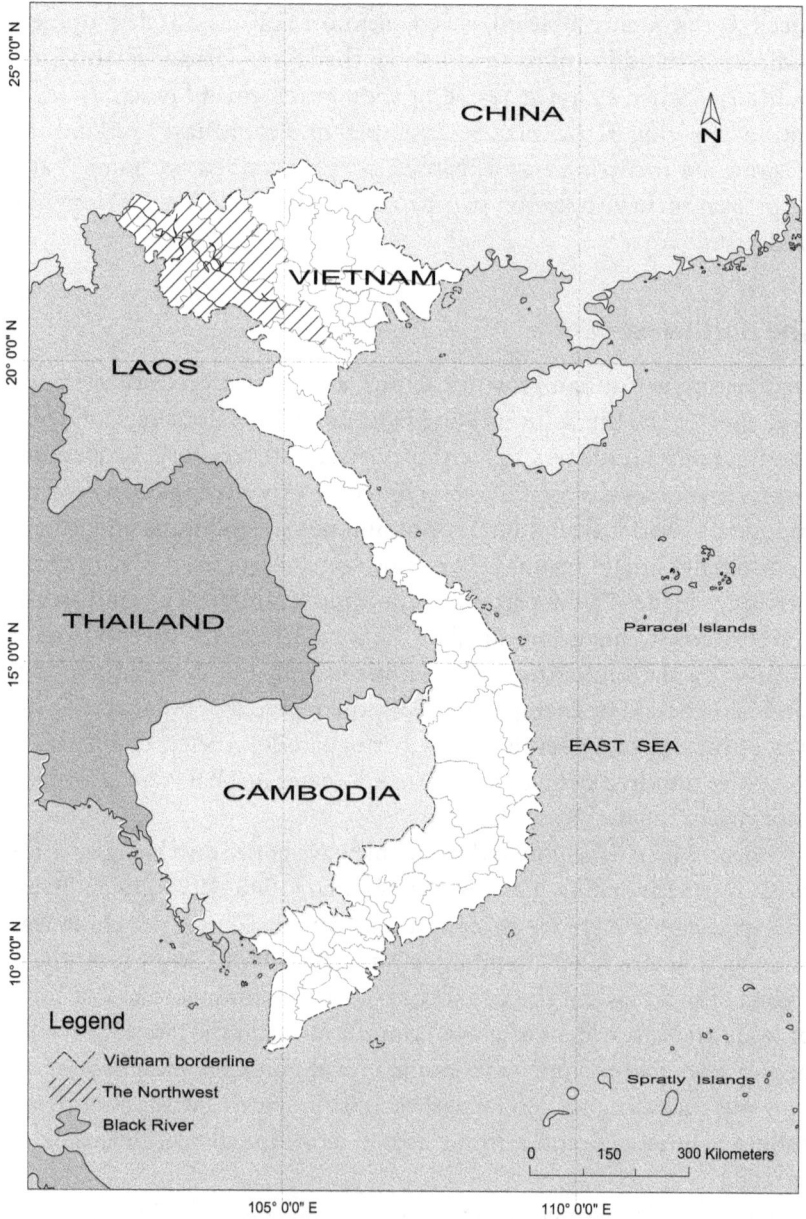

**FIGURE 1.1.** Map of northern Vietnam with the Northwest highlighted.
Source: Adapted from the database of Global Administrative Areas (GADM), www.gadm.org.

financial rewards, the Lý also married off their princesses to powerful chiefs of northern mountainous regions and bound them into a unified bloc around the central monarchy state in the lowland (Thăng Long, or today's Hanoi). Under the Lý dynasty, at least ten princesses were married off to chiefs in northern mountainous regions.[4]

For hundreds of years in the Black River watershed, settlement arrangements have created quilt patches of cultures and farming practices that still persist today.[5] Thái, La Ha, Mảng, and Giáy people live in the river valley or at the foot of the mountains and grow rice. The Khmú/Xá people reside in villages at the middle elevation and are known for their swidden agriculture techniques, a practice often pejoratively referred to as slash-and-burn but is known as "shifting cultivation" in the social science literature.[6] The Hmông choose to live at a higher elevation and primarily grow maize.[7]

Because of natural conditions and the villagers' long-term production experiences, each ethnic group in the Northwest has developed its own niche fit for its people and their daily lives, especially in farming activities.[8] This reality is preserved in a Thái saying:

Xá ăn theo lửa (Xá people live on fire)
Thái ăn theo nước (Thái people live on water)
Hmông ăn theo sương mù (Hmông people live on fog)

Despite the differences across these groups, they share many similarities. Their emotional, cultural, and embodied entanglements with the land, river, and forests were built and strengthened over generations. They lived mostly by agriculture that depended on natural conditions, and they all believed in God (*Then Luông*) and spirits/ghosts. I learned from Khun's father-in-law and other elderly villagers about worshipping practices and various festivals that were celebrated in the past. For Thái people, God above in the sky had the supreme power to govern the land, humans, and everything else in the universe. On land, there were ghosts (*phi*) to control the natural world and activities in it. Thus, to settle in a new village, to build a new house, to clear land for farming, to hunt, or to fish in rivers or streams, one needed permission from ghosts of the land, ghosts of the farmland, and ghosts of the forest or rivers. Ceremonies to worship heaven and earth were organized as annual festivals following agricultural production cycles and integrated with agricultural rituals, mostly to pray to God to protect harvests and people's well-being. These practices of praying to heaven and earth were embedded in people's lives for many generations and quite similar in all ethnic groups in the region.

After 1954, under the new political conditions, and especially after Đổi Mới was instituted, the abovementioned practices began to fade away, as Kinh cadres considered them backward and superstitious.[9] With the increased migration of lowland Kinh people to the uplands from the late 1950s as a key dynamic in the formation of the frontier, and the new reality of Vietnamese as the sole formal language taught in schools as a way of binding together the nation, lowland ways of life have been steadily encroaching on those of ethnic minorities, reflected in how they dress, the meals they prepare, and in the houses they build, among other things.[10] For example, in the 1970s and 1980s, most women still wore traditional outfits even though many men preferred to dress in clothing similar to that worn by the Kinh. Standardizing language and legal discourse were among a number of processes directed by the government that were intended to rein in its subjects and their environment. Change has come gradually in small things associated with uplanders' daily activities.

Government policies have highlighted the formation of new citizens—socialist subjects—who were supposed to actively work to build the nation following a socialist path. Many ethnic groups such as Khmú, Hmông, and Thái joined farming cooperatives, started intensive farming, and reduced their swidden activities.[11] Their control over surrounding forests and rivers has subsided as the government has tightened its control over these resources via the application of sovereign and disciplinary powers. The government does not just control the resources per se, but also controls the discourse regarding their use, management, and meaning. This indicates a tight connection between coercion and extraction in the making of the state.[12]

During my twenty years of conducting research in the Northwest, I learned that since farming cooperatives were introduced to the region, some groups of ethnic minorities such as the Thái, La Ha, Mảng, and Giáy have begun to eat nonsticky rice—sticky rice was previously their staple—and that practice has expanded even further after Đổi Mới, owing to the introduction of many more new hybrid rice varieties. Some traditional dishes that are associated with local resources, such as aquatic plants from the Black River, have disappeared since the dams were built. Young ethnic minority people nowadays use brick to construct their houses instead of raising their homes on stilts, or they simplify house construction by using a hybrid design that integrates traditional features with a lowland brick structure. For example, Black Thái housing designs are no longer required to be ornamented with *khau cút* designs on the roof sides, as they were in the past.[13] The explanation that I have often heard is that the Kinh style of house looks more modern and is more convenient since all the living spaces are located inside the house—including the bathroom. The inability to log the forest for building materials because of the forest closure policy implemented and ongoing since the 1990s has also contributed to this housing adaptation.[14]

After the American War ended in 1975, and following the Border War with China in 1979–1980, the government continued to highlight an urgent need for economic development in the Northwest. In parallel with other policies, the government's development projects in the region, including dams, rubber plantations, and mines, fit into broader strategies to provide energy for national growth, increase exports (rubber and minerals), and enable this poor mountainous region to keep pace with lowland industrialization and modernization. But one of the problems with dams and mines is that they displace people and produce both landscape and cultural transformation in a dramatic way. Displacement divides communities into morsels and destroys their cohesion, which leads to their assimilation into another, more dominant group. From another angle, by turning upland peasants into rubber workers or miners, these projects "modernize" and merge this group into the working class, forcing them to change in culture, lifestyle, and livelihoods, as they are no longer able to practice the ways of farming and living that their families practiced for many generations. This is why territorialization through these development projects has facilitated, more than ever, everyday politics and the formation of differentiated territorial subjects.

## Đổi Mới and Changes in the Northwest

While staying at Khun's house, I often heard her father-in-law say, "When will the old days come?" He was fondly referring to a time when the forests were still abundant and when the river flowed freely, providing them with food and a sense of belonging. Things had changed. The saying offers something more subtle as well, implying that the old days are not in the past, but something to be hoped for in the future. The saying turns the linear assumption of development on its head.

As a consequence of economic reforms in the late 1980s and early 1990s, political and economic changes have increasingly impacted all upland areas in Vietnam. Đổi Mới economic reforms have, in fact, significantly influenced the relationships between ethnic minorities, government officials, and local authorities, since upland peasants began to pay attention not just to subsistence crops but also to market-oriented crops. In addition, development planners and private investors increasingly saw and used upland areas as a potential labor reserve for the region's growing number of rubber plantations and factories. From developers' point of view, uplanders would economically benefit from joining a development project such as rubber plantations, and as a result they should have nothing to worry about.

Đổi Mới has also affected the relationship between the uplands and lowlands. Over the last three decades, economic and social disparities between these two regions have gradually narrowed. Lowland peoples' prejudice against uplanders has been lifted to some extent. The migration of lowland people to the uplands, as well as a large number of development projects in the uplands, has played a key role in introducing modern ideas more intensively to the upland areas, as evidenced in the shifts in clothing styles, the availability of durable goods, new entertainment options, the introduction of hybrid varieties of rice, maize, and cattle, technologically driven agricultural techniques, and more.[15] Nevertheless, despite the changes it may have brought, Đổi Mới did not depart from the earlier processes of exploitation, even as far back as state formation in 1945 and the First Indochina War.[16] Scholars such as Sarah Turner and Christin Bonin have also elaborated on various forms of state control through development interventions that the Vietnamese state adopted, well before Đổi Mới, to integrate upland ethnic minorities into the national economy and mobilize and take control over the Northwest's resources.[17]

The development of the upland areas in the wake of Đổi Mới signals a new kind of connection between Kinh and upland groups, but it is tied to a kind of paternalism.[18] In the last two decades or so, many young lowland people have traveled to the uplands to engage in charity work. They often affiliate with a nongovernmental organization (NGO) or a school, while others set up their own activities. Unlike previous generations, young lowland people no longer consider the Northwest as a land of dangerous forests and poisonous water, although it retains its image as a beautiful but poor, backward region that needs these young people's help. New generations reinforce the idea of development in a different way. Tourism packages for travel to the uplands have increased in popularity since the early 2000s. The attraction of ethnic minority culture helps to drive this tourism boom.[19] The new interest in the Northwest is often a kind of fantasy for "seeing it before it vanishes," where the very people who want to see it are the ones who are then contributing to its disappearance. Meanwhile, for young upland people, their understanding of modernity now includes an urban lifestyle and nonfarming employment. Many young upland people have adopted the same dress as the Kinh youth, and unlike in the past, it is almost impossible to differentiate between them just by looking at their clothes, especially in areas surrounding cities and towns like Sơn La, Lai Châu, and Điện Biên, as well as in other district centers.

Now, children of many ethnic minority groups are attending school; elementary school has been compulsory since 1991.[20] In resettlement sites or around rubber plantations, roads and new schools have been built. The Ministry of Education sends teachers to remote villages so young children do not have to travel too far to attend classes. Khun's husband is one of many elementary school teachers who spend most of their time based in mountainous Hmông villages teaching children how to write and read in Vietnamese. Women's unions at the commune and village levels work to persuade women to have fewer children and increase time between childbirths so the family can invest more in their children's education. Some families keep their children in school through middle or high school; some can even afford to send them to technical schools or colleges after high school. Wealthier families send their children to boarding schools in Hanoi from age twelve. According to national government policy, the college entry requirements for students with an ethnic minority background are relaxed, with the grade-average requirement lower than that for students with a Kinh background.[21] As a result, it is no longer difficult to hire staff who are of an ethnic minority background for government offices, schools, or businesses.

These advances, however, come at a cost. The increasing interactions have resulted in the blurring of identities for many ethnic minority people in terms of housing, attire, food, hairstyles, and their emotional attachments to land, as mentioned above. Government officials see this conversion as a measure of success in bringing different ethnic minorities closer to the "more developed" lowland Kinh. However, while young people regarded these changes as natural and indeed enjoyed the experience, for many older ethnic minority people I interviewed, this was not considered development but conversion. To them, these transformations amount to a failure to keep their culture alive.

Mr. Hin was born in 1945 in Sơn La Province. He is of Thái ethnicity. In February 1964, the eighteen-year-old was drafted into the army to fight in the American War. After twenty years of army service, he returned home to join a farming cooperative for a couple of years before he was appointed as the commune's party secretary, and then its chairman. For him, as someone who has always felt thankful to give and receive support from the government and the party, he was very happy that his people, as well as other ethnic minority groups in the same commune, followed government policies and switched from shifting cultivation to fixed cultivation, ending their nomadic ways. He appreciates the government's support and investment in the Northwest and believes that northwesterners would not be able to have a good life without such assistance. I spent an afternoon drinking tea with him and listening to his story. It was a long story about his life in the Northwest:

> My family benefits a lot from the party and the government. I remember when I was a little boy, we practiced shifting cultivation and moved around very often. When we were told to settle in this place, we were not happy because there was not a lot of water here. The whole commune had only one irrigation system that the villagers built to bring water into the field from a stream up in the mountains over there. Thus, many of us used to solely depend on rain-fed crops. With only one rice crop per year, there was not enough rice for us to eat all year round. Once we were introduced to hybrid varieties that gave a higher yield, we started to do two rice crops per year. We were no longer hungry. But we have to start eating nonsticky rice instead of purely sticky rice. It was hard at first, but it's better to have enough to eat than just stick to one type of rice and be hungry. The government built two other irrigation systems that helped us to irrigate more fields. In 2003, we started to have agricultural extension cadres based in our commune who did help a lot in bringing in new varieties and advanced agricultural techniques, both in cropping and livestock. Our economic life has been getting so much better over the last decade or two.
>
> You know, we are very lucky. While our family benefits from the construction of new roads, bridges, schools, etc., all that came

with the dam and rubber plantations, we didn't suffer impacts, neither from the Sơn La Dam—even though we did have to share a part of our farming land with resettlers—nor the rubber plantations, like many others in my commune or elsewhere in the Northwest.[22]

Although he started by focusing on not having suffered impacts in terms of tangible material resources or agricultural production, Hin's focus changed when talking about intangible heritage:

But it doesn't mean that we didn't lose anything. Oh, look at the young people now, or look at my granddaughter who just got married last month. She doesn't even know how to embroider her own *khăn piêu* [ornate headscarf]. My wife had to sew all of the mattresses that we used in the house when we got married. Even my daughter-in-law, who married my son in 1994, had to embroider more than thirty *khăn piêu* to give to all of the female relatives in my family.[23] That was our tradition. When my wife tried to teach my granddaughter how to embroider, she said, "Why bother, Grandma? We don't need to do it these days. And even if the groom's family asked, we'll just buy them. It's simple." And look around, you don't see that many young Thái women wearing *tằng cẩu* anymore.[24] Almost all of my granddaughter's girlfriends now don't want to do that, as they think it's an old style. Other traditional games and dances such as *ném còn* and *múa xoè* that were once the pride of Thái people are no longer practiced in many of our communities. Many of us also no longer pray to the rice spirit and the ghost of farming fields after harvesting, and I don't know how many people now believe in *Then Luông*. Indeed, I don't even know what most people believe in nowadays.

He then described how ethnic Kinh disproportionately grabbed some of the development opportunities, often at the expense of local people:

Another thing you can see around here is all the businesspeople and middlemen are from the lowlands. We Thái people don't know how to do business as Kinh people do. In the past, we mostly grew crops for our own consumption or maybe traded in the local market. We did not know about fertilizers or hybrid varieties that can give high yield and production. We used our local varieties that gave low production but actually tasted better. No one grows it anymore. We only started to plant crops and fruit trees for commercial purposes in the early 2000s. The middlemen come to buy produce, and they too often would be the ones who have the upper hand in purchasing agreements. As upland ethnic minorities, we are still inferior in many ways.[25]

Hin's feelings are not his alone. At first, he focused on obvious markers of productivity like land, crop outputs, and technology. In terms of these factors, he seemed to be faring better than other people in the region who had suffered more directly from displacement. But as he talked, Hin also hinted at other concerns, related to less tangible values, like the taste of a crop or the style of a garment. He shares these kinds of concerns about intangible losses with others, especially those who were displaced by dam development projects such as Sơn La, Lai Châu, Hòa Bình, Huổi Quảng, Bản Chát, and Nậm Chiến, individuals who suffered cultural and material losses when their land and homes were lost and their social networks disintegrated. Even for affected people who did not have to move, their lives were not the same because of changes in their access to natural resources (land, water, forests). For

**FIGURE 1.2.** Traditional *tằng cẩu* hairstyle and attire of a married Black Thái women. Photo by the author.

people like Mr. Hin or Mr. E, even though their activities and responses were everyday forms of support and compromise, deep down, they were feeling intangible losses.

I still remember back to 2009 when Khun said to me, "If you want to see how people are making Thái traditional rattan stools in Ngọc Chiến commune, you should go as soon as possible before the Nậm Chiến dam floods the rattan forest.[26] Ngọc Chiến rattan stools are special because of the rattan there. Nowhere [else] you can find that type of rattan, but soon they will be gone." I did ride a motorbike to Ngọc Chiến and spent a full day with one of Khun's relatives who was weaving stools with the last rattan collected before the forest was flooded. I bought a few and own them still. Many villagers in Ngọc Chiến lost their income from weaving rattan stools from that moment of flooding onward. However, rattan-stool making was not just a source of income—it was a part of their culture, their link to the forest. Nowadays, even Khun's family uses stools of the same shape and style but made of plastic and imported from China. One can still find Thái rattan stools sold for high prices in souvenir shops in Hanoi or Sơn La; none of them come from Ngọc Chiến. While often seen as separate, the material

**FIGURE 1.3.** *Khăn piêu* is the traditional Black Thái women's headscarf. Photo by Nguyen Vi Linh.

aspects of production and intangible aspects of culture are often entangled, and a threat to a mode of production can impact a cultural tradition. The northwesterners' perception of gain and loss is central to the way in which development is experienced and negotiated. Claims about loss of culture, such as that of Mr. Hin, are not only about culture but also about the northwesterners' subjectivity changing because of their relationship to land, rivers, and other natural resources, about their rights to space and territory, and about their economic and political marginalization within the broader context of development.[27]

## Ethnic Relations—Thái and La Ha People

In the Northwest, Thái is the largest ethnic minority group.[28] There are different names for Thái people, such as Tai, Tày Đăm, Tày Mười, Tày Thanh, Mán Thanh, Hàng Bông, Tày Mường, Pa Thay, and Thổ Đà Bắc. There are Black Thái, White Thái, and Red Thái who live in different locations in the Black River basin.[29] In precolonial times, Thái Mường replaced Kháng and La Ha ruling systems in the Northwest after almost two hundred years of fighting against one another.[30] Thái people (both Thái Trắng and Thái Đen) are formally considered ethnic minority groups in Vietnam, but they are the third-largest group in Vietnam after the Kinh and Mường groups. The Thái people numbered more than 1.82 million (accounting for 1.9 percent of the total population of Vietnam) in the country's 2019 population statistical survey; the La Ha people numbered 10,157 in the same survey (accounting for 0.01 percent of the total).[31] Thái people in Vietnam have maintained their own language and have had their own writing system for centuries.[32] As the name suggests, the language is close to the Thai language, which is the official language of Thailand.

The Đà River basin had long been under the rule of powerful Thái leaders.[33] In 1865, the Nguyễn dynasty ordained for the Đèo family (ethnic White Tháis) to control a vast area of land from Sơn La to Phong Thổ, Lai Châu. Some large Thái clans, including the Cầm and the Đèo, ruled the area for hundreds of years. During the French colonial period, the French supported wealthy clans like the Đèo family, helping them to maintain their power in the late nineteenth and early twentieth centuries.[34] With a policy of divide and conquer, the French formally recognized the Northwest as an autonomous region in 1890, and Đèo Văn Trị, head of the Đèo clan, was made its president. He ruled from Điện Biên to Phong Thổ and presented himself as leader of the

White Thái, the Black Thái, and the entire population of the Đà River basin. To strengthen its relationship with the Đèo family, the French separated the Territoire autonome Tai (Tai Federation or SiPhoc Chau-tai) from Northern Vietnam (1948–1950).[35] During this time, the Thái were ranked by the French (and also considered themselves) as a higher developed group when compared to the La Ha, Kháng, Giáy, or Mảng peoples who also lived in the region. According to other sources, the power of the Đèo clan over the Thái people and other ethnic minorities in the upper Black River could even date back to the fifteenth century.[36]

Before 1954, the diverse upland communities along the Black River were organized as *muang* (in Thái) or *mường* (in Vietnamese), under which the Thái elite controlled relations of land and labor, as well as enjoyed significant benefits, including controlling most of the land and the goods exported out of a muang, commanding labor, collecting tax, and owning Xòe dance teams. A traditional dance of the Thái in Northwest Vietnam, Xòe has long been performed during holidays, happy days in the village, and to welcome guests. Before 1954, only Thái elite could own a Xòe team, which consisted of twelve, twenty-four, or thirty-six (depending on the titles) of the most beautiful girls in a muang. Once chosen, these Xòe girls had to serve until the team owners decided on their release.[37] The Thái elite might also provide land to poor Thái peasants who were not servants. Other non-Thái ethnic groups were either included in the muang on a subordinated basis or lived outside the muang as swidden cultivators.[38]

Right after the First Indochina War ended in 1954, other non-Thái ethnic minority cadres and people in the Northwest were very concerned about the Kinh-Thái alliance as a more "locally specific form of majoritarianism" and feared Thái rule over other ethnicities. The fact that the Thái Mèo Autonomous Zone (TMAZ) was renamed as the Northwest Autonomous Zone (TBAZ, or Khu Tự trị Tây Bắc) in 1962 probably indicated an attempt to assuage "broader concerns about Thái and Kinh rule configured together."[39]

Thái political domination and relative wealth were in fact transformed into the idea that the Thái were more modern, having French/Vietnamese influence and development. I have learned through my trips to the region that even now many Thái people regard other small ethnic groups in the region, including the La Ha, Mảng, and Kháng, as inferior. Many Thái also believe their kinspeople are wealthier than La Ha people because they work much harder—very similar to Kinh people's or lowland cadres' views of upland ethnic minorities in general.[40]

However, even among Thái peasants before 1954, there were three different castes: free peasants (*páy, táy*), who had some freedom to work on the land; semi-free peasants (*cuông, nhốc, pụa*), who were dependent on landlords for their land; and servants (*côn, hươn, khỏi*), who were extremely poor or in debt and had to live with masters.

The La Ha group (also called Xá Cha, Xá Bung, Xá Khao, Xá Táu Nhạ, Xá Poong, Pụa, Xá Uống, Bủ Hà) had long prior to 1954 worked as *cuông, nhốc, pụa*—servants—for Thái families. During that time, they did not have their own villages.[41] It was believed that the La Ha people came to the Northwest before the Thái Đen people arrived in the twelfth century.[42] According to La Ha folklore, during the seventeenth and eighteenth centuries, the La Ha people were equivalent in status to the Thái people before the Thái began to try to dominate the area along the Black River. The La Ha people fought for centuries before finally succumbing to Thái domination. The La Ha had been servants for the Thái people ever since, and on the bottom rung of Northwest society.

The La Ha maintained their language for a few hundred years. However, only some small groups who live in isolated remote areas have managed to retain part of the La Ha language until today; the remaining La Ha speak Thái. They also adopted customs, house design, and dress that were very similar to those of the Thái people, except that La Ha houses were usually much smaller. Thái women—either Black Thái or White Thái, depending on who lived nearby—also influenced La Ha women's hairstyles. In the late 1950s and 1960s the newly formed state required Thái communities to share land with La Ha people, who began to set up their own villages. The La Ha also joined cooperatives and cleared forest for farming.[43]

One further item of note is that uplanders in the Northwest are well known in Vietnam for their alcohol consumption. Alcoholic drinks are an intrinsic part of Thái and other ethnic minority groups' cultural practices, and in the Northwest and upland Vietnam more generally alcohol is commonly offered after group labor exchange, when receiving guests, at ceremonies, or after paid labor arrangements.[44] People distilled rice and maize alcohol at home or bought from their neighbors. Women drink as much as men. Drinking is also the social norm as a way of expressing hospitality. During my fieldwork in the early 2000s, I often observed children—boys and girls as young as seven years old—drinking during dinner when the family was entertaining guests. (Young parents nowadays don't let their children drink until they're twelve or thirteen). I am not sure if alcohol acts to ease anxiety between residents and newcomers or not, but to local people, the more the guest drinks, the better—it is considered as a good sign that the guest is open or honest to the host family. Thái people, like many of us, will talk about many things that they would never normally discuss if they were not drinking. For example, I learned a Thái saying about the La Ha people after a long drinking session in a village: "Thái people eat unclean ginger, but La Ha people eat unclean food all year round."[45] I was unable to memorize how to say it in Thái, so I asked them again the next day; they all laughed but did not repeat the saying. Sometimes I curse my low alcohol tolerance—if I was capable of drinking more, I might have been able to engage in more revealing conversations with the villagers.

In my many visits in Muong Muon commune, it became clear that there was little difference between how Thái and La Ha people answered questions. However, in group meetings, La Ha people were usually shy and quieter, even though they were members of the villages' management boards. There were times when I noticed that La Ha people did not speak at all during the whole meeting if there were also Thái people in attendance. Unequal relationships between various ethnic groups in the Northwest have existed since long before Vietnam's independence and continue to be perpetuated through various forms of dominance and power inequality. These relationships, to some extent, influence the ways that northwesterners behave today, including how they respond to changes caused by dams, rubber plantations, or mines. La Ha and Thái people's experience of development is thus embedded within the legacy of precolonial, colonial, and postcolonial experiences. The cultural politics of development in the Northwest is also the cultural politics of different ethnicities in the region.

## Lives of Resettlers from Hydropower Dam Construction

In Khun's village, Muong Lanh, and in other resettled villages like Muong Nhuong, Muong Ma, and Muong Che that were displaced to make way for the Sơn La Dam (as I will discuss in chapter 3), most villagers were self-provisioning farmers before they were resettled.[46] In the last twenty years, I spent much of my time in these resettlement areas whenever I returned to the Northwest. I learned that before resettlement, household-owned wet rice fields had usually been sufficient for household consumption, and these families had almost never bought rice for their own use. Families that did not own wet rice fields used money earned from selling maize, cassava, soybeans, and other crops to buy rice. Thái people living along rivers and streams fished daily to supplement their meals, their catch providing protein that would otherwise be lacking. Almost every household possessed ponds for fish farming. Families grew vegetables in their gardens and raised livestock. Herds of cattle used to graze freely, without tending, in their pastures. Pigs ran freely in the villages. Wild vegetables and bamboo shoots could be collected in the forest. One of my favorite Thái dishes before their resettlement was roasted aquatic weed (from the Black River) wrapped in banana leaves. The ingredients for this dish disappeared after the Sơn La Dam appeared. Residents of these villages used to go to the market only occasionally to buy items that they could not produce or collect at or near their homes. They were not rich—many of them were quite poor—but my survey reveals that hunger was rare. Similar stories of peasants' lives before development programs came to their villages can also be found in other parts of the country.[47]

Almost every family also used to own a motorboat. As there were no roads in many villages, boats were the main mode of transportation for traveling to the market, visiting friends and relatives, and taking children to school and the sick to the hospital. Using boats for travel was and sometimes still is (mostly upstream of the dam) a very typical lifestyle characteristic of the Thái and the La Ha people living along the Black River. Some individuals used their boats to transport people and goods to earn extra income. Given that they needed very little money for their daily needs, many families had savings for emergencies or to buy new items for family use by the year's end.

For resettlers, the transition to a new place after resettlement was not easy. The loss of a lifestyle and habits to which they were accustomed created an imbalance in their lives and made it harder for them to settle in their new homes. One villager from Muong Lanh told me, "It is scary to think of how much money we need here. In the old village, we did not really use much money. We could provide most of the things we need ourselves like vegetables from the gardens or in the forest, fish in the river and ponds, and so on. We did not have to buy food every day. In the first two years here in the new village, we had to buy everything in the market."[48]

The need to buy food was especially problematic in the first two years after resettlement, and the villagers largely depended on government subsidies. While prior to resettlement, subsistence economies thrived, with little need for money, construction of the Sơn La Dam thrust villagers into a new material reality in which money was essential, even for their daily needs. Another villager shared:

> In the old village, we did not have to worry about so many things like we do here. We had our land and, thank God, we had enough to eat. My family did not own either a motorbike or a TV, but we had a boat. The boat was so close to us. We used it every day. I miss it so much. I wanted to sell it, but no one wanted it. After resettlement it lay unused by the riverbank for a while and probably got rotten by now. I didn't have a chance to go back to see what happened to it from last year. We haven't received compensation for it yet. When we moved here, I had to buy a motorbike. Before we used our legs to walk and used the boat to go everywhere. Now we can't. We need to have a motorbike. And you know what? The motorbike made me dizzy and unbalanced every time I rode it. The boat was so much better. You know we did not work in the field all year round. During off-season time, we rode our boat to go upstream and downstream, visited our relatives and families. It was so much more convenient to have a boat compared to a motorbike.[49]

Even though the infrastructure in their old villages was poor—villagers lived far from hospitals, schools, and markets, and durable goods such as televisions, refrigerators, and motorcycles were often absent—life was secure and followed a seasonal rhythm. While villagers may have been cash poor, their boats and rivers connected them to regional infrastructure, friends, and family.

Ethnic minorities along the Black River used local resources (forests and rivers) to sustain their lives and livelihoods. The upland ethnic people in the Northwest also had customs and regulations for land and resource management. Villagers commonly held and cleared rotating farmland as a common resource; individuals usually held no title for these areas. Each community also had its own informal regulations for land management. Most households farmed a large area of land, six to seven hectares per family on average. Labor availability largely determined land inequality: households with more or stronger workers normally had use of more land, since they put in more work to clear the land. Households with less land were usually newly married couples, smaller households, or those without strong laborers.

For villagers (like those in Muong Nhuong) who used to live near a river or stream and had wet rice fields, wet rice growing methods were passed down from generation to generation; how to move water from the river or stream into the fields and how to farm fish in the rice fields are just two examples of the shared knowledge. As villagers had sufficient accessible farmland, and the patches were scattered, people usually practiced crop rotation. One year they would grow maize, soybeans, cassava, peanuts, and rain-fed rice in some patches and use other patches for grazing. A few years later, when the land was eroding and infertile, they would burn the grazing patches to grow crops on them, while leaving the former cropland for grazing. Usually, after burning the field, they planted the seeds. Then they waited for the plants to grow, weeded two or three times per crop, and then harvested. In their old fields, they did not need to use fertilizer since they incorporated animal manure from grazing and then burned the grass and brush on that patch before planting. They had the opportunity to let patches of land periodically lie fallow to stay fertile, which meant that they also did not use pesticides for their maize or soybeans. Livestock management was also less intensive, since their cattle (normally ten to fifteen, but sometimes up to twenty to twenty-five cows per household) and pigs could graze or forage freely with minimal tending. As mentioned previously, almost every household also managed ponds to farm fish.

Before resettlement, 100 percent of my interviewees (115 households in Muong Lanh and Muong Nhuong) earned income from cash crops (maize, cassava, soybeans, and peanuts) and livestock, while 84 percent had extra cash income from fishing activities along the Black River, and 54 percent earned extra by providing waterway transport. Only 4 percent had to sell their labor for extra income, and most of these villagers worked for wealthier households in the village or in neighboring communities. Most of my interviewees were able to manage their lives without leaving the area for work. As many of the families had up to eight hectares, about 24 percent leased some of their land to outsiders (table 1.1).

As for expenditures, 40 percent of interviewees in the old villages (the same 115 households) spent money on goods such as furniture and other household items (table 1.2). About 78 percent accumulated savings each year, while only 4 percent ended up in debt. Up to 16 percent of households used hired labor to prepare the land and for seeding and harvest. There were no school fees to pay, but schooling was only offered up to Grade 5 in Muong Lanh and up to Grade 2 in Muong Hon and Muong Ban of Muong Nhuong, depending on a village's location and road access. The nearest schools that offered higher grade levels

Table 1.1 Sources of household income before and after resettlement

|  | | | | | | | | LEASE | | | | | | | |
|  | | | | | | | | | | | | | | VEGETABLE | FRUIT |
|  | HOUSE- | WET | UPLAND | CASH | LIVES- | WAGE | | OF | FISH | FOREST | LENDING | WATERWAY | | | |
| VILLAGES | HOLDS | RICE | RICE | CROPS | TOCK | LABOR | TRADE | LAND | PONDS | PRODUCTS | MONEY | TRANSPORT | FISHING | GARDENS | TREES |
|---|---|---|---|---|---|---|---|---|---|---|---|---|---|---|---|
| **Before resettlement** Muong Lanh | 61 | 2 | 10 | 100 | 100 | 5 | 16 | 23 | 57 | 100 | 0 | 57 | 71 | 0 | 0 |
| Muong Nhuong | 54 | 54 | 56 | 100 | 100 | 4 | 24 | 24 | 78 | 100 | 7 | 46 | 98 | 0 | 0 |
| Total | 115 | 26 | 31 | 100 | 10 | 4 | 20 | 24 | 67 | 100 | 4 | 52 | 84 | 0 | 0 |
| **After resettlement** Muong Lanh | 64 | 61 | 2 | 100 | 77 | 36 | 14 | 6 | 73 | 55 | 16 | 0 | 0 | 50 | 50 |
| Muong Nhuong | 59 | 5 | 0 | 100 | 80 | 10 | 9 | 0 | 61 | 61 | 12 | 0 | 0 | 53 | 37 |
| Total | 123 | 34 | 1 | 100 | 78 | 24 | 11 | 3 | 68 | 58 | 14 | 0 | 0 | 51 | 44 |

SOURCES OF INCOME (IN PERCENTAGE OF HOUSEHOLDS)*

Source: Adapted from N. Dao 2012.

Note: The difference in the number of households surveyed was due to the newly married couples in the villages after resettlement who did not answer the questions pertaining to the before resettlement period. Income is broadly defined to include all the products and cash generated from various activities in which households engaged, including products consumed in the household.

Table 1.2  Expenditure of households before and after resettlement

CASH EXPENDITURES (IN PERCENTAGE OF HOUSEHOLDS)

| | VILLAGES | HOUSE-HOLDS | RICE | FOOD-STUFFS | OTHER GOODS | HOUSE REPAIR | CLOTHES | EDUCATION | DEBT REPAY-MENT | HEALTH CARE | SAVINGS | SOCIAL ACTIVITIES | HIRING LABOR | TELE-PHONE | GASOLINE | PRODUCTION INPUTS (FERTILIZERS, PESTICIDES) |
|---|---|---|---|---|---|---|---|---|---|---|---|---|---|---|---|---|
| Before resettlement | Muong Lanh | 61 | 100 | 0 | 41 | 15 | 61 | 20 | 5 | 44 | 71 | 74 | 10 | 10 | 0 | 0 |
| | Muong Nhuong | 54 | 46 | 0 | 39 | 2 | 80 | 39 | 4 | 43 | 87 | 98 | 22 | 0 | 0 | 0 |
| | Total | 115 | 75 | 0 | 40 | 9 | 70 | 29 | 4 | 43 | 78 | 85 | 16 | 0 | 0 | 0 |
| After resettlement | Muong Lanh | 64 | 100 | 100 | 97 | 97 | 86 | 59 | 47 | 56 | 17 | 67 | 0 | 61 | 78 | 72 |
| | Muong Nhuong | 59 | 100 | 100 | 98 | 100 | 90 | 70 | 63 | 54 | 25 | 95 | 0 | 70 | 98 | 70 |
| | Total | 123 | 100 | 100 | 98 | 98 | 88 | 64 | 55 | 55 | 21 | 81 | 0 | 65 | 88 | 71 |

Source: Adapted from N. Dao 2012.

Note: The foodstuffs category equals zero because it refers mostly to nutrition such as meat, fish, egg, fruits, and vegetables. Families did not purchase any of these products because they grew or produced them for themselves. Foodstuffs does not include minor items like salt and fish sauce. Villagers mostly used pork fat instead of cooking oil when they were in the old villages. Also, it is noted that in the before time, people did not spend money on gasoline but did purchase diesel fuel for their boats.

were in the center of Muong Tra commune, more than ten kilometers away; many families were unable to send their children for higher education outside their villages.

After their move, even though more individuals in Muong Lanh than in Muong Nhuong had access to wet rice land, their patches were very small (less than one hundred square meters, and in many cases only ten to thirty square meters). Resettlers bought these wet rice patches from host communities or dug their gardens and diverted water from their ponds if they had one. For them, this rice land, despite its size, provided stable food. Although in the old villages only 4 percent of my survey respondents engaged in paid work, after four years in the resettlement sites that number exceeded 24 percent. Thus, the resettlement process compelled peasants to engage in paid work. Only one family (1 percent) continued growing upland rice, compared to thirty-six families (31 percent) before resettlement. Without access to the river, income available from fishing or from waterway transport has evaporated. The resettlers depend heavily on cash crops, such as maize and cassava. However, with their limited amount of land, income from these crops alone is far from sufficient to help families avoid food insecurity for more than six months a year. Such annual food insecurity forces these villagers to seek out different sources of income and alternative livelihoods, as I will elaborate on in the following sections.

In the old villages, with sufficient land for effective crop rotation, villagers had enough food to eat and were able to provide themselves with their basic needs as well as increase their savings. Only families that did not have strong in-house labor might encounter food insecurity for a short period annually. Even though villagers were self-provisioning, they were partially integrated into markets, mostly via product sales. Villagers were neither dependent on commodity inputs (rice, foodstuffs) for their basic needs, nor did they require inputs (fertilizers, pesticides) for successful production. Their market integration was at a very basic level. The dominant discourse of development in Vietnam highlights dams as a way to improve the livelihoods of ethnic minority people in the Northwest. In this process, however, as development threw people into a new material reality and forced them to learn new skills to survive and more intensively integrate into the market economy, it produced changing territorial subjects and transformed their culture. People had to change the way they worked and lived.

## Engendered River Nostalgia

The displaced people I interviewed, including Khun and Mr. E, shared one thing in common—their longing for the river. Displaced White Thái women formerly from Quynh Nhai district, for example, were no longer able to engage in the traditional practice of washing their hair in the river on New Year's Eve, as they had in the past. The tradition was their opportunity to wash away all the bad luck and hardships of the old year and celebrate a new year with good health and happiness. In an attempt to keep this tradition alive, Quynh Nhai district authorities have recently been organizing this practice on an annual basis for local communities, but not everyone is able to participate, especially displaced people who no longer live near the river. As an activity that the authorities organize, it is also less spontaneous and more structured than the customary activity that ordinary villagers cherished for hundreds of years.

Moving away to new places far from cherished locales can cause many problems. In the resettled villages I visited, men's alcohol consumption had increased, especially in the first two years after relocation. In 2006, when I spent several weeks in Muong Muon, I witnessed men gathering to drink almost every night. Much of the alcohol they consumed was of low quality and was not homemade, owing to a lack of maize and cassava. When I asked why they drank so much, one man commented, "What do you think we can do? I have nothing here except this house. We don't have land. How can I work? We're apart from half of our relatives and neighbors. We miss our home, our village. If we don't drink, what can we do?" Drinking, in these cases, can also be seen as everyday form of resistance. It was villagers' reaction to show anger, disappointment, and opposition to what development projects had brought to them, which they regard as unjust. Excessive alcohol consumption has significantly impacted families. In 2007, two drunk men of Muong Nhuong died in a motorcycle accident. At least three men have suffered brain damage attributed to excessive alcohol consumption. I remember one case in Muong Nhuong village of the husband of the representative of the Women's Union. His drinking led to a stroke in 2007; he became unconscious after drinking for seven days straight. When he regained consciousness, he could no longer remember his name, his family, or his past. His wife became head of the household, and their relatives were unable to support them financially. She worked very hard to allow her children to continue their schooling; for her, better education opportunities for her children was the only benefit of moving to the resettlement site. She dug a pond to stock fish for a few months each year, grew vegetables when it was possible, and raised a pig and a cow. Like many other ponds in the village, her pond had water only during the rainy season (normally May through July), and her window for fish farming was limited. Nor did she have enough water to grow vegetables all year. Her responsibilities in the home meant that she could not leave to sell her labor or engage in other services. As a result, her income was very modest. When I returned in 2009, she was no longer a representative of the village's Women's Union; she instead used that time for farming, tending her cow, collecting fuelwood, and taking care of her husband. For younger people, however, stories often differ. While displacement has created another site for the younger generation to perform new sorts of everyday politics, it also has enabled new types of territorial subjects whose dependency on land and river for their livelihood has changed. A thirty-year-old man shared his views with me in May 2018:

> I don't miss the old village as much as my parents do. Of course, at first it was very challenging. I felt lost. But I've learned to get used to it. After thirteen years, my parents would still rather come back to our old village, but I'd choose to stay. Here it's more convenient than in my old village. We're not by the river, but we're closer to the big road, and Sơn La City. Since I moved here, I have learned to do many different jobs, and now I stay with construction work. It gives me extra income while I can still work with my wife on the farm. Many of us no longer just depend on farming these days.[50]

Changing material reality alters the multiple social and cultural meanings of life, as well as the relationship to surrounding natural resources including rivers, land, and forest, which in turn plays a crucial role in enabling everyday politics and shaping embodied territorial subjects. For many people who were displaced, their subjectivities changed as they lost connections with rooted places and associated tangible and intangible values, values that otherwise serve to drive their cultural transformation. While dam-induced displacement as an external power has influenced all subjects, the experience varied depending on people's gender, age, ethnicity, and access to resources.

## Adapting to Becoming Rubber Workers

While displacement caused by hydropower dams impacts the ways in which women and men engage in production, as well as the realities of their domestic and public spheres, the changes in modes of labor and production brought on by the arrival of rubber plantations in the Northwest are even more substantial. While chapters 5 and 6 directly address rubber plantations, in the next section I will discuss the impacts of these plantations on the culture of the Northwest.

Since 2007, when the Vietnam Rubber Group began to set up rubber plantations in the region, changes to working life have overturned many local ethnic groups' customs and traditions. As discussed above, labor distribution by gender is very common within Thái families and other ethnic groups in the Northwest. Men and women share farmwork in specific ways. However, labor distribution among contract workers on large-stockholder rubber plantations does not follow this traditional pattern, and all workers must comply with the company's rules. The separation by gender of production activities enshrined in traditional family life has been broken. In Sơn La, for example, since a family contributing one hectare of land to the rubber company is allocated only one job on the plantation, the rest of the family is not engaged in the work unless they want to voluntarily help their family's rubber worker to fulfill a daily work quota. Although the husband formally signed a contract with the rubber company (if he received the opportunity) after contributing the family's land, the wife typically accompanied her husband in his work on the plantation.

Rubber plantations have altered relationships among the villagers and destroyed the reciprocity system in the village to a much higher degree than even dam-induced displacement. Before, when households cultivated maize and soybeans, family members and friends used to help each other during planting and harvest. They usually formed a group and rotated between families' fields to prepare the land, weed, or harvest. Now that households work for the rubber company, everyone wants to maximize his or her own working time each day to receive additional payment, and group rotation has stopped. Worse, everyday forms of modifications and evasions, which often occur at the expense of neighbors and other people in similar conditions, are found in multiple sites. For example, villagers have fought each other for more convenient working spots on the plantation. Nobody wants to work on distant or steep plots. In 2012, a rubber plantation worker in Muong

Che was hospitalized after a fight over a good work location, and the commune's police intervened to resolve the situation. In Muong Ma, the headman who had good connections with the rubber company field staff often got better lots to work on for his family and relatives. Colleagues became angry with one another over issues related to the work and were often envious if someone received a more favorable task in the morning assignment.

The local authorities were aware of these problems, and in an attempt to remedy them, district-level officials (both Thái and Kinh) in some locales encouraged villagers to practice traditional activities, such as the throwing balls festival (*ném còn*). Villagers said that they were exhausted at the end of the day and had no interest in practicing these activities. Even though there were *ném còn* games going on in other villages, they had no energy to go and see them. One woman from a *ném còn* team said, "We used to practice throwing, but now nobody wants to see these contests, so we stopped."[51] For a few years now, no one in Muong Ma or Muong Che has shown much interest in practicing any of their traditional activities, including *múa xoè* (Thái traditional dancing) and *ném còn*.

The appropriation of nature and labor is intrinsic to industrial development—a resource-intensive and socially inegalitarian process.[52] Territorialization in the form of destructive development projects marginalizes people through its process, subjecting them to multiple dimensions and layers of cultural transformation, from individual to household to community levels. Under the new conditions, it has been difficult for the villagers to maintain many of their former practices. In general, when they found themselves unable to alter the new rules, they conformed to them. However, not everyone has kept silent; there have been negative reactions to the rubber project. In chapter 5 I will elaborate on the stories of several villagers and their reactions to the rubber plantations that have subsumed their lives.

## Mining-Induced Cultural Changes

If hydropower and rubber plantations have affected northwesterners on a large scale, in terms of geographical area, mining has changed people's lives on a smaller scale, but in ways no less severe. In Yên Bái, the mines polluted streams, leading to fish deaths, while activities associated with the streams, and not just fishing, also collapsed. "Fish from Ngoi Lau stream were very famous because of their flavor," a villager from Au Lau commune of Tran Yen district, Yên Bái Province, told me when we visited the commune one day in May 2018. He continued: "There was a saying, 'Fish from Ngoi Lau stream have always been eaten completely as soon as they're cooked.' But not anymore. We haven't got any fish from Ngoi Lau stream for a few years now." The Ngoi Lau stream originates in Luong Thinh commune of Tran Yen district, Yên Bái Province, home to seven iron ore mining and processing factories. In the past, the stream was full of fish. The water was clean, and villagers living along the stream used it for their domestic needs. Aquatic resources in the stream were a rich source of nutrition for the villagers. Children learned how to swim every afternoon in the summer, while adults used the stream for bathing, cleaning, or washing clothes. These activities have disappeared. In Luong Thinh commune itself, pollution from the factories has changed not only the water but also the air and the land, significantly altering people's livelihoods and ways of living. Water has become a scarce resource, and frequent conflicts over water have damaged social cohesion. At the same time, a lack of unpolluted land for farming has driven young people, mostly Dao (Yao) ethnic minorities, out of their home villages to cities and industrial parks in the Red River delta to earn their living. Villagers' traditional livelihoods, such as paddy rice farming and cinnamon growing, have faded away, making it difficult for them to sustain their lives as they used to. The chairman of Thinh Tam commune complained, "Beside environmental impacts, mining activities in our commune break the custom of our people. From my observations, I found many problems. The villagers' relationship is not the same. I mean it's getting worse. Water, land, and air pollution have damaged people's livelihoods. People are getting poorer. And difficult economic conditions have created social conflicts, and people now can easily fight over small things."[53]

Similar problems related to copper mining activities have affected villagers in Minh Ba commune, Lào Cai Province. Mrs. Dang, a woman from Minh Ba commune, told me, "For us now water is everything. Almost every day, there is some type of fight over water. Everyone is crazy about water. These mining things have seriously degraded our neighborhood relationship." Many young people in the village, regardless of whether they are ethnic Kinh or Dao, had to leave to find nonfarming jobs, while those who remained work as miners because there is no land left for them to farm. With parents struggling for their livelihoods for almost ten years since the mine began operating, many children have dropped out of school, leaving more than a third of the village illiterate.

Finding wage labor is difficult, and villagers no longer have farmland as a safety net. Like dams and rubber plantations, mines play a critical role in forming and shaping local subjects, transforming culture via transforming people's everyday lives. While the dominant discourse highlights the tradeoff in development, the reality shows that ecological sustainability and social justice deserve much more attention from development planners and the wider public.

This chapter has focused on everyday cultural transformation associated with hydropower, rubber plantations, and mines in the Northwest. As territorialization, visible in the creation of new systems of resource control through development projects, has encroached on the Northwest, regardless of whether it has come in the form of state farms, cooperatives, hydropower dams, rubber plantations, or mines, it has resulted in serious unintended effects such as poverty, social problems, cultural loss, and the marginalization of ethnic groups. For many ethnic minority communities in the region, subjectivities have changed when people were forced to switch from basic self-sufficiency to a market-oriented economy after being displaced and resettled because of dam construction or loss of land to rubber plantations, as I will discuss in chapters 4 and 6. Given the limited access these villagers have to formal education and information more generally, this change in livelihood created serious difficulties for many.

In addition to these challenges, ethnic minorities have little influence over the policies and decisions that direct these development projects or allow for the destruction of upland environments, regardless of the effect on people's lives. Northwesterners have been marginalized, not only during the early stage of contemporary nation-building processes after 1954, but in the present day. As territorial subjects, they have constantly been shaped and reshaped as a result of their everyday struggles to maintain their livelihoods, culture, and traditions.

As more and more development projects invade the Northwest region, they are reconfiguring its agrarian and cultural landscapes. The assimilation process that started with the state's formation in 1945 has accelerated with dam-building and the establishment and expansion of rubber plantations and mines. Agricultural land use, as well as forest and river resource management, tightly link with both state laws and local/community regulations. Development planners' failure to pay attention to these regulations, or to longstanding traditions, often leads to adverse impacts on people's lives and community cohesion. Resettlers may be able to continue some of their traditional practices, but as the minority in their new homes, they may soon completely assimilate with their host communities. After a few generations in the resettlement areas, no one may remember how to manage fish-rice fields or run irrigation conduits from the river to the rice fields. Working on rubber plantations failed to help villagers sustain their cultural lives and led to a wave of employment-seeking migration from the uplands to the lowlands, as I will discuss in chapter 6. Cultural changes include not only shifts in dress, customs, and traditional lifestyles, but also changes in resource management, and changes in emotional attachment to these resources and agricultural practices—from the way that people care for their livestock and grow their crops to how they make their living and interact with one another on a daily basis.

The following chapters explore in more detail the three major landscape transformations in the Northwest and everyday politics. The first chapter of each part highlights the materialities and the technologies of production for these resources that help contextualize the external powers on which everyday politics and subject formation depend. These materialities and technologies express acts of territorialization and development by the state and, in some cases, private enterprise, of lands formerly in possession of rural residents thereafter facing displacement and dispossession. The chapters that follow examine everyday politics and agency embedded in processes of territorialization, development, and dispossession.

# PART I

## *Dams*

# CHAPTER 2

# State Power and the Conquest of Nature

In 2004, when I started to work as an activist on hydropower dam issues in Vietnam, I learned that the government had labeled dam-related issues as sensitive, which in practice meant that hardly anyone wanted to discuss it. I remember my first meetings with many of the people who later became good colleagues. Some of them shooed me out the door when I asked questions about certain projects, especially the Sơn La Dam and resettlement issues. In the 1990s and early 2000s, the national government strongly promoted hydropower dams as a renewable source of energy for economic growth. But in the mid-2000s, with the construction of hundreds of hydropower dams all over the country that displaced thousands of people, the hydropower dam became the elephant in the room. Everyone saw it, but as subjectified subjects, everyone avoided broaching the topic because no one wanted to get into trouble for being anti-dam. It took me two years to receive permission to hold the country's first workshop on hydropower development in Hanoi in late 2005. The workshop, named "Hydropower and Sustainable Development after Đổi Mới," attracted almost forty attendees.[1] This event launched the Vietnam Rivers Network (VRN), which soon became a nationwide network of scholars, activists, government officials, and community members who want to protect rivers in Vietnam. They contributed to bringing hydropower into the public eye, and as a result the topic eventually became less sensitive.

The labeling of hydropower as sensitive encapsulates the fact that hydro-social developments in Vietnam are not socially or politically neutral but express and reconstitute physical, social, cultural, economic, and political power relations.[2] Following Vietnam's independence in 1954, the development of multipurpose reservoirs for electricity generation, irrigation, and flood control received much attention from the North Vietnamese government and the governing Communist Party.[3] As in other postcolonial states, hydropower dams in Vietnam have played an important role in supporting the government's political agenda and demonstrating its capacity for independence and modernization. At the inauguration of the Sơn La hydropower project on December 23, 2012, Prime Minister Nguyễn Tấn Dũng summed up the significance of the dam project for the national agenda: "With all our pride, we can say that the Sơn La hydropower project has continued 'the epic conquest of the Đà River' and it has truly become a vivid expression of the revolutionary heroism of a self-strong, self-reliant spirit that overcomes difficulties to rise up in the task of building the glorious Vietnamese fatherland."[4]

This chapter explores hydropower dams as a territorializing development project. It examines how the state used hydropower landscape transformation and the arts of government to strengthen state power and its presence in the frontier. It identifies key external powers at work in the formation of differentiated territorial subjects, which will be the focus of later chapters. As the official discourse of dam development in Vietnam and the Northwest posits dams as a symbol of national development, it suggests that local people, such as those that the Sơn La dam displaced, should be willing to make sacrifices in the national interest. In symbolizing developmental progress, dams play a critical role in the state-building process in Vietnam. Development planners and the authorities herald these projects as a prerequisite for industrialization, modernization, and globalization, as well as a way to improve the livelihoods of ethnic minority people. Moreover, the government highlighted dam development to bring people together to unite the revolutionary spirit, an effort to demonstrate a drive for Vietnam to develop without the help of outsiders. This dominant discourse helps to promote hydropower dams as a must-do development project and normalize any impacts such projects may cause to local people and the environment.

## The Discourse of Nature Domination and National Interest

This section examines the foundations of the dominant discourse of nature control in the national interest that the state deploys. Both the overall project and the nature- and nation-based discourse emerge from broader geopolitical movements. Throughout the twentieth century, global proliferation of large dams and river basin development promulgated a concrete revolution, attributable to tight linkages between geopolitics, technologies, and large dams in the name of development.[5] Large dams were integral to modernization, because engineers and development planners expected dams to generate growth through electricity production, flood prevention, and irrigation development. Policymakers and engineers produced a powerful image of the basin as the key tool for enabling river development, and of dams as the key technological means for achieving it.[6] In his study on hydropower development in Tajikistan, Artemy Kalinovsky points to the ideological underpinnings of dam development, finding that large dams were among "the most dramatic ways to demonstrate man's ability to dominate and transform nature, a significant consideration for postcolonial leaders who promoted dam projects."[7]

In this process of promoting dams, the United States Bureau of Reclamation, the world's premier dam builder, played a crucial role. Viewing the transfer of technological expertise regarding water resources development as a crucial way of solidifying geopolitical alliances with other postcolonial countries, the bureau provided technical support to over one hundred countries, including China, India, and a number of countries in Southeast Asia after World War II.[8] The bureau also helped with the first study on dams as a means to tame the Mekong River in the 1960s, when South Vietnam's government was a member of the Mekong River Commission. In general, governments, particularly postcolonial ones, encouraged hydropower dam construction, not only because dams provide cheap and renewable energy for economic growth, but also because they can channel water for irrigation as well as represent a nation's strength and ability to conquer nature and control people.[9]

In the case of Vietnam's hydropower development, the state had already established the discourse of controlling nature in the national interest as the dominant framing for the territorialization of the Northwest back in the 1950s. In the spring of 1958, North Vietnam's government launched its three-year (1958–1960) economic-cultural development plan for Democratic Republic of Vietnam. The government ordered the 176th Army Regiment (Division 316) to march to Điện Biên, an old battlefield, to establish the first army-run state farm in the Northwest.[10] The government expected that state farms would increase the country's agricultural production, expand agricultural land to produce enough food to feed the state farm workers and local people, and strengthen ethnic minorities' trust in party policies—all while suppressing local forces that followed the Đèo clan or supported the idea of bringing back the old regime.

Promotional materials represented fighting against nature as a glorious task to show strength and emphasized the expectation that everyone on a farm should conform to achieve this task. In his call to arms, to conquer nature and build the nation, "Uncle Hồ" was reiterating the belief that these two ideals were inextricably intertwined. Adhering to these ideals was crucial in this early stage of transforming the Northwest, a change that relied on human willpower, the mobilization of labor, and correct socialist thinking.[11] Administrators used slogans on the farm to encourage workers to work and to stay, such as "Labor is glory," "Land is gold," and "Our hands can build everything; with our strength, we can turn stone and gravel into rice."[12] Leaders employed other slogans to demonstrate the Vietnamese people's determination to conquer nature, including "Force rivers to meander," "Make the mountain bow down," and "Get up before the sun."

Artistic products also reflected the official discourse. In his 1960 collection of short stories, *Mùa lạc* (The groundnut season), Nguyễn Khải wrote about the redeeming and life-affirming qualities of being on the Điện Biên state farm: "Life arises from death; happiness arises from sacrifices and hardships. In this life there is no end, only boundaries. It is essential to have the strength to cross boundaries."[13] Right after the farm's establishment, the state enlisted poets, songwriters, and campaigners to encourage young people in the lowlands to come to work with soldiers in developing the Northwest. Short stories like "The Groundnut Season" or "How the Steel Was Tempered" by Nikolai Ostrovsky were, according to one woman in her late seventies, in the books under the pillows of young people her age.[14] "Heading to the Northwest," by Bùi Minh Quốc in 1958, was a popular poem that many memorized during the period, including a woman who recited the poem to me after I asked her about her memories of the time:

Tilting cars climb the mountain
To the Northwest faraway in the mountain forest

Oh, the Northwest! Leaving the lowlands we were full of
    hesitance
But still eager to come
. . .
At the age of twenty, we now see the direction for our life
We hit the road despite distance and challenges
The Northwest welcomes us
We—the happiest people on earth
Coming to the Northwest with our youth and strength
With a glorious mission: clear wilderness

The Northwest with rich and beautiful land but its people are
    still suffering
I will go to reclaim barren land and wasteland
Will create fields of maize and upland rice
For ethnic minority people in Hát Lót, Mộc Châu having full
    harvest of maize and rice
Bring our lovely *muang* and villages prosperity and abundance
                "Heading to the Northwest" (Lên miền Tây Bắc),
                            by Bùi Minh Quốc, 1958

State media praised young people who volunteered to go to conquer
and harness this harsh and dangerous mountainous region. Mrs. Tuyet,
a former volunteer in the Northwest, recalled her experience:

> I was twenty-two. My house was right in downtown, old Hanoi. Every
> morning we woke up by a loudspeaker calling young people to go to
> the Northwest to build our nation. We were all very excited. Some of
> my friends were scared to leave Hanoi. But I thought devoting our-
> selves to the country was a duty that most of us must do. So I wrote
> a letter to volunteer. My group consisted of 128 young women. We
> left Hanoi in December 1958. Before I left, I thought I would just go
> for a couple of years. But then I fell in love with an officer of Division
> 316. We married and stayed in Điện Biên since then.[15]

The state's efforts to glorify the process of sacrificing for the national
interest by moving to the Northwest in support of building the nation
and developing the Northwest succeeded. In late 1959, Điện Biên State
Farm accepted its first volunteer youth pioneers, a group of 162 young
women from Hanoi, and 50 from Thái Bình Province. With the slogan
"Taking the farm as family, taking the Northwest as a homeland," both
the soldiers and the female youth volunteers were encouraged to bring

their relatives to the Northwest. These lowland workers' primary role was to reclaim and improve fields to expand agricultural production. However, they were also assigned to carry out the tasks of guiding ethnic minorities to engage in advanced and fixed farming, to stabilize their lives, as well as to mobilize the local people to be ready to fight to protect Điện Biên during the American War. The arrival of young female volunteer pioneers buoyed the social atmosphere on the state farm. Women and men teamed up to compete in agricultural production. Soldiers and female volunteers coupled up, and many married, helping to ensure a long-term attachment to the land. After a few years, soldiers formed a new village for married couples who were part of the farm. About 90 percent of those who relocated there were lowland Kinh people; only 10 percent were of upland Thái ethnicity.

After the Vietnamese Labor Party's success with the Điện Biên State Farm, the government and party decided to set up other state farms across the Northwest, including Tran Phu (1961), Au Lau (1962), and Nghia Lo and Lien Son (1965), among many others. The labor strategy was similar to that at Điện Biên. Soldiers from the 85th and 83rd Regiments were transferred to these new farms, followed by volunteers from the lowlands. Common land and forestland that previously belonged to local communities became state farms and state forest farms—or put differently, it all became the state's property. The state has deployed a similar process and discourse frequently throughout historical periods of territorializing upland regions of the country. The discourse peaked with hydropower dams, in which language promoting an ideology of conquering/taming the river dominates. In this way, the state farm created a pattern that was followed by subsequent extractive and territorializing development, under which subordinate subjects' interests are politically and ideologically constructed.

## Regime of Truth and Sovereign Power

The "art of government based on Truth" uses the rationality of science to claim expertise and progressive development to justify improvements and interventions.[16] Truth governmentality requires a politics of acceptance in which incontestable authority derives from unquestionable belief systems.[17] The hydropower dam development discourse constitutes a powerful regime of truth that represents hydropower as a cheap and renewable energy source that plays a crucial role in Vietnam's economic development. The government's development policy highlighted the role of energy production in national economic development, as Deputy Prime Minister Hoàng Trung Hải emphasized on the occasion of the fiftieth anniversary of the establishment of Electricity of Vietnam (EVN): "In any circumstance, the energy sector should always be developed before other sectors. . . . Especially now in the era of industrialization and modernization, the energy sector's role and mission should be the top priority."[18]

Energy demand in Vietnam has increased significantly, in parallel with economic growth in the industrial, service, and agricultural sectors, as well as for domestic use. According to EVN's 2018 annual report, energy demand growth was at 10 percent to 15 percent annually over the previous two decades.[19] The Department of Electricity and Renewable Energy's 2019 calculations emphasized that Vietnam's projected output shortage in 2023 could reach 15 billion kWh (equivalent to 5 percent of demand). By 2030, the annual increase in demand for commercial electricity production is expected to be about 8.3 percent.[20] This framing of energy demand made more visible the impending power shortage, which helped the government and EVN to justify further investment in energy development. When problems are defined and made visible, knowledge production requires experts, and individual subjects become an "essential mechanism by which rule is enacted and people should act on things the ways that they are supposed to."[21] In the case of hydropower dam development, the anticipated future power shortages and high energy demand forecast in the Power Development Plan (PDP) 6 (2007) and PDP 7 (2011) normalized assigning a large share of the national energy structure to hydropower. The government also used environmental impact assessments (EIAs) to justify the claim that that any negative impacts on local livelihoods, on displaced people, and on the environment could be minimized. Vietnam's Adjusted PDP 7 (2016) for the period 2011–2020 targeted energy growth operating on a baseline scenario of 7 percent GDP growth per annum from 2016 to 2030.[22] According to the Adjusted PDP 7, for every 1 percent increase in GDP, power output must increase by at least 2 percent. In order to achieve these energy growth targets, Vietnam has maximized its hydropower development. Indeed, the country is expected to produce 90 percent of its total hydropower potential by 2025.

To meet the country's energy needs, in the late 1990s the government approved master plans for each of the country's large river basins based on their hydropower potential.[23] This planning led to an explosion of dam building across the country, and from 2000 to the present, hundreds of large, medium, and small dams for hydropower production and irrigation have been planned and constructed. In the late 1990s and early 2000s, hydropower produced about half of Vietnam's electricity. In 2018, there were 818 large and medium hydropower projects, with a total installed capacity of 23,182 megawatts (MW).[24] In December 2019, total power production in the country reached 227,421 GWh, an increase from 209,287 GWh in 2018.[25] In that year, investment in hydropower started to slow, largely because development was approaching its limit, even though hydropower still accounted for 39 percent of total energy, second only to coal power.[26]

Government-issued policy divided energy projects into four different categories to support its energy development plan: national-level projects, and projects in groups A, B, and C (see table 2.1). This classification helps define who has the decision-making authority over each type of project (see table 2.2). For non-state-funded projects, investors must request a project appraisal and approval from relevant authorities, including the Ministry of Industry and Trade, the Ministry of Natural Resources and Environment, and the relevant provincial government(s). This policy allows investors to start their projects only after their appraisal. Official policy holds that decisions on dam projects are supposed to be based on scale and impact. Such decisions, however, rarely properly consider the many other factors that affect impacts on people and the environment in the proposed dam's vicinity, as I show in the case of Sơn La Dam in chapter 3.

The prime minster, the Ministry of Industry and Trade (MOIT), and the Provincial People's Committees approve hydropower plans. For hydropower cascades or series of dams on large rivers and their tributaries with a capacity of at least 30 MW, the MOIT appoints EVN to study, appraise, and submit hydropower plans to the prime minister or relevant government authority for approval. Between 2000 and 2013 a nationwide total of 899 large- and medium-scale hydropower projects with a total installed capacity of 24,880 MW were in development; provincial-level authorities approved another 338 small hydropower projects with a collective installed capacity of 1,088.8 MW.[27]

To further support dam development, the formal discourse highlights that hydropower in Vietnam provides several benefits for the nation, including water for irrigation and domestic use, and electricity to light cities and support industrialization. Dams also help prevent flooding downstream. Many of the diverse beneficiaries of the structures do not usually know much about the dams. People who do not live in the vicinity of the dam site normally pay more attention to its benefits than they do to the localized impacts and the costs associated

*Table 2.1*　Dam project classification

| GROUP | CLASSIFICATION |
|---|---|
| National-level project (a project must hold at least one of these conditions to be considered at this level) | • Total investment budget > VNĐ 20,000 billion, of which 30% or more is government funding (approximately US$1.33 billion, 2006 conversion rate of about US$1 = VNĐ 15,000)<br>• Appropriate either >= 200 ha of watershed protection forest; or >= 500 ha of coastal protection forest; or >= 200 ha of special forest land; or >= 1,000 ha of production forest (national reserve and conservation areas are not allowed to be appropriated)<br>• Displacement of >= 20,000 people in the upland areas; or >= 50,000 people in other areas<br>• Project is located in an area that is of special importance to national security |
| Group A | Total investment budget > VNĐ 1,500 billion (approximately US$100 million) |
| Group B | VNĐ 75 billion < Total investment budget <= VNĐ 1,500 billion |
| Group C | Total investment budget <= VNĐ 75 billion (approximately US$5 million) (often these are < 30 MW) |

Source: Adapted from Nguyễn Danh Oanh 2009.

Notes: Dam project classification is as per government's Decision No. 66/2006/QH11 on electricity investment dated June 29, 2006.

*Table 2.2*　Decision-making authority for state-funded dam projects, government's Decision No. 66/2006/QH11 on electricity investment dated June 29, 2006

| PROJECT GROUP | PROJECT APPRAISAL | INVESTMENT DECISION-MAKER |
|---|---|---|
| National-level projects | The National Assembly makes the final decision on investment. The prime minister establishes a National Appraisal Committee. The National Assembly is responsible for organizing a project's appraisal before any approval is granted. | Prime minister approves national-level projects based on the National Assembly's decision |
| Group A | Ministerial level | Ministry and provincial authorities |
| Group B | Provincial level | Ministry and provincial authorities |
| Group C | Provincial level | Ministry and provincial authorities |

Source: Adapted from Nguyễn Danh Oanh 2009.

Note: Provincial authorities make decisions on project investments in Groups A, B, and C based on budgetary availability. Provinces usually support these investment decisions.

with its production. The government's deployment of scientific expertise and complex appraisal systems to characterize the importance of the development plans helped to justify both the massive investment in hydropower it was promoting and the designation of the topic as sensitive and not to be questioned. The success of this regime of Truth is indicated (partly) by the fact that many of the project's beneficiaries paid very little attention to dams' costs and negative impacts until the late 2000s.[28] As hydropower was portrayed as an unquestionable necessity for national growth and improvement of marginalized upland people's lives, its costs, as the costs of development, had to be tolerated, which in return enabled state territorialization with little open resistance, as well as contributed to shaping the ways territorial subjects responded to dams, as I will describe in chapters 3 and 4.

## The Price of Modernization

After Đổi Mới was instituted in 1986, dams became a symbol of development as fuel for Vietnam's economic growth.[29] Development planners justified dams as a way to improve the livelihoods of ethnic minorities in the uplands and narrow economic gaps among various ethnic groups and between the uplands and the lowlands.[30] This idea of dam development embodies Vietnam's modernization process. It expresses how modernity is deeply and inevitably a geographical project in which the entangled transformations of nature and society express changing power positions among different actors in water-related issues.[31] Despite the government's dominant discourse of modernization, this transformation of the social and natural environment comes at a cost to both.

Developmental states (those with state-led macroeconomic planning) find themselves increasingly pulled into the open market with institutional arrangements such as the World Bank (WB), the International Monetary Fund (IMF), and the World Trade Organization (WTO). For a country like Vietnam, having traveled on a long and difficult road of development from a centrally planned to a market economy, the role of these international institutions has been important in the country's reform process. The WB and the IMF's structural adjustment programs in Vietnam were requisite conditions for further loans from the WB and other multilateral institutions to invest in infrastructure, health, and education projects. These development programs and policies have produced widespread indirect and direct impacts throughout the country. In fact, the rapidly transforming landscape of Vietnam has been seen to represent the birth of a hybrid model of development that combines the worst of central planning and control with the worst of capitalist exploitation.[32] In this view, economic transition in a so-called socialist country like Vietnam can, on one hand, be good for the country's economic growth but, on the other hand, not so good for the environment and for communities. The economic transition promotes dispossession processes and further marginalizes certain groups in society. While in the uplands dispossession has been realized through development projects such as hydropower, plantations, and mining, in lowland areas, dispossession has occurred through the creation of industrial zones, especially in terms of urban land development.[33]

The Hòa Bình Dam, Yali Falls Dam, Sơn La Dam, and Lai Châu Dam projects exemplify the ideals and nationalist fervor that dams have come to symbolize in Vietnam. For many people, especially government officials and developers, the negative impacts of these big dams are negligible in comparison to the benefits they have brought, and will continue to bring, to the national economy.[34] During the building of the Hòa Bình Dam in the early 1980s, the Vietnamese government placed a letter addressed to a future generation in a time capsule that was then embedded within a large monument on top of the dam; the inscription, in Vietnamese and Russian, was an attempt to solidify the unity and friendship between Vietnam and the former Soviet Union. Meant to be opened in 2100, the letter refers to the pride of a poor nation that did not have enough food to eat or clothes to keep warm but built the then second-largest dam in Southeast Asia with great determination.[35] Postage stamps of the period featuring images of the Hòa Bình Dam trumpet this potent symbol of modernity.

Dams have caused problems, however, including deforestation and destroyed habitat, at both the dam site and in areas downstream. Social and environmental costs imposed by dam development are far from negligible. Hydropower dams are a form of uneven development, which James O'Connor refers to as "combined development."[36]

By virtue of its location along valley bottoms, land that is now submerged was usually the most fertile for agriculture. Consequently, people displaced from these fertile areas have had to move to places where land is poorer and less agriculturally productive. The government set the compensation prices for land and lost assets at far less than market prices. For example, for the Sơn La Dam, in three districts where I conducted my research, the market prices for lost land were six to ten times higher than the compensation price.[37] Or as a man from Lai Châu Province told me in May 2018, "Oh you know, my family used to have a lot of land, almost three hectares of paddy rice land, not including the upland fields. But now we have nothing. All of our paddy rice land was submerged under the reservoir; upland fields were contributed to the rubber plantations." He continued: "Since the compensation we got from land lost due to the Sơn La Dam was very low, VNĐ 3,000 [about US$2.00] per square meter, we used to joke that one square meter of our land was worth less than an ice cream. Oh well, but that was the province's policy. What can we do?" In addition to the underestimation of dam construction costs, inadequate compensation is another critical factor that makes hydropower projects appear less costly for government officials and dam planners.

Among displaced peoples, most cited land shortages as an issue; lack of adequate farmland after relocation was a shared concern in virtually all instances of dam construction that have resulted in resettlement in Vietnam. Dam development has displaced many hundreds of thousands of Vietnamese, the majority of them in upland areas. The Hòa Bình Dam project, for example, flooded 20,800 hectares and displaced fifty-eight thousand people; the Yali Fall Dam displaced more than six thousand ethnic minority people. The Sơn La Dam resulted in the displacement of more than one hundred thousand people in the

FIGURE 2.1.   Sơn La Dam's construction at an early stage, in August 2009. Photo by the author.

Northwest uplands; and the last big dam on the mainstream of the Đà River, the Lai Châu Dam, displaced almost ten thousand people. In some displaced communities, villagers did not even have access to the national grid for many years after their resettlement.

Building hydropower projects and their related components—roads, transmission lines, and resettlement sites—has degraded upland land-scapes and reduced primary forest cover. Along the Đồng Nai River, for example, an estimated 32,080 to 51,328 hectares of forest were destroyed in order to gain 3,208 MW of electric generation capacity from twenty-six hydropower plants (an average of 10 to 16 hectares of forest for each MW of electricity).[38] While there are no national statistics on forest and land losses linked to hydropower projects, a PanNature study at twenty-nine national parks/reserves reveals that up to 7,277 hectares of forest was either flooded or cut down and 275,889 hectares of land "recovered" (taken or appropriated) to make way for hydropower projects.[39]

The Law on Environmental Protection is supposed to mitigate these costs. Examining the extent to which dam builders obey the law can reveal how mitigation was planned and implemented. Aiming at pro-tecting the environment and mitigating environmental problems asso-ciated with development projects, the Vietnamese government has been updating its Law on Environmental Protection every few years. In the most recent version, approved in 2020, hydropower developers must replant any forest areas lost due to dam construction to ensure green coverage. In practice, this goal seems unattainable. Two principal rea-sons compromise forest maintenance: first, in the hydropower boom, communes often use the scarce land that remains for agriculture rather than forest, and second, investors reduce costs by skimping on refor-estation.[40] A 2013 report by the Ministry of Industry and Trade shows that only about 3 percent of the lost forest was replanted.[41]

By law, developers may not appropriate national reserve and conser-vation areas for hydropower projects. The reality differs. For example, the Sông Bung 4 Dam, funded by the Asian Development Bank, flooded 140 hectares of the core zone of the Sông Thanh National Reserve.[42] The Đồng Nai 6 and 6A hydropower projects on the Đồng Nai River, if built, would flood 197.6 hectares of forest, 86.43 hectares of which belongs to the Cát Tiên National Park.[43] It is clear that in many cases, developers, including the central government itself, do not follow the rules, and project implementation can even go in the opposite direction from environmental law and policies.

An audit report by the Ministry of Industry and Trade submitted to the prime minister in 2010 backs up the reality that some dam projects' developers did not follow regulations on environmental protection, project quality, or even dam security. Although no systematic study of these problems has yet been conducted, many forestry experts believe that such a large loss of forest cover has reduced watershed holding capacity. According to hydrological experts, increased water flows combined with large volumes of water unexpectedly released from dams contributed significantly to the devastating floods in central Vietnam in 2009 that killed 422 people and caused a financial loss of more than US$1 billion.[44] In October 2020, hundreds of people were killed or went missing after severe floods in central Vietnam destroyed about 178,000 houses in less than a two-week period. Environmental groups and scholars attributed the floods to overdevelopment of hydropower dams of all sizes and the resulting serious deforestation in these central provinces.[45]

Other impacts of dams include damage to river ecosystems, reductions in fish production downstream, disputes over water resources, and other adverse downstream effects such as sedimentation loss. For example, the Hòa Bình Dam reportedly blocks 75 percent of the sediment normally flowing downstream.[46] Sediment blockage shortens any given dam's lifespan, risks catastrophic failure, and deprives deltaic plains of fertile soil inputs. A reduction in fish production also deprives local people of an important source of protein.

Under the name of development and modernization, dams serve as a crucial tool in producing state hegemony in upland regions and constructing the frontier. Concentration of local people in high-density resettlement sites makes it easier for authorities to control and monitor frontier subjects.[47] Dams have extensive consequences for the environment and for social and cultural landscapes. They strip land tenure from upland people, as the state and developers claim a right to the land that villagers have held for many generations.[48] Dam development in Vietnam has dispossessed hundreds of thousands of people in the uplands, with accompanying losses of land and livelihoods. Ironically, dam-affected people are the same people who development planners and engineers projected would benefit the most from dam construction. Instead, many have either become landless wage workers or struggle to make a living on tiny plots that they received as government compensation after resettlement. Dam-induced displacement and power generation potentially impact all upland areas in Vietnam with hydropower potential.

## Hydropower Development and the Will to Improve

Vietnam's ten largest river systems have all shown potential for hydro-power: the Đà (Black River), Lô-Gâm-Chảy, Mã-Chu, Cả, Vu Gia-Thu Bồn, Trà Khúc-Hương, Se San, Ba, Serepok, and Đồng Nai (see table 2.3).[49] Of these, the Đà, Lô-Gâm-Chảy, Se San, and Đồng Nai river systems have the highest hydropower potential, accounting for 75 percent of the total capacity.[50] However, small hydropower projects have also spread over all the river systems in Vietnam. Since 2005, the number of small hydropower plants has grown very quickly, with an average of five to six plants per river, throughout the country.[51]

In Vietnam, EVN calculated only about 20 percent of the cost of a hydropower project (equipment purchases) using international market prices; the remaining 80 percent was calculated based on Vietnamese prices, which do not seriously consider the costs of externalities such as environmental and social impacts.[52] This accounting practice esti-mates the stated costs of hydropower investment far below actual and

*Table 2.3*    Hydropower development potential in Vietnam

| | RIVER BASIN | POTENTIAL NUMBER OF HYDROPOWER PLANTS | POTENTIAL INSTALLED CAPACITY (MW) | POTENTIAL ANNUAL ELECTRICITY PRODUCTION (BILLION KWH) |
|---|---|---|---|---|
| 1 | Đà | 7 | 6,800 | 27.2 |
| 2 | Lô-Gâm-Chảy | 9 | 1,500 | 6.0 |
| 3 | Mã-Chu | 7 | 760 | 2.7 |
| 4 | Cả | 3 | 470 | 1.8 |
| 5 | Vu Gia-Thu Bồn | 8 | 1,250 | 4.5 |
| 6 | Trà Khúc-Hương | 2 | 480 | 2.1 |
| 7 | Se San | 8 | 2,000 | 9.1 |
| 8 | Ba | 6 | 650 | 2.7 |
| 9 | Serepok | 5 | 730 | 3.3 |
| 10 | Đồng Nai | 15 | 2,900 | 11.5 |
| | Total from plants with a generating capacity 30 MW/plant | 70 | 17,540 | 70.9 |
| | Total from small hydropower plants with a generating capacity < 30 MW/plant | | 7,000 | 29.1 |
| | Total | | 24,540 | 100.00 |

*Source:* Adapted from Nguyễn Danh Oanh 2009.

accrued costs, and a systematic underestimation of costs contributed significantly to Vietnam's hydropower boom. Hydropower construction projects are expensive—approximately VNĐ 25 billion (US$1.25 million) per MW. Private investors rarely invest in large projects, and foreign investors do not invest in hydropower in Vietnam because the state subsidizes the energy sector and regulates the selling price, cutting into potential returns. State-owned companies, therefore, implement the majority of projects greater than 30 MW.[53]

In 2018, energy from hydropower still counted for 39 percent of the total electricity produced in the country despite the reduction in investment.[54] When Vietnam's Electricity Law was passed in 2005, the lawmakers envisioned major changes for the sector, including extensive equitization of Electricity of Vietnam power generation assets and a greater role for domestic and foreign investors to meet new demand. Nonetheless, EVN dominates electricity production within the energy sector, and in late 2018, EVN and its subsidiaries, Power Generation Corporation (GENCO) 1, 2, and 3 produced 85.72 percent of Vietnam's total electricity; BOT (Build, Operate, and Transfer) and other developers produced 14.28 percent.[55] For hydropower investors, the ceiling price for electricity (not including water resource taxes, forest environmental services charge, the fee for granting water rights, as well as the value added tax) is VNĐ 1,110/kWh (US$0.47/kWh) in 2019.[56] At this price, not many private investors invest in the sector.

From 2016 to 2025, the development of residual hydropower capacity has focused on pumped-storage projects in the country's north and south. In the early 2010s, when domestic hydropower potential started to approach its limit, EVN began to move into Laos and Cambodia to develop hydropower resources. Between the mid-1990s and the late 2010s, hydropower in Vietnam developed at breakneck speed despite environmental groups' efforts to slow down the process. Even though investment began to slow in 2018, when none of the country's rivers remained free from dams, the prime minister still approved two large hydropower projects—Hòa Bình Extension (480 MW) in the Northwest and the Yali Falls Dam Extension (360 MW) in the Central Highlands.[57] EVN is the developer for both projects.

The state's claims on land facilitate hydropower development in Vietnam. The Vietnamese state claimed ownership of all the land within its boundaries immediately after the country's independence from France in 1954. Along with the development of the modern Vietnamese state, a series of laws was promulgated relating to resource governance (such as the Land Law, the Law on Environmental Protection, and the Water Law). In the early 1990s, once the country opened its economy to the world and began pursuing comprehensive development policies, international and environmental groups began mounting pressure on the government to promote better accountability, transparency, and participation in the development process. It had the desired effect, as the government began to pay more attention to development issues, specifically those critical to dam development, such as land tenure, resettlement, local participation, environmental protection, and water management. This was realized in the promulgation of new laws (Land Law 1993, the Law on Environmental Protection 1992, and the Law on Water Resources 1998) and policies, as I will elaborate on in the following sections. Related ministries have constantly revised and amended these laws and policies in order to support the state's goal of more effective resource management.[58] External pressure from donors as well as internal demands from affected people, local authorities, academics, NGOs, and the media have led to these positive changes.[59] The growth of environmental groups in Vietnam and increased access to development policies specified by international organizations allowed a broader audience to compare Vietnam's policies with those of other countries, which in turn stimulated domestic pressure for reform.

The policy and planning process for dam-associated displacement of local populations has also clearly shifted over time. In the past, Vietnam did not have a resettlement program for circumstances in which the state enclosed land for its own interests. For example, the construction of the Hòa Bình Dam between 1979 and 1994 occurred before Vietnam had any policies to support resettlement and rehabilitation or any requirement for an EIA. Consequently, the project's negative impacts on the environment and local people were diverse and enduring. It was a top-down project with no participation of the affected peoples at any stage. NGOs did not exist in Vietnam at this time. The fifty-eight thousand people forced to resettle because of dam construction belonged to Mường, Tày, Dao, Thái Trắng, Thái Đen, and Kinh groups; they did not receive compensation for land loss or aid for their displacement because dam developers did not include these costs into the project's costs. It was only in the mid-1990s that the government started a process of adjusting its resettlement policies to comply with international standards and to respond to internal pressure resulting from the myriad problems stemming from resettlement. The improvement of related laws and resettlement policies, while they did not slow down hydropower development, served as foundation for efforts that, to some extent, would help mitigate impacts caused by dam-induced land acquisition.

## Institutional Structure for River Basin Management

Since the early 1960s, the state's attention to water resources governance has steadily increased, and policies and delegated authority for river basin and water management have continuously shifted. In May 1998, the National Assembly approved the first Law on Water Resources; it came into effect in January 1999. A revised Law on Water Resources was issued in 2012. The Water Law highlights a strategy for dam development, including plans to (1) upgrade and rehabilitate existing dams to increase efficient use of stored water and improve dam safety; (2) build large dams for multipurpose uses, based on integrated water resources development; and (3) minimize dam construction's adverse impacts on communities and ecological systems. Although there are an impressive nine ministries involved in water management, here I focus on the three most important decision-making agencies for river development: the Ministry of Agriculture and Rural Development (MARD), the Ministry of Natural Resources and Environment (MONRE), and the Ministry of Industry and Trade (MOIT).

When the Ministry of Irrigation merged with MARD in 1994, the latter assumed responsibility for the management of water resources. In 2000, MARD established the National Water Council and three River Basin Organizations (RBOs) for the three large river basins in Vietnam.[60] From 2001 to 2008, MARD formed eight river basin planning and management units to act as consulting bodies for the government and provincial authorities. MONRE's founding in 2002, however, led to a dispute over river basin management between the two ministries; MARD had its own plans for managing all river basins, while MONRE formed committees on river basin environment and protection for three river basins.[61] In short, two organizations under two separate ministries coexisted and overlapped in several functions related to river basin management.

The transfer of river basin management from MARD to MONRE in August 2008 put an end to the long dispute between the two ministries. Decree 120/2008/NĐ-CP (December 2008) stimulated the formation of a new group for river basin management—the River Basin Organization— which was expected to work differently from the earlier RBOs that

MARD established. Some of the differences included the way that hy-dropower developers must commit to ensuring minimum flows for downstream areas. Minimum flow ensures that the downstream areas will not dry out and that water demand from people living downstream and for aquatic species is met. Perhaps more importantly, Article 7 of the decree stipulates that all organizations, individuals, and communities can have a voice in water and river basin management. Unfortunately, there were never further instructions on how to implement Decree 120. It is now invalid because it was based on the Law on Environmental Protection 2005, which was later replaced by the Law on Environmental Protection 2012. Between 1993 and 2013, the government, the prime minister, and the three abovementioned ministries issued at least fifty decrees, decisions, and circulars to guide the implementation of policies and laws related to hydropower development.[62]

Bureaucratic wrangling and overlap in responsibilities persist nonetheless, because MONRE is responsible for water and river basin management in general, while MOIT is responsible for dam planning through its subsidiary, EVN. In practice, existing river basin committees and units under MARD and MONRE have played little if any role in dam planning, leading to further problems related to dam construction.[63] As Vice Minister Nguyễn Thái Lai of MONRE emphasized in an interview in 2009, "In reality, our current appraisal procedures face many obstacles because investors only send their project documents to MONRE for appraisal after they were already approved by MOIT." Even though investors are required to request appraisals for their projects from MONRE, this work is normally the last step after MOIT has already approved the projects.[64] This procedure, unfortunately, has not changed in the last decade.

While EIAs have been used as an important tool to justify impacts of dams, they are often poorly conducted. Indeed, it seems that environmental impact assessment has become a bureaucratic formality but not an actual measure to remediate real or forecast environmental impacts. For example, in the case of the Đồng Nai 5 hydropower project, the investor simply copied the EIA of a different project on the Mã River without even changing a number of location names.[65] According to Tuoitrenews, 70 percent of EIA reports have been carried out on paper only—not involving any fieldwork—while the remaining 30 percent are plagiarized.[66] "Such unreliable reports will lead to faulty forecasts that may cause environmental disasters," indicated Nguyễn Khắc Kình, deputy head of the Vietnam Environmental Impact Assessment

Association and a project appraiser for more than ten years.[67] While developers may hold an approved EIA, many fail to follow their own promises within the EIAs to minimize impact.[68] As an official from a provincial Department of Natural Resources and Environment observed, "We have many problems in conducting an EIA. Low-quality EIA leads to false plans to address problems. Investors often avoid following EIAs to reduce their costs. For example, most of them would not do reforestation as required or have effective measures to deal with issues like landslide, biodiversity loss, pollution, etc. Well, even though we have policies in place, enforcement is another story. That's why in many cases, EIAs do not help much in mitigating impacts."[69]

Despite policy improvements, the weak coordination among key ministries in making decisions related to river development, coupled with the bad practices in EIA approval and implementation, has not only accelerated dam development as a territorializing project but has also exacerbated problems that affected people have encountered, as I will elaborate in chapters 3 and 4.

## Advocacy Politics—Environmental Groups' Counterclaims and Increasing Media Interest

Since they were a sensitive topic, no research had been done on the adverse impacts of dams for fifteen years. In 1992, Philip Hirsch and a team of domestic researchers conducted the first study on the impacts of dam development in the country.[70] For the following decade only a few researchers studied this subject, until the Vietnam Rivers Network began to publicize the issue in 2006.[71] There was a rumor circulating in the 2000s about how hydropower dams were approved. It was said that the funds lobbied for a project's approval were based on the dam's capacity (in MW)—the larger the project, the more likely it was to be approved. And once a project was approved by the National Assembly or the prime minister, it became a national project for the national interest; it would be almost impossible to fight against its construction. Thus, the politics of dams in Vietnam is the kind of politics envisioned by central elites for whom economic growth and a vaguely conceived national good matter more than the local people whom these projects disproportionately affect.

In Vietnam, NGOs and social movements have encountered many constraints owing to strict laws that control their effective operation. The public in general views NGOs as an informal channel of information. Nevertheless, in the 2010s NGOs were emerging as a relatively strong voice. During this period, citizens' voices could have an influence in a meaningful but limited way as new spaces for participation opened.[72] The state and NGOs share a dialectic on dam-building issues. While the state has been building an image of dams as a symbol of development and fuel for national economic growth, since the mid-2000s NGOs, the media, and academics have started questioning dam building based on their own studies. The VRN was established to strengthen river protection and has conducted studies on dam impacts across Vietnam.[73] VRN members' studies showed the inefficiency of dams and, worse, their destructive impact on the environment and local people. These studies highlighted uneven development between the uplands and lowlands, showing how dam projects brought suffering to upland marginalized people while dam beneficiaries were mostly in the lowlands and urban areas.

These studies suggested reducing the size of some proposed dams to lessen the impacts on villagers living in areas to be submerged. Scientists and activists shared study results extensively during the VRN's annual meetings, at provincial-level workshops, and in the capital city. VRN and regional and international networks and organizations worked at lobbying and advocacy, providing the public and affected people with comprehensive information about the impacts of specific dams on the environment and local residents. These alliances have also organized campaigns against dam planning in Lào Cai and Đồng Nai Provinces and on the Red River. The government has, in turn, adjusted policies on dam building, resettlement, compensation, and rehabilitation.

The VRN's activities had also encouraged the public and affected people to pursue greater equality in development programs, interests that have shaped the media ecosystem in Vietnam. The VRN had attracted environmental journalists to join and had become involved in river protection work, while media outlets, such as television channels and newspapers, had grown more active in covering these controversial topics.[74] If before 2005 there was hardly any news in any media on dam-induced resettlement or questioning the negative impacts of dam projects in Vietnam, from 2008 forward the media has widely reported on these issues, and the government has begun signaling a growing realization that it may be necessary to reduce Vietnam's reliance on hydropower. While there was almost no media coverage of the impacts of the Hòa Bình or the Yali Falls Dams' construction during the 1980s, 1990s, and even early 2000s, problems associated with dams have been making the headlines in various newspapers since the early 2010s. Examples include "Hydropower in the Central Highlands and Its Associated Problems—Deforestation for Hydropower"; "Dry River—Thirsty People"; and "Gave Land to Hydropower and Went Hungry."[75]

The Adjusted PDP 7 targeted a reduction in the hydropower ratio in electricity production by 2025 to about 20.5 percent from 39 percent in 2018.[76] Whether growing awareness in national government trickles down to provincial authorities remains to be seen. Many medium- and small-scale hydropower plant projects were still being licensed, in Lai Châu, Lào Cai, Quảng Nam, Đak Lak, Đồng Nai, and elsewhere. In late 2009, the prime minister required the Ministry of Industry and Trade to prepare an overall assessment of the country's hydropower situation. Released in 2010, MOIT's assessment suggested canceling thirty-eight small and medium-scale hydropower projects because of their potential negative impacts, and recommended reconsideration of thirty-five others that were already approved for construction. By 2018, after six years of continuous review of hydropower planning, MOIT, in coordination with provincial governments, canceled 8 cascade hydropower dams, 471 small dams in development, and removed 213 dams from the list of potential projects.[77] However, this number is insignificant when compared to the number of dams already built, under construction, or still in the planning stages.[78] The Water Law 2012 maintains the importance of hydropower and encourages its development nationwide wherever possible. Information about the dams' impacts, especially for state-owned projects, has not been made easily accessible. Despite MOIT's 2010 assessment, once a state-owned project has been approved, not one has been stopped. This is not the case for privately funded projects. After several years of concerted effort by the VRN and its allies to advocate against Đồng Nai 6 and 6A on the Đồng Nai River, their construction was halted in 2016.[79]

Despite improvement in land and resource governance policies for compensation and resettlement, decision-making on dam building continues to inadequately and inaccurately account for expenses and to offer poor compensation to the displaced. NGOs and the media remain under the government's strict control. Even though new spaces for the engagement of NGOs were created, the spaces they had for their participation were not neutral but shaped by power relations; activists could only participate in or comment on certain events or topics when they got permission from the authorities. As a result, certain issues related to hydropower development remain underreported.

What follows explores the strategies, institutions, and mechanisms that the state deployed to justify its internal control and resource governance, and the struggle to make the state accountable for the social and environmental costs hidden by these justifications. Territorialization in the frontiers that is associated with the invention of turning a river into energy serves well to demonstrate the state's political and techno-economic power. The construction of dams, while explicitly tied to national economic development and the domination of nature, territorializes the uplands. When it comes to state power and the ideology of development and modernity, even improved policies continue to prioritize economic benefits to nonlocal people and fail to prevent impoverishment of locals. Development policies, justified in the national interest, in practice continue to diminish poor people's ability to control and profitably use the natural resources on which they have depended for generations. Every national project is presented as beneficial to the whole population, even though it requires that some poor people give up their land or livelihoods. Although the greater good of the nation appears to be a worthy reason, it must appear suspect to the rural poor consistently chosen to make sacrifices while the more powerful reap the benefits.[80]

# CHAPTER 3

# Damming the Black River

At the commencement of the massive displacement resulting from the Sơn La Dam construction in the autumn of 2005, I was a member of a group of researchers formed under the auspices of the Vietnam Union of Science and Technology Associations (VUSTA). We were in the area exploring the effects of dam construction on local ethnic minority groups. We moved from village to village, trying to visit and engage with as many villagers as possible and gain a sense of the situation in each locale. Our primary means of transportation was by boat. Everywhere we visited, the only topic of conversation was resettlement. It was chaos. Villagers in Sơn La Province had to abandon their land and relocate to make way for the dam. Houses were taken down. Children stopped their schooling. Crops went untended. I could see startled and worried faces everywhere. Relatives from other villages came to help with the move. These slumbering and peaceful villages along the Black River seemed to be busier than ever. It's impossible for me to put into words; photographs, blog posts, and even video clips equally fail to capture the essence of this time. One needed to be there and experience it.

"Taming" the mighty Black River in the Northwest has been on the Vietnamese government's agenda since the 1960s, not only to provide power generation in support of the country's economic development

**FIGURE 3.1.**    Moving, November 2005. Photo by Nguyen Hoai Thanh.

but more specifically as part of the government's push for social progress and its fight against poverty to uplift this "backward" region.[1] There
are multiple layers of rationalities behind hydropower dam projects.
This chapter examines how the "combination of force and consent"
works to push villagers out of their land to make way for hydropower
dam projects, and which strategies those affected villagers deployed in
their everyday responses.[2]

Hydropower dam development defines people as objects of improvement in an effort to exercise power under the guise of progress.[3] In development planners' reasoning, hydropower dams bring many benefits
to the country and its people—everyone will be better off—for minimal
sacrifice. This dominant development discourse represents a powerful regime of truth with productive or constructive purpose. These
development decisions do not happen in a bureaucratic silo. Indeed,
while hydropower may offer a better life to many people, at the same
time it threatens community integration and citizen livelihoods. Dam
development comes together with contestations, negotiations, compromises, and cooperation at all levels. Peasant societies, as Kerkvliet
argues, are filled with relationships among people with unequal social
and political power, and between ordinary villagers and government
officials or authorities. Dam-affected communities in the Northwest

are no different. Besides resistance, villagers demonstrate compromise, support for, and compliance with those relationships and the distribution and use of resources. Interpersonal relations within households, among neighbors, and between relatives encompass everyday political support, resistance, and compliance.[4]

Over the last few decades, state and nonstate actors have built numerous dams on the Black River. The North Vietnamese government planned the Hòa Bình Dam (1,920 MW), the first large dam on the river, during the late 1960s. The former Soviet Union provided technical and financial support for construction, which started in the 1970s. The Sơn La Dam, the next big dam on the river, with a designed capacity of 2,400 MW, had its diversion sluice closed in May 2010; builders had the first turbine online in December 2010. Construction of the Sơn La Dam began in 2005 and was completed in 2012, but the whole process of preparation to clear the dam site, as well as the displacement and reorganization of resettled villages, took fifteen years (2001 to 2016). The first villages relocated in 2003, while the last families moved in 2012. The last large dam constructed upstream on the Black River is the Lai Châu Dam (1,200 MW). Its construction started in early January 2011 and was completed five years later. Despite many questions regarding security—developers sited these dams within an earthquake-prone area—Prime Minister Nguyễn Tấn Dũng praised the overall project at a celebration of the operation of the first turbine in December 2015: "If the Lai Châu hydropower project is completed in 2016, one year ahead of the Government's decision, it not only benefits the Government VNĐ 7,000 billion per year, but also ensures that the country will not lack electricity." At the ceremony, to applaud the efforts of the energy sector in completing the hydropower cascade on the Black River, the prime minister presented a signboard that read "The project to welcome the 12th National Party Congress" to be fastened to Lai Châu Dam, and he gave awards to individuals and groups at the construction site for their work on the dam.[5]

The Black River's largest branch, the Nậm Mu River, features other dams, such as the Huội Quảng Dam (530 MW) and the Bản Chát Dam (220 MW) (see figure 3.3). Furthermore, dozens of medium and small dams have been built or are planned on the Black River's branches; this does not include dams on the river in Chinese territory, before it reaches Vietnam. After half a century, by the late 2010s, the commodification of the mighty Black River was complete. In the process, government-sponsored dam building on this 910-kilometer-long

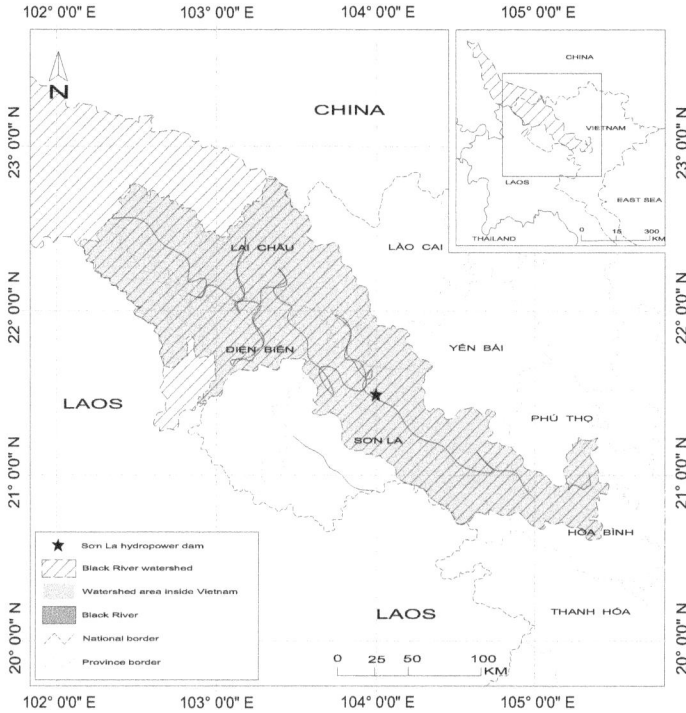

**FIGURE 3.2.**  The Black River basin (portion within Vietnam).
Source: Adapted from Bernhard Lehner and Günther Grill, "Global River Hydrography and Network Routing: Baseline Data and New Approaches to Study the World's Large River Systems," *Hydrological Processes* 27, no. 15 (2013): 2180.

river has alienated northwesterners, provoking debate regarding the dams' impacts on the environment and the Northwest's social landscape.

Regardless of geographic location—the northern mountains or the Central Highlands in Vietnam, the Xekong River basin in Laos, the Narmada valley in India—dams are typically built in upland areas inhabited by ethnic minorities or indigenous peoples.[6] Dam construction has directly or indirectly impacted almost every ethnic minority group that lives in Northwest Vietnam along the Black River. Resettlement drastically alters the resources resettlers farm and the communities they occupy. The elimination of access to the river, a serious shortage of land, and the destruction of important institutions such as communal landownership and arrangements—all these complicate efforts of resettlers to secure lives and livelihoods in resettlement areas.[7] The host communities—the people already living in the areas into which

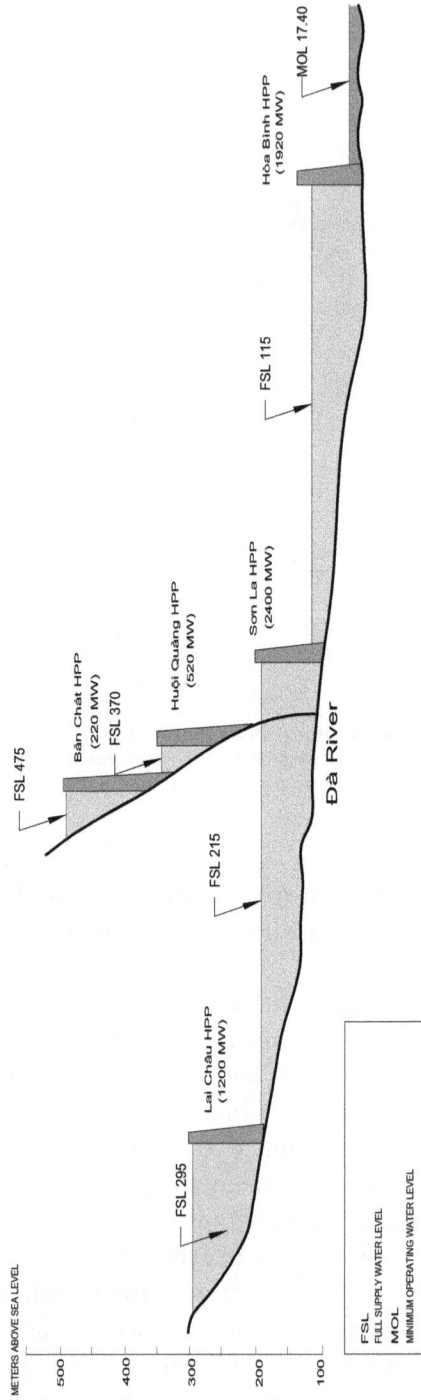

**Figure 3.3.** Hydropower plants on the Black River and its main tributary.
Source: Nguyễn Văn Biểu 2009.

resettlers move—also suffer severe consequences, such as loss of access to land and resources, as well as new problems of community discord and violence.

## Sovereign Power and the Planning of the Sơn La Dam

On June 29, 2001, the National Assembly of the Socialist Republic of Vietnam approved the construction of the Sơn La hydropower project on the Black River, about seventy-four kilometers upstream from the Hòa Bình Dam.[8] The most controversial undertaking of its kind in modern Vietnam, the Sơn La project required the largest resettlement effort—more than one hundred thousand people—in the country's history. The Sơn La Dam's reservoir, with a holding capacity of 926 billion cubic meters, flooded 23,333 hectares, of which almost 10,000 hectares was agricultural land, including rice paddies, gardens, and fishponds. More than 3,000 flooded hectares were classified as forest.[9] Of these, 83.1 percent of the lost land belonged to the Thái ethnic group (both Thái Trắng and Thái Đen); the remainder include La Ha (5.9 percent), Kinh, Mảng, Giáy, and others.

The dam stands in It Ong town, Sơn La Province, 320 kilometers northwest of Hanoi. The plant's power generating capacity is 2,400 MW; dam builders expected annual output to reach 9,429 billion kWh. Since it became fully operational in 2012, the dam has produced about 10,000 billion kWh per year on average, exceeding expectations.[10] According to the government, the Sơn La hydropower project achieves the following key objectives: (1) provides electricity for socioeconomic development, industrialization, and modernization of the nation-state; (2) contributes to flood control in the rainy season, and irrigation in the dry season, for the Red River delta; and (3) helps to promote socioeconomic development in the Northwest and narrow the development gap between the uplands and the lowlands.[11] Since the dam is located in the Northwest, one of the poorest areas in Vietnam, inhabited primarily by marginalized ethnic minority people, its impact on the first and third objectives has drawn particular attention in the Northwest provinces. Banners and slogans about these two objectives and the effort to successfully complete resettlement can be found throughout the three affected provinces: Sơn La, Lai Châu, and Điện Biên.

As initially planned, the first turbine would start to generate electricity in 2012, and the whole plant would be completed and become fully operational in 2015. Electricity of Vietnam, however, successfully

**FIGURE 3.4.** The banners on the truck read "All for the nation's future electrification." December 2005. Photo by Nguyen Hoai Thanh.

persuaded the government that commencing electricity generation one year earlier would bring in an extra US$500 million in revenues. This meant that pushing the project forward by two years would produce an additional US$1 billion for the state. Investors and government officials prioritized economic development and so accelerated the whole process, including resettlement, to enable the plant to be fully operational well before schedule, despite the enormous number of people that needed to be resettled and rehabilitated.

In Vietnam, the authorities often used some special days, including Ho Chi Minh's birthday, Independence Day, and the anniversary of the formation of Vietnam's Communist Party, as benchmarks for significant events, including the inauguration of national projects. In the case of the Sơn La Dam, officials accelerated the construction plan to ensure that the Black River was entirely blocked for reservoir filling by May 19, 2010—the occasion of Ho Chi Minh's 120th birthday.[12] The first turbine started generating electricity in December 2010. In April 2011, engineers connected the second turbine to the national grid. On this occasion, Prime Minister Nguyễn Tấn Dũng told the nation via broadcast on national television VTV1 that "this is a marvelous achievement of our modernization and industrialization process. We should all be proud of ourselves." He continued by praising Sơn La provincial officials for resettling more than 12,500 households within its constituency and enabling the dam project to remain on schedule. By the end of 2011, four of six planned turbines were generating power. According to a 2013 report of the National Assembly's Committee on Science, Technology, and Environment, the Sơn La Dam provides 8 percent of the country's total electricity output and has significantly contributed to Vietnam's GDP.[13]

Planning for the Sơn La Dam reflected improvements in hydropower project planning in Vietnam, a shift from the changes in government policies related to land, resources, and resettlement described in chapter 2. Instead of applying the Soviet Union's economic calculation method, as with previous dam projects such as Hòa Bình, Sơn La hydropower plant planners employed a system called net present value (NPV). A new method for Vietnam, proffered by international agencies, NPV yielded figures used to argue that the project should proceed. The budgeted cost for rehabilitation and resettlement was estimated to be about 29 percent of the total project cost.[14] Inclusion of costs related to displacement helped to ensure the government's budgeting for resettlement expenses, including moving people, compensation, and livelihood recovery.

Concerned about the project's massive and varying impacts, however, most multilateral and bilateral institutions, including the World Bank, the Japan Bank for International Corporation, and the Asian Development Bank, declined to provide funding for the project, even though the World Bank supported the project's pre-feasibility study. China was the only country that expressed support for the project. The dam project was 100 percent state-funded and managed. The international public bid was awarded to Chinese companies, which provided about 90 percent of project equipment (steelworks and generating equipment), while the remaining 10 percent (including powerhouse downstream gates, penstocks, and intake gates) were made in Vietnam.

Ironically, the Asian Development Bank, which strongly supports the World Commission on Dams' recommendations for equitable and sustainable development of water and energy resources, refused to provide funding for the dam because of the massive displacement required and anticipated negative impacts to the environment, but retained its support for the transmission lines for dam-generated power.[15] The Asian Development Bank also provided financial support for technical assistance for capacity building for government and local officers who were involved in the resettlement process.

During the planning phase of the dam, National Assembly members voiced two strong but differing opinions about the dam's size. One group supported a dam with a high-water level of 265 meters above sea level (expected capacity of 3,600 MW), arguing that a larger dam would bring more benefits to the national economy; another group argued for mitigation of any negative impacts and supported a dam with a high-water level of 215 meters above sea level. According to the government's master plan for the Black River, in addition to the decision of having one large dam with high-water level of either 215 meters or 265 meters above sea level, there were options for developing smaller dams (roughly 150 to 170 meters). While the government considered opposition to the dam's height of 265 meters, it did not consider the option of the considerably smaller dams.[16] Development planners argued that the larger the dam, the more economic benefit it would bring to the economy.

Although a master plan for resettlement was prepared in the late 1990s, detailed planning for most of the sites remained unfinished when mass displacement began in 2005. By the end of 2006, detailed planning for only seventy-three resettlement sites had been approved (accounting for 25 percent of the total project sites).[17] Fifty-five resettlement sites lacked surface water but were still included in the master plan, because otherwise there would not be enough space for all the resettlers.[18] Thus, despite claiming to have better prepared this time around, authorities in reality conducted resettlement for the Sơn La hydropower project in a fashion largely unchanged from earlier, haphazard dam resettlement programs.

In the late 1990s and early 2000s, a number of overseas Vietnamese and members of a Thái study group sent letters to the prime minister's office, calling for the project's termination and expressing their concerns about its potential impacts on the Thái ethnic people, including historic and cultural sites that would be flooded, as well as concerns about other social and environmental problems. A number of scientists and academics from VUSTA worked together to push for the 215-meter option. In response to VUSTA lobbying, the government agreed to switch the dam high-water level from 265 meters to the smaller dam of 215 meters. In the face of growing criticism from financial institutions and environmental lobbyists, as well as public outcry, the government also appeared more responsive to concerns about the project's safety and its impacts, compared to its record with previous dams, including the Hòa Bình Dam and the Yali Falls Dam. While the government and development planners ultimately imposed Sơn La Dam construction in the Northwest, the project planning process was not one of life-threatening force but instead an expression of sovereign power that was contingent, multiple, and contested, yet at the same time both jeopardizing and accommodating interests of subjects.[19]

## Everyday Politics of Resistance and Territorial Subject Formation

We arrived in Pa Ha village late one evening in November 2005. An uphill walk of about four kilometers from the riverbank to the village consumed my remaining energy for the day. By the time we reached the headman's house, we were all exhausted. It was dark, and we didn't see much of the village until the next morning. Most the village's seventy-five wooden houses had been disassembled—ten remained standing, scattered across what remained of the site. The headman explained to us that those houses belonged to twelve families of a clan fighting forced relocation:

> Most of the villagers followed the direction of local authorities and project officers and were preparing to move to a designated resettlement site in a different district. But these families want to stay no matter what happens. I've tried to explain, but they don't understand that they have no choice. It will be painful if you don't follow your village, because you won't get farming land the same time with your neighbors, or even worse, you may not get compensation land at all, as when you agreed to move, there would be no land available for you. Without land, how can peasants live? It's no point to be stubborn, as they will be forced to move before their land will be submerged under the water.[20]

No one wanted to move, but families adopted different methods to deal with the change, and all followed the decision of the head of their clan.

Resettlement is one of the most profound impacts on territorial subjects and landscape transformation caused by large-scale development projects such as the Sơn La Dam. Dam introduction not only transforms the landscape, but it forces whole populations to move, changing their physical and social landscapes. In many instances, authorities do not allow entire communities to relocate together to one new location, owing to insufficient land availability at the resettlement locale. Torn into many groups and moved to different locations, communities lose access to places dear to them—their home, their town or village, their entire surroundings, locations in which generations of their families had lived and loved. Northwesterners do not consider their land or their forest simple resources; they do not hold a "user-to-resource" relationship with the forest and the river. These communities use no language for taming or exploiting nature. It is very simple, one villager said: "The forest, the river is everything to us, is Mother, is the source of life that we respect and worship."

Among the more than one hundred thousand people in nineteen thousand households displaced in the three provinces of Sơn La, Lai Châu, and Điện Biên, in Sơn La Province alone thirty-one communes (including 248 villages with 14,993 households) moved.[21] The project's most challenging task was to organize this resettlement.[22] All resettlement sites required two types of infrastructure. First, they needed infrastructure for receiving resettlers (to be completed before people moved in, per government policy), including roads, water, and electricity. Second, resettlement sites required infrastructure for livelihood rehabilitation (not required until after resettlers moved in), including health clinic stations, schools, irrigation facilities, and more.

Before resettlement, the project and district and commune authorities struggled to convince affected people that they should move. Armed with slogans like "All for the future electrification of the nation," "If you want to resettle people, you must settle with their consent first," "Eat together, discuss together, do it together, and speak the same language [as villagers]," "Life in the resettlement site must be better than in the old village," and "People know, people discuss, people implement, people monitor," cadres who were either from the same ethnic groups or fluent in local languages were sent to villages to persuade people to move. Obtaining affected people's consent to give up their land was one of the first priorities in an otherwise top-down process, as it was impossible to use force to evict one hundred thousand people from their homes. One Kinh official at the district level told me on November 2009, "If all of a hundred thousand affected people refused to move, this project would never happen. But if only a few hundred individuals refused to do it, it would not be a problem." District authorities traveled to each commune to announce to authorities there the latest information on the move, related plans, and resettlement.

Representatives of the villages' administrative bodies—headmen and village party secretaries, as well as representatives of the Farmers' Association, the Women's Union, the Youth Union, the Veterans' Association, and the Fatherland Front Committee—were all required to attend these meetings. These representatives then returned to their villages to persuade other villagers to follow the plan. The local village administrators were supposed to set an example by pioneering the relocation process. Everyday forms of compliance by both village representatives and villagers, therefore, enabled the whole process of resettlement and strengthened the power of the authorities.

Again, the Sơn La Dam resettlement process was clearly more organized than earlier displacements to make way for the Hòa Bình Dam and the Yali Falls Dam.[23] As early as 1995, professional institutions like the National Institute of Planning and Projection and the Institute of Geography began to conduct master planning for resettlement and rehabilitation before dam construction began, which included extensive surveys and investigation of resettlement sites.[24] The national government made the decision to decentralize resettlement implementation responsibilities from the province down to the district, commune, and even village levels.[25] Resettlers were informed of the compensation policy and procedures prior to their move. By the time of my research trip in 2009, most of the villagers who lived below the 140-meter water level of the dam had moved to designated resettlement sites. They were encouraged to visit these sites before moving day.[26] Critically, the resettlement program's officers also paid attention to the need for land suitable for both housing and farming.[27]

In order to identify potential problems before massive resettlement began, officials conducted a pilot resettlement move for villagers in the It Ong commune, where the dam is located. After test runs in the Muong Ta and Muong Phin communes, where displaced people moved into already-built concrete houses, the provincial authorities faced strong resistance from resettlers. For almost one year, they constantly sent requests to the authorities and the project's Resettlement Management Board to demand policy changes. One villager remarked, "We had no choice. We needed to fight. It's not our tradition to live in already-built concrete houses. The house is not just the house. It's our home and tradition."[28] The authorities then accepted the resettlers' request to change the housing policy. This was the first time in the history of resettlement projects in Vietnam that authorities adopted a suggestion for change from affected people. Everyday resistance indeed has brought welcome changes to resettlers. A new policy of dismantling a family's old house and transporting it to be rebuilt in the new location helped resettlers keep customary forms of housing. This support for house relocation, according to most of the resettlers that I interviewed, was useful and even necessary to make resettlers more comfortable in the new location. The resettlers recognized this change as a major improvement in the resettlement policy for those affected by the Sơn La Dam, and they were happy with it.[29] However, with more than one hundred thousand people to be resettled, and as the government accelerated the whole process by two years, resettlement morphed into chaos. Affected people did not simply passively follow the procedures that the authorities put in place.

Those to be displaced by the Sơn La hydropower project dealt with the news of their displacement in various ways. While most of them would experience ex situ displacement, forced to move from their homes, communities, and livelihoods, some would experience in situ displacement: they would be able to remain in their house if it was above the new waterline but would lose their land and other support systems.

As Dominique Caouette and Sarah Turner suggest, resistance, as part of power, is "context-dependent and a force that is changing relative to dominance and within a dynamic network of power which can gather strength, diminish, and shift positions."[30] Even though those affected did not act against the dam itself, they were against the idea of moving out of their homes and communities, locations that held memories of their entire lives. According to resettlement officers, those impacted often refused to sign the papers to instigate their relocation; in other cases, the papers were signed, but the villagers then refused to move.[31] Many resettlers even argued that it did not matter if they signed or not. Without realizing exactly what a hydropower plant and its reservoir were or how their homes would be submerged, these villagers believed that if they just stayed put, nothing would happen, and nobody would kick them out of their houses.

In some villages, people persisted in not signing the moving agreements until the local government sent officers of the same ethnic group to persuade them. In this way, strategies and tactics were adjusted to induce ethnic minority people to sacrifice for the national interest. An official of the Lai Châu Resettlement Board provided a firsthand example:

> I was transferred to this position from a different district because I am a Thái person, because I know the language and the culture,

and because my people trusted me. If a Kinh cadre came to the village to convince villagers to move, for sure no one would agree. I had to travel from village to village for months. There were countless nights I've spent in villages, drank with villagers, sang songs with them, and told stories of our land, our river, our forest, our lives. Everyone cried, including me. They agreed to move and signed the paper, but when the time came, they might still resist. I was under so much stress having to do the job.

In a number of village meetings I attended, villagers admitted that they were afraid of moving. My survey of 123 households in Muong Lanh and Muong Nhuong villages in 2009 showed that 59 percent of the villagers worried and were afraid of moving, and 39 percent felt sad but not too worried, because they believed that the government would do anything to help them resettle and that their lives in the new locales would not be too difficult. Only 2 percent were not concerned about resettlement. These were young people, and they earned their living mostly by engaging in service activities such as the transport of maize, soybeans, and foodstuffs on the Black River. For this very small minority, their livelihood before resettlement did not depend heavily on the land.

Some families reacted to the approaching dam project by ceasing to work on their houses or to invest in their businesses. Their lives were uncertain, and they had a hard time dealing with this uncertainty. The chairman of a commune in Lai Châu Province where I visited in 2008 is one example. In his garden, there were piles of big logs to be used for house construction. He said that he had bought them in 1995 intending to build his own house. Then he overheard the news about the dam project, so he just stored the logs and waited. The house that his family was living in at that time was just a cottage, not a real Thái house with a staircase. Other families, even though they were very upset about moving, simply ignored the displacement news or did not pay much attention to it. Their lives continued undisturbed as if nothing would happen. They built new houses and invested in businesses. When asked (in May 2008) why they did that, a food store owner in Lai Châu answered my question with one of his own: "What do you think is real: our existing lives or the dam?" He continued: "We don't know when the dam will be built, but one thing we know for sure is we need to live. And if we don't work and keep our life going, then we will sure be in trouble, as we will not have enough to eat. When the time comes close, then we'll see what we can do."

In fact, during my trips in 2008 and 2009, I learned that in many villages, people were telling each other that in order to get increased compensation for the move, they should plant fruit trees, lumber trees, increase their cattle herd, and build good quality houses. Results of this strategy showed in villages in all three provinces in the form of more trees planted, cattle procured, and new houses built before resettlement. To their credit, the strategy worked quite well for a number of families in these areas.

When the time to move neared, those who would be affected were allowed to visit their designated resettlement sites. At this time, they began to realize the potential difficulties, including land and water issues. Their reluctance to move increased. Even though they had already signed papers authorizing their displacement, they did not pack or dismantle their houses. The government then promised an extra VNĐ 4 million (US$350) to any family that moved on time. Resettlers were also promised an advance of 50 percent of the compensation amount (averaging about VNĐ 15 to 18 million—about US$1,000 to $1,200) to buy durable goods and logs for housing. Some resettlers even refused an advance payment; they did not care about the money. As a village party secretary stressed, "Who would want that amount of money to move early? That's where we were born. Our life is there. Moving out of our homeland was the biggest pain we ever experienced. If you have never been through it, you can't understand. I would have done anything to slow down the moving process. I'd rather have lost my position in order to stay. But we had no choice."[32] We may be able, in part, to understand how this felt. Sentimental connections with the land of one's ancestors, with the place where one was born and grew up, with the neighboring communities, as well as ties of kinship, were key factors creating resistance to the move, alongside concerns about land and water shortages at the resettlement sites. While disciplinary governmentality induced norms for proper, ethical behavior, putting pressure on village representatives to be the first ones to move, some of these representatives were nevertheless the first to refuse.

One of the prevailing problems associated with displacement is that land compensation usually fails to provide enough land for people to produce their food, and villagers' landholdings generally decrease after resettlement.[33] For villagers displaced by the Sơn La Dam, it was common that a household's farming land might be reduced from, say, five to seven hectares prior to resettlement to only one to two hectares after resettlement, depending on the number of household members.

Ordinary northwesterners with little formal education had very few options after their displacement and often became impoverished landless laborers. In cases in which farmers were resettled in ecological zones where none of their previous farming practices were relevant, their previous knowledge and their assets—seeds, tools, and other resources—became devalued. Thus, regardless of the form of displacement they experienced, their subjectivities changed as they worked to find ways to respond and adapt to new living conditions. They developed new livelihood strategies out of necessity. Once they were no longer able to produce a sufficient part of their daily consumption needs, they had to sell their labor to earn money to buy food, clothing, and even shelter—necessities that they could provide for themselves prior to their displacement.

Land shortages and soil infertility at the resettlement sites left resettlers facing limited livelihood choices. In order to adapt in their new locations and environmental conditions, newcomers have had to learn new skills. As they no longer lived by the water, they needed to learn new agricultural techniques. In rural resettlement sites, the farming practices were also different, and the resettlers' skills and knowledge of how things were done in their old villages were of less use; knowledge of the old ways began fading away as a result. Those who, like villagers in Muong Lanh, used to live by rivers and streams but did not own wet rice fields have had the opportunity to buy patches for wet rice cultivation in their new area but had to learn a new planting cycle: plowing, seeding, transplanting, watering, weeding, and harvesting. And since land was now scarcer, resettlers had to learn techniques for intensive farming. Host communities could direct newcomers on when and how to apply fertilizers and pesticides in order to achieve high yields, but as resettled farmers adapted to these new ways, they could find their land exhausted after a few years of intensive cultivation. Villagers understood that crop rotation allowed the land to rest, but for resettlers, leaving a new, smaller tract of land fallow for one year could be an unaffordable luxury.

Although the displaced upland people may not have had the power to alter the decision to construct the dam in their area, they demonstrated a wide range of responses not limited to "weapons of the weak."[34] Affected people came up with a variety of strategies to undermine the process and maximize their benefits. People wrote petitions to request policy changes, refused to sign relocation papers or move, or gathered money to invest in tree planting or construction of new houses on the original sites before resettlement in order to get higher compensation. Some community representatives even took the side of locals against the government and dam builders. Villagers, on the one hand, resisted, via micropolitical behaviors, changes imposed on them whenever possible, and, on the other hand, negotiated and adapted to life in the new environment through continuous learning. Their everyday politics stretched from resistance to compliance, negotiation, compromise, to modification and evasion to adapt to the life in resettlement sites: a life without having enough land to farm, not close to the river, fighting over land among neighbors, abandoning their old skills and learning how to use chemicals for intensive farming against their will, and so on.

Despite a number of policy and planning changes around hydropower dam development, many aspects of the state's approach on the ground remain unchanged. According to the government, the Sơn La Dam is a key asset for the country's energy security and plays a vital role in modernization, industrialization, and ensuring economic growth in the Northwest.[35] Decision No. 10 of the Communist Party Congress affirmed that the construction of the Sơn La Dam was a historic opportunity for the Northwest region in general, and Sơn La Province in particular, to transition toward modernization, rearrange labor and population, and enable the province to develop rapidly and sustainably in the near future. The dam also serves to raise Vietnam's status in competition over development with its large neighbor, China. One could hear a very common argument during that time among high-ranking government officers: "Why can China have the Three Gorges [Dam] and Vietnam can't have the Sơn La? We are not less developed than China."[36]

According to the Vietnamese Law on Environmental Protection, any development project that impacts the environment or people's livelihoods must have an environmental impact assessment (EIA) conducted by independent experts before the project can be submitted to the relevant bodies for approval. Construction of the Sơn La Dam began in December 2005, well before the final review of its EIA in May 2007. This suggests that the EIA was only a cursory requirement, a procedure on paper that may not affect practice.

Even though the Vietnamese government claimed to support the World Commission on Dams' recommendations and emphasized that dam projects were to follow that direction, resettlement for the Sơn La project, much as with other past dam projects in Vietnam, was still a top-down process in many ways. There was no public hearing about the

*Table 3.1*  Public acceptance and implementation of Free, Prior, and Informed Consent (FPIC) for the Sơn La project

| KEY DECISION | PUBLIC PARTICIPATION AND PRIOR INFORMED CONSENT |
|---|---|
| Decision about whether the dam should be built | None. The Politburo and the National Assembly made the decision. Only some NGOs and scientists were able to raise their concerns. There was concern that creating a large reservoir that holds a large amount of water could be a national security issue in case of war or other conflict. |
| Technical issues including dam height and other design features | Affected people, who were mostly from upland ethnic minority groups, were not allowed to voice their views, as they were considered poorly educated and with little knowledge about technical issues. Some NGOs and scientists were able to advocate on their behalf, and there was some success regarding dam height. |
| **Resettlement issues** | |
| Site choice | Some resettlers were able to visit some of the sites before moving, but their choices were limited. |
| Choice in land price and lost crop price | No participation at all |
| Housing design | Yes. Resettlers were allowed to build their new houses using a design of their choice. |
| Water supply systems | No. The government employed engineers to design water supply systems. In many cases, when people moved to a locale and found that there was no water, they had to find their own solutions. |
| Amount of compensation for land and other lost assets | No participation at all |
| Options for land compensation | In some cases, affected people could request how they would like to be compensated (i.e., they could choose either to receive money and find land themselves or to wait for the local authorities in the new locale to allocate land). |
| Host communities' opinion about receiving resettlers | Yes. But their responses did not matter much if there was land available in their village. Mostly for mixed resettled villages where resettlers moved into the same village as the host community. |
| Host communities' opinions about the amount of land and resources that they would have to share with resettlers | This depended on the political situation in the area. Some communities were difficult to convince. In general, host communities were usually told about the project and their responsibility to share resources at the same time as workers were about to start measuring and leveling the ground for resettlement sites. Host communities were expected to follow the authorities' decision. |

Source: Adapted from N. Dao 2012.

project or for the decision to speed up resettlement by two years. The "free, prior, and informed consent" (FPIC) implemented in the Sơn La project was reduced to one procedure: affected people were informed about the schedule for moving their households. They were not consulted to determine if they agreed or not. Despite a certain amount of opposition in some areas, authorities persuaded people to sacrifice for the sake of the national interest.

Among the displaced households, more than 80 percent engaged solely in farming and thus depended entirely on arable land.[37] Since in Vietnam the land essentially belongs to the state, no matter how long a family and their ancestors may have worked the land, if the state or state-backed developers say that the land is needed for the national interest or development purposes, the users will lose their homes and their farmland. The principles of FPIC are not followed, in large part, because the users do not have the right to refuse. Their sacrifice is necessary for the sake of the state.[38] In turn, a number of government officials resisted acknowledging the sacrifice. In formal conversations that I had with at least ten high-ranking government officials, a common reaction was, "What sacrifices are you talking about? Don't use that word. Nobody has to sacrifice here. It's for the national interests, which means it's for everyone's interest." In short, despite improvement in resettlement policies, the government failed to improve its approach to resettlement, and created challenges for affected people in recovering their livelihood after the displacement.

## Compensation and Challenges in Resettling

"Oh, Sơn La should build more prisons, as now the provincial authorities are in charge of implementing [the] resettlement component of hydropower projects. There will be more corruptions," joked a district vice-chairman one day in September 2006 as we talked about the challenges of facilitating resettlement for those displaced by the Sơn La Dam and the related corruption. To support the one hundred thousand impacted locals in the Northwest, the government had set aside thousands of billions of Vietnamese dong (hundreds of millions of US dollars) to relocate and help people recover their lives after resettlement. By 2014, the budget for the resettlement component of the hydropower project was VNĐ 26,457 billion.[39] In 2018, the government added another VNĐ 2,662 billion to support the resettlement program.[40] However, compensation has always been very controversial, and its disbursement was glacial. In Muong Muon commune, for example, Khun's family and other resettlers received the last installment of their compensation in early 2020, fifteen years after they moved to their re-settlement sites.

The sluggish pace of land allocation in resettlement sites, coupled with delays in land loss compensation, intensified the villagers' concerns about their means of living in their new homes. Before Khun and other villagers in Muong Lanh and Muong Nhuong moved to their new villages in 2005, they memorized the promised terms of compensation and support in the central government's early policy, called Decision No. 01. It bases the area of land loss on land-use-right certificates, the land that project officers determined using measuring tapes, or simply on an interview with the villagers without any formal measurement of their lost land.[41] None of the land-area figures were derived from measurements of former land with actual land survey equipment.

In January 2007, a change in policy featured in Decision No. 02 required project officers to use survey equipment to measure both the land lost in old villages and the land received in new villages.[42] Resettlers displaced by the Sơn La Dam could now only receive government compensation based on measurements obtained from land survey equipment. Land was classified as wet rice land or hilly land, and compensation was also based on this classification. The area of land, ignoring its quality or productivity, was the main criterion for land compensation in the new village; all wet rice land was valued the same, and all hilly farmland was valued the same. According to Land Law 2003, the provincial authorities set land prices; affected people had no say in this matter. This reflected the state's view of land compensation and highlighted the resettlers' marginalization. People were upset but unable to do anything to change the compensation structure.

For the Sơn La project, the government applied a standardized egalitarian policy for several kinds of compensation, including land distribution and food support, among others. However, resettlers in different provinces received different amounts of land, depending on each province's land availability. In Muong Muon commune, where Muong Lanh and Muong Nhuong villages are located, the amount of land resettlers received for compensation was far from enough to allow the displaced to sustain their lives if they relied solely on cultivation of the provided land.

In the Northwest uplands of Vietnam as in most other parts of the country and in Southeast Asia in general, land carries particular importance in social as well as economic terms. Land is not only a means of livelihood but also an indicator of security and happiness, with emotional and spiritual attachments. It connects people to places that are associated with their identities. In dam-affected areas, residents face a shortage of land for cultivation, largely as a result of land limits at all resettlement sites. In most cases, resettled communities and the host communities that received them were composed of farmers dependent on land for food and livelihood. Only with a large area of land for growing a variety of crops can these farmers sustain their families without hunger. Most villagers who cultivated wet rice before being resettled no longer had access to this type of land after their move; they were allocated only hilly subsidiary croplands.[43] Their wet rice farming experience was of no use in these new locations. In some exceptional villages, like Muong Lanh, villagers bought a certain amount of land for wet rice cultivation from the host community. However, these very small patches normally provide only enough rice for a family of four people for two months. Lacking irrigation systems, these wet rice patches often do not produce as expected during drought.

In Muong Lanh and Muong Nhuong villages, even after four years in the resettlement sites, villagers indicated that they most missed riverine land and dry fields where they would conduct extensive farming and rotate crops in multiple patches. One villager in Muong Lanh village said, "When I was in my home village, I could never imagine that one day I would not have enough land to grow my crops. I used to wish to have more strength so I could work harder on my land. We were only afraid of not being strong enough to work, never worried about not having enough land."[44]

The contemporary shortage of farmland manifests itself in land scarcity at all resettlement sites in the Northwest, especially in Sơn La Province, where the government relocated more than fourteen thousand households. In planned rural resettlement areas, the most challenging work has been to redistribute land from host communities to resettled communities. Understandably, host communities saw no benefit in sharing scarce resources with the newcomers, and community members wanted to receive compensation for their land before giving it up to the resettlers. Both groups depend on farming for subsistence and livelihood. According to my interviewees, young people (under twenty-five years old) from host and displaced groups fought regularly in the first five years after the move. Host communities considered newcomers as outsiders who came to take their land and competed with them for water resources. In resettlement sites, such as Muong Nhuong, the farming system is particularly unsustainable because the resettlers received only infertile hilly farmland with very steep slopes (35 to 40 degrees) featuring low green-coverage rates and high potential for erosion, landslides, and flash floods. Resettlers' attempts to make a living on this marginal land would eventually lead to further land degradation, because they would have to adopt intensive farming practices that require far more chemical inputs than they were accustomed to. The tension over land among the two groups (host and resettled) has produced new territorial subjects in the region as a result of everyday modifications and evasion practices, people who sometimes became newly unfriendly to one another.

The space allotted to the displaced groups, potential degradation aside, remained inadequate to their needs and previous standards. In Sơn La Province, for example, resettlers were allocated approximately 0.25 to 0.3 hectare per person, depending on the land availability in different communes. This allotment included arable land and fishponds. In this upland area, an average family of four people consumed about seven hundred to eight hundred kilograms of rice annually. If they don't have access to or own wet rice fields, they grow maize. A family of four would need a successful maize crop from about 1.5 hectares to buy sufficient rice to feed themselves all year. By late 2009, the price of rice was VNĐ 10,000 to 12,000/kilogram (US$0.55 to 0.67), and the maize price was VNĐ 3,000 to 3,200/kilogram (US$0.17 to 0.18). The land doled out as compensation (1.0 to 1.2 hectares for a family of four) was insufficient to sustain a family if they relied only on this land for their livelihood—and that is just for food. The calculations do not include other expenses—clothing, school fees, medicine, and more.

Babies born in the post-resettlement period did not receive a land allocation in the new village. As a consequence, young couples with two children born after moving to the resettlement site, for example, would receive only about five thousand square meters (half a hectare) of land. According to my interviewees, these young families complained to the project management board and local authorities but had not received any adjustment. In most of these cases, the husbands left the village to seek work as porters or other forms of employment to mitigate needs unmet by additional land. Those unable to do this would be forced to rely on social networks for support—their relatives and neighbors—or otherwise deal with family needs for food and supplies. In the early days after resettlement, a number of families returned to their home villages (about forty to fifty kilometers from the new village) in order to grow crops on their old land. In Muong Nhuong, before the water submerged the old site in late 2009, ten households regularly returned to their old land to farm and to raise livestock, leaving their children alone in their new homes. When asked, most said that they would rather be farming in their old pre-submergence lands than live in the new village, have nothing to do, and suffer from hunger. After their old land was submerged, these people had to remain in their new villages. During my trip to this area in late 2009, I met two men whom I had never met before in the village, since previously they had been away to work their old land. The men revealed that their options were now limited to (illegally) cutting down trees in the nearby forests or gathering in the commune's central market to wait for offers of day labor. It did not always work out, as some days they earned nothing at all. By 2020, in villages like Muong Ta, half of young people, mostly men, left the village to find employment in industrial parks in the Red River delta.

Livestock husbandry proved no less complicated. Because livestock provides financial security and can be easily liquidated for urgently required cash, almost every household rears one or more types of livestock. In the new villages of Muong Lanh and Muong Nhuong, the common area was too small to accommodate every household's grazing needs. As a result, each household usually had only one or two cows, a significant drop from up to ten before resettlement. Many resettled villagers had to purchase new cows, as many animals died during the move to the new sites. Pigs roamed freely in the old village, but at the resettled sites they had to be confined to pens. Families raised a hybrid breed that grew faster and could be sold after about four months, instead of their former local breeds, which required eight to twelve months before sale. In order to raise swine in the new location, resettlers either attended extension training courses or learned rearing methods (e.g., how to build a good pen, what to feed the animals, how often to bathe them, when to call a veterinarian) from host community members. Such changes not only significantly impacted resettlers' income and expenditures after resettlement but also altered the way they lived their lives.

In brief, dam development and territorialization in the Northwest have reshaped land use and driven the marginalization of the resettled in resettlement sites. Forced migration has dramatically transfigured resettlers' lives and livelihoods.[45] Forced migration, insufficient land compensation, and marginalization conspired to create obstacles to resettlers attempting to reconstitute their lives in their new villages.

## Remaking Gender Labor

The daily activities of the resettlers in their old villages were organized into simple patterns of labor division, and gender played a clear role. Only men engaged in work that required interactions with people beyond the village's boundaries. Only men dealt with outsiders or did heavy manual labor, including forest clearing and fishing. Women were responsible for work inside the house, including cooking, taking care of the family's daily meals, washing clothes, and cleaning the house. If the family practiced wet rice farming, the husband plowed the land, and the wife transplanted the young rice into the field. If the family practiced hillside farming, the wife used a stick to make holes, and the husband followed and put seeds in the holes. According to these families, putting seeds in the holes was hard work. It required constant work in a bent-over position over several hectares of hilly farmland, work that often caused back pain. Women did most of the weeding. The husband and sons never engaged in the tasks identified as women's work, especially the indoor activities. The gendered labor division in this region was also inseparable from and shaped by people's relations with the natural conditions in which they were embedded.

Changes in resource availability and natural conditions have significantly shaped people's behaviors and livelihood strategies. After resettlement, the ways in which resettlers reconstituted their lives and livelihoods have not been uniform, and women have often disproportionately suffered. Resettlers devised different strategies to fit various individuals, families, groups, and villages. While before resettlement, women mostly worked on their farm and inside their homes, in the new villages, because their subsistence has become more commoditized, women became more involved in outside work. Women joined training courses in new farming techniques and spent more time engaged in livestock husbandry. When possible, they brought their garden products to local markets to sell. If their families opened convenience stores or engaged in service businesses, the women worked as cashiers and bookkeepers. In 85 percent of the 123 interviewed families in both villages, the wife kept the household's money. In Muong Nhuong, Muong Ma, Muong Che, and Muong Ta villages, many women were having difficulties in adapting to their new location. Only in Khun's Muong Lanh village, which suffered less severe water shortages than the other villages, did women seem to adapt faster because they could grow vegetables and livestock. Women of Muong Lanh were also nearer the market than women in other villages and could easily bring their produce to sell. In Muong Ta and other locations, life was more difficult. A woman (age fifty-plus) recalled,

> My husband bought a motorbike and returned to the old village to work as *xe ôm* [motorbike driver]. I had to stay home and take care of everything. It was similar for many other families here back then. Every day I got up at 6 a.m. to cook for three children, clean the house, then I went around to ask if anyone needed labor. I tended cows, I did weeding, applying fertilizers, and planting for other families in the host community who hired me. Some days I got about VNĐ 150,000 [about US$12]. Some days I got nothing. I was not used to that type of life. Some days I was too tired and did not know what to do, so I cried. I cried because I missed my home village, because I never thought my life would be that hard, because I worried if I did not work that much, my children would go hungry. I missed my husband. We used to do everything together.[46]

In general, within the first three years after resettlement, villagers shared a widespread concern about not having enough land to farm and having to spend money on almost everything. Women experienced hardships in managing their households. As Khun said, "Oh, women suffered more because women would have to worry about [many things], from what to put on the table for dinner for the whole family to taking care of the young and the elderly. Men only worried about if they had alcohol for them to drink. And when we first moved here, we did not have land to work on, so men tended to drink more. They were sad and missed their old home."

## Power Disparity and Corruption

On the night of August 7, 2016, arson in the main building of the Muong Muon commune People's Committee burned to ash all the papers, data, and files related to Sơn La Dam resettlement and compensation in the commune. To date, no one has been arrested. Khun told me that the commune's chairman was later fired as a result of corruption allegations related to resettlers' compensation money. But Khun was not exactly sure what was going on. No government officials were ever sent to prison for charges or allegations related to the Sơn La hydropower project. The act of erasing evidence, like what happened in Muong Muon, was not unique, given the large number of people to be resettled because of hydropower projects in the Northwest and elsewhere in Vietnam.

Officials in Sơn La, Lai Châu, and Điện Biên Provinces were entirely responsible for the implementation of resettlement within their respective constituencies, and each provincial government issued its own related resettlement instructions. Provincial authorities worked closely with relevant ministries in Hanoi—Investment and Planning, Finance, Agriculture, and the Environment—during the resettlement process to adjust and implement policy. This cooperation enabled provincial and district authorities to more effectively connect with the central authority and increased space in which these local authorities could exercise their power, which in turn spawned corruption. As the state gave provincial governments the green light to select contractors for all projects with a value less than VNĐ 5 billion (about US$300,000), provincial and district authorities increased their power by selecting bids for infrastructure work in resettlement sites, determining the kinds and amounts of compensation, and supporting rehabilitation efforts.[47] Only projects valued at more than VNĐ 5 billion were required to follow formal bidding procedures. Districts were responsible for most of the projects related to resettlement, including roads, schools, water and irrigation, ground leveling for resettlement sites, compensation, and so on.[48] Keeping a large amount of money at provincial and district levels also created opportunities for corruption. One official in charge of resettlement at the district level, whom I interviewed a few times in 2008 and 2009, was later promoted to the provincial level. I visited his new house in 2018 (his family was also displaced in 2009) and was amazed at its luxurious interior, especially compared to his pre-resettlement home. In response to my surprised look, he said, "Well, this whole resettlement process has been very hard for all of us, but not everyone suffered the same way. For some of us, it was a good change." I did not dare to ask where he got the money for such a house.

Most of the resettlement sites experienced delays in compensation for lost assets and property (such as houses, gardens, boats, crops, fruit trees). Resettlement officers usually blamed complicated and lengthy administrative and disbursement procedures for the delay. However, there was a rumor that resettlement officers had simply put the money into the bank to earn interest, although no one knew this for sure. In most of the cases, villagers would wait; the most they could do was to send requests or petitions to officials at the commune and district levels. However, in some places, people (mostly Thái ethnic groups) could not wait any longer and decided to fight for their money. The action taken by Thái villagers in Chu village, Muong Muon commune, to collect the compensation money owed to them for livelihood recovery offers dramatic evidence. After four years of filing complaints and making inquiries without success, the villagers traveled in late 2010 to the district center and seized a local official who was a member of the district's resettlement board. They took the official to the office of a deputy head of the resettlement board and locked up both men. The villagers took turns guarding the locked office while sending demands for their compensation back to the district authority. They refused to accept the promise of the vice president of the district's People's Committee to provide compensation within ten days. The villagers wanted their money within two days, and they received it. In Phong Tho district, resettlers actually threatened resettlement officers who had offered false promises about post-resettlement compensation, especially regarding land. In Quynh Nhai district, resettlers dug trenches across the road that went by their village to highlight their demands for a higher level of compensation. They repeated the trench digging on a nightly basis for quite some time until the local authority finally met some of their demands. People in Quynh Nhai district even cut down swaths of bamboo trees in reaction to what they called unfair resettlement.

While provincial and district authorities may have strengthened their positions thanks to the dam's construction, commune-level authorities in submerged areas faced a different situation. For many commune leaders from resettled communes, there was a chance that they might be able to continue their work in their new area—but only if there were vacant positions in the host communes. If not, they had to retire.[49] People who used to be headmen and representatives of political associations in the old villages usually did not have the opportunity to continue in their positions when their village relocated to a host community.

For the host communes, the authorities faced different types of challenges. They were supposed to follow provincial and district governments' resolutions and directions. If there was land judged to be available in their locales, it was almost impossible for them to refuse incoming resettlers. Commune authorities were responsible for persuading their villagers to share land with the resettlers. They also had to deal with all kinds of post-resettlement problems (such as land and water shortages) as well as deal with tensions between the two merged communities, host and resettled.[50]

It is important to reiterate that there were significant improvements in resettlement and compensation policies for the Sơn La project, compared with previous dam projects. During certain stages of the project, authorities incorporated (to an extent) affected people's opinions into recommendations to policymakers. For example, in the pilot resettlement projects in Muong Ta, instead of "land for land," the government resettlement policy described "land for infrastructure," meaning that host communities had to relinquish part of their land to resettlers in order to gain improved infrastructure (roads, electricity, etc.). As we have seen, the resettlers did not receive accurate compensation for land losses because there was no detailed measurement of the land they had lost in their old villages. Those affected were very unhappy and complained to local authorities, who considered these complaints and referred them to higher authorities. As a result, the compensation policy for resettlement changed—resettlers received cash compensation for the difference between the area of land in their old villages and the land received in resettlement sites. Host communities received cash for the land that they were forced to share with resettlers. For people in Muong Ta, the provincial government finally proposed a solution to compensate both resettlers and host communities: each resettler received VNĐ 10 million (equivalent to about US$670), regardless of how much land that person lost, and host communities received 70 percent of the total value of the land granted to resettlers. In addition, as a result of experiences with resettlement at the pilot sites, potential resettlers were later encouraged to visit the resettlement site chosen for them—and were provided with bus transport to do so—before they agreed to move.[51] While the affected people had the option to say no to the new site, it was not really a viable choice, because those who tried to resist usually faced difficulties later in finding a place to settle down, as in the case of the twelve families in Pa Ha I mentioned at the beginning of this chapter.

Though there have been important strides in project planning and implementation, problems remain. Affected people must conform to the state's overall development plans. Their influence over a particular project remains limited to only a few stages during the implementation process. In addition to the problems that the Sơn La Dam has posed to resettlers, it has presented difficulties to local authorities on multiple levels. With one hundred thousand people who needed to be relocated in a very short time, resettlement units at the district level had to recruit a large number of contract staff who had no or very limited knowledge of resettlement. As a result, many of these new personnel were not competent enough to efficiently handle the workload. At certain sites, resettlers arrived at their new villages and found no roads, water, or electricity. In areas such as in *di vén* (villages relocated higher up on the riverbank) and *di xen ghép* resettlement sites (resettlers moved into the same village with host communities), it took more than a year for roads and electricity to arrive. Support programs for livelihood rehabilitation were slowly rolled out and were inefficient from the start; provincial-level extension officers who designed them did not adequately account for relevant social, ecological, and cultural factors.

During the long process of resettlement, people with more political power, such as government officials at the district level, took advantage of the situation. Local officials, including officials from ethnic minority groups, wielded corrupt power in managing a large amount of money for compensation. Conspicuous power disparity not only between affected people and the authorities, but also between district and commune authorities, between host and resettled commune authorities, and among affected communities, impacted relationships, actions, and the formation of territorial subjects.

Regardless of the sacrifice borne by thousands of local villagers, from the government perspective Sơn La Dam has always been a symbol of progress and development. Hoang Van Chat, secretary of the Sơn La Province Communist Party and chairman of the province's People's Council, said, "The company [EVN] has made practical contributions to the socioeconomic development and the industrialization and modernization of the country in general, and Sơn La Province in particular. In 2018, the company contributed VNĐ 1,345 billion to the provincial budget, helping the province to invest in infrastructure, serving poverty reduction for people of ethnic minority groups in the province."[52]

Sơn La Dam, as well as other dams on the Black River, compressed different models of state control: conquering nature, generating power for economic growth, formulating policy, obtaining consent and participation of subordinate northwesterners, and making territorial subjects. "Power generation" means the creation of electricity, but it can also be interpreted as the making and remaking of relations between the center and the periphery that strengthens the party-state's capacity to control resources and further territorialize upland regions. These power relations have varied, depending on the spaces and the places. They have been exercised in different forms and at different levels. Local authorities, especially at the commune level and largely from ethnic minority backgrounds, were disempowered by their communities' displacement and the marginalization of their political opinions. Yet not all local people suffered: dams, as well as rubber plantations, have actually strengthened relations between the central authorities and some regional powerbrokers in the Northwest. Local or ethnic minority leadership in the Northwest, in this case, emerges through economic and political exchanges against the backdrop of constant change, transformations, and threats.[53]

Planning or dam-associated displacement of local populations has clearly shifted over time. Important changes include compensation policies (subjects to be compensated, compensation for both directly and indirectly affected people), improvements in subsidies and rehabilitation support (time and level), and levels of participation, among others. Policies have changed owing to various contributing factors, including international pressure and domestic social pressure, although it is not clear which factors are most important. Officials learned from the displacement caused by the Sơn La Dam and many other large-scale projects. As a result, Vietnam's Constitution (2013) and Land Law 2013 have strengthened legal protections for people affected by development displacement, with provisions to identify them, inform them, and consult with them prior to any acquisition; to recognize certain customary land-tenure rights; to recognize and compensate for loss of economic activity on land; to provide replacement land as a compensation option; to compensate before possession; and to pay a relocation allowance when people must relocate. However, how effectively this new policy has been implemented on the ground remains a point of contention, as we will see in the case of mining-induced displacement in chapter 8. In order to make way for dams, hundreds of thousands of hectares of land were taken from upland peasants and small farmers. Displaced peasants, who have limited levels of education and face constraints in terms of access to capital, have a difficult time finding livelihood alternatives. Via their practices of everyday politics, territorial subjects were forming and shifting because of changes in their relationships to land, being forced to share land with others, changing their farming practices, living and interacting with different others, and developing relationships with authorities. Accumulation is not simply about the concentration and centralization of the power of capital but is also, as Philip McMichael argues, about "dispossessing alternative practices."[54] Accumulation takes away people's various means of livelihood and their ability to ensure food security, and in this process often disproportionately affects women.

# CHAPTER 4

# Subject Making, Market Integration, and Differentiation

"Ah, do you know that Mr. E's family now is the wealthiest in our village? And not just our village, he is even wealthier than any other families in our neighboring villages." Khun told me this news when I visited Muong Lanh in 2017. "His family just bought two new trucks." She continued: "So they have three trucks now. They have expanded their business, and both of his sons were able to buy houses in Sơn La City. But look at Mr. Ghin's house, it's about to collapse. Mr. Ghin's situation is probably worse than the last time you saw him. We have become so different compared to the life in the old village before resettlement."

As differences in livelihood strategies inform diversity in rural areas, shifts in land use, capital, labor, and agricultural technique facilitate and shape the emergence of varied access to capital, technology, and labor, as well as the differentiation among the upland villagers in Vietnam. Before the development of the Sơn La Dam and rubber plantations, villagers in the Northwest were self-provisioning peasants. Their methods of farming resulted in low-cost production, but in ways unlike the input cost reductions of large-scale farming. When a family is self-provisioning, it supplies inputs for production with minimal market dependence. Van der Ploeg ties self-provisioning to "provisioning of all the resources required for the unit of *production* (as opposed to the unit of consumption)."[1]

A large body of literature focuses on agrarian transformation, transition, and peasant incorporation, examining what happens to farmers, farming systems, food security, consumption, etc., in the process, and what happens when subsistence-focused systems turn into market-focused ones.[2] Henry Bernstein calls the process of agrarian transition from subsistence agriculture to agricultural production for the market "the commercialization of subsistence."[3] In his research on the processes of rich peasant accumulation and mechanisms of social differentiation in Vietnam, Haroon Akram-Lodhi highlights that a group of higher-income peasants may have emerged after the changes in access to land following decollectivization in the late 1980s. This group had relatively larger landholdings and used advanced farming techniques, as well as hired labor power, which resulted in higher yields per unit of land and allowed for a greater degree of market integration and diversification for their production.[4] The differentiation in that case, therefore, was mostly a materialist distinction. However, social differentiation has always been both sociological and material.[5] Ben White, for example, highlights differentiation as not about income inequalities (i.e., some peasants become wealthier than others) but about changing relations between peasants or between peasants and non-peasants in the context of commodity relations.[6] Among villagers who have lost access to land and other resources in the Northwest, differentiation has occurred in both the sociological sense and the material sense.

The processes of differentiation among resettled people who appear to start with roughly equivalent social relations is this chapter's focus. I argue for differentiation—the *process* by which people's class positions change with respect to one another over time—as an integral part of everyday subject making. Changes in the nature and intensity of market integration as well as in production relations (changes in the control of and access to labor and capital) drive differentiation in these locales. Ecological changes due to megaproject development and resource extraction have constrained livelihood choices, while agrarian changes have produced new forms of inequality, including spatial inequalities.[7] When forms of capital-intensive agriculture (like plantations) or non-labor-absorbing projects such as mining or hydropower seize land, the struggles of increasingly proletarianized or semi-proletarianized agrarian populations over both means of production and social reproduction became acute.[8] Because resistance, collaboration, and/or compromise might occur in particular contexts, it becomes crucial, when analyzing people's livelihoods, to recognize elements of local everyday politics and critical points of intersection between different values, interests, and knowledge. Important insights can be gained about how macro-policies concerned with the development of the nation in general and the Northwest region in particular—such as the promotion of hydropower dams—are negotiated at individual, household, and village levels.[9]

## Diversification of Livelihood Strategies in the New Villages

Changes in resource availability and natural conditions significantly shape people's behavior and livelihood strategies. For villagers displaced by the Sơn La Dam, for example, the ways in which they reconstituted their lives and livelihoods after resettlement have not been uniform. Resettlers have devised different strategies to fit various individuals, families, groups, and villages. In the new villages, since their subsistence has become increasingly commoditized, women are also more involved in outside work.

In my friend Khun's Muong Lanh village, resettlers received hilly farmland from the host communities two years after resettling. Maize was the only crop grown on this land. In the third year, authorities allocated the resettlers small patches of land to grow wet rice. In the

**FIGURE 4.1.** Resettlement site, December 2005. Photo by Nguyen Hoai Thanh.

absence of an irrigation system, rice crops relied on rainfall. During the 2009 drought, families did not have enough water for their rice fields; the rice withered, and the families were left with no food or crop for their own consumption. Some families managed to buy pumps to bring water from their ponds to the fields, but this strategy was not always successful. Pumped water is only useful during land preparation; the seedlings need rain, since the ponds are empty during the growing season. As a result, the farmers have good harvests only in non-drought years. This offered further incentive to fight for an irrigation system to support resettler wet rice patches. After four years (2009 to 2013) of arguments between villagers, the district's Resettlement Management Board had the construction company install a small system with funding from the resettlement project.

The villagers organized Muong Lanh into three groups, based on house location, to increase community cohesion and support. Each group accepted responsibility for cleaning public spaces in its part of the village and supporting its neighbors with housework and child care and social activities such as visiting the sick. When the village created its own regulations for environmental protection and social support, villagers encouraged one another to follow these regulations. Such actions help to keep the village's reciprocity networks viable and encourage a spirit of communal support. Kinship relations also help hold the village together through various means of support. My survey of sixty-four households in Muong Lanh in 2009 showed that 27 percent of resettlers supported their relatives financially when necessary. In Muong Lanh, reciprocity and social networks play key roles in survival strategies.

The village also sent representatives of the Farmers' Association and the Women's Union to participate in extension training courses to learn about the proper use of fertilizers and pesticides for growing maize. As the villagers did not have to use chemicals on their crops in the old villages, these techniques were new to everyone. After the training courses, the representatives passed on their new knowledge to their fellow villagers. A villager in Muong Lanh recalled in 2009,

> In our old village, when it's time, we cleared the trees and plants in our fields, let them be for about one week, then we burned them [the fields]. The next day, we used sticks to make holes and put seeds in. No tilling or anything else. After about one week, the maize sprouted. We weeded twice: the first time was two weeks

after the sprout, then the second time was after one month. That's it. Then we waited for harvest. We could have two crops per year. We never used fertilizers or pesticides. One kilogram of seeds planted in a thousand square meters and we got a three- to four-hundred-kilogram harvest. Here in the new village, from one kilogram of seeds we got a four-hundred-kilogram harvest, but we needed to apply fertilizers and pesticides. And since we have much less land, we cannot depend only on farming anymore.[10]

Villagers have started to diversify their activities, combining agricultural with nonagricultural work, and focusing on commercial services. At the resettlement site, as part of their "plural activity"—their combination of agricultural and nonagricultural work—some villagers have become petty commodity producers who maintain their subsistence through integration into wider social divisions of labor and markets. As their families' livelihoods no longer depend entirely on farming activities, many villagers are now part-time farmers or marginal farmers—the term that Peter Hazell and colleagues use to refer to farmers who cultivate small tracts of land and have livelihoods that depend on various activities besides farming.[11] In Muong Lanh in 2008, more than two years after their resettlement, villagers produced enough vegetables for their families' consumption and were able to sell two tons of additional produce in the local market along with bamboo shoots that they collected in the forest. This extra income from their gardens would not have been possible in the old, pre-resettlement village because of two factors: (1) in the old village, people mostly produced for their own consumption; and (2) they were not located close to the market, which made it difficult to sell their produce.

Now located on a steep slope, the resettled villagers at Muong Nhung village were not as lucky as those in Muong Lanh, even though they originally came from the same Muong Tra commune. Hunger immediately threatened after their relocation. The area is comparatively dry and lacks a major water source, so gardens did not thrive as they did in Muong Lanh, and villagers were unable to earn extra income from produce sales. However, every family managed to grow some vegetables to support its daily consumption. As the village is near a small water source, some households chose to plant their vegetables on the village path, leaving a small space for walking (figure 4.2). In order to deal with water scarcity, resettlers dug ponds. These were empty during the dry season (October to March) but supported fishponds and water storage

**FIGURE 4.2.** Growing vegetables on the village path, Muong Nhuong village, August 2009. Photo by the author.

during the rainy season (April to September). Resettlers also made use of the forest, gathering bamboo shoots for sale and collecting bamboo and rattan to make household items for the family and to sell in the local market. Villagers that I spoke with longed for larger patches of land for farming, like those they possessed in the old village. They wanted to be able to sell their garden vegetables and secure land to cultivate wet rice. Many of them (mostly Thái) complained that their wet rice farming techniques would soon be forgotten in the village, and they were justifiably concerned about how the next generation would survive without enough land to feed themselves.

On the hilly farmland that the villagers received as compensation for their displacement by the Sơn La hydropower project, they intercrop maize and cassava. In the first few years after resettlement, the villagers were learning how to effectively engage in intensive farming on their small patches of land, a significant change from the extensive farming that they practiced in their old village. Villagers moved to Muong Nhuong from two small villages in Muong Tra commune—Muong Hon and Muong Ban. In the new village, they did not want to just take the new name given to them—Muong Nhuong. So they chose to build their houses in two separate areas of the village and have created two small hamlets, keeping their old names—Muong Hon and Muong Ban. Villagers in each of these hamlets dealt with the change quite differently.

Muong Hon hamlet's headman took responsibility for learning new techniques and traveled within the commune and the district to learn the optimal time for seeding and fertilizer and pesticide application. He also consulted with several families in the host community who were known for their success in breeding and raising hybrid pigs. He then shared his newfound skills with the villagers. The headman told me that "whoever pays attention will likely have more chance of success in doing new things." Muong Ban villagers employed a different strategy. As individuals or families, they consulted with members of the host community to learn methods that were tailored to their specific needs and strategies. In both hamlets, while some of the resettlers were successful in their attempts to raise the faster-growing pigs, others have returned to the familiar breed and traditional rearing methods, having accepted that their pigs will not reach a salable size as quickly. With their resettlement compensation money, two families opened convenience stores, and one has done quite well in this business.

In general, the villagers have employed various strategies that depend on their family's composition and labor availability. These strategies have been conditioned by particular social, cultural, and economic relations. Each family and every village has a unique story. In general, intertwined relations within and outside their villages put various pressures on families and individuals. Strategies shift with changes in the labor situation, capital investments, productivity cycles, reproduction within the family, and even social relation priorities—like caring for children, the elderly, or the sick—each generating alternatives that increase or decrease dependency or autonomy.[12] All these activities have contributed to the transformation of agrarian landscapes in the area and the creation of new territorial subjects. Changes in land use such as converting farmland or forestland to plantations or mining sites or being submerged under a reservoir follow from intentional human activities, the interaction of different institutions, or changes in the mode of governance over land, water, plants, and animals.[13]

## Plural Activity as New Trajectories

Immediately after moving, resettlers in Muong Bung commune relentlessly struggled for their livelihoods, trying to secure their daily needs, many suffering from hunger. In the new conditions in resettlement sites, plural activities have become commonplace. Villagers have combined different ways of earning a living, including working the tiny land plots they received after resettlement, renting farmland from the host community or from wealthier village families, and selling their labor—working for wages within and outside their village. Villagers engage in multiple activities tied to the labor market. Even though work as a porter or selling one's labor in the local labor market is not an option that villagers prefer, many of them earn an important portion of their income in this way. This plural activity has produced positive outcomes, including desired income growth, an important facet of economic independence.

The phenomenon of engaging generally in plural activities may also be partly stimulated by the government policy of promoting diversification in rehabilitating livelihoods. Through various agricultural extension training programs, cadres from the district level came to promote a model of "progressive farmers," which encouraged resettlers to learn new techniques and diversify livelihoods.

Defying ethnic stereotyping as "lazy," resettlers of all ethnicities worked hard and tried to grasp any economic opportunity that they could find. Working as a motorbike driver was quite common for men before they had received their compensation land. Others sought jobs nearby or in other areas. Some illegally engaged in logging. This illegal activity was not always met with punishment; forest rangers chose to ignore such activities, as they felt sympathetic with resettlers.[14] A forest ranger said "[resettlers] only [logged illegally] for survival. They had already been through too much due to the displacement."[15]

In some cases, villagers cleared some parts of common land to grow their own trees. A man in Muong Ta said,

> When I moved here, I had to learn to do many different types of work, from construction worker to motorbike driver, to potter, and paid labor on other people's farm. I also started to clear common land to grow plums. Of course, the authorities did not like it. Growing your trees on common land was not allowed. They summoned me to the office and asked me to stop. But I told them that I was hungry. My children were hungry, and we were miserable. If I did not do it, what was my family going to eat? So, they let me do it. Most of my neighbors saw me doing it, and they followed as well.[16]

Thus, plural activity became more than a purely economic activity; it was political and social behavior that played a critical role in both landscape production and the making of territorial subjects in the Northwest. Villagers themselves through their labor contributed to landscape production by clearing forest or turning common land into their own. They actively sought means to assert new forms of land control and to earn livings for their families.

Not every household has successfully diversified its income sources, but most attempt to and learn to do so in different ways. Household composition partially governs this trend.[17] Families with young and strong sons appear to be more successful in diversifying to increase the family's income, mostly by out-migration of some family members to find employment in industrial zones in other provinces. The number of family members, their level of education, and social networks also drive success at diversification. Young women with a high school diploma have opportunities to train as nurses, pharmacist assistants, or daycare and preschool teachers. They may find nonfarming work but still remain involved in their family's farming activities. The integration of the peasantry into the labor market either as labor suppliers or buyers "most closely characterizes the process of class formation among direct producers and hence, their incorporation into the dominant capitalist mode of production."[18]

Villagers with different resources have involved themselves in various nonagricultural activities, depending on their skills, health, and fitness. If we consider plural activity a combination of agricultural activities and nonagricultural activities within a production unit (a household), about 62 percent of the sixty-four surveyed families in Muong Lanh and 36 percent of the fifty-nine surveyed families in Muong Nhuong can be considered as engaging in plural activities. These activities include handy work or services, such as carpenter, painter, or porter (36 percent of households in Muong Lanh reported this kind of work and 11 percent in Muong Nhuong); commerce services (14 percent in Muong Lanh, 8 percent in Muong Nhuong); and public services, such as government employment as teacher, nurse, etc. (12 percent in Muong Lanh, 17 percent in Muong Nhuong).

Resettlers experimented with various economic activities to identify those that best suited their families' situations. When they failed at one activity, some tried other activities, while others gave up attempts and slid into drinking, as I recount in chapter 1. Plural activity thus offered potential to meet the needs of resettled families for new income sources.

It also affirmed their self-control and rise from difficult circumstances. However, while plural activity has led villagers to greater market integration and changes in access to capital, it has also accelerated differentiation within the community, as only few households could manage to do well, depending on their labor and available resources.

## Dynamics of Village Differentiation

Like other communities, an upland peasant community has never been a community of equals. Some households possess a larger pool of in-house labor and reclaim a larger area of land. Some wealthier households inherited land from their ancestors and did not have to work as hard as others to clear new land for rotational farming. Since the development of capitalism and commodity production was not uniform or uninterrupted, the expansion of commodity production did not always suggest the material impoverishment or worsened vulnerability to food shortage experienced by peasants. Some peasants thrived at times, while many others did not, and a state was often incapable of effectively helping those who struggled.[19] In general, for peasants, risk and subsistence security are central in their lives. They find it natural to be preoccupied with subsistence. James Scott calls the technical arrangements of the "safety first" principle that correspond to a "subsistence ethic" within peasant social structures a moral economy—the notion of economic justice and their working definition of exploitation.[20] This logic does not mean that peasants incline toward accumulation of land and wealth when they have the opportunity, but it does argue that subsistence or survival is the first priority in precarious situations.

For resettlers in Sơn La, the most salient change that everyone recognized and felt uncomfortable with in the new villages was the need to purchase everything, from rice to eggs, fish, and even vegetables in some places like Muong Nhuong, Muong Ma, and Muong Che. My surveys show that if before villagers went to the market only once or twice a month for leisure or to buy items, such as oil or salt, that they could not produce themselves, after resettling, these villagers went to the market almost daily to purchase food. All the resettlers had to buy rice, regardless of whether they had access to wet rice patches. This increased market interaction dramatically reshaped villagers' daily lives, putting heavy pressure on them to pursue various livelihoods in search of additional income. They also had to borrow money more frequently—55 percent of villagers were in debt, compared to only 4 percent before the move. Schools were now accessible, so education expenditures were accordingly higher. As time passed, the villagers learned to adapt to their new way of life, just as they learned to adapt to new farming methods and to a life without the river. But differences in control over capital and production resources brought differential control over other issues in the village, such as decision-making on shared village matters like installation of water pipes and organization of community events.

In order to illustrate a more comprehensive picture of differentiation in Muong Lanh and Muong Nhuong villages, I investigate the circumstances of villagers in three categories of wealth—the wealthy, those of middling means, and the poor—through the triple lens of causes, processes, and indicators.[21] Although differentiation is based on production relations and relations to capital and state, rather than income differences, I use these categories because this is how the resettlers divided themselves in their new location; the same categories existed in their old villages. Before resettlement, the wealth dynamics were largely attributed to access to land; and in general, the more labor a family had—that is, the size of the family—the more land they would be able to clear for farming. For those families, the amount of compensation for land loss was higher than that of other families who used to own less land. However, the amount of financial compensation families received from resettlement (for lost crops and trees on their land, boats, etc.) was not the key factor in wealth stratification in the resettlement villages, because some families used most of their compensation money on housing or other durable goods. I use the group data provided by the headmen, and from villagers via group ranking exercises.[22]

According to the latter, wealthy families include those who have savings at the end of the year to buy more production materials, durable goods, and more land than the area given to them after resettlement (twenty-five hundred square meters per person), and/or were able to hire labor for their farming activities. Medium families were identified as stable—they had enough to eat year-round without suffering from food insecurity but were unable to buy more land. Poor families suffered from food insecurity and fell into the government's criteria for the poor, which meant they had an income of less than VNĐ 400,000 (about US$40) per person per month. This group also included those the local authorities rank as poor and eligible for government food subsidies. I will examine their access to resources and capital, network availability, market integration, and the ways that they spend their compensation and savings.

### Differentiation in Muong Lanh

The authorities and the Resettlement Management Board in Sơn La consider Muong Lanh one of the best resettlement sites in Sơn La Province, and the provincial government often lauds it as a model resettlement site to visitors from foreign embassies and potential donors like the World Bank and the Asian Development Bank. Good infrastructure, including roads and schools, contributes to Muong Lanh's reputation for success. Most of my interviewees expressed happiness with the village's infrastructure. Muong Lanh is on flat land, which meant it was easier there than at other locations for the families to dig fishponds and run water pipes to their houses. This topography proved beneficial for gardening and raising livestock. Despite fierce disputes between the host communities and resettlers when the latter moved in, the villagers now enjoy friendly and respectful relationships after several years of cohabitation. The village also maintains a good relationship with the commune's administration. One person from the resettlement village works as a commune legal officer.

In 2011, villagers ranked 40 percent of the village as wealthy. When resettled families first moved to Muong Lanh, each received the same amount of land per person for housing and farming. Although land for housing was intended to be distributed by lottery before the move, many families simply seized land on a first-come, first-served basis—those who moved earlier snapped up the choice locations, usually with a pond, to build their houses. One woman explained, "We were voluntary to be the first ones to move. We had to do lottery for our housing lots before we moved, but since the others did not want to move and we were the first ones here, we just grabbed the best lots. Indeed, no one followed the lottery result."[23] Thus, these families enjoyed more favorable conditions. Other families, including the headman's household, were able to buy ponds and paddy rice patches from members of the host community, thanks to compensation money or savings, or connections that include those formed via children's marriages. The survey revealed that one-third of the families employed the former method, using compensation money or savings after a few years of diversified farming in the new village.

As cash became the most urgent need in their new home, villagers developed different strategies to raise the money for their families' needs. After moving in, a few families quickly adapted to the land shortage situation by starting small businesses instead of solely relying on farming and, as a consequence, made themselves the wealthiest families in the village. Most shifted from farming alone to diversified farming and business or service work—raising livestock, providing transportation, or starting small shops—to divest their livelihoods from a dependence on land. These resourceful families often had good connections with people running businesses outside the village, had young and strong labor, and were willing to risk investing in new business activities. For example, seeing that maize was a dominant crop in the area, Mr. E—the man who had the village's first bathroom—and his family used most of their compensation money soon after arriving to invest in a maize milling machine to serve their village and the neighboring villages (host communities). They successfully grew vegetables in their garden, raised chickens and pigs, and made alcohol to sell at the local market. Using income from the milling machine and selling their pigs, in 2009, Mr. E and his two sons were able to purchase a large truck to transport maize. A year later, in 2010, another family in the village invested in the maize milling business but went out of business in 2016. By 2017, Mr. E and his family bought two additional trucks and expanded the mill's capacity. They were even able to sell their maize alcohol to people in Sơn La City and as far away as Hanoi. Theirs is a success story. They farmed the small plot of land to support their daily needs, diversified their income, and steadily built their businesses. Such families supported their relatives with jobs and cash, including purchasing wet rice land for their children from host communities. Such families have started to accumulate more land than their fellow villagers.

Those who have family members with higher educational levels and stable jobs like teaching elementary school (Khun's family) or working as a commune officer also do well. In the first few years, these kinds of families farmed their land, grew vegetables in their gardens, and raised animals, just like their neighbors. With additional stable income, however, they earned extra money by lending it at high interest rates and could afford to occasionally hire laborers to work on their land. By 2018, thirteen years after moving to the new village, Khun's family no longer farmed its land, instead leasing it to neighbors. A few families even purchased water pumps to divert the water from their ponds to their nearby rice patches. Other families used their compensation money to invest in planting fruit trees or raising hybrid pigs. As newcomers, the resettlers were unfamiliar with raising a different breed of pigs and in different surroundings, but by 2012, those in the host community, who initially guided the newcomers' efforts in rearing these animals, sought them out for advice. Two households were thriving thanks to their neighbors' need to buy food and other goods; these families opened convenience stores in the village. Many maximized their garden space and earned part of their income from selling vegetables.

During my visits to Muong Lanh village, I spent many hours with Mr. Nu. Even though he was one of the village's leaders, he had been against the resettlement plan and was very concerned about the changes that his villagers faced in their new home. His family was quite successful in the new location, but he loved to reminisce about the old village—it was his favorite subject. This suggests that doing well in a new location does not equate to happiness. One afternoon, I visited him in his home to learn more about the resettlers' lives before the move. As we drank our tea, he told me his story:

> Oh, you want to know about life in the old village? I can spend days to tell you about it. The life there was quite different. You know, I have been through a lot, from the farming cooperative period in the 1960s until now. I used to be a head of our cooperative during the 1970s. The land in our old village was unlimited. You just did not have enough strength to clear it for your farming, otherwise you could have ten hectares or even more than that. And the fish, oh my gosh! I miss the fish. Just a few years ago, I caught an eighteen-kilogram carp. Oh, it was huge. My family had four ponds. I caught fish every day in the Nậm Mu River [a big tributary of the Đà River], even in the winter. We had fish in our meals every day. I have two sons, so we all could work together in our field, catching fish, and so on. We had enough food and were able to have extra for saving every year. I didn't want to move here, but what could we do? We're lucky that our house is near a pond, and we could clear the other patch [pointing to a rice patch near the house] for growing wet rice. Well, it's just a small patch but better than nothing. My wife and I work in our field. We grow maize. We also grow vegetables in our garden for selling. We have a buffalo and some pigs. Things are OK here. We have enough to eat. It's convenient as it's close to the market, close to the provincial and district centers. But after four years I still don't feel that it's home yet, and there is so little land for everyone in my village.[24]

Families like Mr. Nu's diversified their income and adjusted their livelihoods to compensate for the limited land they received in the new village. This diversification took many forms, including different farming activities, from growing rice, maize, and vegetables to raising pigs, cows, and chickens, as well as engaging in services such as running convenience stores, milling, and transporting. With the resulting income, these households were able to purchase more wet rice land from the host communities. Perhaps, for some families, they have simply been luckier in their agricultural activities than their neighbors.

These families began to enjoy the fruits of their production labors, especially in terms of physical items that did not exist in their old village: computers, gas stoves, refrigerators, and freezers. However, not all these families were able to sustain this prosperity. By 2019, four families in this group had borrowed from the bank to invest in larger businesses, had lost most of their money, and were unable to repay the bank. Two families mortgaged their houses and left the village to work as paid labor in Bắc Ninh Province in the Red River delta. Indeed, in 2021, all the villagers in Muong Lanh, including Mr. E's family, borrowed money from the bank in five-year loans, with amounts ranging from VNĐ 20 million (about US$900) to VNĐ 100 million (about US$45,000).[25] The practice of borrowing money from the bank to invest in business emerged with the increase in market integration—the tight

FIGURE 4.3.    A vegetable garden in Muong Lanh, August 2009. Photo by the author.

link with the market for both inputs and outputs of their business and everyday lives—that followed resettlement.

In 2011, almost half the village fell into the medium wealth group (46 percent). Most villagers depended on their farmland, gardens, and livestock and worked as wage laborers during their free time. Living close to the market has its disadvantages and its advantages. On the one hand, villagers spent more money, since it was so easy to get to the market. On the other hand, everything they produced could be sold in the market, from garden vegetables to bamboo shoots to fuelwood collected in the forest. Raising cattle, pigs, and goats as an economic strategy differed among households. As there was not enough land for grazing, each household usually raised only two or three cows or a water buffalo for plowing. Not everyone was as successful in raising pigs as were the villagers in the wealthy group. Those in the medium group usually invested in a smaller number of animals, just enough for them to have extra income to buy rice and other necessities. With their moderate income, most of the villagers in this group were unable to purchase more land from the host communities and did not have the means to enjoy as many luxury items as those in the wealthy group. Sometimes the boundary between the medium and poor groups blurred; even though they earlier had enough to eat, these groups were not able to save for emergencies. A suboptimal harvest, a livestock failure, or a family member's illness could trigger a food shortage.

Mrs. Bin was thirty-five when her family moved to Muong Lanh. She is married and has two children. This is her story:

> When we had just arrived here, I cried a lot. We all missed our old village dearly. We used to live right by the river. Everything was attached to the river. I never had to worry about not having fish to eat. Moving here, we don't even own a pond. My husband told me we could not just sit there and cry. While we were waiting for receiving our farming land, my husband went to work as a motorbike driver in It Ong. It Ong is near the dam site, so there were many construction workers there. There was high demand for motorbike drivers [xe ôm]. I started to pick up work in neighboring villages. I took whatever opportunities I had, from land preparing to transplanting rice. I also learned to grow hybrid pigs and chicken. When we received our farming land, we both spent more time working on our farm, but my husband still went out for labor jobs. We don't earn a lot, but it's enough for our expenses.

Things are now not too bad for us. But we still dream about our old village.[26]

After the move, 14 percent of the families in Muong Lanh reported that they were miserable, due in large part to the lack of arable land in the new village. These families usually faced labor and capital shortages and had only minimal savings from the pre-resettlement period. Without savings or other sources of income, purchasing wet rice land from the host communities was impossible. Resettlers' lack of good connections or networks was an additional barrier. The land offered as compensation in the new village was not sufficient for food crops (maize and cassava) to sustain their family throughout the year, let alone offer any extra crop for sale. Luck also played a role, especially in raising livestock. Some families borrowed or used all their compensation money to invest in pigs, but the animals died. Cows died during the cold winter months. One man in this situation saw all his animals die while his neighbor's livestock thrived. He said, "I don't know what to do, whom to blame, maybe just blame why God is so cruel to me."[27] He could not even consider borrowing and investing in livestock again, as he was unable to pay his existing debt. He left the village in 2012 to work in Vĩnh Phúc, a neighboring province of Hanoi.

A number of families in this group had many small children or lacked strong labor in the house, which limited the opportunities for wage work or employment as a porter. Some in this group were too weak to work the land, so it was leased to other households. These families mixed cassava with their rice as a staple food for one to six months a year. They frequently bought food on credit at the village convenience stores; the debts for these purchases accumulated until payment at harvest time. Most of these households resided in the higher, hilly areas, and they didn't have ponds for raising fish. In 2010, the government implemented Program 30a, which supported poor families in the uplands with twenty kilograms of white rice per person per month in the three months preceding the harvest.

According to my interviewees, some villagers saw individuals of the poor group as lazy, spending their compensation money on rebuilding their house or buying new consumer goods such as televisions or motorcycles instead of investing in production. Neighbors typically held little respect for these poor families, who longed to return to their old villages.

Mr. Ghin was the first person I interviewed during my first trip to Muong Lanh in 2005. He approached me as soon as I arrived at the village. He had just finished building his house at the resettlement site, and he wanted to access some of his resettlement money in advance so he could complete his new bathroom. He thought that I might know the cash compensation schedule. The headman told me that Mr. Ghin was one of the poorest people in the village. When I returned to the village four years later during my dissertation fieldwork, he was still one of the poorest in the village. His voice always sounded bitter when he told me about his life, but there was a glimmer of hope for a better future.

> I served in the army when I was young. Ah, that was at the end of the American War. After I finished my term, I came back to the village and got married late. Unfortunately, we did not have any children. We had to adopt two children. But when they grew up, they did not live with us. I worked hard most of my life but did not meet my fortune. However, in the old village, things were not that bad, as at least we had our land. We could work on it and survived. We did not have enough food all year round though, just nine or ten months. Here, I don't know what to do. The land is so small and not very productive. The only thing we can grow is maize, and it's not enough for us to survive more than six months. I don't like it here. There is no river. You know, the river is so important to our life, and I miss it so much. Well, but here I have a new toilet. Oh, I also have a new and bigger house. We did not have a toilet in the old village. The problem was because we were poor and did not own a large area of land in the old village, the compensation for land lost that we received was less than other, wealthier families who owned more land in the old village. And I spent all my compensation for rebuilding the house, building a new toilet, bought a TV, furniture, and I don't have anything left. Now I want to raise pigs. I see Mr. E could earn a fortune from raising pigs. But I need to go to the bank to borrow money for it. Hmmm, not sure how it works, but I'll give it a try.[28]

His family's fortunes had not changed when I last visited the village in 2019. His plan to raise pigs was largely unsuccessful, though he had a couple of them in a pen to sell once they matured. It seemed very hard for Mr. Ghin and his family to escape this cycle of poverty. Unfortunately, his family's case is not unique. A few other families in the village faced similar problems responding to the dramatic changes in their lives after resettlement and beyond.

Little evidence suggests that poor people in the villages have become landless; they instead seem to try to hold on to the tiny piece of land they received as compensation. Families sometimes lease their land, but most of them do not sell it outright. Members of the wealthy group may possess more land, purchased from the host communities with extra income, but this advantage has not resulted in large differences in landownership, because the amount of farming land for sale in a commune is limited, and most of the families who were able to buy more land did it within the first five years after resettlement. Group discussions revealed that in the case of Muong Lanh, landownership and farm size proved fairly stable, and any agricultural surplus supported other production resources like trucks, water pumps, fruit trees, and livestock. Several factors contribute to differentiation in a village, but the most important include access to capital, land, and resources; the availability of labor (extra income from selling labor and/or increased effort in different farming activities); and social connections and networks. As the whole village of Muong Lanh is Thái, ethnicity alone had no bearing on who received better land or house plots. Families with good connections, who moved earlier, or who had more land in the old village enjoyed an advantage from the start. Overall, I have seen no significant movement of families between these three categories of villagers' wealth in the eighteen years since I first visited. Resettlement has deepened existing inequalities, as evidenced in Mr. Ghin's plight. When a couple in the old village had no children and/or owned less land, their situation did not improve in the new village—they still had less labor and received less compensation for land lost.

Resettlers in Muong Lanh have fairly successfully reconstituted their lives overall, with a high percentage of households in the wealthy and medium wealth groups. Since the village is close to the commune's center and market, it is easier for villagers to sell their produce and earn extra income. Successful households often have better access to resources and capital, have stronger networks, and prove to be more strategic in spending their compensation and savings. Luck may also be a factor in these stories. This success does not scale; livelihood recovery has not met this level of success throughout the 276 of the Sơn La hydropower project resettlement sites.[29] Muong Lanh, a special case, enjoyed favorable conditions. Not so the Muong Nhuong resettlement village and the two small hamlets within—Muong Ban and Muong Hon. The case of Muong Nhuong more accurately reflects conditions faced by many resettlement villages, not only in Sơn La Province and the Northwest, but elsewhere in Vietnam, including the central area and the Central Highlands.

## Differentiation in Muong Nhuong

Villagers in the Muong Ban and Muong Hon hamlets in Muong Nhuong village appear to have faced greater difficulty than resettlers in Muong Lanh. The village is located in a dry and hilly area and has poor water access. Villagers can walk across dried-up ponds in October and November. Critical water shortages have made both raising pigs (especially the new hybrid variety) and gardening a challenge. Some villagers cultivate drought-tolerant plants. Such livelihood strategies appear unavoidable given the dramatic shift from life by the river to life in an arid, hilly area. The geography of their new area has influenced opportunities and outcomes for the resettlers' production strategies.

During my first day in Muong Nhuong in 2008, I did not purchase any vegetables to bring to the village, thinking that I would be helping if I purchased them from the villagers. It turned out to be very difficult to find vegetables to buy in the village, because of the water shortage. As I walked around the village, I saw a woman with her baby. I asked her what kind of greens she had in her garden. She told me that the only thing she had was morning glory (*rau muống*). "Great! That's one of my favorite veggies," I thought. But when I asked if I could buy some from her, she said, "No way. These greens are not for selling. They are for my pigs." I stood speechless while my research assistant Lien burst into laughter. After searching for a while, I finally managed to purchase some young pumpkin leaves from the village's Women's Union representative. Since this experience, I have always remembered to bring extra vegetables and other food when traveling to that village. A few years after the resettlement, the situation had not improved; Muong Nhuong villagers needed to purchase almost everything at the market, including vegetables.

The rocky land assigned to resettlers in Muong Nhuong has yielded little agriculturally; villagers have been unable to clear it and turn it into arable land. According to my interviewees in Muong Nhuong, at the time of resettlement, the land was allocated to villagers via a lottery. Resettlers cannot access areas nearby for clearing and cultivation, as that land is managed by the host communities. Conflict erupted between the hosts and the newcomers whenever the latter attempted to use these lands; efforts soon ceased. The resettlement families' access to the forest has also changed. The nearest forest contained mostly bamboo trees. It normally took almost a day to collect bamboo shoots and fuelwood; only families with stronger labor resources could do so with any frequency, despite concerns shared by most families that both commodities would soon be in short supply. Households did not leave their land idle, even though it was not fertile—they grew maize or leased the land to another family. None of the households sold their land, and all longed for more land for cultivation, or at least water to grow vegetables in their gardens and raise pigs and chickens. Born as peasants, many told me that they wanted to continue as peasants even though they had a very limited amount of arable land—they loved that way of life. Others simply had no alternative, since they did not know any other way to earn a living.

For my analysis in Muong Nhuong, I used criteria similar to what I used in Muong Lanh for grouping families into wealthy, medium, and poor. In 2011, the villagers categorized as wealthy 20 percent of the families in Muong Hon hamlet (one family of La Ha ethnicity) and Muong Ban hamlet (where half the hamlet is La Ha); that was half the rate of perceived wealth in Muong Lanh, even though incomes were much lower than the same group in Muong Lanh. Some were able to lease or buy small patches of farmland from the host community. As families in the host communities owned quite a large area of land (as did the resettlers before their move), selling a small piece did not impact their income, and the revenue from the sale could be used for expenditures like fixing houses, weddings, or durable goods.

Resettlers in these hamlets received the same amount of land per person as did their peers in Muong Lanh. These families also diversified their income—none relied solely on farming. A few households spent their compensation/savings to buy wet rice patches from the host communities, while others had strong labor in the family and earned extra wages as porters. Some families had more savings from their old villages and/or received more cash compensation, as their farmland was larger. Some of these wealthier families, in turn, lent money to other people in their village or in neighboring villages at high interest rates. One village man said that "my fellow villagers now don't like us because of what we do—overcharge for lending money. Oh well, everyone has their own way of surviving. This is ours."[30]

The villagers in this wealthier group usually have more advantageous social networks outside the village, such as family or relatives who run successful businesses that the resettlers can join. They are also more business-minded as compared to their neighbors. The headman of Muong Hon is one example. In addition to growing maize on the plot that his family received as compensation, he raised pigs and chickens. His wife planted cassava in plots around the house and in many small patches that he was able to clear in the area. They used the cassava to feed the livestock. The headman is a son-in-law of Mr. E, the family who owns big trucks and a maize milling machine in Muong Lanh, so he was able to join his in-law's business. Later, he worked as an intermediary in the maize business; he bought maize from other villagers and sold it at a higher price. Some of his brothers in the village also joined him in this business. They routinely supported one another with money when needed, and the headman also invested in pigs. Since 2011, he has kept ten to fifteen pigs in his barn and earned money from their sale. By 2018, he was the wealthiest man in the village. His success meant that he gave up his job as headman to spend more time on his businesses.

Outside of their farming activities, some families in Muong Ban chose different strategies for making money, not all of which are pleasing to their neighbors. One family moved to live along the big road that runs through the village and opened a small convenience store. They became a village debt owner. Villagers buy supplies on credit, sign a debt book, and pay off the debt at the end of the month or at harvest time—at a high interest rate. Arguments happened every now and then between the debt owner and villagers unable to pay the debt when due. This debt-owning family had not been considered wealthy before resettlement. Also in Muong Ban, a couple of families in the wealthy group often bought maize from their neighbors—those who were in financial difficulty—at a low price (often about 60–65 percent of the price at harvest time) and then sold the maize later to intermediate agencies for a profit. For the last ten years, these maize traders have been controlling others' labor using agricultural surpluses since resettlement. A traditional system of reciprocity seems to have been abandoned in these hamlets.

Every time I visited Muong Nhuong, I stopped by the house that served as the village's convenience store. It was far from the rest of the village, located alongside the long and lonely road to Thuận Châu district. There is an interesting story of how the store's owners became one of the wealthy families in the village, which proves that sometimes what seems to be bad luck proves not that bad after all. The family used to be in the medium-income group prior to resettlement. When they first arrived in the village, their house stood in the highest area of the village, right next to the mountain. A few years after their initial resettlement, a landslide damaged their house. They asked the commune to allow them to relocate to a site next to the road where they could rebuild their house.

As they did not have sufficient arable land to survive from farming, the husband, Mr. Lam, searched for temporary work, without much luck. One day, a car stopped to ask for directions; the driver asked Mr. Lam if he sold water or snacks. He did not have anything to sell, but this spurred the family to open a convenience store to meet the needs of travelers and villagers. The family took out a loan from the Bank for the Poor and used the remainder of their compensation money to purchase a refrigerator and food items to sell. They started with instant noodles, eggs, vegetables, and snacks for children. Later they added ice cream, yogurt, cooking oil, fish sauce, and basic groceries that villagers needed. The business grew quickly, and they became one of the wealthy families in the village.

When I asked Mr. Lam why they needed to offer credit to villagers who bought from the store, he said, "I can't do it any other way, since I have to sell stuff to anyone who needs it. But many people in the village don't have money available when they need to buy things. If I did not sell to them, I might not be able to keep the store. So having a debt book is a good way to do it. They can always pay me later when they have cash."[31] When I saw him in 2019, Mr. Lam was still doing well with his store.

About 35 percent of the families in Muong Hon, and half of those in Muong Ban, fit into the medium-income group. They work hard all year and have just enough to eat. They intensively farm their compensation land and raise livestock: pigs, cattle, goats, and chickens. To get extra income, a few of them work as motorbike drivers in Muong La town. As everything can be sold in the market, families collect bamboo shoots and vegetables and sell them in the market whenever possible to provide extra income. A couple of families in Muong Ban intercrop vegetables in their maize fields. Only families with strong labor are able to go to the forest for bamboo shoots, as the forest is several kilometers from the village.

This group less commonly benefits from kinship support in the form of financial assistance than do individuals in the wealthy group; families struggle to meet their basic needs, let alone support their relatives. This group does not maintain an effective reciprocity support system; they cannot help one another with farming work, building houses, or caring for the sick when needed because they are too busy working for their living. Members of this group lack resources for reciprocity support. For example, the husband of the village's Women's Union representative (who sold me the young pumpkin leaves) had a stroke in 2007 and lost his memory, as I mentioned in chapter 1. His wife became the head of the household. Their relatives in a similar income bracket were unable to help support this family.

In Muong Ban, my research found that eight resettled households (about 14 percent of hamlet households) have had no money for their daily food for a few months each year. These poor families used their compensation money to buy consumer goods, and then needed to borrow money from lenders at the commune's center for their food, seed maize, fertilizer, and pesticides; the interest rate on this loan runs about 4 percent per month. At harvest, lenders visited the fields and collected the debt in kind, taking the maize right from the field. These villagers have repaid their debt but are left with little or nothing to show for their labor, and the cycle continues year after year. Other families, who chose not to borrow from lenders, sold their young maize to their neighbors in the high-income group. Other families in this group chose not to engage in intensive farming and did not purchase fertilizers and pesticides for their crops. These families could not afford these inputs. Their maize production was low, and their earnings from selling their crop were not sufficient to buy food until the next harvest. As the village faces water shortages, families reverted to raising their local variety of pigs that require less water for bathing and cleaning barns than the hybrid variety. They let the pigs roam in the village and fed them whatever was available.

Each family has its own story, and not every household classified as poor in the new village was in the same category before resettlement. The move and coping with the associated changes varied widely from family to family. One day I visited a house where the husband, Mr. Thinh, was weaving a basket, and the wife was babysitting their grandchildren. They were both about forty, but already had three grandchildren. Mr. Thinh told me that he was lucky to find this special bamboo in the forest to make the basket. From the family's photos displayed on the wall, it seemed to me that his family had not always been this poor. When I asked him why he did not work in the fields that day, he sighed.

> Well, we have only one hectare of land for four of us. Not much to work on. We used to have nine hectares in the old village. We also had a number of patches for wet rice growing. We grew rice, soybeans, maize, and had more than enough to eat. When we moved here, my wife was very sick. We had to spend quite a large amount of our cash savings and compensation during her hospitalization. Now we have nothing. No water for a fish pond or for raising the hybrid pigs. Do you see our traditional pigs running over there? It will take a while until we will be able to sell them—well, if nothing goes wrong. We have nothing in our garden either. No water, and the land is so poor. You know, I want a patch of wet rice so badly. I want to be able to move water from the spring to the rice field again.[32]

Ten years later, his family's situation had only marginally improved. Mr. Thinh has not been able to afford the wet rice patch that he longed for. Since his wife's death in 2017, he has become resigned to the situation and his circumstances. "Now," he said, "it's my children's turn to worry about earning a living."[33]

According to my survey, in both Muong Ban and Muong Hon, about 40 percent of the resettlers splurged and spent their compensation money buying durable consumer goods such as televisions, motorcycles, refrigerators, freezers, and furniture, among other things. After two or three years, most of the families who bought freezers ended up selling them; freezers were not of much use anymore with little food to freeze and few customers for frozen treats. When I asked about their post-settlement financial choices, most of them told me that they hadn't known what to invest in, given the limitations caused by the lack of water in the village. As a consequence, many of these resettlers faced food insecurity after their government subsidy ended in October 2007. Many, though, have received rice support in the pre-harvest months since 2010 through the government's Program 30a.[34] Eight years later, half of these families still benefited from the program. Even though these villagers were poor, they did not receive the whole of their promised relocation compensation for fourteen years. Only in 2020 did these families, as well as other resettlers in Muong Bung commune, receive their remaining compensation, following a decade of fighting the district government.[35]

Ethnicity has also played a role in differentiation in Muong Nhuong. Thái people seemed to secure better land after the move and settle down faster than La Ha people. As a result, there were more Thái (85 percent) than La Ha in the high-income and medium-income groups. All the people in the poor group were La Ha. These families were poor even before resettlement, and the situation was exacerbated by their limited access to land and capital post-resettlement, as well as by their inherited limited social connections and networks.

This chapter has focused on how resettlement has reinforced the villagers' differentiation. However, the process is not linear—some wealthy people became poor (like Mr. Thinh) in their new village, while some others became wealthier (like Mr. Lam, owner of the convenience store in Muong Nhuong). Labor availability or good social networks, as in the case of the Muong Hon headman, were important conditions for them to raise their income status. The level of market integration and the way people spent their compensation and savings also played crucial roles in this differentiation process. Resettlement also changed relationships within the village, making it even harder for people to settle down. Social relations through reciprocal exchange had eroded. The headman of Muong Ban hamlet spoke of the upheavals. "Things have been changing so much, even the relationships among us," he said. "Before, if one family had some important work to do, such as building a house, the whole village and relatives would come to help. Now, if one family wants to build a house, they just go out and hire someone to work on it. Neighbors and relatives are busy earning their living."[36]

A casual inquiry might suggest that residents had basically the same start in their new home. They all suffered land scarcity compared to the situation in their old villages, as well as changes in control over and access to surrounding resources in their new locales. After resettlement, the host communities mediated their access to land and forest resources. Yet resettlers started with different capacities, resources, and networks, all of which have influenced differentiation among them in sociological and economic senses. In the new area, as in the old, human activities interacted with natural conditions and shaped cultural and agrarian landscapes. Resettlement has not only transformed the landscape but also produced differential subjects and beneficiaries. As dam-induced territorial subjects, villagers also participated in producing material landscape through their labor. By clearing the forest, encroaching on common land, digging ponds, building irrigation canals, and planting fruits trees and vegetables to sell in the local market, resettlers—women, men, young, old—contributed to ecological changes, enabled new production relations, and accelerated market integration as well as spatial and social inequality within the community. Their everyday politics, stretching from resistance to compromise to collaboration, were embedded in this process of subject making, under which nostalgia for their homeland and the beloved river remained unchanged.

The next two chapters turn to another type of resource commodification in the Northwest—rubber plantations, a second form of landscape transformation, which serves as a key technology of state territorialization and enables differentiated territorial subjects. Under the direction of the central government, rubber companies in collaboration with the Ministry of Agriculture and Rural Development and provincial authorities declared that rubber plantations would support dam resettlers and modernize northwesterners. This hegemonic project reiterates the government's dominant discourse—that northwesterners need development.

# PART II

## *Rubber*

## CHAPTER 5

# The Politics of Rubber Plantations

I returned to the Northwest in May 2019 to learn that both the Sơn La Rubber Joint-Stock Company and the Điện Biên Rubber Joint-Stock Company had recently started to tap the latex after more than ten years of growing rubber trees in these provinces. It was the time when villagers who had contributed land to rubber plantations were supposed to receive their 10 percent revenue from the sale of the latex. Back in 2007, the government encouraged each family in Sơn La to contribute at least one hectare of land to the rubber project, and in return one family member could sign a contract to work as a rubber worker. The value of the contributed land was calculated at VNĐ 10 million per hectare (US$650), corresponding to one thousand shares (with each share valued at VNĐ 10,000, or US$0.65).[1] According to the company, the latex quality in Điện Biên was very good, but villagers complained that they received very little revenue. One villager said,

> We were told that if we contributed land and became shareholders, we would receive 10 percent of the revenue annually after seven years, but it took 10 years until the company could do the tapping, and it has been three years since they started to tap the rubber, and our villagers got almost nothing. When the company just started to clear land for their rubber trees, we got some

compensation, and that's it. My family contributed close to ten hectares and got compensation for the crops on that land. Nothing else since then. Such a long and frustrated wait![2]

At the commune level, authorities were very concerned about the struggles that villagers have endured because of land shortages; villagers had contributed much of their farming land to the rubber company and were having trouble earning their living. A commune chair of Thái ethnicity told us,

> Most people who contributed land have been in difficult situations because of lack of land for farming. At the commune level, we don't know what to do to help our people. It's the national government's policy, the province's strategy and direction. What do you think we—the authorities at commune level—can do? The most we can do is to complain to the district authorities. But even the district authorities can't do anything to help. They have channeled our complaints to the provincial government. We need to see what the province will decide. I've heard that the province has frozen all of the land that was already given to the rubber company but hasn't been used for growing rubber trees. Imagine, just two years ago, rubber trees were still a multipurpose and strategic tree in our province. Not anymore. My people are fighting to get their land back. But I am not sure how much hope we can have. The rubber company got so many favors and so much support. They got our land.[3]

The terms "Land acquisitions/appropriation," "land grab," and "land deals" commonly depict processes in which empowered forces such as large corporations take land from the commons or from smallholders, either through purchase or lease (for commodity crops or fuel crops), or by state appropriation (for reservoirs or national reserves).[4] These processes open the way to "a truly wide-ranging global 'land reform' ... [or] regressive land reform where governments take land from the poor and give (or sell or lease) it to the rich."[5] Such land appropriation—a transfer of land-use rights and ownership from the poor to the powerful—usually implies injustice.[6] This process alters land tenure relationships that have existed in these localities for a long time and further marginalizes poor local people. The literature on land grabs also reveals the role of both international and domestic drivers.[7] More particularly, a large body of studies on agrarian change and rural transformation in Southeast Asia in the last decade has emphasized crop booms and their impacts on local livelihoods.[8] These crop booms include coffee, shrimp, cocoa, rubber, oil palm, and fast-growing trees, and highlight that large international and domestic investors, but also smallholders, have driven this expansion in the region.[9] Land acquisitions, indeed, also help to strengthen a state's control over its people and transform agrarian settings in the affected areas. Wendy Wolford and her coauthors highlight the role of the state in global land grabs. They argue that many states are "active, calculating partners in land deals, negotiating the costs and benefits of the contemporary moment in order to maximize returns on what are considered marginal lands or marginal communities."[10] According to the authors, in order to fully understand contemporary land deals, we must contextualize the issues and analyze them as fixed in a particular place and time to apprehend influencing factors such as "institutions, practices, and discourses of territory, authority, and subjects."[11]

This chapter examines how, in support of the rubber project, the Ministry of Agriculture, provincial governments, and the rubber company adopted all four arts of government—"regime of Truth," "sovereign power," "discipline power," and "neoliberal power"—to classify a large area of land to be used for rubber plantations as "barren land" and force villagers to comply with the project. The chapter also explores how the combination of both external and internal power has shaped and reshaped territorial subjects and their everyday politics. It did not matter that, in reality, fallow land is not empty land; rather, it has been cultivated in the past and intentionally left to rest by previous users. This act of creating new systems of resource and spatial control in the frontier served to undo established territorial orders in this region.[12] Rubber plantations have subsumed thousands of hectares of farmland and forest in several provinces in the Northwest: Sơn La, Lai Châu, and Điện Biên. Similar to what Jennifer Sowerwine argues about Vietnam's forest classification and reallocation in the late 1990s and early 2000s, these processes of state territorial control are informed by a long history of nation-building tactics and state making to stabilize the frontier through controlling the rational use and exploitation of resources and the rearrangement of minority populations for strategic national purposes.[13] This process also parallels how the state defines land as available for urbanization in the lowlands, revealing how the

**FIGURE 5.1.** "Vườn cao su tổ"—the original rubber garden in Sơn La Province where high-ranking government officials who visited the site planted a rubber tree. Each tree has a sign to indicate who planted it. Photo by the author.

government seized land that had been used for a long time by poor and marginalized people and categorized it as idle land so it could serve the purpose of development and urbanization.[14]

## Terra Nullius and Turning Land into Capital in the Northwest

The idea of turning "idle land" or "wasteland" into "productive land" was popular in Southeast Asian nations and China in the 1950s and 1960s. Erik Harms and Ian Baird found that there was a similar way of defining "wasteland" in Southeast Asia, and only those who had power could define degraded land/forest and the applications and boundaries of these terms.[15] Making a component of nature, such as forests or land, visible to shape their existence and to use as a "problem" in need of a solution requires nature to be defined as a target for intervention, visualized with plans for actions, and as Pamela McElwee insists, these processes of change must be named.[16]

In the case of state farm building in the Northwest in the 1950s and 1960s, and later the migration of lowland laborers to the uplands, authorities had first to define land as an object of action—classifying land into categories such as empty land, unused land, farmland, or forestland—and visualizing land categories in maps designed for the purpose of management by the state and authorities.[17] Subsequently, authorities had to define action for environmental change. They named and identified "wasteland" or "empty/idle land" and forced these lands to become productive through the act of "clearing the wilderness" in service to the nation-building process. This notion of wasteland echoes that of John Locke, who highlights in *Two Treatises of Government* that wasteland and common land could be used in opposition to land that was privately owned, cultivated, or commodified.[18]

It is worth noting that wasteland or terra nullius narratives have been around for centuries; rulers and colonizers have used them to justify expansion of their lands. The colonial logics for development have been deployed for contemporary projects of development not just in Asia but also in other parts of the world.[19] For the Điện Biên State Farm as well as other state farms in the Northwest in the late 1950s and during the 1960s, the government saw most of the land taken for the farms as empty, unused, and uninhabited.

Back then, in Điện Biên alone, a large area of land (five thousand hectares) was considered empty or idle land, consisting of unused land on hillsides, abandoned fields (even though farmers there practiced shifting cultivation, and the land was idle as part of its rotation), and pastureland adjacent to the forest.[20] Authorities saw these large areas of "idle" land as having great potential for expanding state farms, despite the fact that the lands were scattered. Land for the Điện Biên State Farm, for example, consisted of many small parcels. These parcels were mostly of five to ten hectares, and the largest section was one hundred hectares—all interwoven with villagers' farmland. The farmworkers' tasks included fence construction to prevent entry of free-ranging cattle and pigs.[21] Rubber plantations first established in the Northwest in 2007 followed a similar pattern. Most of the land used for the rubber trees either belonged to villagers or was land that the government classified as common or idle land, again interspersed with villagers' farmland. The same way of defining land continues into the 2020s; the government continues to take land that poor and marginalized people have used for a long time and categorizes it as idle land so it can be used to serve the dual purposes of development and urbanization.[22] In brief, the practice reveals how a contemporary socialist state has been employing the same sort of colonially acquisitive logic regarding its own territory as Europeans did throughout the world with the terra nullius principle.

In the early 2000s, as a result of strong lobbying by the Vietnam Rubber Group (VRG), the Vietnamese government saw rubber as a strategic commodity and the expansion of rubber plantations as an economic development opportunity for the poor in this region. This point of view can be clearly seen in the words of Communist Party general secretary Nông Đức Mạnh during his trip to Sơn La Province in 2010:

> The Vietnam Rubber Group is a big corporation of the country, and it is looking to become a powerful corporation, not only in Vietnam but also in other countries. Today I came here to see a very new image of our farmers. Building rubber planting teams with land contributed by the local people—this is the right policy, it is one of the issues that we want to discuss in the 7th Resolution of Section X on agriculture—farmers, and rural areas. I highly welcome and appreciate this model. I hope that the rubber group perseveres in doing this. This is a major policy, the leading role of a state-owned enterprise.[23]

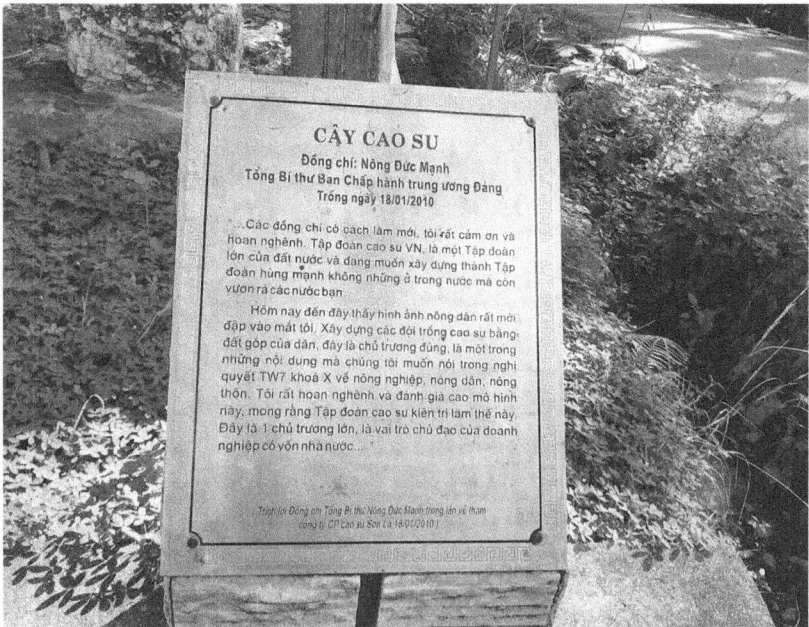

**FIGURE 5.2.** A quote from the speech of Communist Party Secretary Nông Đức Mạnh during his visit in 2010 is engraved on a plaque in front of a rubber tree he planted.

With this strong support from the party and the central government, Sơn La provincial officials targeted more than 30,000 hectares of rubber trees by 2020.[24] In the same period, Lai Châu Province was even more ambitious, seeking to increase its rubber tree plantings to 65,000 hectares, well above the central government's expectations. Điện Biên Province aimed to plant 20,000 hectares. In reality, companies had planted 13,220 hectares of rubber trees in Lai Châu by 2018, while Điện Biên had 5,000 hectares, and Sơn La had about 7,000 hectares. This development, just like dam-induced displacement, raised questions about land rights and livelihood concerns among the area's ethnic minority people (mostly Thái), including concerns about food security, employment opportunities, and cultural degradation.

Since all of the land in Vietnam belongs to the state, authorities only sanction land acquisition on a large scale if it is for the national interest, like government projects or defense. Rubber plantations in the Northwest did not quite fall into these categories. Thus, without central government support, VRG could not obtain the needed land for its project. Before 2007, the plan to bring rubber trees to the Northwest was quite controversial. Many people, including officials from the Ministry of Agriculture and Rural Development (MARD) and from line agencies at provincial and district levels of Sơn La Province, harbored concerns about the suitability of soil and climate conditions in the area, as well as about the inevitable changes to ethnic minority groups' farming practices and livelihoods.[25] Local resistance to the plan lasted for a few years until 2006, when Prime Minister Nguyễn Tấn Dũng visited the Northwest and reaffirmed that rubber plantations should be developed in the region.[26] The rumor among the public at the time was that VRG officials had a very close connection with the prime minister, who, during his visit, pointed his hand to China and asked the people surrounding him, "Why can China plant rubber successfully on the other side of the border and we cannot do it here?"

Groundwork began almost immediately after this speech. Since its inception, the rubber plantation project has been integrated into and now plays a role in the decades-long plan to industrialize and modernize the Northwest, as well as transform small upland farmers into workers in concentrated large production units.[27] Since the local government already had access to state funds to support the resettlement of those displaced by the Sơn Lam Dam, it decided to use a large portion of this funding to promote rubber plantations as a means of livelihood recovery for the resettlers.[28]

As alluded to earlier, the process of acquiring land for the rubber plantations was not linear. Local authorities, through their institutions, played a key role in this process. For example, in Sơn La Province, beginning in 2007, the provincial government directed its district officials to base task forces in each of the communes and villages that had the potential to host a rubber plantation, in order to propagandize and persuade villagers to contribute land to the rubber project. The provincial government then formed the Rubber Development Steering Committee to supervise and guide the project. Communist Party general secretaries Nông Đức Mạnh, Nguyễn Phú Trọng, and many other high-ranking government officials in Hanoi took turns visiting Sơn La Province and its rubber plantations in support of these propagandizing efforts. As a gesture of strong support of the project, each of them planted a rubber tree in an area called the "original rubber garden" in It Ong commune, Sơn La Province.[29]

Under the central government's direction, the provincial governments did whatever they could to fit a rubber project into their economic plans. Pressure from rising prices of rubber on international markets in the early 2000s, as well as from domestic investors, catalyzed policies pushing for increasing land appropriation for rubber plantations. Authorities at lower levels were placed in a situation in which they had to create favorable conditions for domestic investors to expand their businesses. The entire process reflects the close links between the state and its large companies (both state-owned and private) in pursuing development policies. Rasmussen and Lund's cycle of frontier-territorialization-frontier-territorialization, in this case, reflects well territorial dynamics in relation to the commodification of resources in the frontier. It shows how state power remains fluid and constantly under negotiation through a process of establishing and wearing down social orders of property systems, legal identities, and political structures.[30] With the rationality of science to turn "wasteland" and "barren land" into productive land to justify the promotion of rubber plantations, the government at all levels has supported rubber companies to seize thousands of hectares for their project, which indeed enabled the establishment of new territorial orders and shaped northwestern territorial subjects.

## The Political Economy of Rubber Development in Vietnam

The French colonists brought rubber production to Vietnam in about 1897 as France expanded its military power in Indochina.[31] Colonists established plantations primarily in the southeast, where the soil and climate (temperature and annual rainfall distribution) were considered more suitable. By 1930, the French had planted 10,000 hectares of rubber trees and were harvesting 11,000 (metric) tons of latex per year. In 1950, the planted area was 70,000 hectares.[32] By the 1970s, the total area of rubber plantations nationwide was about 76,600 hectares (of which only 5,000 hectares were in the north; the majority were in the southeast and the Central Highlands), with an annual production of 40,200 tons of latex.[33]

Since the early 1990s, the Vietnamese government has embraced rubber as a strategic crop and has created favorable conditions for the sector's development in response to the world's increasing appetite for rubber, which grew at an average rate of 5.8 percent annually between 1900 to the 2000s. In 2010 the annual growth of rubber consumption reached 15.3 percent but then fell to 4.8 percent in 2011 as a result of economic problems in the US and European countries.[34] The price of rubber continually rose at the beginning of the twenty-first century, further encouraging the expansion of rubber plantations in different regions throughout Vietnam, including the mountainous Northwest, where rubber trees were introduced. As a result, the area dedicated to rubber plantations in Vietnam increased almost fourfold, from about 250,000 hectares in the early 1990s, with total production of 103,000 tons of latex, to 965,000 hectares, which yielded 1.1 million tons of latex, in 2018.[35] Despite the competition for cultivated land for various industrial crops with similar ecological requirements—coffee, black pepper, and fruit trees, among others—the central government established a policy to further develop the rubber sector.[36] Historically, the price of rubber has risen and fallen in part because of the relatively long period before a tree becomes productive; farmers and planters react to high prices by planting a lot of trees, leading to a large drop in the price of rubber when these trees start to produce seven to ten years later. The increase in prices at the beginning of the century, especially around 2010, was huge—they rose to three to four times what they had been a decade earlier—in part due to demand in China. This led to a major planting wave in these monsoon zones, which was followed by a collapse in prices when the new trees started to produce.[37] Rubber is highly susceptible to boom and bust cycles.

In 2012, owing to a rapid rise in production, Vietnam rose to fourth (ahead of India and China) in output among rubber-exporting countries, ranking behind only Thailand, Indonesia, and Malaysia. It continued in that position until 2018.[38] In 2019, Vietnam exported more than

1.2 million tons of latex, valued at around US$6.2 billion, and became the third-largest rubber exporting country, accounting for 7.7 percent of the world's total rubber production and 5.6 percent of the world's total cultivation.[39] Currently, more than 80 percent of Vietnam's latex is produced for export; of this total, VRG—the largest state-owned rubber company in Vietnam—accounts for 70 percent of production.[40] VRG planted more than 400,000 hectares and produced about 300,000 tons of natural rubber in 2018, accounting for 41 percent and 27 percent of rubber area and production respectively.

The government considers rubber not only a strategic crop but also an important commodity for developing the country's economy and improving the lives and livelihoods of upland ethnic minority people, helping to narrow the economic gap between the uplands and the lowlands. Prime Minister Nguyễn Tấn Dũng, at a rubber sector meeting in 2005, put it clearly: "Over the last 10 years, VRG has achieved leaping steps with a high growth rate, especially in production, income, and revenue to the state budget. It has created jobs for tens of thousands of people and significantly contributed to economic development in remote and mountainous areas where ethnic minority people reside. Their achievements deserve high respect and compliment."[41]

Authorities framed the promotion of rubber plantations in the upland areas as a strategy to create jobs and to improve the lives of the upland people. Both the government and the rubber company promoted market forces and revenue as incentives for villagers to join the project. Notably, the government encouraged large-scale plantation creation, arguing that even though small growers require less input, the rubber they produce is grown in isolated and distant areas, where it is more difficult to apply advanced technologies. Additionally, small stockholders' rubber plantations are scattered across unconnected plots, making it harder to gather latex, lowering the quality of the latex and raising the production costs.[42] Thus, the government prioritized large-scale plantations instead of encouraging smallholder rubber farmers, despite the fact that in neighboring countries such as Laos, China, and Malaysia, smallholder rubber outcompetes rubber plantations for a number of reasons, including greater flexibility in withstanding booms and busts as smallholders increase or decrease tapping efforts based on price.[43]

The politics surrounding the government's rubber project have never been simple. Increased international demand for rubber, as well as lobbying by domestic rubber investors, drove the government's interest in rubber. When the global demand for rubber increased in the 2000s, the government prioritized rubber development. Higher prices on the international markets increased revenues for domestic rubber investors. According to Nguyễn Đình Trạc, general director of the Duc Long Gia Lai Group, one of the largest rubber groups in Vietnam, the investment in rubber plantations in 2012 was VNĐ 130 million (US$6,500) per hectare.[44] After seven years of initial tree growth, tapping could begin and continue for twenty-five years. At the end of a project's life, logging the rubber trees brings in additional revenue sufficient to cover investment costs for clearing the land and planting and raising the trees. According to my interviews with VRG officials in Sơn La in 2011, even if the price of latex decreased, the expected revenue from rubber logging alone would be significant and justify investment in planting the trees.[45] Growing rubber therefore was increasingly considered as an agricultural practice with superior revenue, and rubber companies actively lobby the government to obtain access to more land in order to expand their plantations.[46] It is worth noting, however, that on one hand, Nguyễn and other rubber investors overstated the expected revenue from the plantations (overestimating sales prices and expected production), while on the other hand, investors relied on the state to secure poor-value forest or "wasteland" from its current users in order to justify its seizure. This need for land, rather than any assessment that small rubber farms introduce inefficiencies, drove lobbying efforts, which in turn captured government support for large companies over smallholder farmers. This uneven exercise of power has played out time and again in rubber development. By 2010, for example, the Vietnamese government permitted large-scale rubber companies to convert to plantations most of the land intended for a national, five-million-hectare reforestation program in the Central Highlands, central, and southeast areas of the country. In response to the government's demand for expanding rubber plantations, the Ministry of Agriculture and Rural Development issued guidelines for planting rubber on forestland.[47] Furthermore, in 2013, the prime minister signed a new decision on restructuring the agricultural sector, which increased focus on the expansion of the domestic rubber industry.[48] As a result of this combination of factors, the land area cultivated with rubber in Vietnam broadly, and in the Northwest in particular, has been steadily increasing since 2010, as it has in the neighboring countries of Laos, Cambodia, and China.[49] In addition to the development of domestic rubber production, Vietnamese rubber companies have been investing in new plantations in neighboring countries, with promotional assistance from the Vietnamese government. As of 2015, Vietnamese enterprises had planted about 50,000 hectares of rubber in Laos and 150,000 hectares in Cambodia.[50]

Thus, the Vietnamese government has played a critical role in enabling the expansion of rubber plantations within Vietnam and in neighboring countries. Some may simply interpret this support as the government helping its large companies respond to world market demand; however, the role of rubber plantations in the government's development strategy, as well as the centralization of investment policy, raises political questions about Vietnam's development priorities. In addition to imposing the rationalities of a "regime of Truth" regarding the need for making land more productive and boosting national economic growth, development planners and investors also assumed, in a display of neoliberal power, that northwesterners were rational economic agents who would benefit when joining the project, either via becoming rubber workers or shareholders. Establishment of rubber plantations has created new territorial subjects, who no longer have any control over their land, who no longer work for themselves but work instead under supervision of team leaders assigned to them by the companies.

## Governmentality and Rubber Plantations in the Northwest

"You know, if there was no Sơn La hydropower project, there would not be rubber plantations here in the Northwest, and our villagers' lives would probably be better in many ways," an official of Tu La district told me when I visited him in May 2017. I was surprised, because the first time I met him, in 2009, he enthusiastically described the bright prospects of the rubber project. Now he sounded very disappointed:

> The project was promoted as a way to support livelihood recovery for displaced people from the Sơn La Dam and improve people's lives. But now it's still very far from that goal. Have you visited the original rubber tree garden of the Northwest yet? If you haven't, you should, and you will understand why I said that. There is live evidence there about the project support. I don't need to explain to you. Every single one of the national government leaders planted a rubber tree there when they came to visit us. You will see the signs and their autograph.[51]

I had visited that original rubber garden previously on a few occasions. I visited it again with this official after this talk in his office.

Rubber trees from Quảng Trị Province in central Vietnam were first introduced to the Northwest in 1959.[52] Planted on the Điện Biên State Farm, they failed to produce any latex. Since the early 2000s, with the aim of expanding rubber plantation acreage to take advantage of high rubber prices, scientists and the Vietnam Rubber Group have actively sought out new land for rubber plantations, including nontraditional environments such as the Northwest, where climate conditions do not favor rubber trees. Indeed, the move to the north occurred after the Chinese started to successfully plant rubber on the other side of the border in Yunnan in southwest China.[53] At the same time, the central government in Hanoi and the provincial governments of the Northwest have faced challenges in finding livelihoods for hundreds of thousands of people displaced by the Sơn La hydropower project. The central government set aside millions of dollars for livelihood recovery programs for resettlers through agricultural extension services, but none has proven successful.[54] This was a golden opportunity for VRG to step in and lobby the government. Its efforts were rewarded, and the Northwest became a new strategic region for rubber plantations, regardless of the fact that virtually most of the land that VRG lobbied for was already allocated for the resettlers' use. In 2006, the first three thousand hectares of rubber trees were planted in the region, with the very first seventy hectares (called the original rubber tree garden) located in It Ong commune, in Sơn La Province, the same commune in which the Sơn La Dam is located.

Since 2007, Prime Minister Nguyễn Tấn Dũng had directed and held a deep interest in the development of rubber production in the region. The Communist Party, the provincial people's committees, and their policies, as well as government and functional offices involved in rubber plantation development in the Northwest provinces, made clear that they linked this project with the region's socioeconomic development plans. As the central government had already allocated funding for livelihood recovery, it decided to use a large portion of these funds to promote rubber plantations as the livelihood solution.[55] Since the dominant narrative framed the rubber plantations as necessary for the region's socioeconomic development, this linkage suggested that it would be morally suspect to say or do anything against it. Here, the neoliberal governmentality, built on the state's "unceasing vigilance, activity, and intervention,"[56] approached villagers as rational agents who would benefit economically from becoming rubber workers. Everyone gains. Villagers would, reasonably, contribute their land and join the rubber company. This massive resource territory project converted tens of thousands of hectares of forest and farmland into rubber plantations and created new territorial subjects and different beneficiaries.

In this project, the provincial people's committees of Sơn La, Lai Châu, and Điện Biên Provinces closely collaborated with VRG. In 2011, the Sơn La Province People's Committee (PPC) issued a book for its cadres' use, a compilation of the policies that various levels of government had issued between 2009 and 2011 related to rubber.[57] The book indicated that villagers contributed their land and thereby became shareholders of the Sơn La Rubber Joint-Stock Company (SRC).[58] Workers are employed on contract. The SRC holds responsibility for the production costs. Once the rubber trees mature and produce latex, all investment costs are factored into the total cost of production for the purpose of calculating dividends. The Sơn La PPC has the responsibility of supporting the plantation, both in policy and in implementation. The District People's Committee and Commune People's Committee are responsible for coordinating land measurements and allocation and for informing and mobilizing the local people to contribute their land. In other words, following the central government's direction, local authorities at all levels were in charge of appropriating land from farmers to give to the Sơn La Rubber Joint-Stock Company. Authorities applied this mechanism in the neighboring provinces of Lai Châu and Điện Biên as well.

Each province set up its own rubber steering committee with the province's party secretary as the chairman. Nguyễn Thế Luận, deputy head of Sơn La's Rubber Development Steering Committee, indicated in a meeting in 2011,

> Our province issued new policies, which in principle satisfactorily addressed issues related to the rights and interests of farmers. We also successfully organized a workshop on how farmers contribute their land-use rights in return for shares in the rubber development project. This model is relevant to the practical conditions of the province, contributing to the industrialization of our agriculture and modernization of our rural areas, which creates motivation for sustainable development, building favorable conditions for propagandizing and persuading people to join the rubber development program.[59]

Joint-stock rubber companies in Sơn La, Lai Châu, and Điện Biên directly implemented the development of large-scale rubber plantations in their provinces. However, these companies planted rubber not only in resettlement sites and areas that the Sơn La hydropower project has impacted, but also on the land of host communities, as well as in forested areas that the government itself classified as having poor or low value.

While rubber plantations, unlike the Sơn La Dam, were not explicitly framed as established for the national interest, the central government, as well as the three provincial governments, bestowed on the rubber tree the status of a multipurpose tree. This places a burden on the humble tree, while conferring power to those engaged in rubber production. The national government saw rubber projects as a way to help alleviate poverty for ethnic minority groups residing in this region, especially the Sơn La hydropower project resettlers. Provincial governments saw the project as a provincial revenue source via the rubber companies' taxes, and highlighted the trees' green coverage as a way to improve the environment.[60] The benefits that the rubber trees were intended to bring to investors and locals are summarized in a 2011 *Rural Economics* newspaper interview with Nguyễn Trí Ngọc, head of the Department of Crop Production: "The Ministry of Agriculture and Rural Development issued Circular 58/2009/TT-BNNPTNT dated September 9, 2009, providing specific guidance on rubber plantations on forest land, accordingly, recognizing rubber as a multipurpose tree, both to bring profits to the company and contribute to poverty eradication in the northern mountains. Rubber trees are also for logging. Thus, rubber trees should be grown on forest areas that were allowed to be converted . . . and should be properly planned."[61]

The Sơn La PPC issued a decision in 2011 to emphasize that "the development of rubber trees is a focal task of the province's Communist Party, and of administrations at all levels, in order to realize and implement the Party's and the State's development strategy on agriculture, farmers, and rural areas for the aim of improving the material and spiritual life of our ethnic minority people."[62] Echoing the Sơn La PPC, the PPCs of Lai Châu and Điện Biên issued their own policies to support rubber plantation creation in their provinces.

The documents related to rubber plantations in the Northwest do not address the risk of growing rubber in that region. Rubber trees stop producing sap at around four degrees Celsius (about 39°F), and they will die if the temperature drops below zero degrees Celsius. In

2009–2010, extreme cold weather killed 95 percent of the rubber trees planted in Phú Thọ, Hà Giang, Yên Bái, and Lào Cai Provinces, as well as 5 percent of those in Sơn La, Lai Châu, and Điện Biên Provinces.[63] Even the government's will is not enough to ensure the success of rubber production in nontraditional environments like the northern uplands of Vietnam.

In 2014, after seven years of growth, the first rubber trees planted in the Northwest produced no latex, despite the company's many tapping attempts. Party General Secretary Nguyễn Phú Trọng still planted a new tree during his 2014 visit to Sơn La Province, despite witnessing firsthand the failure of this first attempt at rubber production. He remarked in the meeting with representatives of Sơn La Rubber Join-Stock Company:

> Now the final result is unknown, but I see the rubber trees are good and prepared to be exploited, which is a good development trend. I highly welcome the spirit of leading the pilot policy of farmers' contributing land to our state-owned company as a model for planting rubber trees. Of course, there are difficulties at first, but the important thing is that VRG and Sơn La Rubber Joint-Stock Company get strong support from Sơn La Province. You have a direction, good policy, formed a mechanism, and you have your own team of workers. Now there are only seven thousand households contributing land, [and] with more than four thousand employees [you] are very well-organized. I hope you take good care of the rubber trees that you have planted, and further expand the area. If you have good results and make the model replicable in many places across the country, that would be great.[64]

By 2019, there were more than fifty thousand hectares of rubber trees under cultivation in the Northwest. Even though this number might represent a small footprint on the landscape, many people's livelihoods depend on it. The government took many thousands of these hectares from villagers to give to the rubber companies, which then left the land idle when plantation development stalled. Villagers remain unable to reclaim their land and at the same time earn little income from laboring for the rubber company, on top of having little or no means to grow their own food. These three provinces also host latex processing factories. In Sơn La, a factory constructed in 2018 subsumed sixteen hectares of arable land in Tông Lạnh commune, Thuận Châu district, and cost more than VNĐ 109 billion (almost US$5 million); it is able to process nine thousand tons of latex annually.[65] As of June 2019, the province of Lai Châu had 13,220 hectares of rubber trees in four sub-regions either under cultivation or ready to harvest latex.[66] The province's first processing factory was also constructed in 2018, on 14.5 hectares in Nam Tam commune, Sìn Hồ district.[67] Điện Biên Province's 2009 plan set a goal of twenty thousand hectares of rubber trees under cultivation by 2020; as of 2018, it had only reached one-fourth of this goal, due in large part to villagers' resistance and some key provincial leaders' concerns about the project's effectiveness and local people's livelihoods.[68] Nevertheless, in 2020, VRG planned to invest in three new rubber processing factories in Lai Châu, Lào Cai, and Điện Biên Provinces (one per province), with a total processing capacity of eleven thousand tons of rubber latex annually.[69]

To create a legal corridor for this rubber development model in which villagers contribute land, become rubber company shareholders, and receive 10 percent of the revenue from selling the latex, the prime minister issued Decision 990/QD-TTg on June 18, 2014. This made way for a pilot model of farmer households to contribute land and cooperate with companies under the VRG umbrella to develop rubber production in the Northwest. The decision states, "Annually report to the Prime Minister on the pilot implementation for households contributing land; summarize and evaluate at the end of the pilot implementation period and submit it to the Prime Minister in the fourth quarter of 2018." In June 2019, six months after the deadline, VRG had not submitted its evaluation of the pilot model to the central government.[70] An interesting point from my interviews with district officials in Sơn La, Lai Châu, and Điện Biên in May 2019 was that the majority denied that their provinces had adopted rubber as a strategic and multipurpose tree. They affirmed, rather, that the central government had imposed this decision. With the project's failure to bring stable income to all villagers who had contributed their land, the dominant narrative of the rubber tree as a multipurpose tree started to shift. The different rationalities that the government used in taking away land from villagers and promoting the rubber project have shaped everyday subject making in the region. With the claim that the project was to help resettlers who were affected by the Sơn La Dam, the government and rubber companies further upset territorial orders in resettlement sites by forcing resettlers to contribute the land they received for resettlement, as I will elaborate in the next chapter.

## Coercion, Consent, and Power Inequality in Decision-Making in the Rubber Project

Researching this topic has never been easy or straightforward, given the central and provincial officials' strong support for the rubber project. Every time I visited the Northwest, I had to be very careful with wording my requests for permission to conduct research in these provinces, for fear of not getting the permit.[71] At the beginning of my trip to Sơn La in May 2013, I found myself sitting among a few nervous-looking individuals in a meeting room at Sơn La PPC headquarters. "Are you a journalist?" one person asked. "No, as indicated in my request document, I am a researcher," I replied. The cadre seemed at ease with this response. "Oh, OK, but why did you say that you wanted to interview us? Why do you use the word 'interview' if you are not a journalist? We don't want to answer any interview questions. We can provide you some data and reports, but not interviews. We don't like journalists. We have enough to cope with." They refused further attempts at conversation and quickly gave me reference papers to take to the district level. When I arrived at the office of the Sơn La Rubber Joint-Stock Company, its director stated that he had nothing to share, and if the provincial authorities had issued my paperwork, I could ask them for a report. In other instances, district police questioned Binh, my local guide, about me and my activities. When I returned to Hanoi from Muong Bung, Binh called me. He had accompanied me on my visits to various villages in the commune where rubber trees were planted. Binh was worried. "Sister, please note that police from the district have called me many times since yesterday. They asked for your number, and I gave it to them. But they keep calling and said they received reports that you came and asked questions about the rubber project and people's livelihoods, which they said you were not supposed to, as rubber was a sensitive topic. They asked a lot about you, but I said you had permission to do research here and you came back every year. So be prepared that they'll call you or may be after you." Luckily, this was the extent of our contact with the police, but it made me nervous each time I returned to Sơn La. I was not afraid of the police calling me in for questioning; rather, I was concerned that individuals like Binh would get in trouble for helping me conduct my research.

For rubber development in the Northwest, the Ministry of Agriculture and Rural Development was responsible for issuing policies to guide the rubber project's implementation. The MARD sent

Document No. 3492/BNN-NT (December 20, 2007) regarding direction and policies for rubber plantations in the Northwest provinces to the prime minister: "The development of rubber in mountainous provinces should focus on large-scale plantations at the beginning stage. Once the large-scale plantations become stable, small rubber farms will be developed and serve as satellites for the large-scale businesses. The state will give favorable investment conditions."[72] MARD officials were also the first to define rubber as a multipurpose tree for this region. The list below summarizes the roles of various stakeholders in rubber plantations. In this process, the authorities find the land, the company invests in land preparation and planting, and local people contribute the land and become shareholders and rubber workers.

The summary of different stakeholders' roles in the rubber project at the local level in Sơn La Province was as follows:

- Provincial authority: provide funds to support conversion of lands to rubber plantations (mostly in terms of advancing money to purchase seeds and fertilizers for intercropping maize in rubber plantation during the first three years, give loans of VNĐ 5–10 million [US$260–520] to poor households for livestock raising, build new kindergartens for rubber workers' children, and train farmers to be rubber workers). These works are implemented by the Sơn La Rubber Company (TLHD No. 98/DC NCDD-PTCCS [Tài liệu hướng dẫn Số 98-ĐC-BCD PTCCS], page 7).
- District and commune authorities: implement the province's policies in terms of reviewing plans, preparing cartography, redistributing land to the rubber company, and persuading local people to contribute their land (Decision No. 197/TB-UBND, dated November 20, 2007).
- Sơn La Rubber Company: invest in the entire production circle from land preparation to seedlings, planting, and harvesting (Decision No. 98/DC-BCDD-PTCCS, page 10).
- Local people: contribute land for rubber plantation. One hectare is valued at VNĐ 10,000,000 (US$650) or 10,000 shares. Local people receive benefits from company dividends, and from payment for contract work with the company (Decision No. 98/DC-BCDD-PTCCS, page 9). Local people also supply their labor to the project via contract work.

In fact, local peoples' participation in this plan was very limited. As in the past, officials employed a top-down approach to persuade locals to voluntarily take part in this project. The project's district management board coordinated with the commune management board. The Communist Party secretary acted as the head of the propaganda team to divide the households into small working groups—four villagers per group. The district management board prepared communication documents for these activities. In most villages, however, the locals did not passively follow the order to contribute their land to the project. Concerned about losing precious farmland, villagers felt uncertain about their future if they participated. Many first refused to participate, and it took time for the local authorities and the rubber company to prod villagers to join the project. This was especially true in resettled communities where the displaced people had only been allocated a scant amount of land. According to one member of a commune's project communication team, its members usually had to hold between five and seven separate meetings with villagers to explain how the project could be beneficial to them. In some cases, mobilization was very difficult. For example, when I was staying at Khun's house, I often visited Muong Ma and Muong Che villages and learned that the communication team held twelve meetings in each village. For villages without resettlers, fewer meetings were required, as each household had several hectares of farmland; contributing one or a few of these would still leave families with usable farmland in case the rubber trees did not produce. Questions that villagers often raised in these meetings included: What does shareholding mean? What benefits would I get? What would other members of my family do without land? Could I get my land back if I wanted to? What will happen if the rubber trees do not produce enough latex?

Muong Ma and Muong Che house villagers displaced by the Sơn La hydropower project. These resettlers had already lost their more-extensive farmland; in their new villages, each household received approximately one hectare of arable land as compensation. Understandably, they wanted to hang on to this small piece of land to grow maize, cassava, and other crops to feed their families. One villager said, "We only have one hectare after the resettlement. The land is something real and tangible that my family depends on. If we contribute it to the rubber company, we do not know what will happen in the future."[73] In the authorities' push to include villagers in the rubber development project, many resettlers were losing all their land and, with it, their traditional way of living. Within only three years, after suffering from ex situ displacement caused by dam development, villagers in Muong Ma and Muong Che experienced in situ displacement caused by rubber plantations when they lost control over their land and environment entitlements. The processes of land dispossession and displacement associated with hydropower development and rubber plantations have also led to the reduction of labor opportunities and an increase in indebtedness, social problems, and greater rates of out-migration in the Northwest, as I will elaborate on in chapter 6.

In the case of Muong Ma and Muong Che, commune staff had to visit each household to persuade them to participate in the project. Many refused and were then told that opting out meant that they would lose access to benefits such as health care and education for their children. Specifically, their children would not be able to go to school, because the rubber company would build the new schools. When they were sick, the villagers were told, they would be denied access to medical care.[74] Village leaders and Communist Party members were asked to become the first participants to hand over their land in order to set an example for other villagers to follow.[75] These activities had the aim of encouraging the local people to contribute their land. However, the villagers did not seem to have a choice in the matter. In the end, most households agreed to do so, even those who originally were strongly opposed. According to my interviewees, two important concerns informed this acquiescence: villagers feared losing the abovementioned benefits, and feared that if their land was located in the middle of the proposed plantation, it would be impossible to access their fields without damaging the young rubber trees in the surrounding acreage—for which the penalty was well beyond their means (VNĐ 200,000, or US$11 in 2012). Only one family successfully refused, as their land was not on the hill that the rubber company intended to use. They were able to continue farming and did not encounter as many difficulties regarding income stability as did the families who joined the project. Other families whose land included sections not on the same hill were also doing better, as they were still able to grow maize and other crops on their remaining land.

Indeed, not everyone suffered from their engagement with the rubber plantations. Some people enjoy being rubber workers. The headman of Muong Ma is an example. He was very supportive of rubber and actively pushed his villagers to participate. He was also very close to the rubber company's representatives, who were stationed in the neighboring Bu village. Thanks to the connection he had built with the rubber company's representatives, he and his family always had more convenient plots to work on. He said to me in a 2011 interview, "I think the rubber project is a great idea for promoting development and progress in our village. We can work as workers now and have income. Indeed, now we don't have to worry about things like where to buy the seeds, if it rains at the right time for the maize to sprout, or when to spray to avoid pests. People shouldn't complain that much." Many other villagers in Bu village also showed enthusiasm about the project. As they were not resettlers, each family already held a few hectares of farming land. For them, contributing one or two hectares to the rubber plantations would not have the same effect, since they retained land to work on.

While the rubber companies promised to create jobs for villagers who contributed their land, in fact many villagers did not want to work on the plantations. They quit and out-migrated to find work in other provinces. As a result, the majority of the rubber workers migrated to the area from the lowlands. When I asked a villager in 2017 why this was the case, he said, "Working in the rubber plantations is very hard. You don't have control over your time. It is very different from growing corn. We're not used to it." His answer was not unique; I repeatedly heard similar responses: "Working as rubber workers is killing our culture," or "It's heavy work." Many shared that "people became competitive and did not support each other as we used to when we worked on our own farm." Outsiders' perspectives differed. A representative from SRC said, "Oh, ethnic minority people are lazy. They don't want to work hard." Provincial government officials held similar views: "Oh, well, villagers like to complain. We all know that. They'd complain about just anything." Or, "Becoming rubber workers is a big step for villagers to be modernized. It takes time. Some villagers complained, but some have adapted well. In general, they'll have to get used to it, or they would have to quit." Or, "Many people from the lowlands are lining up to get the job, but we asked the company to prioritize local villagers. They should see it as a privilege and stop complaining." In short, the official position was that villagers should appreciate the opportunities given to them as their land was taken away.

How should we understand villagers' complaints or reasoning about their inability or trouble adapting to being "modern workers"—a life-altering reality that such development projects have brought to the region? My conversations with villagers during my annual trips to the region revealed that the difficulties they experienced in participating in the transformation of the Northwest's landscape were not limited to changes in their economic circumstances; more important to them were the changes in their ways of living, of associating with the land, the forest, and the reciprocal working relationships that they have built with their relatives and neighbors for many generations.

The extensive government involvement detailed above was a critical precondition for forcing households to join the project. Government policy was indeed a critical dynamic that changed the uplands in many ways, especially in how resources—in this case land—are governed in agricultural settings.

## Counternarratives and Everyday Resistance

State hegemonic development projects, such as rubber plantations, promote territorial reconfigurations, subjecting spaces and their inhabitants in various ways, including economically and materially, legally and administratively, culturally and politically, but not without provoking resistance.[76] As I discussed above, for almost ten years after the first rubber trees were planted in It Ong commune in 2007, the local government considered rubber in the Northwest a sensitive topic. Gaining access to research sites and meeting with provincial officials have been extremely difficult for researchers. WARECOD was the first NGO conducting research on this topic in the Northwest, in 2009.[77] For many years, no other NGO in Vietnam conducted research on this topic. Furthermore, as rubber production in the Northwest is a central government project, and provincial authorities have been very cautious when addressing this issue, for many years the media did not cover related problems that local communities face. This changed in 2017 when the rubber companies started to tap the trees. A widespread outcry from villagers in the Northwest about the rubber project's impacts on people's lives and livelihoods then caught the public's attention. In May 2019, VUSTA co-organized a workshop with the Center for Indigenous and Rural Development and invited villagers from all three provinces as well as researchers and representatives from rubber companies to attend and share their opinions on the project's effectiveness.

Even though policies linked to rubber development in the region were accepted and formalized at the central and provincial levels, settling disputes over land allocated for rubber plantations has proven to be a difficult, and slow task.[78] The same can be said for the authorities' struggles to persuade villagers to contribute their land. Moreover, the

monitoring of project implementation has not been completely effective. Delays in execution and the lack of monitoring have directly affected the interests of rubber workers and their families. In some cases,
it has stirred quite a strong reaction from villagers. In group discussions at the village level in Muong Ma and Muong Che in 2017, villagers
indicated that if they were to begin again, most of them would refuse to
contribute their land to the project.

In other villages of Muong Bung commune, village leaders persisted
in refusing to contribute land. This was the case with Khun's village—
the village's leaders were aligned with the population and refused to
sign a contract with the rubber company, no matter how many times
the district and commune authorities held meetings to explain the
project's benefits to their lives and the national economy. The local authorities gave up, and no land from Muong Lanh village was included
in the project. This result is due in part to the village's resistance,
but pushback from authorities may also have been muted, given that
Muong Bung commune had already met its assigned quota for land
contributions.

Another special case is Tinh village in It Ong commune, which borders Muong Bung commune. In Tinh village, villagers took matters
into their own hands and cut down all the young rubber trees (already
two to three years old) in their village, arguing that they saw no benefit
from the trees for their community. These lands were returned to the
villagers for farming soon after. The fight did not end there. The rubber
company filed a grievance letter with the PPC, demanding compensation for its loss of investment in land preparation and for the young
trees. The local authorities did not want to apply legal procedures to
the Tinh villagers, who were considered unable to compensate the company. One of the government officials at the commune level told me,
"You cannot ask the villagers to compensate for the rubber trees that
they cut down, as they have no money. They are so poor already."[79]
To avoid similar incidents in other communes, the authorities and the
company strategized to protect the rubber plantations from this sort
of action.[80] Signs with the words "state property" were hung on plantation borders and in various public spaces as a reminder of the rubber
trees' importance. The signs also remind the villagers that the trees do
not just belong to the rubber company, but to the state; damaging state
property is a serious crime.

In It Ong commune, where the original rubber garden is located,
the government had taken twenty-seven hundred hectares for the

construction site of the Sơn La hydropower project. (Villagers were displaced to Muong Ta commune in Moc Chau district, more than one hundred kilometers away.) The dam itself does not cover all twenty-seven hundred hectares, but the provincial government did not return the unused land to the villagers; instead, the government offered it to the rubber company.[81] The villagers have been protesting this move ever since, claiming it is their land. In an area where there were no rubber trees, villagers camped on-site to grow and watch over their own crops. Villagers stated that they agreed to give their land to the hydropower plant for the sake of the national interest, but not to the Sơn La Rubber Joint-Stock Company.[82] In Sơn La, provincial officials planned to plant ten thousand hectares of rubber trees on land that the villagers had "offered" and given to the rubber company. However, resistance has grown, and villagers know that rubber development has not proven itself to be in villagers' interests, let alone alleviated any poverty. Villagers demand a clear explanation about the use of the land that has not yet been planted with rubber trees. They also demand that provincial authorities set out clear procedures to allow landholders to regain their land if it is not planted as promised.[83]

The rubber development project fits well with the central government's goal of transforming small and scattered upland production into concentrated large-scale production, and it also makes it easier for the state to control the uplands. Both central and provincial governments interpreted any resistance to the project as a criticism of "the state's will and power." Since Prime Minister Nguyễn Tấn Dũng initiated the rubber project, it immediately became a "must do" project, shoving aside other concerns. Both central and provincial governments proclaimed the project to be for the uplands' development and modernization in particular, and the country's in general. This may explain why even reluctant district officials concerned about villagers' welfare still put in their best efforts to persuade villagers to contribute their land.[84] One official said, "That's part of our job. What do you think we can do? You see even the Ministry of Agriculture and Rural Development did not agree with the project at first, then later had to support the project and issue documents describing how to implement the project. Hopefully the project will bring benefit to people in the end."[85] During my visit in July 2009, one Kinh official in Tu La district described skepticism. "I worked here almost thirty years, and I know the soil, the weather here. Mark my words. As long as you and I live, we'll see the failure of this massive project." He was not afraid to strongly express his concerns about its feasibility. On my return two years later, I learned that he had been transferred to another job. Overall, the social response to the project has been relatively weak. However, many people do respond to this project in one way or another. Even though villagers' reactions make no headlines, it is not surprising that most hold strong feelings about the conversion of their agricultural lands into rubber tree plantations.

We have seen in this chapter that, in the name of development, economic growth, and improvement of ethnic minority lives, rubber development has increased the role of government agencies, local authorities, headmen, and state-owned and joint-stock companies in villagers' access to land and livelihoods. The rubber plantation projects have enabled new territorial orders and produced new territorial subjects in the region. In this case, the "regime of Truth" highlights the need of turning barren or low-quality land into productive land and emphasizes the rubber tree as a multipurpose tree. At the same time, disciplinary power is characterized by the state and the rubber company's control over space for development. Within the boundaries that the rubber plantations create and with the labeling of rubber trees as the state's property, the rubber company, on behalf of the government, applies sovereign power by punishing (via fines) those who commit the crime of damaging rubber trees—the state's property. Rubber plantations demonstrate, on the one hand, the close intertwining of development as an intentional project of improvement and progress, and on the other, the commodification of resources, capitalist expansion, and market value production in the frontier. Using rationalities for neoliberal governmentality, rubber company officials consider the project as a favor to and a good opportunity for petty peasants to improve their lives. Officials reserve concern for tree growth rather than for villagers' livelihoods. Local authorities have different views about the project, and not all of them were supportive of this land contribution scheme. State officials were not entirely indifferent to villagers' welfare, either. Some that I interviewed genuinely cared for and supported the villagers. Local authorities, especially at the commune and district levels, only had limited ability to influence the central government's strategic project. Such officials showed caution in what they said and how they reacted, reluctant to bear any negative consequences. We found different forms of everyday politics, especially everyday resistance, performed not only by affected villagers but also by local authorities who cared. For villages in the uplands, if the headman strongly supported the project, he would find a way to push other villagers to join (as in the case of Muong Ma). If the headman refused to join the project, it is likely that other villagers would follow his lead (as in Muong Lanh and Tinh villages). Villagers forced to join the project openly fought back when possible, even though they did not always succeed. Given the many factors that impacted this land dispossession process, including the location of the villages' farmland and the targeted land quotas, each village's reaction was unique.

# CHAPTER 6

# Rubber Workers and the Making of Modern Subjects

I have returned to Nam Nang commune in Lai Châu Province only a few times since my first visit in 2005. Every time I visited, some familiar faces were missing from the group of people with whom I had discussions. On my first visit, many villagers were preparing to resettle, while others were preparing to share their land with the resettlers whose land was about to be flooded to create the Sơn La Dam reservoir. My other visits came right before and one year after the same people sacrificed again; this time they had to contribute their land to the rubber plantations. Quang Van Giang was the headman when I first visited Pa village, Nam Nang commune. He had been retired from his position for a good number of years by this time. The last time I saw him was in May 2019. He asked me,

> Did you see the rubber trees on the way here today? They are big now, but we still don't see income as promised. In the last fifteen years, first, we were asked to give up our land for the Sơn La Dam, and then we contributed to the rubber plantations. We were told our lives would be better with the rubber plantations, but now the situation is not even close to what we were promised. You can't see many of the people you saw last time today because people are all over the place now. A half of the village has left home to work in some industrial park or as seasonal labor somewhere else.

According to Mr. Quang, to make way for the Sơn La hydropower plant, Nam Nang villagers lost 80 percent of their land—largely agricultural fields for rice and maize. Since the Sơn La Dam resettlement in 2009, locals' income has been very unstable because of a lack of farmland. When the rubber plantations started in the Northwest in 2007, Lai Châu Joint-Stock Rubber Company asked villagers in Nam Nang, just like villagers in many other communes of the three provinces of Sơn La, Lai Châu, and Điện Biên, to contribute their land and have family members work on the plantations. Given the very poor pay, however, this type of work did not allow workers to afford all their basic expenses. As a result, villagers, especially men, had to leave their village to work, leaving older people, women, and children at home. This chapter explores how local villagers' participation or nonparticipation in the rubber project is a product of multiple entangled factors such as economic pressures, livelihood maintenance, and everyday gendered struggles over place and space. My research demonstrates that we cannot understand one issue without taking the others into consideration. Analyzing interweaving forces of both external powers and agency in everyday subject making provides insight into how northwesterners become who they are and what they are.

In Vietnam, land rights are a key arena, not only for policy making but also in the quotidian dynamics of state domination. Land rights closely connect with the exercise of state control.[1] In many cases of land use and development, it does not matter who holds the land title; rather, it matters what the state wants to do with the land. Land, however, is not just a physical resource or a space for state activity. Land, according to Wolford and colleagues, is "life, stability, livelihood and social reproduction."[2] Thus, "identities and subject positions are constituted through relationships on and with the land."[3] In the case of rubber plantations in the Northwest, rubber investors and the government at all levels use land to bind people to policies that are not their preference or in their interest, policies that push them to become landless paid workers against their will.

## The Technology of Rubber Plantations

In Sơn La Province, upon agreeing to contribute their land, villagers had to complete a "Registration form for land contribution as holder for the Rubber Joint-Stock Company." This form contains the following requirements: (1) to register to contribute land to the planning area for the rubber plantation, and (2) to observe the rights and obligations of shareholders as mentioned in the labor contract. The form not only was evidence that villagers were voluntarily contributing the land, but it also formally bound the villagers to the rubber project.

Joining the rubber project exacerbated the villagers' struggle over land-use rights, especially for the resettlers who had been displaced to make way for the Sơn La Dam. As each displaced person received only about twenty-five hundred square meters of farmland at the resettlement site, the amount of farmland available to grow food, let alone cash crops, was significantly reduced when they had their land taken for the rubber project. Despite having received the promised land as compensation, the resettlers had yet to receive the red book—the legal title land-use document. Villagers expressed concern, but officials reassured them that the paperwork would be forthcoming once the land contribution issue was settled. Several problems soon arose. First, the resettlers' red book documented only the land contributed to the rubber project, *not* their total land allocation, including residential land. Second, the district's People's Committee kept the original red books; villagers were given a photocopied version. This practice was applied only to those households that had contributed land for the rubber project. The district authority stated that it would hold these red books for thirty years for safekeeping, but in reality, this was to ensure that the villagers would not be able to reclaim their land if they changed their minds.[4] Thus, despite having land-use rights, these villagers were effectively made landless. These families lost the right to determine how their land was used.

The Sơn La Rubber Company is the party on the no-risk side of the rubber plantation contract. In Lai Châu and Điện Biên Provinces, such practices differ slightly among communes even in the same district. For example, in Nam commune, Su La district in Lai Châu Province, and Thanh commune, Đa Binh district in Điện Biên Province, commune authorities defined the land given to the rubber companies (Lai Châu Joint-Stock Rubber Company and Điện Biên Joint-Stock Rubber Company) as collective land, which means that no individual households signed an agreement with a rubber company. Instead, the communes' People's Committees, on behalf of those they represent, signed these agreements.[5] Thus, commune officials offered the land to the company without clearly identifying its rightful holders. The red books in such cases bear the name of each commune's People's Committee. Villagers have no right at all to claim their land, nor have they had access to or even seen these documents. A commune chair explained to me later that the commune offered up a large area of land so that the rubber company could begin planting as soon as possible. This avoided the delay that would be caused by actually measuring the land area belonging to each household. This haphazard and rushed solution meant that some families lost all their land, while others lost none. Using such methods, the rubber company obtained land sufficient for tens of thousands of hectares of rubber trees to be planted in Lai Châu Province between 2009 and 2012. A similar method was employed in Điện Biên Province. This arrangement also excludes the binding agreement of "one hectare contribution, one worker per family" as occurred in Sơn La Province. The Lai Châu Rubber Joint-Stock Company made it very clear from the beginning that villagers were not obliged to work for the rubber company to receive the 10 percent dividend from their land contribution. It went further to state in the agreement that it would return villagers' land only once it halted rubber production. The company also indicated that when it harvested the latex, it would inform the villagers of their portion and its value. In terms of the dividend, the company stated that it would divide the total revenue received annually by the total land area. This would be further divided by the commune's population, then multiplied by 10 percent of the total revenue. Villagers would receive a 10 percent dividend regardless of whether their family contributed land. Unfortunately, things did not go as planned, and by the first rubber harvest, villagers who contributed more land were angry at the decision, as I will elaborate on later in this chapter.

The government's support of the rubber project buttressed companies in conflicts with villagers. This favor raised questions about issues of injustice and exploitation—taking from the poor to give to the rich. In addition, rubber companies benefited from various conditions surrounding land acquisition that enabled them to avoid some of the government's own land-acquisition policies. For example, state policy set the compensation price for production-land acquisition in 2009 at VNĐ 48 million/hectare (around US$2,700), and land that had been cultivated for food crops was paid for in cash.[6] However, if acquisition was for the rubber project, this same land was valued at VNĐ 10 million/hectare (US$562), and the companies did not pay villagers with cash but with shares, and only after the trees matured and could be tapped.[7]

My surveys in Muong Ma and Muong Che villages in 2009 (table 6.1) revealed that 49.3 percent of households in the study site contributed

*Table 6.1*    Land contribution in Muong Ma and Muong Che villages

| VILLAGE | | NUMBER OF SURVEYED HOUSEHOLDS | AREA OF LAND TO CONTRIBUTE (%) | | | | |
|---|---|---|---|---|---|---|---|
| | | | *0* | *1–20* | *21–50* | *51–80* | *81–100* |
| *Total* | Households | 75 | 1 | 1 | 10 | 26 | 37 |
| | % | 100 | 1.3 | 1.3 | 13.3 | 34.7 | 49.3 |
| *Muong Che* | Households | 37 | 0 | 0 | 6 | 15 | 16 |
| | % | 100 | – | – | 16.2 | 40.5 | 43.2 |
| *Muong Ma* | Households | 38 | 1 | 1 | 4 | 11 | 21 |
| | % | 100 | 2.6 | 2.6 | 10.5 | 28.9 | 55.3 |

Source: Survey by the author, Sơn La, November 11–13, 2009.

almost all their land for rubber production, and 34.7 percent contributed half their land. Only 2.6 percent of the households contributed little or no land, but they would eventually have to do so if their land fell within the planning zone. In the long term, therefore, the livelihoods of the two villages become reliant on the rubber plantation. In some special cases, landowners were over sixty years old and/or had disabled children; members of these households were unable to work for the rubber company. They were promised local government support, and once the trees could be tapped, they would receive income from their company shares like their neighbors. In the meantime, they were landless, unable to grow food crops, and unable to act on the situation. Even though investors in collaboration with the local authorities implemented community consultations, they were the ones who made decisions on how to proceed with the rubber project. And local villagers, once again, had few opportunities to voice their opinions on development projects that took away land and resources they depended on for their everyday life and livelihoods.

## Livelihoods before the Tapping

In order to promote the rubber plantation project, each province (Sơn La, Lai Châu, and Điện Biên) set up its own steering committee to direct land "mobilization" and persuade villagers to join the rubber project. I attended meetings where district and commune-level cadres, along with representatives of the rubber company, painted a picture of prosperity and a bright future for villagers who joined. While the central and provincial government officials argued that the rubber project could play an important developmental role in the Northwest, including in job creation, food security, and modernization, the actual outcome followed a divergent reality.

Food insecurity became an acute issue only a few years after the project was inaugurated. Indeed, shifts in income and livelihoods in the area reflected the problems associated with rubber plantations across the region. The situation changed only gradually after the villagers' land was given to the rubber plantations—it took time for all the problems to manifest themselves. My surveys show that in the first three years of growth, before the trees developed a canopy, households were allowed to intercrop maize and soybeans on the plantation, but not cassava. They were required to keep their distance from the seedlings. Weeds had to be removed by hand instead of by burning, and the land had to be worked with hoes instead of plowed with buffalo power. These physically demanding requirements meant more man-hours of agricultural labor, resulting in lower yields. Even though the first few years were difficult on many plantations, the Muong Ma and Muong Che villagers' problems were further aggravated by a lack of government support during this period. Households found limited alternative livelihood options, and many failed to find an additional source of income to supplement their work on the rubber plantations.

Work on a rubber plantation is demanding and has never brought sufficient income to the villagers. Locals describe the jobs of watering, weeding, and road construction between rubber fields as very difficult; one standard man-day of labor was very hard to complete (in 2009 one standard man-day, or eight hours, of labor in Sơn La earned VNĐ 57,000, or US$3). For example, to water the trees, workers had to climb the plantation hill while carrying water on their shoulders. Few water sources meant workers had to convey the water from far away, sometimes kilometers—arduous labor, which limits the amount they can haul per trip. Performing such labor on the steep hills requires workers in good health. For weed removal, the company requires that sixty trees be weeded per man-day. The area's steep and rocky terrain makes challenging rubber-field road construction even more difficult. Many workers were unable to perform the required man-day in a twenty-four-hour period and therefore earned only VNĐ 17,000/day (less than US$1). Villagers quickly began to worry about how they would support themselves. One person complained that "every day, we have to go to Lieu Tra market, fifteen minutes by motorbike, to buy rice on credit for eating. Now all of the land has been contributed [to the rubber plantation]. Also, how can I have land for building a new house for my children when they get married, and there is even no land for growing vegetables?"[8]

After three years, people experienced further challenges in income and working conditions. First, they were no longer allowed to intercrop within the rubber plantations, leading to a further reduction in family income and food. Second, the paid work available for them decreased drastically, as the trees were no longer saplings and did not require watering, required weeding only twice annually, and needed fertilizing just once a year. In 2013, the average salary of a rubber worker in Muong Ma and Muong Che villages was VNĐ 600,000 per month (about US$30). The villagers were unable to earn enough for a minimum subsistence salary, even though pay for one standard man-day of labor in Sơn La by 2013 had doubled since 2009 to VNĐ 120,000 (US$6) for all types of work.[9] Lower income equates to food insecurity for these families. In the first three years, when they were able to intercrop maize, they could purchase basic foodstuffs at the local convenience store on credit and repay the debt when they harvested their crops. The new reality meant that they now depended entirely on daily work on the rubber plantation. In 2013, the owners of the area's convenience stores stopped permitting rubber workers to purchase on credit.[10] According to some villagers, this new rule was implemented because the store owners were unsure if they would be able to recoup what was owed them—workers might not have enough money to pay their debt at the end of each month.

When compared to income from maize cultivation, income generated from rubber is lower and uncertain. In the past, if villagers were sick or busy with other activities and did not attend their maize fields for two or three days, the crop's yield or income showed little adverse effect. After they became day laborers for the Sơn La Rubber Joint-Stock Company, their income declined after even one day's absence. If they did go to work but their output did not meet a satisfactory standard, they were not paid at all. With maize cultivation, villagers could generally estimate their expected income so that they could budget for annual household expenses as well as other expenditures, such as house repairs or renovations. For example, according to a member of the village management board in Muong Che village, his family produced seven tons of maize per hectare in 2008, which meant his family had a fairly stable budget, receiving VNĐ 18 million (US$1,060) per hectare after six months of work.[11] It is much more difficult for villagers to forecast their annual income when they are employed as rubber workers (see table 6.2, comparing maize growing and rubber planting).

Mr. Tien of the neighboring Hoa Muong village contributed all four of his family's hectares to the rubber company in 2009. Mr. Tien, who was not a resettler, told me that his family used to grow upland rice, and each year they harvested about five hundred bundles of rice, enough for the family's needs. Although the economic value of the crop was minimal, they never had to worry about rice self-sufficiency. Since contributing their land to the rubber company, the family of four had to depend entirely on their remaining, much smaller wet rice area. While waiting for the latex to be tapped, family members took different jobs to make ends meet and to buy rice. In the rainy season, Mr. Tien and his wife traveled to the Sơn La reservoir to fish, but income from fishing was unstable.

The agrarian setting and people's working habits in the field completely changed once they joined the project. One villager shared the traditional schedule of terrace farming for the Thái people as an example. For each maize crop that his family planted, the work was concentrated

*Table 6.2*   Comparison between crop cultivation and rubber planting

| | RUBBER PLANTING | MAIZE, CASSAVA, AND SOYBEAN CULTIVATION |
|---|---|---|
| 1 | Long and difficult work:<br>- Trees need watering<br>- Cultivation done by hand<br>- Requires digging holes for planting<br>- The same work is assigned to men and women | Much less effort:<br>- No watering<br>- Buffaloes for plowing<br>- No digging<br>- Men are responsible for heavier work; women have other tasks at home or on the farm |
| 2 | Time, work:<br>- Determined by the company<br>- Whole working day, more time required<br>- Year-round work | Time, work:<br>- Independence, self-management<br>- Shorter working day: 6–9 a.m., 3–5 p.m.<br>- Intensive work but only for three months per year in the cropping season |
| 3 | No previous experience:<br>- Need to learn new skills<br>- Yield and income decreased<br>- Increased working time<br>- Decreased time for rest and taking care of family | Have previous experience:<br>- No new skills to learn or master<br>- Higher yield<br>- More time for rest |
| 4 | Income:<br>- Unstable<br>- Unable to estimate<br>- Unable to make plans for future expenditures<br>»» »» **Very worrying** | Income:<br>- Relatively stable<br>- Able to estimate<br>- Able to make plans for future expenditures<br>»» »» **Less worries** |

Sources: Surveys by the author in Muong Ma and Muong Che, 2009.

in the first three months after the fields were planted. From the fourth to sixth month, they only needed to work with the crop occasionally. September was the month of harvest. After harvest, the family visited friends and relatives, repaired or built houses, collected fuelwood, or gathered forest products for sale. When working for the rubber company, however, they were no longer able to control their time. According to my interviewees, because of the company's lack of advance planning, laborers trekked up the rubber hill every morning without knowing whether work would be available. They waited for work at the plantations. Those who arrived first might find work, while those who came later might find no work or have to wait for possible assignments. Most often, the workers returned home empty-handed. Northwestern villagers, who for many generations relied on farming for their livelihoods, now turned into "modern workers"—rubber workers. They had to learn to work under pressure and deal with daily uncertainty in making their living. These resettled villagers' lives have changed from a manageable seasonal rhythm of cropping and balancing daily activities of choice to having to do intensive everyday work at the plantations without being able to control how they use their time.

## Marginalized Modern Workers

Land seizure for development in Vietnam involves dispossession, expelling many villagers from agriculture without absorbing their labor into the economy, and creating new territorial subjects in the region. This has greatly transformed the agricultural structure and agrarian settings in the area. Tracing agrarian transformation and changes in labor settings in the project sites helps us to understand how state policies that promote accumulation drive people away from their familiar daily practices that are dependent on access to land. Drawing on Karl Marx's concept of "relative surplus population," Tania Li argues that the accumulation process can create an agrarian labor question that involves a large "surplus population" of rural people who were dispossessed from the land and abandoned.[12] Or, according to Henry Bernstein, accumulation has created "classes of labor" when people lose their land and get into various forms of petty production and wage labor that are informal and precarious.[13] When they become landless, the majority of these people also become unemployed, and in many cases they turn to migrant labor in desperation. This illustrates how the powerful discourse of development and progress fails to deliver its promises.

In order to obtain land for rubber plantations, company and government officials promised villagers a good future if they joined as rubber workers; this rosy future was based on best-case scenarios, and reality has proved to be different. At this time, villagers were also told that the rubber price was very high—up to VNĐ 150–170 million (US$8,100–9,200) per ton. Local cadres and rubber companies called it "white gold."[14] Even the villagers' 10 percent of revenues would exceed what they earned from growing maize. Thus, authorities set up a scenario to turn peasants into rubber workers in all three provinces where rubber trees would be planted. Apart from the rights listed in the official documents guiding rubber plantation establishment, staff at the provincial, district, and commune levels also verbally promised local people that they would receive other benefits, including buses to bring them to and from the rubber area, and trucks to transport fertilizer and seedlings across large and hilly plantations. These promises created a strong sense of hope for a better life, if not for adult villagers themselves, then for their children and grandchildren.[15] Unfortunately, these promises were unfulfilled, leaving local people to question the actual benefit of the rubber plantations for the development of their households' economy.

The rubber company was not transparent in its process for signing contracts with the villagers. By 2012, the Sơn La Rubber Joint-Stock Company had recruited twenty-two hundred long-term workers and twenty-four hundred temporary workers—more than four thousand workers in Sơn La Province alone.[16] When asked, however, most of the villagers said that they had never received a copy of the contract they had signed with the company; others had never even signed a contract. According to a staff member of the Sơn La Rubber Joint-Stock Company, the delay in signing contracts was due to a lack of consensus between the provincial government and the company on the contract's contents.[17] In addition, the project documents and labor contracts that officials read to the villagers in community meetings were in Vietnamese, a language that was not well understood by some participants. My survey shows that there was an overall feeling of confusion among villagers about their interests and responsibilities, as well as the expected benefits. Further, the project's management board did not clearly articulate these points in the contract created to facilitate land contributions and detail stakeholders' responsibilities and obligations. The final article of the labor contract, for example, states that "rights, obligations, legal interests, and legal consequences of the signing of this contract are well understood by the two parties."[18] This raises important questions: How can villagers confirm the contract if they do not fully understand the contract language? How will they be able to deal with any disputes that may arise in the future? Signing the contract meant that the household could not ask for their land back until the end of the "agreed-upon" terms—twenty-five to thirty years later.

Working conditions on the rubber plantation have also been controversial. The villagers work thirty days per month. Even though each household has one person employed as a paid worker for the rubber company, the payment is based on the amount of work completed daily, and usually the whole family contributes to completing the work assigned to one person. The tools required to complete the labor are not sufficient and are not always available when needed. Two households might be provided with only one crowbar and one hoe to share, for example. The company does not provide all the tools required to complete tasks, including hoes, shovels, and knives for hole excavation, hole filling, and weeding. Local people dealt with the tool scarcity issue by waiting until the tools became available, which impacted their daily income, or by acquiring the tools themselves.

These difficulties affected workers' incomes and health and caused conflicts between households. When asked about such problems, one representative from the Sơn La Rubber Joint-Stock Company said, "Hmm, people like to complain no matter what. You know, they are farmers; hoes and shovels must be available in their houses. The project doesn't need to provide all these tools for every household if they already have the tools at home."[19] Interviews with company staff show that, in general, they believed that this opportunity for villagers who used to be peasants to become workers on the plantations was a big improvement, and the villagers should be proud instead of complaining about the tools and equipment provided. This lack of tools, however, also affected relations between laborers and with the Sơn La Rubber Joint-Stock Company. Workers told the research team that after eight months they had received from the company only one of the two sets of work clothing that were stipulated in the contract: one pair of boots, one raincoat, and 1.5 kilograms of laundry detergent. The allocation of only one set of work clothes made it difficult for the workers to come to the plantation daily and maintain adequate hygiene; if they washed their work clothing, they had no clothing to wear to the plantations the next day.

The ethnic minority groups living in these three provinces were not accustomed to the intensive work schedule that the rubber company

**FIGURE 6.1.** Rubber plantation workers in their uniforms, July 2009. Photo by the author.

set. They were working the same land, but in worse conditions, where the type of work differed radically from what they were used to. Employment as rubber workers did not equate to these groups becoming modernized, as the government and the rubber company boasted. Villagers were confused about their responsibilities, including what they owned and what they were supposed to receive. By 2018, half the young people in Muong Ma and Muong Che had moved to Hung Yen, Bac Ninh, or other industrial parks in the lowlands to work in factories. These shifts led to a major transformation of agrarian settings in these provinces.

## Tapping the Latex, and the Lives of Rubber Workers

One day in early May 2015, a friend in Sơn La called me. "Are you planning to come visit us anytime soon?" she asked. "You should come ASAP." I was surprised, as she had never before approached me in this way. I quickly realized why. Locals reported that the Sơn La Joint-Stock Rubber Company had just chopped down about seventy hectares of eight-year-old rubber trees in Sơn La Province. I was shocked to hear this news, given the villagers' stake in the plantation's success. With this loss of trees, how would these families cope? The company explained its action—the trees showed no sign of producing any latex after eight years of growth. A rubber company's staff in the village told me that the company would replant a different variety of trees with a shorter development period.

By May 2019, Sơn La Province had almost seven thousand hectares of rubber trees, half of which were being tapped. These lands belonged to 7,210 households. However, the effectiveness of this program for ethnic minority people in Sơn La in particular and the Northwest in general fell far short of what villagers and local authorities expected. Among the 7,210 households, only about 900 have an income of VNĐ 2 million (US$87) per month. The remaining households have a much lower monthly income.[20]

The first rubber trees in Sơn La were successfully tapped in 2017, ten years after planting. By the end of 2018, households received low dividend payouts of US$65–80 per hectare, and villagers were extremely disappointed. One district official in Tu La explained, "Now the company said they could only sell the latex at the price of US$1,087 per ton, not US$8,100–9,200 per ton as they said when persuading villagers to contribute their land back in 2007–2008. But you know what, if that's the case, then our villagers should receive 50 percent of the revenue. Otherwise, there's no way they would be able to sustain their life. They would rather keep their land and grow maize or cassava."[21]

During the May 2019 VUSTA workshop, villagers complained that their income from work on the rubber plantation was reduced compared to working with maize; for some families, earnings had dropped 40 percent. Dividends that villagers received from contributing one hectare to the rubber project only amounted to 2–3 percent of what they received when they grew maize on that land.[22]

One day in May 2019, I visited Hoa Muong village, Sơn La Province. The headman rummaged through his documents relating to the procedure for contributing land to the rubber project, showing us the list of households in the village who received dividends for rubber latex production in 2017–18. Mr. Thi contributed about two hectares to the project, but the total area of rubber ready to tap in 2017 and 2018 was only 0.78 hectares. Mr. Thi received a payment of just over VNĐ 600,000 (about US$30) after a ten-year wait on his investment. Mr. Du's household contributed 1.8 hectares, but in 2018, tapping was limited to 0.05 hectares of his land; he received only VNĐ 370,000 (US$18.50).

Other households that contributed between 0.2 hectare to 1 hectare per household received a payment of only VNĐ 100,000 to 200,000 (US$5–10) per household, and some were paid as little as VNĐ 2,000 to 3,000 (US$1–1.50) per household.

One villager said,

> My family took very good care of the rubber trees. We contributed 0.3 hectares to the rubber company. In 2018, the whole area was under tapping, but the amount of money we have received for both 2017 and 2018 was only VNĐ 235,000 [about US$11.70]. It was a good thing that we only contributed that much land; compared to other families, we are still lucky to have land to grow other crops. At the beginning of 2019, when we were told to come to receive our dividend, many households had to ride a motorbike three to four kilometers to the receiving point, but the amount was only tens of thousands of VNĐ [US$0.50], so many households did not even bother to take it.[23]

Worse, rubber trees of the same age growing on some other families' land did not produce any latex, and these families received nothing. Mr. Hien is an example. The rubber trees on his land have been thus far unproductive. He said that before he contributed his family's land to the rubber project, he planted cassava on his 0.6 hectare. Each year he harvested six to seven tons of the tuber; he sold some and kept the rest to feed his pigs. Thanks to this cultivation, the family always had dozens of pigs in the yard, a few sows, and a few hundred chickens. Over the past ten years, without that upland field, his family of four people has relied entirely on 720 square meters of paddy rice. They do not even have sufficient land to graze their four cows. This is a shared plight for the nearly one hundred households that contributed about forty-three hectares to the rubber project in Hoa Muong village. The whole village relies on 6.5 hectares of paddy rice land. The poverty rate of Hoa Muong village is close to 50 percent. Hoa villagers have received their share of the rubber revenue, even though it is paltry. Many other villages that contributed land at the same time were still awaiting their first payment.[24]

When I returned to Muong Ma and Muong Che villages in May 2019, I learned from my focus group discussions that only 144 people, down from more than 600 in 2009, were still employed as rubber workers across Muong Muon commune, while villagers contributed 1,301 hectares to the rubber plantations. In Muong Ma, only nine out of the sixty-five workers still work on the plantations; the other fifty-six quit to look for work elsewhere. One man told me, "You know, you would never get their labor contract. They kept telling us to go through a probation period and called us 'temporary workers.' It's like four, five years and then ten years, you're still not qualified to be their workers." He laughed bitterly.[25]

While in 2014 there were close to four thousand rubber workers across Sơn La Province, five years later more than thirteen hundred had quit because of low wages or a lack of available work.[26] When I broached the issue with a district official in Tu La a few days later, he said,

> Well, the good thing is not all of the villagers contributed all of their land. Unfortunately, most of the people who contributed all of their land were resettlers of the Sơn La Dam. In these cases, they had to go far from home to do labor work. No other choices. Work for villagers has been one of the main issues here. Indeed, we have many times sent recommendations to the provincial level and to the rubber company. The most important thing is income for villagers. Once villagers became workers, they need to have an agreement, a work contract, and have a salary. That's how you call them "workers." They need to have health and social insurance. And if there was not enough work to do, they must be able to receive or claim for employment insurance. Everything needs to follow legal procedures. Here you find nothing like that in the way the rubber company treats our villagers.[27]

He went on to criticize the company and did not seem to care that in his position, he probably was not supposed to say such things.

> The company has been doing wrong the whole time. They keep saying that villagers are not qualified enough to be workers. All necessary procedures to protect villagers' labor rights have been ignored. Villagers contributed land and signed up to work for the company, but soon they realized that they did not earn enough to feed their family, they did not have a work contract, they did not have health and social insurance; one day they have work to do, the next day they have nothing. Of course, they quit. That's inevitable. The last time I had an opportunity to be in a meeting with the company's representatives, I said, "You guys should go to restudy our labor law." But they did not care. Even the province's Department of Finance did not think I was right. Ha ha ha! I said:

"There is no such thing called temporarily recruited workers here. Workers are workers. Workers need to have full rights and responsibilities as defined by law. Employers need to be responsible for their workers if they don't have enough work to do. I don't know. If your company is at a loss, you need to work with the government to get a subsidy, so you can have the money to pay for these ethnic minority workers. Otherwise, what would they eat?

And that was the first time I heard an official in such a position admit a mistake.

The thing is our province also made mistakes. We were too easy on the rubber company and gave them so many favors. Unlike Điện Biên, in Sơn La, the rubber company did not have to compensate villagers for crop loss when they took the land. All the money to support villagers comes from the province's budget, including support for production, vocational training, etc. That was because the rubber has affected Sơn La resettlers. Now they started to tap the latex. The work is very hard, and on top of that villagers did not get what was promised.

When the workers started to tap the latex in 2017, there was not much sap, so they only worked for ten days each month. They received VNĐ 600 (US$27) for those ten working days, which is also their monthly income. With 572 hectares available to tap in 2019, Muong Muon produced 172 tons of dry latex, but villagers had no clue of its value. The company did not share their financial statements. Even the district authorities were left in the dark. In early 2020, as the trees were producing more latex, a full-time worker could earn VNĐ 10 million (US$440) per month, but most were already employed elsewhere, leaving only those who could not leave. To tap the latex, villagers, both men and women, need to begin work before 3 a.m. and work until sunrise. On the first day, they tighten the band around the tree. On the following night, they tap the latex, which was then collected on the third day. Even though the monthly salary for tapping was vastly improved compared to before tapping, many did not want this work, as it was very laborious, must be done at night, and compensation was received only every two months. Villagers still have to sign debt books with interest at local stores for food, gasoline, and other necessities. As families have had to work very hard for a hand-to-mouth existence over the past decade, many young people had to leave school early. In 2018, up to 80 percent

of the villagers in both Muong Ma and Muong Che were illiterate, most
of them women. If someone became ill and needed to travel to the hospital, they required either the head of the Women's Union or a Vietnamese speaker to accompany them. One could argue that this illiteracy
rate was similar to that of the village before resettlement, but resettlers
moved here thirteen years ago with the promise of having a better life
and better opportunities for women and girls in terms of education and
other social services—promises unmet. These troubled times also saw
increases in drug and alcohol use.[28] Villagers became more vulnerable
to scams. For example, in 2017, a number of villagers in Muong Muon
commune lost their money to a corrupt district official who coerced
them to give him their savings for farmland being opened up thanks to
a land-clearing project. He said that each household would be eligible
to buy one hectare at a cost of VNĐ 100 million (about US$4,400). He
could even help buy two hectares for VNĐ 100 million. Many villagers
believed him and mortgaged their homes to borrow funds for the project. Their money and the official disappeared, and as of 2019, villagers
still expressed hope to me that he might be caught, and their money
returned.

The situation in Lai Châu and Điện Biên Provinces was not much
brighter. In more dire situations, like in Nam commune in Lai Châu or
Thanh commune in Điện Biên, villagers are struggling for their livelihoods. They have not received any rubber revenues, as they have been
unable to reach a consensus on how to share what little revenue has
been forthcoming. Villagers contributed their land to the rubber companies under the commune's name instead of by individual landholders. In 2019, the Lai Châu Rubber Join-Stock Company claimed that
they had not been able to sell their latex, so they had nothing to pay
the villagers. The chairman of Nam commune had run out of options:

> Our villagers work very hard, but their income is only enough
> for gasoline. Once the company could sell their latex, they paid
> workers VNĐ 2 million [US$87] per month. When they said they
> could not sell the latex, they paid villagers VNĐ 300,000 [US$13]
> per month as an advance. Then they pay one time at the end of
> the year. Many families have been in hunger. We lost 80 percent of
> our land to the Sơn La hydropower project. So we have nothing
> left. Before, when there were only Sơn La and Hoa Binh Dams,
> we were able to grow some crops in the semi-flooded land in the
> reservoir [area]. But now Lai Châu Dam is under operation, [and]

all the hydropower projects on Nam Na tributary upstream are also completed and under operation. The semi-flooded lands are of no use at all because the time [that] water is low is too short. It doesn't give us enough time to grow anything. I am stressed. I will have to resign at the end of this term. I can't take it anymore.[29]

## Differentiation in the Village

"I wish we could still have our land, so I didn't have to leave our village to earn my living like this."

I was listening to a young man in his mid-twenties on an early June day in 2018 when I returned to visit Muong Ma and Muong Che villages in Muong Muon commune. The man and his wife had to leave their ten-month-old daughter with her uncle's family so the couple could earn a living working in a shoe factory in Bac Ninh Province in the Red River delta. They reported that they each earned VNĐ 6 million per month (US$267), but they had to pay for rent and food, leaving little savings. Once a month, they returned to the village to see their daughter. "In terms of the income, it's still better than if we stayed," he said. "But the problem is our family has been separated. I hope we can have enough savings to come back and buy a piece of land to farm."

Unfortunately, he did not realize his dream. When I visited Muong Muon a year later, I learned that the young father had lost all his savings as well as the money he had borrowed from relatives and the bank. He was one of the villagers who gave his money to a corrupt officer who offered the false promise of purchasing cheap farmland.[30] Similar stories were not difficult to find in his village and others across the Northwest, especially in those where families contributed land to rubber companies.

In 2013, there were 80 households in these two villages (46 in Muong Ma and 34 in Muong Che), and by 2019 there were 112 (65 households in Muong Ma village and 47 in Muong Che village). Since the families lacked land for farming and struggled with the little income that each household could earn from work on the rubber plantations, many children had to drop out of school each year, and most of them married at a young age. In 2019, for example, six couples under the age of eighteen married, seven children ages thirteen or fourteen had to drop out of school, and more than fifty people left their village to seek employment—six couples left together, and fifteen women went alone, leaving their husbands and children in the village (six of these women abandoned their husbands because of the men's drug use). In Muong Ma village, 70 percent of the women are illiterate. As they do not speak Vietnamese, they required assistance communicating with a doctor if they or a family member fell ill.

Life has been very difficult for villagers in the post-resettlement period, owing in large part to the need to contribute to the rubber project most of the land they received as compensation for resettlement. By early 2020, among the 112 households in these two villages, only 3 were considered wealthy by the village's definition—these households have extra savings at the end of the year. They have recently invested in goat and cricket rearing and sell their products to restaurants in Sơn La City, which is eighteen kilometers away. These three households saved enough money to purchase farmland from Ang, a neighboring village. The former headman of Muong Ma village, who was a strong supporter of the rubber project, is a member of one of these three households. He pushed other villagers in Muong Ma to contribute their land and become rubber workers back in 2007. In the first few years of the project, when work on the rubber plantations was still readily available and was providing a good income for villagers, his role as headman and as a project supporter solidified for him very good connections with rubber company staff in Muong Muon commune. Using such connections, he secured more work and favorable working conditions for himself and his family. I later learned that he was the one who reported on my research activities to the police at the district level each time that I visited the villages. Before latex tapping began in 2017 and work on the plantations was scarce, the headman quit and started raising goats and crickets. He was quite successful in connecting with restaurants in Sơn La City and has stable buyers for his crickets and goat meat and milk.[31] I asked his wife one day in May 2019 why other families in the village were not following their path, and her response was,

> Oh, we could only share a little bit of techniques in raising goats and crickets. Not more than that. Our buyers are our secret. We don't want to have too many producers in the village. If too many people are raising goats and crickets, there won't be enough buyers, and we will be in trouble. Whoever is smarter and faster will be successful. On top of that, other people are quite lazy. They don't want to learn new things or take risks. That's why there are only three families in the village that can do well.[32]

Muong Ma and Muong Che villages share similar topographic conditions to Muong Nhuong and also lack secure water sources. Small gardens produce small crops, with little extra produce that villagers can sell for additional income. In 2021, six households (four in Muong Ma and two in Muong Che) have been in extreme poverty and constantly suffer from hunger.[33] These families do not have land or the labor to work it, so their opportunities to earn an income are very restricted. Most of the time when I was in the village, I would see them eating only rice with salt and hot chilies. Fish and meat were almost totally missing. For another five households, the husbands have become drug users and do not work or support their families. These households suffer from hunger for extended periods each year. Another twelve households manage to secure food year-round, thanks to strong laborers in the family and resourcefulness in securing work outside the village. The remaining households are in a similar situation to the poorer families, lacking food for one to three months every year. Even though the work of tapping the rubber trees seems to have brought employment for some villagers since 2017, it is physical work in which not everyone can engage, especially those with health conditions or with small children they cannot leave home at 3 a.m. for five hours. Most of the households in these villages, except for the three wealthier households, continue to sign debt books on a daily basis for basic necessities.

When compared to other villages in the commune such as Muong Lanh or Muong Nhuong, whose members did not contribute their land to the rubber project, the majority of villagers in Muong Ma and Muong Che have become impoverished. As the rubber project transformed the material landscape by turning thousands of hectares of forest and farmland into monocrop rubber plantations, it not only caused ecological degradation but also produced new landless territorial subjects, people who struggled to make their living and keep their families together, and who also experienced changes in how they interacted with one another and with the authorities.

## Gendered Subjectivities of Rubber Plantations

Land dispossession, agrarian changes in the region, and the promotion of misguided development programs can all result in changes in gender relations, roles, and responsibilities.[34] Men may not be able to continue in their leading role in the family, and women may become increasingly involved in the labor force; this in turn may bring changes in relationships within the home as well as undermine masculinity and male status. Gender and identity are relational, and gendered subjectivities are contested in relation to changing environmental, economic, and production conditions linked to livelihoods, natural resources, and wider development programs and policies. Gender and gender relations are not only the products of social and cultural processes but are also products of economic transformation. Thus, once gender is considered as a process, the dynamic relationships between gender, environment, and other aspects of social and cultural life can be brought into view and examined. In order to understand the gendered dimension of struggles over power, justice, and resource governance, feminist political ecology undertakes to "focus on resource access and control, gendered constructions of knowledge, and the embeddedness of local gendered environmental struggles in regional and global political economic contexts."[35] In reality, both men and women can be disadvantaged by social and economic structures. Changing gendered divisions of labor and social practices both benefit and disadvantage men. When changes happen, men deal with a new situation differently from women, and men are not necessarily less vulnerable. Differences occur not only between women and men, but also among men and among women. In examining the differences among men, it helps to understand the diversity of masculine practices. Men are not always the winners, and ignoring this risks overlooking gender-specific inequalities and vulnerabilities.[36]

Since social values are fundamental to "men's and women's identity, self-esteem, and also to gender relations," it is important to understand these values in their particular context in order to unpack the various factors that affect the relationships between men and women in changing situations.[37] For example, Bonnin and Turner explore the case of some upland groups in Vietnam in which cultural norms reconfigured local realities even though state law aimed to maintain equal rights for men and women. Vietnamese law dictates that women and men have equal rights to landownership. Specifically, the law stipulates that both husband and wife should register and be named on the land use certificate. In reality, however, it is very common that only the male head of the household's name appears on these certificates. This issue is not limited to upland people but is certainly significant for this case. Research also shows that in the context of rural Southeast Asia, the modernization of agricultural work has significantly impacted gender roles and relations in ways that strengthen hierarchical relations and marginalize women.[38]

Just as with many other economic policies, the rubber project is gendered in the sense that it has arisen out of gendered economic processes that disproportionally impact men and women as well as their roles and opportunities to participate in decision-making processes. In 2015, 2016, and 2017, I visited Muong Tro village in the same Muong Muon commune. Muong Tro village was not affected by the Sơn La Dam, so the villagers there had more farmland compared to villagers in Muong Lanh, Muong Ma, or Muong Che villages. When asked about her role in the decision to contribute land to the rubber project, Mrs. Ninh recalled, "Well, I was worried and did not agree at first. We discussed it for some time, and my husband finally convinced me." Other families have different stories: "Here in Muong Tro village, we had quite a large area of land because we were not resettlers. My family had six hectares. I saw that most of our relatives agreed to contribute the land. So, my husband and I discussed it, and we decided to contribute two and a half hectares. We kept the remaining area to grow our crops. Good thing that we kept part of our land, otherwise now we would be in a more difficult situation."[39]

Even though structurally subordinate to men, women have proactively responded to the challenges of economic hardship in order to support their families. In a majority of families (forty-five out of sixty-five households in my survey in Muong Tro village in 2016), while the husbands work only on the rubber plantation, the wives work both on the rubber plantation and in their own gardens or small farming patches. Some families—3 percent—have opened small convenience stores to earn additional family income. Women have become more active in working outside the home; in thirty-five out of sixty-five households surveyed, women embraced training and potential income-generating activities, such as partaking in agricultural extension training (activities only men engaged with in the past) and learning to grow mushrooms or raise frogs and hedgehogs. None of the women I interviewed complained about the amount of work they do, but they all long for the past when they were able to freely work on their land. The rubber project has intensified women's labor while diminishing their land-use rights. This has sometimes led to escalating domestic conflict and violence over the control of income from rubber, which is similar to what happened on oil palm plantations in Indonesia.[40]

Indeed, the rubber project has brought many social problems to the village, affecting relationships within families and in the community. Before the introduction of rubber in the region, these families usually received compensation for their work after the harvest. At that point they knew how much they had earned, and the husband and wife often discussed how to allocate those funds throughout the year until the next harvest. If the money they received from their crops was insufficient for family expenses, they would confer on how to earn extra income. In such cases, the husband often worked as a farm laborer for a neighboring family or in other villages; many also worked outside of farming. In the first three years after offering their land to the rubber company, villagers had a lot of work on the plantation. Both husband and wife worked and received monthly payment for their labor. As the payment was based on productivity, most people worked thirty days per month. While both men and women were absorbed into the plantation labor force, the husband most often received the payment, since his name was on the contract. In this way, the rubber plantations have reinforced patriarchal social relations in the village.

With the introduction of monthly wages, families tended to spend more, especially men. Simple availability made cash and cash purchases more popular than ever. To meet the demand, more stores popped up in the commune, opened by villagers and outsiders, to sell alcohol to men, sweets for children, food, and other goods. Families who contributed more land and therefore produced less of their own food needed to spend more of their wages buying their daily food. In 2009, Muong Tro village had no heavy drinkers, and neither women nor men were drunk on a daily basis. A villager told me, "Brewing had long been an important activity in our life, from going to the forest to pick the right leaves to selecting the right maize, cassava, or banana for the alcohol. We brew mostly for family or village events. Our alcohol is tasty and safe. It's very sad that this tradition is now fading."[41]

The arrival of the rubber plantation, and the resulting reallocation of land, has meant that many families stopped distilling alcohol because they did not grow enough maize and cassava for this purpose. Moreover, alcohol of low quality, imported from China, has become readily available in convenience stores.[42] Lower-grade drinking options have not stopped many men from developing heavy drinking habits, as I learned from our interviews. Thus, while drinking alcohol has always been part of the culture in the region, alcoholic beverages have progressed from locally produced, mildly alcoholic drinks used to

entertain guests to a kind of industrial opiate of the masses for plantation laborers—from a delicacy to an object of dependency.

In the years leading up to the arrival of the rubber plantations, some
men left the village to work as paid laborers in a nearby town. Shortly
after, heavy drug use started for some of these villagers. A recovered
drug addict recalled, "My former employer gave me free methamphetamines. He told me not to worry about the money, just try it. At first,
I liked it, as it helped me work long hours without being very tired. But
when I got used to having it, I had to pay for it. I was unable to work as
hard as before and was unable to control myself when my body needed
it. It was terrible. Luckily, I didn't go too far. My wife helped me a lot.
She urged me to join a rehab program held by the local authorities, and
finally I was able to quit."[43]

For most men who became addicts during this period, their employers or friends offered them drugs for free to start them using. Once
they became addicted, the free drugs stopped; to find the money to feed
their habit, many men helped their dealers to lure other men from the
village into drug use. The drug users in Muong Tro village and neighboring Muong Ma and Muong Che villages included these men, but
especially younger men or teenage boys.[44] This rise in addiction is not
unusual in this region; researchers have observed similar phenomena
wherever rural farmers become industrialized laborers. As indicated in
a United Nations news article in 2018, this has been particularly problematic in Vietnam, where drug addiction was rising.[45]

Once the rubber trees arrived, men needed to work hard to meet
daily work quotas. They learned that drugs like methamphetamines
could help them work tirelessly for longer periods of time. During the
first three years, the men could make more money from their work on
the plantations, and many spent it on drugs. An addict said, "Most
of us can only afford methamphetamines, so that's why you see more
people using it, especially younger people." Our interviewees did not
reveal any information about where they purchased the drugs.

After the third year of planting rubber trees, when the pace slowed
and the number of working hours fell, villagers received lower wages
than they did previously. This reduction in income, coupled with farmland shortages, has discouraged men in many ways. Their leisure time
increased when compared with that of women, especially men who had
less land, as their plantation work required only a few hours each day in
the morning, and they would arrive home before lunch. Some ventured
into the forest to collect bamboo shoots or traveled to town to sell their

labor for extra income, but a number of them became bored and hope-less with the undesired spare time. They ended up gathering together more often, where they drank, used drugs, and gambled.

My focus group discussions revealed that once these men began us-ing drugs and/or gambling, they cared more about obtaining drugs or gambling earnings and losses than they did about anything else. These group discussions pointed to a number of other unwelcome, harrow-ing behaviors and responses by family members. Drug users had to ask their wives for money; if the wife would not give them money, the hus-band might steal some or take items from his wife or his parents to sell; if he was unable to steal anything worth selling, he might sign a debt book at a local store or pawn the family's motorcycle. The wife, depend-ing on her resourcefulness, would then have to borrow money some-where to retrieve the motorcycle. If she was unsuccessful, the family would be unable to travel to work on the plantation—the distance from the village to the plantation is three to seven kilometers uphill. Given the limited amount of wage work available, if the family had to walk to the plantation, there would be no work on offer by the time they ar-rived. A woman in her thirties said, "I am very upset. But I don't think I have choices, unless I want to divorce. But if I did that, what would happen to my children? Now I need to take care of the family and find ways to help my husband back to the right path. I sought help from the commune Women's Union. Some men made it. Maybe my husband can do it too." This reflects an increase in women's disproportionate share of the "altruistic burden" within low-income households at the study sites and across Vietnam.[46]

Women reported that men would drink at home, at a neighbor's, with friends or without. Some described men becoming physically abu-sive when drinking. In one group discussion, a woman said that "men now do not care whether the family has anything to eat, all they care about is if they have alcohol for the day. Men drink to drown their prob-lems." A man in his forties responded, "Not all of us drink all the time, and not only because we're sad, even though we tend to drink more when we're sad. We also like to drink when we have nothing to do."[47]

When the husband does not help with housework, women handle that along with other productive and reproductive work, as well as involve-ment in community management work related to common resources—all, they report, with limited support from their husbands. In particular, subsistence agricultural activities (in forty-two out of sixty-five house-holds surveyed in 2017) have quickly become the women's domain as men either do not do much to help, according to their spouses, or go to work nearby during the day. More women at the study sites report taking the lead in making decisions on domestic issues, and since many of them are now their family's provider, they are in a better position to negotiate with the rubber company when necessary. All these changes have led to family crises. According to the villagers, before the plantations' establishment, there were no divorces in Muong Tro village. By 2016, there were eleven divorces, and in five of these cases the wives simply left to find employment as domestic helpers in town or fled to escape their husbands' drug use or drinking habit. A woman who lives in the neighboring village of Muong Che said, "There have been so many social problems since we joined the rubber project. The government said that the rubber plantation is for poverty reduction, but we have become impoverished because of the rubber trees. Since we have joined the rubber project, the whole village is deepened in sadness."[48]

Responses to changes in economic conditions have also encouraged changes in gender norms. In the past, men rarely did housework such as washing clothes or cleaning. Now in some families (31 out of 114 households in my survey in 2016), husbands help their wives with housework. In these families, husband and wife share most of the work. No fighting was reported in these families. A man (age thirty) said, "Our life has been getting very hard, and if I didn't do more to help my wife, things would be more difficult for all of us, especially the children. So, I do my best to help out."[49] This fact highlights the diversity within groups of men and masculinities as men and women negotiate the varying demands of everyday situations.[50]

During my 2019 trip to Muong Muon commune, I did a survey with sixty households in Muong Ma and Muong Che villages and learned that because of the lack of work on the rubber plantations, up to 50 percent of young couples (in which both partners were under thirty-five years of age) left their children at home with their parents or relatives to find work in industrial parks in Bắc Ninh, Hải Dương, or Hưng Yên Provinces—all lowland provinces in the Red River delta. These couples only returned to see their children monthly or even every two months. The number of addicts in these two villages had also grown, including up to 35 percent of male teenagers, helping to make Muong Muon the commune with the highest rate of drug users in Sơn La Province.

Rubber plantations have not only driven land acquisition in the Northwest but have also led to transformation of gender roles and responsibility. Both women and men experienced difficulties in adaptation. At the same time, while gender stereotypes may have been reinforced in a number of cases, changes in household economic and production conditions have opened up spaces for changing gender norms in which women and men could work together in their struggle against land dispossession.

## Subject Making under State and Rubber Plantations

Upland ethnic minority people in the Northwest have not only been subjugated by the process of state formation and socialist development, but they have also been divested of their lands for the national interest through hydropower development and for development through the rubber project. Under the central government's direction, provincial authorities did whatever was needed to fit the rubber project into their province's economic priorities. Pressure from an increase in the price of latex on the international market in the early 2000s as well as from domestic investors catalyzed particular policies that increased instances of land appropriation for the rubber project and changed resource governance in the Northwest. The authorities at lower levels were pressured to create favorable conditions for domestic investors to expand their businesses. This whole process highlights the close links between the government and large companies (both state-owned and private) in pursuit of development.

The PPCs of Sơn La, Lai Châu, and Điện Biên Provinces issued their own solutions on rubber plantations. It was the province's decision that those who contributed land would also become rubber workers; local officials were left to mobilize households to contribute land. This model is not a market mechanism, operating under civil transactions; rather it was implemented at the provincial government's direction and with its intervention throughout the process of acquiring land from villagers. The responsibility for outcomes lies at the feet of the provincial governments, not just the rubber companies. Authorities allowed rubber companies to determine which trees to plant, how to market the crop, and how the original landowners would be compensated for their labor. Local authorities and state agencies did not cooperate effectively to look after local people's interests, social, economic, or physical. In terms of labor issues, authorities failed to clearly define the interests and responsibilities of farmers and the rubber companies in the various land contribution contracts. People's land rights and ownership were distorted. Even though farmers theoretically retained land-use rights, they lost the ability to control their land and decide how it will be used. As a consequence, labor issues and food insecurity will continue to be critical problems in these areas until effective solutions can be found and a consensus on the matters reached.

Rubber plantations in the Northwest region are enclosures of land that has been dispossessed of its previous users (in this case, villagers/resettlers), in turn subjecting them to new production and labor regimes. The provincial governments and large corporations have collaborated in creating a new mechanism to seize land and to control the populace. Stated differently, the state's vision of industrialization and modernization favors a kind of state-capitalist politics of possession, functioning through shareholding and labor contracts. Local authorities bound villagers to these projects by retaining the villagers' red books, a method new to Vietnam. These politics of state formation help strengthen the state's power and its sovereignty over the people. Institutional control over land and over political subjects produces and strengthens the dominion of the state and of large investors in the upland areas. Even though people, including villagers and NGO workers, consciously or unconsciously react to the project's unjustness, they have limited large-scale options to change the situation. The production of state space has altered villagers' relationships not only to land and surrounding resources but also among themselves and with the authorities. The effects of the rubber project on the division of labor at my study sites are complex and varied. Gender relations are subject to continual renegotiation. Under these new conditions, when the majority of women and men encounter similar economic hardship, the ways that they deal with problems differ. In the face of these socioeconomic changes, gender relations—traditionally relatively egalitarian, with complementary roles for women and men—have been dramatically impacted by changes in access to and control over land, by new relations of production, and by the creation of state-business alliances that control land and labor. In these processes, villagers are not passive victims of the state-capitalist project. Their agency, conditioned by their age, gender, and access to resources, plays a crucial role in their everyday life subject making, and many continue to take any opportunities they find to fight for their rights and justice.

# PART III

*Mines*

# CHAPTER 7

# Materialities and Politics of Mining

At the seventh session of the 14th National Assembly meeting in 2019, the minister of natural resources and environment highlighted: "Minerals are 'public assets' that are under the ownership of the whole people, uniformly managed by the State, tangible but limited, most not renewable, so they must be exploited, used reasonably, economically, and efficiently in serving the immediate and long-term economic development of the country."[1]

In line with this view at the national level, the dominant discourse of development in the Northwest posits minerals as an economic pillar of the region. Even though in most cases the landscape transformations from mining are enormous, potential profits can be even higher. Despite the fact that mineral extraction continues to pollute air, water, and land, as well as displace communities residing near large mines, most provincial governments in the Northwest consider mining a stable and crucial way to ensure local revenues and contribute to the state budget via taxes on resources, licensing fees, and environmental protection fees.

During the global COVID-19 pandemic that began in 2020, the government further promoted resource extraction, including mining and hydropower. An official from the Lào Cai provincial government confirmed this practice in 2021: "In the context that revenue from trade and services continues to decrease deeply owing to the impact of the global pandemic, mineral exploitation and hydropower have brought a relatively large and stable source of income to the provincial budget and contribute to the accomplishment of [the] province's economic targets as well as the state budget revenue."[2] In Lào Cai Province in 2021, for example, its tax department estimated that the province's revenue from mining activities was VNĐ 1,500 billion (approximately US$65 million), accounting for 10 percent of the province's total budget. It can be broken down as environmental protection tax, approximately VNĐ 214 billion (US$9.3 million); license fees, approximately VNĐ 370 billion (US$16.09 million); mining companies' payments into a fund for road improvements and environmental restoration, about VNĐ 119 billion (US$5.17 million); and others. In Yên Bái Province, officials have praised mining projects for their contributions to the local and state budgets as well as for creating jobs in the province. Mining was one of the most stable income sources for Yên Bái during the pandemic, as it was for Lào Cai. A representative from Yên Bái Province's Department of Natural Resources and Environment explained that "the mining projects put into operation have created jobs for local workers, [and] contributed to the state budget through taxes as well as various types of fees, including fees for environmental protection and license granting."[3] In 2020, mining projects in Yên Bái Province contributed more than VNĐ 500 billion (US$21.7 million) to the state and province budget, employing about twenty-three hundred workers. Provincial leaders understandably consider mining projects a crucial catalyst in the province, enabling industrialization and modernization. These leaders herald the industry's impact on changing Yên Bái's economic structure, specifically by expanding the industrial sector and creating conditions for other service industries to develop.[4]

This chapter focuses on mining as the third of the key contemporary territorializing development programs in Vietnam that have transformed the Northwest's landscape and its territorial subjects. While the massive expansion of rubber plantations in three provinces in the region—Sơn La, Lai Châu, and Điện Biên—responded to the world's demand for rubber and fundamentally changed local villagers' ways of life, the discoveries of iron ore in Yên Bái Province and copper in Lào Cai Province have dramatically changed local access to land and clean air and water and damaged the surrounding environment—all with the provincial and central governments' blessings as they support these mineral extraction projects. The chapter will explore how territorialization, under the name of development, associates with the production of new frontiers when mineral ores are discovered. It will examine the political economy of mining in Vietnam in general, followed by scrutinizing how disciplinary power generates "subjectified subjects" where both government officials and mine investors aim to induce the norm that mining means progress, which subdues antimining behaviors. Finally, the chapter discusses political technologies of mining in the Northwest with detailed elaboration of how copper mining in Lào Cai Province and iron ore mining in Yên Bái Province have caused significant environmental, social, and cultural damages in the mine vicinity.

## Mines as Resource Frontiers

Globally, mining has resulted in different types of accumulation by dispossession. Rasmussen and Lund argue, "Frontier spaces are replete with physical and symbolic violence . . . [where] land and resources are 'freed up' for new forms of appropriation."[5] When a mining company, private or public, discovers a valuable mineral, it works to acquire rights to mine the mineral, regardless of the impacts mining may cause to local landscapes, to people's access to the land, and to surrounding resources. Thus, "when new resources are discovered or become valuable, landscapes change and new opportunities arise; new frontiers emerge and the interest in the (re)territorialization of space becomes acute."[6] This process produces new resource territorial subjects, whose lives and livelihoods are disrupted in unprecedented ways. Rasmussen and Lund's cycle of "frontier-territorialization-frontier-territorialization" shows how the discovery of new resources—minerals in Northwest Vietnam, in this case—undoes existing social orders and subsequently creates new systems of resource control. In the Northwest, the land that local villagers have used for generations is placed, with the authorities' support, under the mining companies' control. This shift in power or control alters villagers' access to forest and rivers via deforestation and pollution. These frontier moments of creation or installation of dams, plantations, and mines continually negotiate the constitution of political authority and cannot be understood as separate processes, but rather as processes that work in sync to weaken certain forms of political power and reinforce others.[7]

Although mining takes place in all six provinces in the Northwest region, I will focus on the situation in Yên Bái and Lào Cai Provinces, the most active mining areas in the Northwest, where iron ore and copper are being extracted. In Yên Bái, private mining companies involved in iron ore extraction account for most of the extraction activity. In Lào Cai, however, copper mining is managed by a state-owned corporation, the Vietnam National Coal and Mineral Industries Holding Corporation Limited (Vinacomin). Like Electricity of Vietnam (EVN) and the Vietnam Rubber Group (VRG), Vinacomin is one of the nineteen largest state-owned corporations in Vietnam. Private mining companies in the Northwest receive licenses for smaller mines, while state-owned companies get licenses for large mines. The active involvement of private mining companies in the Northwest proves that territorialization is not necessarily reserved for the state. Other non-state institutions, especially private companies that enjoy close connections with high-ranking governmental officials, also find ways to territorialize resource control in this region. In these cases, non-state actors often "mimic state institutions and enroll state actors in making [their] territorial realization possible."[8] This situation plays out time and again in countries across the world.[9] Territorialization emerges out of new relationships between the state, extractive processes, technologies, and affected local villagers.

Mining, by its very nature, radically transforms landscapes; all extractive activities must move earth. Gavin Bridge, who has conducted extensive research on mining, highlights this impact. "A frequent entry point for considering the environmental impacts of mining . . . is to consider the physical landscape modifications that occur in the process of extracting and refining valued materials from the earth," Bridge writes.[10] Researchers estimate that the amount of earth moved for mining and excavating activities worldwide exceeds 57 billion metric tons per year, 4 billion tons more than the materials shifted by water erosion.[11] Annually in Vietnam, mining activities provide the economy with at least ninety million tons of cement limestone, seventy million cubic meters of common construction materials, nearly one hundred million cubic meters of sand, more than forty-five millions tons of coal, and over three million tons of iron ore.[12]

The impacts of mining on the environment are not confined to the mine and its vicinity. Contamination can spread via waterways and travel tens of kilometers downstream, generating secondary and tertiary contamination in rivers, groundwater, soil, and air. Mining not only transforms the local topography by altering land use and vegetation patterns, erecting structures, and creating dump sites, but also

**FIGURE 7.1.** Tailing (mining residue) pond at a copper mine in Lào Cai Province, May 2019. Photo by the author.

alters local history and forms new territorial subjects, while stirring tensions and conflicts among and between affected communities and other stakeholders.[13] As a result, environmental conflicts are often significant surrounding mining issues. Armin Scheidel and colleagues in their recent research on environmental conflicts show that among 2,743 cases documented worldwide in the EJAtlas (a global environmental justice atlas that documents and catalogs social conflicts around environmental issues), the mining sector accounts for 21 percent of cases, compared to 14 percent for water management (dams). Issues caused by mining are significantly deadlier than other types of environmental conflicts, such as fossil energy installations or dams.[14] At the global level, mining activities, very similar to hydropower dams, often are sited in remote areas where ethnic minorities or indigenous people reside—individuals whose livelihoods are resource-dependent. These people also suffer from displacement and pollution, unequal power distribution, and social inequalities.[15] The impacts here are broader than environment and health—mining has changed ethnic identity/relations and created new territorial subjects in the frontier. In the Northwest uplands, mining-induced destruction paved the way for the development of a new landscape in a very different way from the changes brought about by hydropower dams or rubber plantations, as I describe in previous chapters. Even though both state-owned and private companies can get licenses to mine, the procedures vary. So does mine size for each company. Government and state-owned companies, especially big ones like Vinacomin, consider large mines as strategic development projects for national growth. That is why state-owned companies get the right to develop large mines. Private mining companies often get licenses for smaller mines and cannot apply the discourse of national interest as justification for their projects. Policies and requirements for mines, including environmental impact assessments (EIAs), licensing, mitigation, and compensation, differ depending on a mine's size, as I will elaborate in the following sections.

## The Political Economy of Mining in Vietnam

Vietnam is a country with diverse mineral resources—more than five thousand mines extracting sixty types of minerals were active in 2018.[16] The mining industry began to take shape under French colonials in the late nineteenth century.[17] In 1955, the Democratic Republic of Vietnam took over mining operations in the north. It maintained and developed mineral exploitation and processing facilities until the American War ended in 1975. In the post–American War period, especially since Đổi Mới in 1986, the demand for minerals from Vietnam has grown rapidly, both for domestic consumption and for export.

Since the beginning of the twenty-first century, an increase in global mineral commodity prices, combined with technological advances, has put pressure on the Vietnamese government to further promote its investments in mining through its state-owned corporation, Vinacomin, as well as through private companies and foreign investment. Vinacomin claims to have conducted basic investigations and explorations, and discovered deposits, at over five thousand sites to date. It has evaluated a number of minerals of high industrial value, and estimated reserves of oil and gas (at 1.2–1.7 billion cubic meters), coal (240 billion tons), iron (2 billion tons), copper (1 million tons of metal), titanium (600 million tons of heavy minerals), bauxite (10 billion tons), zinc, lead, tin, and apatite (2 billion tons combined), rare earth (11 million tons), minerals used as construction materials (52 billion cubic meters), as well as others in smaller quantities. Most of the extracted ore is used to meet domestic demand, but a growing portion is for export (mostly to China), including copper, bauxite, titanium, and rare earth.[18] Its wealth in mineral resources and government-backed production have made Vietnam the third-largest mineral producer in Southeast Asia, after Indonesia and Malaysia.[19]

In 2020, some of the key minerals being extracted included bauxite, nickel, coal, gold, copper, iron ore, chromite, aluminum, and titanium. Mining is the third-largest contributor to the country's GDP, and the industry has a high average annual growth rate of 8.15 percent. In 2008, mining (including oil and gas) contributed 9.07 percent to the nation's GDP; five years later, in 2013, that figure increased to 11.49 percent. In 2018, mining—excluding oil and gas—contributed 5 percent of the total GDP.[20] As a result, the government considers mineral extraction a strategic sector that significantly contributes to the country's economic development. However, mining activities have posed serious challenges to sustainability and development across the country. The environmental impacts of mining activities in Vietnam include erosion, land subsidence, and loss of biodiversity, as well as soil, groundwater, and surface-water pollution caused by chemicals from ore excavating and processing. In some cases, forests in the immediate vicinity have been cut down to create tailing ponds, including for bauxite mines in the Central Highlands and Nghe An Province.[21] According to the Ministry of Agriculture and Rural Development's 2014 annual report, 11,312 hectares of forest and forestland were converted to mining that year, while there was no activity to recover mined land or reforest areas where mining had ended.[22] While there is no data on total amount of soil that mines excavated each year in Vietnam or in the Northwest, the Sin Quyen copper mine in Lào Cai alone excavated 12.5 and 10 million cubic meter in 2019 and 2020, respectively.[23] Besides damaging the environment, mining-related chemical pollution also affects the socioeconomic conditions and health of the affected people. Mining has affected ethnic minorities' livelihood security and contributes to changes that make it extremely difficult for them to continue practices tied to their ethnic identities.[24] In wilderness areas, mining can wreak havoc in or otherwise alter ecosystems and habitats, while in farming areas, it can disturb water, arable land, and grasslands, as it has done in Yên Bái, where mines flooded and washed away rice fields, polluted the water to unusability, and damaged cinnamon trees by coating them in dust. These impacts, in fact, prevent villagers from maintaining their livelihoods in sustainable ways and impede the government's development goals.

National and provincial bodies, specifically the Ministry of Natural Resources and Environment and the provincial Departments of Natural Resources and Environment, are the decision-making bodies responsible for controlling mineral extraction. Directive No. 02/CT-TTg and Decree No. 15/2012/ND-CP detail how the Mineral Law of 2010 is implemented in practical terms. The highlight of the Mineral Law of 2010 is the financial policy on minerals. The law specifically proposed a new framework for the management of minerals and the mining business to adapt to a socialist-oriented market mechanism. Authorities implemented regulations on granting mining rights for the first time since 2014. The Adjusted Mineral Law 2018 further added regulations on mineral planning and requirements for environmental protection in mining.[25] By the end of 2020, the total revenues earned, from 2014 to 2020, from granting mining rights exceeded VNĐ 52,000 billion (approximately US$24 million): more than VNĐ 37,000 billion was funneled to the central government's licensing authority, and VNĐ 15,000 billion found its way to local authorities.[26]

The Adjusted Power Development Plan 7 and the Vietnam Mining Development Strategy have set out the following objectives to be achieved between 2016 and 2030: (1) developing a sustainable national energy and mining industry; (2) diversifying and securing energy and resource supplies; (3) making refinery and downstream processing of minerals mandatory; and (4) addressing, in some fashion, political and environmental pressures to ensure economic returns to the nation.

According to Article 1 of the Vietnam Mineral Resources Strategy up to 2020—aiming to achieve its goals by 2030—minerals, as nonrenewable resources, must be "managed, protected, excavated, and used rationally, economically, and efficiently" to meet the requirements of Vietnam's industrialization and modernization.[27] Since its issuance, the Mineral Law and mineral resources strategy have helped to set a direction for sustainable mining. Issues such as environmental protection, improvement, and restoration after mineral extraction have received increased attention from involved actors. As a leader from Vietnam's General Department of Geology and Minerals affirmed in 2021, "With more than 76 years of establishment and development of the sector, the legal document system on minerals management and extraction has basically been completed, creating [an] important legal corridor to improve the effectiveness and efficiency of state management of minerals. And at the same time, the law and legal documents promote the sustainable development of the mining and mineral processing industry, environmental protection, and national security protection."[28]

Nevertheless, the concept of responsible mining has not seemed to gain much traction or attention in Vietnam.[29] Indeed, a significant gap stands between environmental policy adoption at the national level and its implementation at the provincial, district, and commune levels, especially when it concerns responses to environmental incidents or stakeholder involvement and participation.[30]

In order to initiate a mining project in Vietnam, a company must obtain two different licenses—one for exploration and a second for mining, including mineral processing.[31] The Communist Party committees and the Provincial People's Committees (PPC) issue licenses to explore and mine minerals for construction, while the Ministry of Natural Resources and Environment (MONRE) authorizes exploration of all other types of minerals. Mining licenses are granted through frameworks that regulate the rights and obligations of the state and the companies. However, research by the Vietnam Chamber of Commerce and Industry and the Consultancy on Development show that progress in achieving good mining practices in Vietnam has been slow, owing to insufficient and inconsistent implementation of the legal framework by mining companies.[32]

To receive approval to undertake mining activities, the mineral and environmental protection laws require companies to undertake and submit the results of an environmental impact assessment (EIA) or an environmental protection plan (EPP), depending on the size of the project. The EIA content should allow for the identification and assessment of all potential environmental impacts and risks associated with the proposed mining process. MONRE's appraisal department and the PPC assess and approve these reports. Companies must also develop an environmental rehabilitation plan to leave the mining site in a well-organized state after mining ends, and to prevent and deal with emergencies. These plans (EIAs and EPPs) should safeguard the rights of local people living in proposed mining areas, including compensation in case of displacement, investment plan development for localities, and the prioritization of local employment.[33] In practice, however, many companies do not follow these plans as required, leading to serious adverse impacts on local communities and the environment, such as loss of livelihoods, displacement, landslides, deforestation, and land, air, and water pollution. In practice, pre-mine institutional order has been replaced. Villagers lose their farming land to mining companies. Their access to forest and water is compromised by deforestation and water pollution.[34]

According to MONRE's 2014 statistics, about three thousand organizations and individuals nationwide conducted mineral exploration and exploitation under 4,320 licenses. MONRE granted 559 licenses that year.[35] Recent 2018 data provided by Duane Morris LLP shows more than fifteen hundred registered mining companies in Vietnam: about 55 percent are state-owned, 36 percent are owned by private Vietnamese companies, and 9 percent are foreign enterprises.[36]

At the national level, Vinacomin dominates Vietnam's mining industry. Established in 1995 as a mineral corporation under Decision No. 1118/QD-TCCBDT of the Heavy Industry Ministry (today's Ministry of Industry and Trade), Vinacomin officially took its current name and began operations as a joint-stock company on October 6, 2015.[37] In 2018, Vinacomin's total revenues were VNĐ 103,081 billion (approximately US$4.5 billion).[38] However, shortcomings afflicted Vinacomin's operations in particular, and the mining sector of Vietnam more generally, including the use of obsolete technologies, lack of mechanization, inadequate infrastructure, a large workforce with low productivity, excessive energy consumption, numerous safety deficiencies, and environmental pollution and related social consequences. In 2016, Vinacomin set priorities on technological innovation and proposed various approaches to environmental problems, including pollution mitigation, reforestation, and generally restoring the land to the conditions before the mine.[39] Nevertheless, the problems largely remain, and Vinacomin's progress at setting and implementing policies to mitigate adverse impacts and set good practices for other companies to follow seems to be glacial. According to my interviewees, in many cases mining companies barely meet targets in reforesting old mining sites after closing the mines, fail to effectively deal with pollution (for example, sprinkler trucks are not enough to help mitigate dust), do not resolve impacts from mine explosions to nearby villagers' houses, and rarely provide adequate compensation for affected villagers. The Mineral Law, the Law on Environmental Protection, and the Mining Development Strategy, while they created legal frameworks for mining development in Vietnam, failed to ensure sustainable mining. Mining as a territorializing development project continues to significantly impact the environment and frontier subjects.

## Power and Silence

"Can you please not call in the media or post anything about the mining situation online?" After I had left Yen Be district of Yên Bái Province in August 2018, I received this request from a friend of a friend who worked for the province's police department. He continued, in reference to the research I was conducting on mining in the province: "I've heard that there were a lot of problems down there, especially after the flood two weeks ago. The company will find ways to solve them, but they need time. Please don't make it messier." The mining company he was referring to was the Ngoc Thanh Company, one of the seven private iron ore mining and processing companies located in Thinh Tam commune. When I returned to the area in early May 2019, I learned that the company's support for flood-affected villagers had so far been minimal. Some did receive nominal compensation for the losses incurred in 2018, but villagers suffered from new problems that the Tan Tien mining company had caused; it not only had dumped mud from its mining activities into the Ngoi Lau stream, but conducted mining activities beyond its permitted area and continued operating after its license had expired. A commune chairman, who is a Dao (Yao) person, told me,

> Actually, this will need a state management agency at a high level involved, and we really need government officials who care. We at the commune level are very concerned and feel that the situation is very urgent. All we could do was to send requests to higher levels, but we didn't have much progress yet. I have a thought that if needed, I would be advising villagers to sue the company in the provincial court. Otherwise, things may never change. You know, people here are already very vulnerable and marginalized. They have nothing. Their lives depend entirely on farming, and now their fields are gone. What are they going to eat? To tell you the truth, villagers brought petitions to us, we had to take them. But we at the commune level also had to give up, as we did not know how to solve the problem as we did not have a budget for it.[40]

It is true that villagers in the Northwest need government officials who not only care about their lives and about the environment but are also keen about finding solutions to problems instead of hiding them. The commune chairman's point reminds me of my trip to Lào Cai Province earlier that year. When sending my request to provincial officials for permission to conduct research in Lào Cai, I expressed the need to learn more about the impacts of development projects on water resources in the province. The response I received upon arriving at the PPC office to collect my referral document was surprising. "We here in Lào Cai don't have any problem with water. Everything is fine. I don't understand why you need to do research on our water." He refused to give me the document. Unable to convince him otherwise, I left. He called me an hour later and said: "Fine. You can come back to get the paper." I collected the document and immediately traveled to Ty Ba district to apply for permission to conduct research in Tu Lan commune, where the Sin Quyen copper mine is located. Similar problems occurred every time I came back to these two provinces to conduct research on mining. Obtaining data from the provinces' environmental monitoring centers has often been very difficult, as are interviews with provincial and district authorities. Even at the commune level, it is not easy to find officials willing to express what they really think about certain situations in their locales. For example, the chairman of Tam Luong commune, a neighboring commune of Thanh Tam commune, avoided my questions and did not want to speak about the situation in his commune. Foucault's "disciplinary power" clearly applied in this case. The notion of progressive development generates "subjectified subjects," in which everyone is under the pressure of being watched by the authorities, and that prevents free and open expression. As mining means progress, anti-mining is morally wrong, and people are not supposed to speak against progress. In formal meetings, most government officials appear to always support the idea that all development projects are important for the country's economic growth, though in informal conversations outside their offices, some may express personal reservations. For example, one official shared with me over lunch one day, "If we express our opinions against government's development plans, it doesn't matter if they are national or provincial plans, we may lose our position. So, better always show that you're supportive of governmental development plans, even when you find them problematic or unreasonable, like mining or rubber plantations."[41]

Thus, to promote development projects, the government does not use force or coercion to obtain compliance but instead relies on everyday institutions (like workplaces or community meetings) and interactions (formal and informal among colleagues or community members) to induce individuals to govern their own behavior. State power, even if unseen, informs consent and fosters certain conduct.[42] Strangely, the only time that breaching this reluctance to speak openly seemed a bit easier for officials and other workers was after I broke my ankle in the middle of my fieldwork in Ty Ba and had to continue my work in a cast. Wherever I went, people would start our conversation with a comment on my broken ankle, which seemed to relax them, and we could talk easily about various issues that they normally may not have been comfortable discussing, including the politics surrounding the mines, rumors about corruption, or pressures they felt in following directions from higher authorities and, at the same time, coping with problems that affected communities face.

## Political Technologies of Mining in the Northwest

According to Vinacomin's analysis, the Northwest region has numerous large-scale mineral deposits. Many of these have not been explored or assessed to identify their true size or the value of their reserves, making it hard for the corporation to develop a plan for concentrated mineral processing based on raw material sources.[43] Development of mining in the Northwest therefore became a priority of both central and provincial governments in the 2010s. In 2013, the Department of Natural Resources and Environment (DONRE) of the northwestern provinces granted 1,518 licenses for mineral exploration and exploitation for companies that had submitted proposals. MONRE also granted 118 licenses under its authority. By 2020, both entities had granted more than two hundred additional licenses.[44]

Since national mining experts and managers consider mineral resources limited assets, they have emphasized the importance of having timely and relevant solutions to strengthen state management of minerals to ensure that minerals will be used and exploited effectively. The central government suggested to Northwest provincial authorities that they not grant permissions for investments in small and fragmented projects. Another requirement is the need for all Northwest provinces with mineral reserves to coordinate with MONRE in zoning scattered mineral areas and national resource reserve areas to guide development for each area. Provinces are also required to collaborate to build concentrated, large-scale, mineral-processing industrial parks with advanced technologies in order to ensure investment efficiency and production capacity.[45]

At the provincial level, under pressure from both the central government and mining-affected people, the provincial DONRE has been working to improve its mining policies over the past few years. For example, the DONRE of Lào Cai, Yên Bái, and Sơn La have been advising their

Provincial People's Committees to issue directives on strengthening mining management, including licensing and monitoring pollution. Accordingly, each division and people's committee at every level (province, district, and commune) now takes a role in the management of minerals in its locale.[46] The DONREs also advised the PPCs to issue plans to protect unexploited minerals, and to require coordination in mineral management with neighboring provinces. During my trip to Lào Cai in 2018, I learned that since there are many large mining sites in the province, DONRE has also coordinated with the provincial Department of Finance, the Department of Industry and Trade, and the Tax Department to regularly review the actual selling prices on the market to enable the Lào Cai PPC to change tax policies and adjust resource taxes accordingly to help the provincial government avoid unnecessary tax losses. In addition, the authorities have been disseminating propaganda and educational materials about the law on minerals to a variety of subjects—including representatives of state agencies, businesspeople, community members, and those who live where minerals are mined—aimed at increasing awareness of the importance of mineral resources and of the mining industry.

To further promote mineral extraction in the Northwest as a tool to serve the region's economic growth and in support of exports, the prime minister approved Decision No. 1266/QD-TTg (August 24, 2017) on the "overall survey of mineral resources and finalizing the geological map of ratio 1:50,000 of the northwest region in the service of sustainable socioeconomic development planning." The prime minister has tasked MONRE with this project, which has five specific objectives: (1) to complete geological mapping—a mineral survey at 1:50,000 scale; (2) to clarify the potential capacity of mineral reserves and other geological resources; (3) to delineate geological structures to assess deep hidden minerals and identify geological formations containing deep hidden ores; (4) to summarize, measure, and draw geological and mineral maps at a scale of 1:250,000 for the Northwest region in general, and for each province; and (5) to provide training for geological technicians through the project's implementation, with the participation of domestic and foreign geological scientists, and build on-staff capacity for geological investigation, assessment of mineral potential, sample analysis, and information technology application.[47] In July 2019, Tran Quy Kien, a MONRE vice minister, led a briefing to report results of the above plan after its first eighteen months of implementation. Once again, the meeting highlighted the importance of constructing geological and mineral maps as a foundation to boost the Northwest region's mining industry.[48]

Even though there are different types of minerals scattered across the provinces in the Northwest, mining has significantly contributed to only two provinces' economic growth—Lào Cai (over thirty-five different types of minerals) and Yên Bái (seventeen different types of minerals). By 2021, Lào Cai had about 150 active valuable mines with high-quality and large reserves, including apatite, iron, copper, gold, rare earth, and graphite, among others—all possible to be extracted on an industrial scale. In particular, three types of ores—apatite, copper, and iron—are being mined on a large scale, reaching tens of millions of tons of ore annually. According to a leader of the tax department of Lào Cai Province, enterprises operating in the field of mining and mineral processing in the province play a key role in the province's economic development, accounting for 20 to 30 percent of the province's annual contribution to the state budget. As of October 2021, the tax department of Lào Cai had collected revenues amounting to about VNĐ 4,787 billion; for Yên Bái, the revenues were VNĐ 130.1 billion.[49]

While mining in these provinces has been profitable, it has also caught the public's attention because of its impacts on local people's lives and livelihoods, such as displacement, pollution, or land loss, and associated stresses. Over the last ten years, more and more media outlets, including newspapers and national television channels, have been covering these problems.[50] But government officials have different opinions on these matters. At the district and commune levels, it is not very difficult for me to find officials who sympathize with affected villagers. But at the provincial level, officials often do not dare to say things that may cause them trouble. When I described my research to a provincial official in Lào Cai and asked about the impacts of mining activities on local people and the environment, he said,

> There are always tradeoffs in development. That's a dilemma we're in. Without budget coming from activities such as mining and hydropower, how can we develop? Where will we get money to improve our roads, build bridges, not talking about schools, hospitals, and other social programs? Mining companies have also created thousands of jobs. Affected people got compensation for their land loss. That's good enough. You know, you can't have everything. If we want to develop, we will have to sacrifice certain things. We need to educate people about the importance of mining so they'll understand.[51]

This discursive framing insists development is still much needed in the Northwest region, and mining plays a key role in this framework.

Vimico, the Sin Quyen–Lào Cai Copper Mining Company under Vinacomin, has created a website for the Sin Quyen copper mine that highlights its role in creating jobs and training local villagers to become miners, as well as its contributions to social programs in the area where the mine is located. Through claims of job creation, compensation measures, training, education, and policy improvement, the government and mining companies try different territorial governance tactics and create new imaginaries and territorial subjects to legitimize mining development in the Northwest. Unfortunately, not all villagers could or wanted to become miners. While the mine produced new subjects who could no longer live by farming and in forests as they used to, most of them became migrant workers by necessity, as their land was polluted, and their forest was degraded.

Unlike those affected by hydropower and rubber plantations, however, in which officials persuaded villagers to move or contribute their land, either for the "national interest" or for future "economic benefits" of holding shares in rubber companies, mining-impacted villagers were not aware of these adverse impacts until they experienced them. Before mining began, companies provided no community meetings to inform locals or win consent for mining in Lào Cai or Yên Bái. A villager in Yên Bái said, "At first, we knew nothing about the mines. There were only rumors. And then we have a few enterprises operating at the same time: extracting and processing businesses. Everything changed."[52] While mines dispossessed people and altered the way they lived and interacted with the surrounding environment, mine developers did not consult with affected people before they started their projects, which made it more difficult for people to reorganize their lives to accommodate mining, and so further marginalized them.

### Copper Mining in Ty Ba District, Lào Cai Province

On September 17, 2003, the Mineral Corporation, a unit under Vinacomin, launched the Sin Quyen copper mining complex project—the biggest nonferrous-metal project in Vietnam at that time. The project covers 830 hectares, stretching across Minh Ba and Tu Lan communes of Ty Ba district in Lào Cai Province. To make way for the project, hundreds of households in these two communes had to give up their land and move to resettlement sites. The mining capacity of the Sin Quyen mine ranges from 1.1 to 1.2 million tons of raw ore per year. The mine annually produces 47,000 tons of copper concentrate with 24 percent copper, and 75,000 tons of iron ore with 64 percent iron. The ore deposits were discovered in 1961 by Geological Delegation No. 5, but a detailed exploration only began in 1969, and it took more than four years for the group to complete its initial report on the site. Further detailed exploration continued from 1976 to 1982. To geologists involved in this process, the mine was the proud result of many years of research, collaboration, prospecting, and exploration. The National Mineral Assessment Committee finally approved a comprehensive report on the mine site that certified there were seventeen ore bodies with 53,505,759 tons of ore reserves in the Sin Quyen copper mine, with average content of copper of about 1.01 percent, yielding 521,426 tons of copper metal.[53]

With a domestic investment of nearly VNĐ 1,300 billion (US$867 million), the project includes a copper mine and smelting factory. In 2013, Vietnam Eximbank provided VNĐ 1,500 billion (US$800 million in 2013) for Vinacomin to invest in a mine expansion in terms of excavation area and capacity, which was subsequently increased more than twofold.[54] The company planned to implement this extension project in twenty years, starting April 1, 2013, but the province issued the appraisal on October 31, 2022, nine years after its commencement.[55] Vinacomin was very proud of its work. Its representatives boast that the complex meant that they had a "closed" mining production line, one that managed the entire process from ore sorting to copper smelting, serving the cause of the country's industrialization and modernization. Since then, copper mining has accelerated in this area, due mainly to Sin Quyen Copper Mining Branch activity.

The Sin Quyen Copper Mining Branch was established on July 1, 2005—it was formerly known as the Lào Cai Copper Joint Venture Enterprise, and then the Sin Quyen Copper Mining Enterprise–Lào Cai. On August 1, 2006, it became a unit under Vinacomin, renamed as the Sin Quyen-Lào Cai Copper Mining Company. On October 15, 2015, when Vinacomin began operations as a joint-stock company, Sin Quyen-Lào Cai Copper Mining Company became a branch of the corporation, with the full name of Sin Quyen Copper Mining Branch, Lào Cai (Vimico). Vimico tasked its 773 employees with exploring, excavating, smelting, and refining copper ore and other minerals. The branch has contributed about VNĐ 350 billion (US$15.6 million) annually to the state's coffers. In the second quarter of 2018, the branch doubled its production capacity to 2.5 million tons of raw ore per year and opened Mineral Sorting Plant No. 2. On May 19, 2019, on the occasion of Ho Chi

Minh's birthday, Vimico celebrated its first batch of copper ore from the Vi Kẽm mine (capacity of 350,000 tons of ore per year). The construction of two more ore transportation tunnels began in early 2020. After the completion of Mineral Sorting Plant No. 2 and the extraction of copper from the Vi Kẽm mine, the corporation expects to contribute about VNĐ 650 billion (almost US$30 million) to the state while raking in over VNĐ 2,000 billion (US$900 million) in revenue with its workforce of fourteen hundred.[56] Vimico claims that its projects have created a breakthrough for Vietnam's nonferrous-metal industry by meeting one-third of the domestic production demand and reducing the need to import copper metal, thereby saving the government over US$40 million per year. It also lauds itself for its contribution to the socioeconomic development of Lào Cai, a Northwest border province. For Vimico, economic development plays a vital role in the region's development and modernization.[57] Vimico's website claims that "every year the company pays special attention to supporting activities of the province, ranging from building infrastructure for socioeconomic development, to promoting local culture and education. This attention has been realized in terms of constructing inter-village roads, clean water systems, schools, medical clinics, public service houses, and cultural houses for some communes in the province. We also provide financial support for charity activities, sports and art for local agencies and mass organizations."[58] With its contributions to the local and national economy, the company enjoys strong support from central and provincial governments. While the Sin Quyen mine's expansion has caused a wide range of environmental problems and had a significant impact on local lives and livelihoods, triggering pollution, land loss, and job loss, there was no separate EIA finalized for either the expansion or the ore transportation tunnel project before their commencement.[59] Vimico, as a state-owned company, faced no penalties for this violation of law.

Mining in Lào Cai has polluted the environment, reduced the area of arable land, and threatened local people's lives with thousands of unsafe mine explosions. PanNature is one of the few NGOs that has conducted a study of mining in Vietnam. Its research confirms that individuals resettled as a result of mining activities face extreme difficulties, including a lack of farmland and access to clean, potable water, as well as exposure to severe air and noise pollution.[60] Media outlets such as VietnamPlus or Nong Nghiep highlight that villagers who live near mining sites have suffered on a daily basis as dozens of ore-bearing trucks stir up dust and emit exhaust, and the mines continue to trigger explosions that one villager likened to lightning. These problems affect not only the villagers near the mine but those who reside along the roads on which mining trucks travel. Every day ore trucks drive by, raising dust. Villagers close all the doors in the house to cope. On many days, dust in the house impairs residents' breathing. Even worse, at around 3 p.m. every few days, the mines conduct controlled explosions, shaking nearby houses.[61] A villager who lived next to Sin Quyen mine told me that villagers had repeatedly appealed and sent petitions to the authorities and the mining company, but nothing changed. When I asked about the problem, a representative of the Lào Cai DONRE said that enterprises in the province had invested in sprinkler trucks to wet the road in order to reduce dust pollution. This was far from sufficient, and according to local residents, there is still excessive dust on the road to the sorting factories. Local authorities have also admitted that mining produced a huge amount of dust, a source of environmental pollution. Ore transportation activities also damage the roadway surfaces. Some mines flooded rice fields and polluted people's water sources. Unfortunately, the ways in which authorities and the company have responded to villagers' complaints have been ineffective and unhelpful,

FIGURE 7.2.   Wastewater from the mine near Mrs. Dang's house, May 2019. Photo by the author.

according to those affected. According to my interviewees, the company was very slow in responding to the villagers' requests, and most of the time it ended up not solving the problems. The territorial expansion of mining has continued. The opening of a new mine and the construction of necessary facilities, including temporary containment reservoirs, have expanded the mine's territorial footprint.[62] While many accepted the situation without much resistance, many others fought by all means possible with hope that the authorities would listen to them and pressure mining companies to mitigate impacts, as I will elaborate further in the next chapter.

### Iron Ore Mining in Yen Be District of Yên Bái Province

"You know, our minerals are a curse." I was interviewing a man of Dao ethnicity in Thinh Tam commune, Yen Be district, in Yên Bái Province in May 2019. He continued: "Because of the iron ore mining here, we now have lost our livelihoods. Our cinnamon trees stopped growing. Our rice fields have been buried under mud. We have no water to grow anything. We have become so poor now."[63]

According to the province's Department of Industry and Trade, Yên Bái's minerals are diverse in type, but most of the deposits are small and scattered; the level of geological investigation is rough and uncertain, especially for iron ore minerals. Private companies carry out most of the mining activities in the province. According to the province's planning document on extraction, processing, and use of iron, copper, gold, lead-zinc, and other minerals in Yên Bái Province in the 2011–2015 period—a document approved in 2010 and projecting activity to 2020—iron ore reserves were estimated at two hundred million tons. Iron ore mined in Yên Bái is mostly used to meet domestic demand.[64]

MONRE and Yên Bái provincial officials have approved a plan licensing iron ore mines. As of March 2015, 121 mining licenses were granted to ninety enterprises for activities in the province, including 34 licenses that MONRE granted and 87 that the PPC issued. Most of this iron extraction in the province relies on open-pit, semi-mechanized construction methods—a rudimentary mining technology known to expose eight to ten times more waste material to the environment than underground mining, with substantial damaging effects on soil, air, water, and living beings near the mining area.[65] In Yên Bái, a handful of companies—including the Tan Tien Son Company, the Hoang Minh Anh Joint-Stock Company, the Minh Duc Mining Joint-Stock Company, the Ha Quang Joint-Stock Company, the Northwest Mining Investment Joint-Stock Company, and the Ngoc Thanh Mining Company—have completed the construction of refined ore sorting plants within mine sites.[66] There are also some companies investing in iron ore processing as shown in table 7.1. Unfortunately, since many companies operate in the same areas at the same time, it is difficult for local communities and authorities to identify the responsible company if pollution, such as dust covering cinnamon trees or river contamination, occurs.

In addition to licensed mining activity, illegal mining activities are well documented in Yên Bái. The biggest culprits appear to be companies with expired mining licenses that continue to operate without permits. According to an official report from the province, over the last five years, Yên Bái Province's responsible offices, in collaboration with environment police, worked together to stop many infractions. Rumors persist, however, that these unlicensed miners bribe local government officials and get away with their illegal acts.[67]

To help boost the mining sector's development, the Yên Bái PPC has since the early 2000s issued a number of policies supporting mining planning and development.[68] In 2013, with the aim of mitigating problems that mining and other industrial activities inflict on local water resources, the PPC issued a decision on planning, extracting, and using water resources into 2020–2030.[69] The decision highlights that (1) 100 percent of industrial complexes must have waste treatment systems that meet national environmental standards. and (2) for watershed

Table 7.1   Companies investing in post–mining iron ore processing in Yên Bái Province (by 2019)

| COMPANIES | CAPACITY (TONS/YEAR) | INVESTMENT (BILLIONS VNĐ) |
|---|---|---|
| Cuu Long Yên Bái Steel Joint-Stock Company | 200,000 | 597 |
| Development Company No. 1—one-member limited company | 100,000 | 600 |
| Hoa Yen Joint-Stock Company | 100,000 | 61 |
| Ha Quang Joint-Stock Company | 150,000 | 31 |
| Hung Phat Joint-Stock Company | 18,000 | 35.8 |
| Thuan Thong Dat Mining and Commerce Joint-Stock Company | 250,000 | 55.8 |
| Hung Thang Company | 150,000 | 70.3 |
| Hoa Yen Mining Company | 500,000 | 194 |
| Yen Bai Steel Join-Stock Company | 60,000 | 55.3 |

Source: Sở Kế Hoạch và Đầu Tư Yên Bái 2019.

areas, 100 percent of mines, mineral exploitation, tourism, and services must have waste and wastewater treatment areas and protection infrastructures as prescribed in their EIAs.

As in the Tu Lan and Minh Ba communes of the Ty Ba district in Lào Cai Province, villagers in the Thinh Tam and Hung Tam communes in the Yen Be district of Yên Bái Province have suffered water, noise, and air pollution and have lost their farmland. As mentioned above, in 2018, mud from a tailing pond that belonged to the Ngoc Thanh Mining Company buried villagers' paddy rice fields. During my trip to the area in 2019, I learned that this incident was not unique. Heavy rains caused the burial of fishponds and rice fields belonging to families living near the Minh Duc iron ore refining factory. Villagers no longer grow anything on the land. One man said, "The iron ore refining factory of the Minh Duc Mining Joint-Stock Company did not do their job in containing their waste. Rock and dirt overflowed and caused much damage to us."[70] His family's compensation from the company for their rice fields and fishponds was limited to the monsoon paddy rice crop when the field was first damaged but did not compensate for spring crop losses or for damage to the land itself, since they no longer grow paddy rice on this land. Another man complained, "My family moved here, [and] for forty years, our rice fields and fishponds had never been flooded, no matter how heavy the rains were. Only when the Minh Duc Company came to exploit the ore, they excavated the dirt and made a massive mess of land and rock drift, and now their dirt buried the whole rice field."[71] All the villagers told me that their water source was exhausted since the mine began its operations. Many of their wells were polluted and unusable. In response to villagers' complaints, the Minh Duc Company bought rice fields that were buried by rocks and mud after the floods. Most of these areas were then abandoned. A few households did not agree to sell their land to the company and instead asked the company to restore the rice fields and fishponds to their previous state. In summer 2020, two years after the mud spillage, they were still awaiting a response.

Central and provincial governments regard mining in the Northwest as a starting point for a series of economic and social changes that, for them, constitute development, much the same way they had regarded hydropower and rubber plantations. Over the last three decades, the mobilization of mineral wealth has been a steady theme of development policy for Vietnam in general and the Northwest in particular. In this view, mineral extraction and processing precede industrialization and unlock the region's buried treasure.[72]

The chapter reveals that, enabled by a wide range of political technologies, forms of dispossession vary from place to place, project to project. For mining in the Northwest, these forms vary depending on both the mines' sizes and private or public structure of the company. The ways mining companies work with affected communities also differ, whether it comes to communicating with affected people, to implementing compensation or responding to local requests, to collaborating with local authorities in solving problems, and so on. While the motto of national interest has not been used in the same way as it has with hydropower dams, officials have employed economic development catchphrases. Claims of job creation and local infrastructure improvements were used to justify mines. Meanwhile, regular improvement of legal policies on environmental protections associated with mining activities has allowed the government at all levels to show willingness to more effectively deal with the negative impacts of mining. Mining activities cause air, water, and land pollution, fundamentally altering access to livelihood-encouraging resources, leading to unsustainable intensification of land use, increasing livelihood insecurity, and differentiating local communities, as I describe in the next chapter. Depending on the context, authorities and/or powerful developers have set up institutional orders in response to a new type of resource commodification, which can sometimes either undermine or erase the old orders completely, or take them apart and reorganize or reinvent them.[73] At the same time, in these processes of reorganizing institutional orders, the mechanisms of truth and power and people's agency bring about new resource territorial subjects who are further marginalized in their homeland.

# CHAPTER 8

# Surviving the Mines, and the Everyday Politics of Marginalization

I was in Ty Ba district of Lào Cai Province in May 2019. A local guide was telling me stories about villagers digging trenches across a road, which was the main route for truck convoys carrying minerals from the mine to the nearby processing factory. He was laughing. "Oh, you know, these mining companies, they think they can just do anything here because they got their license. Look at the road. The road was new and got destroyed in a very short time because of these trucks. Some may argue that the money to build this road came from mining taxes. So what? The trucks carry heavy ores, and with the intensity they run every day, no road can last. And see the dust? Of course, to a certain point, people have to react."

When I asked him if he thought the situation would be improved anytime soon, he shook his head and simply answered with a question: "How?" He was right: How?

As the mine continues to expand, it is hard to see opportunities for improvement. One year later, in May 2020, villagers in Minh Ba commune, Ty Ba district, were fighting hard again, this time not against the trucks causing dust and destroying the road, but to prevent different trucks from the Sin Quyen copper mine from dumping rocks and dirt in their fields. A mere five hundred meters away from the site is a discharge tunnel for the Sin Quyen Mineral Sorting Plant No. 2, from which flowed toxic waste that polluted the commune's pond. The village's chickens and ducks that drank the water all died, and villagers dared not use it. They complained to the local authorities, and the mining company finally filled the pond with rocks and dirt. The company truckers' carelessness led to rocks and dirt also being dumped on the rice field adjacent to the contaminated pond. The rumor was that the Sin Quyen Copper Mining Branch was planning to build a structure on that land. As truck after truck filed through, the pile of rocks and dirt grew, and the air became increasingly polluted with dust and exhaust fumes. The villagers decided to fight back to stop this rock dumping, this "development." Their everyday resistance took many forms—from sending petitions to the authorities, working with media, to chasing away the trucks and even threatening the drivers. While many villagers were fighting against the mine, or migrating away to find work, others enjoyed new employment opportunities that the mine brought. Together these trends have amplified dynamics that shape and reshape landscape production as well as resource territorial subjects. In this chapter, I examine the politics of the livelihood dispossession, differentiation, and environmental degradation in the Northwest caused by mining. The chapter reveals how people's agency, conditioned by their age, gender, ethnicity, and access to resources, plays a key role in their everyday politics in responding to changes.

## Mining, Water, and Landscapes of Livelihoods

In mineral extraction activities, waste outputs vary from mine to mine as a function of the range of mineral substances extracted from the earth and the diversity of the environment in which extraction takes place. The most important characteristic of metal mining, however, is the process by which a relatively small amount of a valued substance is isolated from a much larger mass of less valuable material.[1] Segregating the valued component occurs through a series of steps, each producing a separate waste stream. According to Douglas and Lawson, in general, 3,138 million metric tons (MMT) of iron ore material yield only 604 MMT of usable iron ore. The net production is even lower for copper—4,190 MMT copper ore material results in only 9.3 MMT of usable copper ore.[2] Thus, huge amounts of waste will be disposed of into the local environment, which causes significant problems for local socioecological systems and livelihoods. And waste volume is often only part of the problem. Pollution caused by chemical reactions from mineral processing or by a material simply being exposed to air, as well as the accumulation of contaminants, further harms humans, animals, and the surrounding environment.[3]

Mining adversely impacts local livelihoods, primarily through its effects on land and water resources. Local communities have access to land and water that serve as livelihood assets, reserves for future use, items of consumption, and sources of cultural identity.[4] In his research on the impacts of mining on local water and livelihoods on the Bolivian Altiplano, Perreault highlights that one of the fundamental conflicts between the agricultural and mining economies lies in their dependence on water. Both are water-intensive activities and therefore highly sensitive to water availability.[5]

Mining activities in Northwest Vietnam have increased the risks and vulnerabilities of marginalized communities and may also deprive local villagers of the opportunity for a sustainable livelihood. In Thinh Tam commune alone, there are seven iron ore mining and processing factories. Three villages—Luong Tam, Thien Tam, and Mon Tam—have borne the brunt of this industry in the area, with three of these factories on their land. In Thien Tam village, for example, 90 percent of the population is Dao (Yao) ethnic minority people, 7 percent is Tày, and 3 percent is Kim.[6] Their livelihoods have long depended on cinnamon trees and paddy rice cultivation. The quality of their cinnamon is well-known in Vietnam. Mr. Trieu, a villager in Thien Tam village, told me about his situation:

> My family used to have three *sào* [1 *sào* = 360 square meters] of two-crop paddy rice land and three hectares of cinnamon trees. We also did cattle grazing in the community land. We never had to worry about food. But now we don't have water to grow two rice crops per year anymore. No more cattle either, because the factory was built on the grazing land. They said it was barren land and did not belong to anyone. It was the commune's land. Our cinnamon trees have stopped sprouting new leaves because the trees have been covered with dust. That made our income from cinnamon very marginal. Just about VNĐ 1–2 million [US$44–88]. Much lower than what we had before. Many of us are in hunger, especially the ones whose fields were buried in mud from the iron ore mining and processing.[7]

According to Thien Tam village's headman, in this village alone, five hectares of paddy rice that belong to forty-four households were flooded by waste from the Ngoc Thanh Mining Company's tailing pond. Another 19.5 hectares of two-crop paddy rice have no water for rice production because mining has contaminated the Ngoi Lau stream (also known as the Thien stream in the commune), the main surface water source for the rice, but now unusable. As Mr. Trieu recalled, when the villagers complained and pressured the company, it took months before they received compensation for only one lost crop—VNĐ 1 million (US$45) per *sào* (as they estimated, 1 *sào* could produce 0.2 tons of rice, on average valued at US$45)—but they were never compensated for the loss of the land's fertility resulting from contamination.

Mining activities have fundamentally altered the spatial availability of livelihood resource bases, leading to unsustainable intensification of farming and increasing livelihood insecurity. Resource scarcity may also trigger conflicts within otherwise peaceful communities. My 2019 trip to Luong Thinh commune revealed that households in the three affected villages were struggling to maintain their farming activities. According to its headman, Thien Tam village had 240 households in June 2019, 44 of which became much poorer because of land and livelihood loss. Followed by the headman, I walked across Thien stream to visit Mr. Trieu's cinnamon trees. My feet were engulfed in a thick layer of yellowish mud as soon as I stepped in the stream. The headman explained that it was the result of iron ore mining and processing, and my skin might become itchy and form a rash. "You see, with this type of water, how would our villagers be able to grow anything? We don't have water for our crops. Villagers are fighting over water." He continued:

> Our village used to be living in peace. There was never a fight in the village. But not anymore. At the beginning of this crop [of rice and other subsidiary crops], water was a very big thing. Two families were in a serious fight, as one family whose field is closer to the water source had released a lot of water to their field, [while] the family whose field is farther away from the water had very little for their field. The latter family was very angry, and they fought. First verbally, and then physically. It was awful. The commune's police had to come to calm them down. They were very close neighbors before. It was very sad.[8]

On the other side of the stream, the cinnamon trees looked very sad, as a thick dust covered their leaves. No young leaves could be seen. Two women carrying a cinnamon tree walked by, and I asked them why they had cut down the tree, as it seemed to be young. The older woman, the mother, said: "Well, we had no choice but to cut it because it almost died. The iron ore dust is killing everything here." Her seventeen-year-old daughter-in-law nodded and added, "If you walked along the stream, you'd see our paddy rice fields now abandoned. There is no way to grow anything, as both the soil and water have been contaminated." I asked the headman if the villagers had any form of recourse. He shook his head sadly: "We did make a lot of complaints to the commune, to the district, and to the companies. It took a very long time without any proper responses. Finally, the district sent an irrigation company to come to find solutions for water to irrigate the remaining fields that are not covered by mud. But nothing really worked out yet." Back at the headman's house, he made us some tea using water from a twenty-liter bottle. As expected, almost every house in the village now buys water, which impacts their already stretched budgets. According to the headman, before the factories began operating, the villagers used water from a hand-dug well about ten meters deep. Now every household has had to pay for a well to be drilled to reach at least thirty meters. Even then, the water smells like iron ore, so most do not dare to use it for cooking or drinking.

In Lào Cai Province, for the communities affected by the Sin Quyen copper mine, the situation is worse. As the mine stretches 830 hectares over two communes, more households have lost their land.[9] The mine extension project took additional 245 hectares that were villagers' planted forest and cash crop land.[10] A Ty village of Minh Ba commune, for example, is located right behind the main factory. While the EIA approved in 2016 clearly indicates that wastewater in the tailing pond of ninety hectares in Minh Ba commune should be treated to meet Vietnam's environmental standards before being discharging into the environment.[11] Villagers in A Ty complained that seventy households in the village lost all their land—at least three or four hectares per household—as a result of pollution caused by the tailing pond and other mining activities. Vimico, the company in charge of the mine extraction, was supposed to find land to resettle these villagers and hundreds of others, as well as compensate them for land lost. Unfortunately, not all affected households have been able to resettle yet, owing to a lack of land for resettlement sites. My focus group discussion participants shared a story about the commune's cadastral official, who embezzled the compensation; she faked half the villagers' signatures and stole their money. The other half of the villagers who did receive compensation were offered only 50 percent of their land's value. According to Mrs. Dang, a villager in Minh Ba commune, her family and neighbors have been suffering from noise from mine explosions twenty-four hours a day, dust from mining trucks, and a lack of land for growing food. Villagers complained that they were no longer able to raise free-running chickens, ducks, or pigs, as the animals died from drinking contaminated water released from the mine. The walls and roof of Mrs. Dang's house have been cracking because of the constant explosions. Every time it rains, she uses buckets, pots, and pans to catch the water leaking into the house. She shared her frustrations with me:

> When they started to build Mineral Sorting Plant Number 2, they kept telling us that they would resettle us to a safer place, but it has been a few years now and we're still waiting. They told us we could resettle right next to a brick factory, but we don't want that. The brick factory has been polluting the air over there in the last few years. Oh, no. "Avoiding watermelon skin, and stepping on a coconut's skin." We would like them to arrange a better place for us. We're tired of complaining. They, the authorities and the company, have abandoned us; [those] who die, just die, who can live, then live. My family has sent petitions continuously since 2014

FIGURE 8.1.  Mrs. Dang's house is cracking from the constant underground explosions. Photo by the author.

up to now. I sent everywhere possible, including to journalists so they could help cover our story. I am not afraid. We're already dying here. We just want to have some support for fixing the house and have clean water for our daily use so we can live like normal people. Now they all tell us opposite things. We don't know how to think and what to believe.[12]

Since the mines began operation, and throughout their continued expansion, they have dramatically affected villagers' lives and livelihoods. The villagers' adaptation has been unnecessarily difficult because of the lack of support from the authorities and the mining companies. In these cases, the dispossession of collective rights and access to water and land has followed from the privatization or marketization of these resources. Water and land dispossession can take the form of contamination, which effectively removes water and land from the public sphere and encloses it.[13] Thus, the powerful alliance between the authorities and the mining companies in the name of economic advancement has further marginalized people in the Northwest. For mine-produced territorial subjects, living conditions resulting from pollution are far worse than those of people displaced by dams, or rubber workers. While mine operations make it hard enough for villagers to sustain their livelihoods because of land loss, the mine-generated noise and air and water pollution exacerbate the problem on a daily basis, impacting people's physical and mental health as well as their relationships within the community. Lack of clean water for both farming and daily use has been one of the most serious issues faced by local villagers. Aside from everyday resistance and compliance, everyday politics manifested itself in forms of everyday modifications and evasions, such as the case of the commune's embezzling cadastral official, or the fight over water among community members. Instead of targeting people in superior positions, this form of everyday politics came at the expense of neighbors in similarly dire conditions.[14]

## Land and Labor Issues

Worldwide, mining occupies considerably less than 1 percent of the earth's land surface. In the United States—a country with an extensive mining history—metal mining occupies only 0.025 percent of land surface, in comparison to 70 percent for agriculture.[15] Even though mining occupies a relatively small land area in Vietnam and elsewhere compared to rubber plantations, the comparative impacts of mining on the environment cover a much wider area of land and water, and these impacts prove more severe than those from rubber or other crops.

Just as in some parts of Indonesia, and in other places where rural dispossession created "surplus population," in the Northwest of Vietnam, where resources are "discovered" and become commodities, such resources are considered useful, while the people who live in these areas are not.[16] As Tania Li points out, two main vectors of rural dispossession in Asia today include the seizure of land by the state or state-supported corporations, and the piecemeal dispossession of small-scale farmers who are unable to survive when exposed to competition from government-backed industrial agricultural systems. Unfortunately, land dispossession does not have any intrinsic link to the prospect of labor absorption.[17] Rasmussen and Lund explain this reality as the "dispossession of land and livelihoods [which] becomes detached from any prospect of labor absorption."[18] As a result, affected villagers suffer; they either become miners or paid workers somewhere else and/or have no land to work on.

Land along a river is considered highly desirable, both for agriculture and for living. But once the river is contaminated, so is the land. When there is no usable land for farming, villagers have no choice but to leave the village in search of a job—any type of work that can bring them an income. In areas where mining activities take place, like in areas where rubber plantations and hydropower sources are developed, investors often promise to bring development and jobs for locals. These are not the only similarities. While mining activities do create jobs and develop additional services, they do not guarantee work for local communities. At the same time, adverse impacts on water, land, and air from mining activities lead to the degradation or destruction of local production, animals, and crops.[19] Yet, according to my interviewees, compensation from investors is insignificant and meets only a small portion of the affected people's immediate needs, not enough to help them recover from their loss or ensure their long-term livelihoods. In order to survive, many laborers clear forest to gain more land for farming, participate in illegal mining, or leave their hometown to find work. My research in Thien Tam village reveals that in 2021 only seven villagers out of 240 households found employment with the mining company. Even then, they are only temporary workers, who are not afforded any benefits. According to one mineworker I interviewed in May 2019, workers are underground in three shifts. Each shift includes thirty people of different skills, but most workers come from outside the commune. Work in the mine is very hard and yields a monthly average income of about VNĐ 5 million (about US$220). Typically, only young men take this type of job. In Luong Thien, labor scarcity and danger have pushed almost half of the village's young people under the age of thirty out of their homes and villages; they now work in industrial parks in the Red River delta.[20]

By early 2020, A Ty village of Minh Ba commune had suffered the same fate. More than half the young people left the village to find work, while others found employment in the Sin Quyen copper mine. The fight to secure these young people's jobs in the mine was not easy. A villager said, "At first, none of the kids of affected families in my village were able to get a job in the mine. The company brought in workers from somewhere else who had connections with the company. For a few years, we sent many petitions and even protested. Finally, since late 2014, Vimico started to receive some of our kids to be their workers. The salary is low, about VNĐ 4–5 million per month (US$170–220). But they have benefits. When they are retired, they can have pension money."[21]

For people unable to find a job at the mine, they either go to Sapa (a famous tourist site of Lào Cai Province) or out-migrate to Hưng Yên, Hải Dương, Bắc Ninh, or Nam Định Provinces in the Red River delta, looking for work. In May 2022, my research assistant Lien reported that none of the villagers in A Ty stayed in the village to work as miners, even though many of them had been fighting for that opportunity eight years earlier. Only the ones who work as technicians or truck drivers stay. Other people left because the work was too hard and very different from the farming they used to do. Payment from mining labor was also much lower than what they could receive working as migrant workers in other provinces.

Mining projects in the two Northwest provinces that I discuss in this chapter have caused dispossession of both land and livelihoods in local communities. Affected villagers lost much of their land as well as their access to clean water for farming and domestic use, which has pushed many of these peasants out of their home villages to become paid labor. Their everyday politics stretch from resistance to compliance, modification to evasion and even support—the micropolitics of shifting and producing territorial subjects to resist and/or adapt to changes. Increased migration of young people to find work elsewhere has altered the local population structure and placed more burden on the women and elderly who stay, as I will discuss later.

## Mining-Induced Displacement

Mining in Lào Cai has polluted the environment, reduced the area of arable land, and threatened local lives with daily mine explosions. As mentioned in chapter 7, to make way for the Sin Quyen project, hundreds of families of different ethnicities, including Dao, Tay, Kinh, Hmông, and Giay in Minh Ba and Tu Lan communes, have been resettled. The PPC of Lào Cai Province's master plan of mineral management, extraction, and processing for 2007–2015, with an eye on 2020, states that "mineral exploitation and processing activities in the locality of the province must ensure the interests of the state, businesses, and people in the areas with minerals." This suggests that the process of resettling locals, which is essential for mining activities, is completed before mining commences, in order to help stabilize affected people's lives. However, the resettlement process associated with Sin Quyen mining project fell far below such standards. In reality, owing to a lack of vision by planners, villagers still have not, after many years and many moves, settled and returned to lives approximating those they enjoyed before the mines. Their resettlement opens up no new economic opportunities for them; rather it makes their lives more miserable. Research by PanNature confirms that individuals resettled due to mining activities face extreme difficulties, including a lack of farmland and clean, potable water, as well as exposure to severe air and noise pollution.[22]

It seems that no comprehensive plan or proper organization for resettlement was in place before the project started. The company dealt with resettlement in a choppy and careless fashion. More than fifty households in A Ty village of Minh Ba commune had to move three times. According to the village's headman, the first move was in 2003, when the Sin Quyen copper mining complex started construction. In this first instance, the resettlement site was only a few hundred meters away from the old residences. The second relocation was in 2009 and coincided with the mine's expansion. The resettlement site was once again only a few hundred meters away from the first resettlement site. Because the copper mining generated a large amount of dust, this short distance between the site and villagers' homes made environmental pollution in the village inevitable. Mr. Hu was one of the first people displaced from Minh Ba commune. He now lives in the Minh Tra resettlement area, which is located on an old landfill that covered a swamp. Here, both groundwater and surface water are polluted, and the ground lacks stability. The resettlers continue to suffer from noise and vibrations of daily explosions in the mine; many report that they live in fear of becoming sick because of the pollution and of having their houses damaged because of shockwaves from explosions. Mr. Hu said, "Since we moved here, we have never had a good night sleep. My wife wanted to start a new business here, like raising pigs and distilling maize alcohol, but we had to give up because of no water. We all lost our land, and now can't really do anything in this resettlement site. We're dying."[23] Although villagers did not have to move far, their frequent relocations have affected their children's education. As most families could not secure stable livelihoods, they could not ensure financial support of their children's schooling. Furthermore, pollution from the mines has affected people's health. A villager in Minh Ba said, "We don't know if it's because of the air and water pollution, but half of our village got sick often. Nine people in our village were diagnosed with cancer. Nobody tells us anything about the impacts."[24]

In order to deal with the problem, in 2016 Ty Ba district officials implemented a policy to support the relocation of these households to new resettlement areas. I visited Mr. Ha's house in May 2018 and learned that in July 2017 villagers were told to move for a third time, to a new resettlement area in Minh Ba commune, a few kilometers from their current village. He said, "We are very tired of moving because we have had to move three times in just over ten years. It is extremely difficult to stabilize our lives." Mr. Ha's neighbor added,

> We find it strange that under the same project, why did people in charge not have a long-term plan in the first place, anticipating that the factory would expand its scale? Why didn't they foresee that the mine would cause problems such as dust, water pollution, noise, smoke, etc., affecting the living environment of local people? As they were incapable of doing it, they failed to arrange proper resettlement for us. Now we had to move so many times, how can we live our lives when we have no land and no job?[25]

Faring even worse than people who were displaced by the Sơn La Dam, many people in Ty Ba who were displaced by mining operations did not receive any farmland at all when they were resettled, even though 100 percent of them were engaged in agriculture and had no side jobs. Participants of my focus groups shared that the amount of land that resettlers received for housing in resettlement sites varied depending on land availability in the new village. Some households received one hundred square meters, while some other households received slightly larger lots for their houses. At the commune level, the authorities were planning to persuade villagers to move away from farming. A commune leader rationalized: "Our villagers will be resettled in Minh Ba commune, and since Minh Ba commune is located right at a border gate with China, there are always a lot of paid workers who work as porters unloading and uploading goods. There are also hundreds of trucks carrying goods from lowland areas. We have oriented resettlers so that they can open shops, grocery stores, etc., and do business in the new place. They don't have to farm anymore."[26]

Such rationale failed to convince villagers, who were very worried about their future. For individuals whose lifework has been farming, the idea of suddenly becoming retail store owners seemed unfeasible. Many villagers of Dao, Tày, or Giáy ethnicity told me that engaging in businesses like trading or operating a retail store only suits those of Kinh ethnicity or maybe Hmông people. At the same time, many Kinh ethnicity villagers said that they also had no clue how the proposed solution would work for them—if every household opened a store, who would be their customers? In early 2022, these households remained reluctant to move. Development-induced displacement, most of the time, creates chaos among affected populations and disrupts their lives, livelihoods, and relationships to one another, as well as to land and natural resources that they depend on. As a result, resistance and negotiation become indispensable political responses to dealing with displacement, to making their livings, to struggling with their daily livelihoods and interacting with authorities, mining companies, and other affected villagers.

## Participation, Conflicts, and Social Responses

In Luong Thien village of Yên Bái Province and A Ty village of Lào Cai Province, not one villager told me that they were informed about the proposed mining project before it was implemented. In accordance with the Law on Environmental Protection, the investor needs to prepare an EIA before being granted a license. Environmental and social issues and risks should be identified in the assessment, together with feasible and appropriate mitigation measures. Communities should be informed about the project's content and effects. For their project to be approved, developers need to gather the opinions of people in the area through community consultation on related issues like environmental impacts, land compensation, resettlement, or mitigation plans.[27]

Most people living nearby seemed unaware of community consultation opportunities during the EIA phase. As mentioned above, the Sin Quyen Copper Mining Branch did not even complete its EIA before commencing extraction. As of July 2020, the company was still finalizing its EIA, which needed to include impacts of the mine expansion and construction of Sorting Plant No. 2. About half the people that we interviewed did not even know the full name of the mining companies that were upending their lives. In Yên Bái, for example, most of the commune officials we interviewed said that they did not have access to the EIA report and did not know the details about public consultation during the project's construction period. The lack of transparency by multiple levels of governing authority in disclosing information on companies' mining activities deprived people of any opportunity to comment on and oversee mining project planning and implementation.

Even though not all communities affected by mining resist, when they do, the objectives, narratives, and intensity of this resistance vary. Through their everyday resistance, which at times can be direct and confrontational, villagers struggle to affirm claims to what they believe they are entitled.[28] As Anthony Bebbington and Jeffrey Bury highlight, conflicts are linked to the mining-sustainability relationship and are motivated by concerns about livelihood security, environmental degradation, and the perception that well-being has not improved in proportion to mining companies' profits. Bebbington and Bury argue that maps of mining concessions can be viewed as maps of uncertainty that lack a transparent mechanism to illustrate how money from mining can be transformed into human development and environmental justice.[29] Indeed, these institutional constraints help explain the social unrest "driven by greed, grievance, uncertainty, and fear that often accompany mining expansion. That such arrangements persist reflects the political power of those who benefit from them, as well as central government commitments to prioritize institutions that promote foreign direct and large-scale investments as pathways to economic growth."[30]

Struggles over resources entail questions concerning political communities as well as the relationship between citizenship, territory, and the nation.[31] Similar to hydropower dams and rubber plantations, mining projects (re)produce territories, redistribute resources and decision-making power, and reconstruct subjects and identities—but again, not without igniting resistance.[32] The new "territorial moments" of mines

in the frontier, on the one hand, reiterate power inequality among involved actors, and on the other hand strengthen villagers' agency in
their fight against injustice. As mentioned above, villagers in Thien
Tam village were fighting over water. Their everyday politics in the form
of resistance included protesting against the company and marching to
the commune's center to demand support and compensation for their
losses, among other demands. Villagers in Minh Ba engaged in similar
activities. They even wielded knives to chase the trucks that choked
their fields, and demonstrated at the district office seeking a safe resettlement site. Villagers in Minh Ba sent petitions to the local authorities every ten days. Mrs. Dang and a few of her neighbors went as far as
the provincial level to complain, talked to journalists, and cried out for
help to anyone who would listen to their story. As a result, the media
have started to cover stories of affected people. For example, headlines
included, "Pollution from the Largest Copper Mine," by Nong Nghiep
newspaper; "The Largest Copper Mine in Southeast Asia Causes Pollution" and "Mining Companies in Yên Bái Turned Rice Fields into Abandoned Land," by Vietnamplus; as well as "Tan Tien Mining Company
in Yên Bái Ignored Laws," and "Villagers Cried Out for Help in Dealing
with Water Pollution Caused by Mining," which were posted on the
MONRE website.[33] News spread via television and newspapers, in con-
cert with everyday political efforts by villagers, helped to put increasing
pressure on mining companies to address villagers' demands.[34] Mining
Alliance, which comprises seven NGOs and is coordinated by PanNature, also helped raise the issues to the wider public through various
activities, including research, workshops, and media collaborations.

The people's fight was not entirely in vain. In March 2018, Luong
Thien villagers protested when there was no clean water for their rice
seedlings. They marched to the commune's center and refused to leave
until someone talked to them. Commune authorities had to invite
mining company representatives to attend a meeting. Even though the
company initially refused to compensate the villagers or to clean up
the mud that had choked the fields, district authorities later sent an
irrigation company to construct a new irrigation canal for villagers and
to clean the fields. In response to the generally negative impacts of Yên
Bái's mines, the province's Department of Natural Resources and Environment requested in 2018 an investigation of seven mining companies
in Thinh Tam, as well as compensation for the buried agricultural land
in this village.[35] In Document No. 165/BC-STNMT (May 7, 2019), the
provincial DONRE required the Tan Tien Mining Company to (1) seal

and consolidate all bottom drains that connect its Pond No. 3 with the Ngoi Lau stream; (2) repair the drying system of water and sewage treatment before May 25, 2019; (3) dredge all waste mud in water treatment and sludge treatment plants before July 10, 2019; (4) recycle wastewater back to production; (5) perform environmental protection measures according to the EIA report; and (6) regularly check to detect and solve problems of water and sludge treatment systems.[36]

When the company did not follow these requirements, on March 12, 2020, a DONRE inspection team sent a report to the Yên Bái PPC highlighting the Tan Tien Mining Company's many violations against articles in the Law on Environmental Protection that occurred during mining activities in Luong Thinh commune.[37] The Yên Bái PPC decided to close the mine. It issued a decision that required Tan Tien to level the land and restore the environment. The decision gave the company two months to implement these steps.[38] If the company did not voluntarily comply within the given time frame, it would be forced to comply with regulations.[39] Many people argued that the fine issued to the Tan Tien company was too low—VNĐ 15 million (US$660)—stressing that there must be something wrong with the system. Some questioned the power behind the company and its connection to Yên Bái PPC or those at a higher level. In the end, the company would continue the mine's operations after it paid the fine, and the land was never restored as required by law.[40]

As for the Sin Quyen copper mine, the villagers' grievances have not resulted in any change, likely because the mine belongs to one of the largest state-owned corporations.[41] Still, the People's Committee of Ty Ba district has been actively working for people impacted negatively by mine activity, demanding that the mining company solve resettlement issues and address villagers' complaints. The People's Committee of Ty Ba district issued Document No. 373/BC-UBND on July 20, 2020, to the Lào Cai PPC to request the provincial government's help in pressuring Vimico as well as its mother company, Vinacomin, to finalize the EIA for the Sin Quyen copper mine extension and address the petitions from Mrs. Dang and her neighbors as soon as possible.[42] Most recently, in a meeting between the People's Committee of Ty Ba district and representatives of Vimico on December 11, 2021, the company once again promised to address problems that the villagers raised. The company again highlighted its willingness to create jobs and to provide training for young local villagers to become technicians and find employment in the mine.[43] The difference in the way that local/district/provincial authorities dealt with private mining companies in Yên Bái and the large state-owned Vinacomin in Lào Cai in responding to social pressure highlights the fact that mining capital is itself highly differentiated. Differences in ownership structure, a company's connection to authorities, objectives, and constraints can shape degrees of motivation for adopting environmental mitigation plans. Since the authoritarian government in Vietnam makes it difficult to openly resist or criticize, Mrs. Dang and her neighbors' modest achievement stands out. Indeed, pollution issues have recently received more attention from the government, especially after the Formosa incident in 2016, when pollution caused a mass fish kill in four central provinces of Vietnam.[44] Thus, even though villagers' acts of everyday politics in the form of resistance involve both little or no organization, they feed into forms of advocacy politics that have driven changes in policies and practices, however small. In contrast to what Kerkvliet argues—that the persons or institutions targeted by everyday resistance typically do not know, at least not right away, what has been done at their expense—in this case the authorities and companies were aware of the larger problems with mining issues and villagers' reactions but failed to solve them.[45] Concern about being constantly watched or of being seen as behaving irregularly constrains the way the individual acts. This concern informs the difficulty in obtaining permission from the authorities to conduct research on this topic, or in getting access to community members.

## Negotiating Differentiation and Inequalities

Vimico claims that it has facilitated jobs for more than four hundred people with permanent residence in Ty Ba district, offered vocational training courses on smelting, mechanics, and auto repair, and employed more that one hundred people who are children of households in Minh Ba and Tu Lan communes.[46] While mining companies emphasize their contributions to job creation through technical training that qualifies local youth to work in the mines, employment issues have not been without controversy. Participants of my focus group discussions complained that the majority of the four hundred people that Vimico congratulated itself for employing were not actually from affected communities. Roughly more than half of the other one hundred local young people from Minh Ba and Tu Lan employed at the mine are Kinh ethnic people who likely had better connections to the company or to authorities and who are more likely to hold high school diplomas; people otherwise eligible for employment but from other ethnic groups like Tày, Giáy or Dao, often drop out of school before the end of grade twelve. Few families have the financial resources to keep their children at school until grade twelve or provide postsecondary education; the opportunity to earn a college or technical diploma remains rare. For those fortunate enough to gain postsecondary education, they face an additional obstacle after graduation in the lack of access to a social network that might help them find a relevant job. While government policies at all levels often highlight the need to give priority to job applicants with an ethnic minority background, as we saw in chapter 1, connections play a key role, and in these cases, people of Kinh ethnicity, who often have more connections with the mine's personnel, may have an advantage over people of Dao, Tày, Hà Nhì, or Giáy ethnicity.[47]

Even though the central government has historically strongly promoted gender equality in education in Vietnam, for many families in the Northwest, female educational support rarely weathers governmental financial difficulties.[48] In Minh Ba and Tu Lan communes of Lào Cai Province, as well as in Thinh Tam commune in Yên Bái Province, the rate of girls dropping out of school before reaching high school is higher than for boys, and that rate among non-Kinh ethnic minority groups is higher than among the Kinh.[49] Although the legal age of marriage in Vietnam is eighteen, among many ethnic minority groups in the Northwest in general, and in these communes in particular, it is not uncommon for girls to marry at age sixteen or seventeen. Mining impacts dropout rates and associated dislocation. In the past, while girls may have dropped out of school early, it was likely in order to take care of younger siblings, help their parents with farmwork, or to marry, rather than to travel far from home in search of employment to support their families. With a reduction in available farming land because of the mines, many of these girls travel to nearby towns or as far away as the Red River delta in order to work at street food stands or as nannies, helpers, or live-in caregivers for middle-class families. In 2019, border police rescued two girls from Ban Chuoc village who had been working at a karaoke bar in Hanoi and were in danger of sex trafficking into China. Many believe this is not an isolated case but a reality demonstrating how differing success at ensuring children's education has exacerbated gender inequality in these communities and harmed the most vulnerable, forcing them to leave their villages and relocate to towns and cities outside the protective reach of their families.[50]

The mining-affected areas in Yên Bái and Lào Cai Provinces demonstrate significant social differentiation. In Yên Bái, mining companies employ a small number of villagers, likely because of the locals' lack of connections with company officials, their uninterest in taxing physical labor, the low wages, or the absence of health benefits.[51] In Thien Tam village, villagers' situations failed to improve after the mines began operation. Villagers have suffered to varying degrees depending on their access to farmland and water, and conflicts over these resources have intensified. More than half the village's young people have been forced to migrate to find employment. A young woman complained, "I wish I could finish high school and get a degree in early childhood education. But since my parents could not afford keeping me in school, I quit when I was at grade nine and was [instead] working as a maid in Lào Cai city for five years." She laughed. "My parents wanted me to go back home and get married, so I went back home," she said. "If I find someone who wants to marry me, I may say yes. But most of young men are away working somewhere now. It's not easy to find a good one."[52] In A Ty village of Lào Cai Province, the mine has damaged community cohesion. Tension has grown among villagers over various issues, including access to clean water, and resettlement arrangements. Differentiation also occurs between families who receive benefits from the mines, including their children's employment, and those who provide services—such as supply produce, open food stands, or run convenience stores—for the mines or its employees.

During my several trips to Ty Ba, I became a friend of Mrs. Dang, the Minh Ba villager. Mrs. Dang is forty-eight, and she already has two grandchildren, five and seven years old. Her husband abandoned the family for a younger woman when Mrs. Dang was pregnant with the couple's second child. She stayed in the village and raised her children on her farm. She also worked as an intermediary, buying vegetables and bamboo shoots in the local area at low prices and selling them at a street market in Ty Ba town at a higher price. Mrs. Dang shared her concerns with me when I talked to her in early 2020:

> You know, even within one village like A Ty, we are at different stages: Some families were already resettled, but their lives are not much better. They were the ones who agreed to move first. But at that time, seventy families in my cluster refused to move. We did not want to move to the site designated for us, as we saw it as no better than here. We [seventy families] worked closely together to

fight. But now you know what happened? Three men were appointed to join the commune authorities, and they abandoned us. They never open their mouth to speak against the mine. . . . The chairman of the commune is corrupted and never expressed his will to protect us. Then half the families have at least one of their kids to work in the mine. They stopped complaining as well. Some families whose children left the village to find jobs somewhere also got tired of fighting. The village gets so divided.

She continued bitterly:

For me, as long as we have clean water, I don't mind staying. As a single mom, moving is a lot for me. Since we lost our land, I've been earning by selling bamboo shoots. I have also been working as paid labor in a low-quality restaurant. It's not ideal, but we survive. Now we're stuck. Now there are only nine families left to fight for our rights. We constantly send petitions to the authorities at all levels. Not sure how they [the authorities and the mining company] will actually solve this problem.[53]

Among the young people in the village who work in the mine, several work as technicians. They are all men. At least five attended technical college and earn VNĐ 8 million (US$350) per month instead of VNĐ 4–5 million (US$175–220) per month that unskilled employees earn. Three other young females found administrative positions at the mining company through connections and told me that they were happy with their jobs. One shared that "the work I do is much better than farming. I love it. I don't have to worry about if I could have a good harvest this year or not. I get my salary every month. It's like a dream comes true. The mine has brought many benefits and development in our hometown. Now we have better roads, everything is more convenient."[54]

The conditions in A Ty village contrast starkly with those in Thien Tam village, even though mining activities have impacted both villages. The tactics that the mining companies use to deal with local issues depend on mine ownership—state-owned or private. Both communities, however, are divided. Young people cannot earn a living from the land because they do not have access to resources. Two options remain: work for the mining company, or migrate away. Not everyone can secure a good job in the mining company, and many had little interest in the hard work and low pay of the mine, so they chose to migrate. Older villagers either compromise or continue to fight over resources. Community cohesion has been shattered. In both villages, women suffer disproportionately, taking on larger roles in households and communities without their husbands, away at the mine or migrating away for work, by their side. One woman described this challenge: "One time, it was a heavy storm, and my roof was damaged. Water poured into the house, and I had to manage all by myself. My parents-in-law were old and could not help. Another time, my son got sick at night, [and] I had to drive the motorbike to take him to the hospital in Ty Ba, more than twenty kilometers away. It has been hard without my husband home."[55]

Mining in the Northwest accumulates or incapacitates space or land around it, and its territorial expansion increases over time. Mining impacts landscapes and waterways for the long term, despite the government's requirement for all mining companies to rehabilitate the landscape after mining activities end. The impacts of mining activities in Lào Cai and Yên Bái Provinces resemble those of communities displaced by the Sơn La hydropower project or those whose land became entangled with rubber development. All in these communities were dispossessed of their collective rights and their access to land and water. Mining activities have occupied or degraded an important part of local land and forests, directly impacting people's livelihoods in exchange for negligible compensation to offset livelihood losses experienced in the wake of dispossession of land. Land and water dispossession can also take the form of pollution. Contamination of land and water effectively removes these resources from people's lives. Tom Perreault argues that various forms of accumulation have driven livelihood dispossession: accumulation of toxic sediments in farmland and floodplains, accumulation of water pollution, and accumulation of territory.[56] While resettlement and the failure to resettle both lead to major impacts on local lives and livelihoods, problems caused by mining have been much worse compared to those resulting from hydropower dams, due to the extent of the resulting pollution.

Mining activities in the Northwest have not had a positive effect on local communities. Mining companies do not recruit most mine workers locally, reaching out to few from local areas. Companies rarely guarantee the rights of workers, offering irregular work schedules and no labor contracts, as in the case of the private mining companies operating in Yên Bái. At best, affected villagers receive limited compensation for losses and often have to force (limited) government action to constrain the pollution that mining companies cause. Mining certainly does not produce development commonly understood as improvement in the lives and well-being of upland peoples.

The mining industry plays an important role in the economic growth of these provinces, but mineral mining and processing companies offer limited support to local communities in the Northwest. This repeats experiences in other provinces across Vietnam where mining activities are ongoing. While mining can be beneficial for the national economy, at the local level mining may not contribute to poverty reduction, and mines have little positive influence on income generation for affected people.[57]

Deleterious effects on people's livelihoods and the environment aside, the operations of processing and transport of minerals degrade local infrastructure. Throughout the entire mining process, a lack of access to information about mining operations has profoundly inhibited people's roles and voices in monitoring mining activities in their communities.

"Accumulation by dispossession" and uneven development have been closely associated with all three key development projects in the Northwest—hydropower, rubber plantations, and mining. Mining as a hegemonic project imposed on local people has transformed their ways of living and interacting with one another. Local communities, while only minimally integrated into the mining economy, have nevertheless been subject not only to mining's boom-and-bust economic cycles but also to its pollution, which has increased since the mines first became operational. Mining in the Northwest—the process of extraction and export of mineral commodities—is structured by laws in ways that produce uneven forms of development.

Marginalized populations in this upland region suffer the most. Their subjectivities change because the deep emotional connections that people have with their land, their forest, their rivers—these vital sources of their cultural identity—have been disrupted or even lost through dispossession. Environmental degradation caused by extractive industries in remote regions can be particularly acute because property rights are often poorly defined, the market valuation of land for non-mining purposes is low, and monitoring and enforcement costs in the periphery of national territory are high.[58] Regardless of the conditions villagers find themselves in, they continuously struggle for their rights. Their everyday politics stretch from support to compliance, modification, evasion, and resistance. We can see close links between mineral extraction, political-economic marginalization, environmental conflicts, ethnic identity and relation, well-being, and environmental degradation, including the government's role in both mediating tensions and facilitating resource access and control. These links also highlight broader concerns about social and environmental justice and the resistance of marginalized people to mining operations, as well as structures of power in relation to identity, social interactions, and internal colonialism.

# Conclusion

When I was a child, my brothers and I always waited in anticipation for my father's stories every time he returned home from his trips to the Northwest. And it was not just stories that he brought. It was fresh plums, peaches, mangos, or sometimes, on very special occasions, pork jerky. This was a very difficult time in the early 1980s when food shortages and hunger were prevalent in most parts of the country. As we, like everyone else in the country who was not a farmer, had to use food coupons, these treats from my father's trips were a big deal for us. My father was an agronomist, and his first job was with the Việt Bắc Department of Agriculture in the early 1950s; a few years later, he began working in the Thái Mèo Autonomous Zone.[1] Even though it was only for a short period, he made friends and became very close with "Uncle" Sinh, who was Khmu ethnicity, and "Uncle" Dinh, who was Thái ethnicity. My father returned to the region frequently to work with various government agricultural departments. People like Uncle Sinh and Uncle Dinh taught my father about their land, their culture, and inspired his love for the Northwest, which he nurtured in me. My father's stories about the people, the mighty Đà River, and the forests from that time differ from what I have observed over the last twenty years since I began conducting research in the Northwest. But these stories, conversations, and tall tales have all helped me to better understand the changes in the Northwest that people and their land have experienced since state formation in 1945.

In this book, I have examined the production of landscape and resource territorial subjects in the Northwest uplands of Vietnam. Tracing territorialization in the region through the experiences of development—of Khun, Mr. Hin, Mrs. Dang, and other northwesterners I have met over the last twenty years—reveals deeply unequal power relations among stakeholders in the region. People like Mr. E have shared stories with me that capture how the very things that we consider to be development indicators—like a bathroom, a motorbike, or a bigger house—can actually be distractions. I have also uncovered connections between development-induced displacement linked to hydropower dams, rubber plantations, and mining, and agrarian change, everyday politics, differentiation, and the creation/modification of ethnic identity in upland spaces. Vietnam has witnessed unequal development not only between the lowlands and the uplands but also among upland communities. This socially unjust and disproportionate allocation of benefits, costs, and risks arises for the many reasons I have examined, including ethnicity, gender, and access to resources.

I have advocated for a concept of state territorialization as a political project of exclusion through inclusion. It is a process of making territory, one that in turn creates and controls both resources and subjects. As a frontier in the making, the Northwest has experienced commodification through processes of resource extraction, land dispossession, and accumulation. The inclusion of northwesterners in the nation-building process explicitly excludes the majority of them from participating in political decision-making about how the region's space and nature are or will be managed. In short, these northwesterners' inclusion in the nation's plans depends on their exclusion from the political process. State territorialization as a project of exclusion through inclusion is not unique to Vietnam or to the Northwest but occurs in many other parts of the world where the cycle of "frontier-territorialization-frontier-territorialization" has prevailed.[2]

Emphasizing that everyday politics, entangled in the process of territorialization, is the product of the ongoing fight to survive and to thrive, the stories here have shown that territorial subject formation has always been made and remade not simply because of territorialization and external powers, but because of the key role played by people's agency. For northwesterners, traditional cultural practices including *múa xòe* and *ném còn* have faded away because of changes in the living environment and surrounding resources. Housing, hairstyles, cloth-ing, dining, and farming practices have all been altered. Development produces complex and confounding subjects with differing subject positions. They are no longer either self-provisioning peasants or so-cialist subjects who, in the 1960s or 1970s, conducted intensive farm-ing and reduced their swidden activities or joined cooperative farming for socialist construction. After Đổi Mới and since development proj-ects such as hydropower dams, rubber plantations, or mining arrived in their villages and intruded on their lives, many northwesterners—post-socialist subjects—have become landless, jobless, migrant workers, marginal farmers, rubber workers, miners, store owners, debt owners; they have become involved in plural activity and have to constantly fight for themselves, for their children, and for future generations.

As I bring my story to a close, I return to a question that I asked in the introduction: How do different resource materialities contribute to different forms of state territorialization? I have argued that the so-cial relations of territorialization in the Northwest of Vietnam since 1954 are complicated, especially after Đổi Mới in 1986. Since this pe-riod, three specific development projects in the trajectory of landscape production in the Northwest have shown that territorialization has no discernible limit, nor is it reserved for the state alone in making and remaking resource territorial subjects. Each of these particular ma-terialities and its associated state extraction regimes has a distinctive relationship to or effect on the land and its people. In this process, po-litical technologies continuously produce territories and guide subjects whose agency the government "deployed rather than destroyed."[3] The territorial subject-making that occurs does not produce monolithic post-socialist subjects, but fractured plural subjects who must con-stantly find their own way. Not simply adapting to confusing, barely workable circumstances imposed on them, they must also make the best of their lot through continual everyday processes of negotiation, compromise, and resistance.

Development planners' dam discourse has been dominant and ubiq-uitous among related actors since the 1950s, and dams have endured as a symbol of Vietnam's development and modernization. Driven by this dominant development narrative, national planning and develop-ment continue to narrowly privilege economic growth and accumu-lation. However, planning and decisions about dams—as with rubber plantations and mining—continue to neglect affected people's voices. External and internal social pressures for policy improvement have led to a number of changes in Vietnam's policies, including those concerning land, resettlement, water, and environmental protection. Indeed, as the Sơn La case study shows, there have been some improvements in the participation of affected people in certain stages of the resettlement implementation process. Such minimal progress, however, has been far from sufficient to help ensure affected people's fair and meaningful participation throughout development projects. The participatory rhetoric that dam planners invoke, in fact, masks the actual social exclusion of people that the dam displaces, thus further silencing voices that have been muted historically. Thousands of people were displaced to make way for the Sơn La Dam and were only informed about the project and their need to relocate—let alone given a say in the matter—years after officials made the decision to build the dam. Although different stakeholders in Vietnam have been devoting increased attention to the issue of participation in decision-making processes related to resources management (for example, river/land governance), there remains a dearth of clear mechanisms through which to engage people. The existing policies have made assumptions about resettlers' ease of adaptation to a new environment and have failed to address consequent impoverishment, among other life-changing impacts.

Despite the importance of hydropower projects for Vietnam's economic success, the government and dam developers have consistently underestimated costs associated with dams, as well as their impacts on people and on the environment, overemphasizing dams' benefits compared to costs. The government, through its Ministry of Investment and Planning, has approved the construction of hundreds of dams since the 1990s, despite causing resettlement, changes in local communities' livelihoods, forest and biodiversity losses, and serious soil erosion due to water flow and sedimentation changes, among other problems. As with many development projects in the Northwest, the benefits of dams, including electricity generation, flow to the lowlands, while the costs fall on upland resettlers' shoulders. Broadly speaking, Vietnam's current dam policies have two cost-benefit problems: the first is the unequal distribution of costs and benefits; the second is the hidden costs of losses in cultural diversity, ethnic identities, and social tension that may affect the country as a whole. These cost-benefit problems point to the need for the government to properly address questions of social difference and inequality in resource use and access. At the same time, these also highlight issues of geographic injustice, social inclusion, and ethnic identity transformation in contemporary Vietnam.

Everyday politics that links to territorialization through the government-promoted expansion of rubber plantations in the late 2000s and 2010s has complicated the government's attempts to modernize Northwest uplanders. Rubber plantations in this region have dispossessed people from their land and pushed them into impoverishment without preparing them to adapt to changes. It has turned thousands of northwesterners into paid laborers, many of whom have been forced to travel far from home to find employment, fundamentally changing their cultures in the process. Land dispossession in this case has not only impoverished people but also undermined their land rights. And as I have shown, losing farming land increases work burdens on women. Under such conditions, women and men deal with problems differently in the face of shared or similar economic hardship. In the face of socioeconomic changes, gender relations—traditionally relatively egalitarian and complementary in the Northwest—have been reshaped by changes in access to and control over land, by new relations of production, and by the creation of alliances between state and business in controlling land and labor.

Finally, the processes of dispossession and accumulation in locations where mining activities have upended people's lives have reinforced and expanded the scope and scale of both territorialization and the practice of everyday politics. Ethnic minority communities, barely integrated into the mining economy except through the odd family member lucky enough to secure a company job, continue to face myriad issues related to the contamination of their land, water, and air. They have also suffered from land and livelihood losses, as well as community disintegration. Similar to hydropower dams and rubber plantations, mineral extraction activities have reproduced exclusion through inclusion. Different forms of power produce, diffuse, and reinforce uneven development in the Northwest uplands. This power inequality has not only deprived villagers of their land but also deepened their hardships and struggles to simply survive.

Dam building, rubber plantations, and mining in the name of development have unmade and remade spatial orders in the Northwest, upending established rights that local villagers have been holding on to for many generations, creating replacement of the existing rights.[4] Through the continuous cycle of "frontier-territorialization-frontier-territorialization," the state and allied elites use new and old political technologies to strengthen their control over land and other resources. The national economy's demand for electricity, and the world's demand for rubber, iron, and copper, have forced thousands of upland villagers into the labor market. While displacing people from their land—either ex situ or in situ—neither the dam, the plantation, nor the mine generates adequate jobs, and they close land frontiers for smallholders who might otherwise use the land to create jobs for and feed themselves.[5] Thus, with ongoing dispossession in the Northwest, where resources— but not people—are needed, there has been a creation of a surplus population, which has led to an increase in indebtedness and out-migration. Similar situations have occurred across Asia—including in Indonesia, Malaysia, and Thailand—where poverty has not been reduced but has rather expanded and intensified under development policies, despite claims by the architects of development that their projects will bring benefits to everyone involved.[6]

The emergence of neoliberal governmentality in post-socialist Vietnam has added to a complex web of interests evidenced by corporatism and the rise of powerful interest groups with rent-seeking activity.[7] Indeed, it has deepened the inequality and exploitation in development and domination in politics. The diverse governmentalities employed in development politics in the Northwest, applied in the cases of hydropower dams, rubber plantations, and mining, have steered northwesterners' conduct as well as the multidimensional counter-conduct responses. Many sources can inspire and influence "conduct of conduct." The first are state agencies and various government-employed technologies used to control resources including rivers, land, forests, and mines. However, fluid regulatory norms and institutions also "affect the very thoughts and experiences of persons; authoritative figures as within a community or family; or as importantly, one's own self."[8] With many actors involved in each of the above three types of development projects, governmentality is not only accomplished through government technologies of rule but also through nonstate actors, such as local people, private investors, nongovernmental organizations, and international donors.

Scholars of resource politics strive to deepen our understanding of the connection between development and differentiation. My ethnographic approach has enabled me to explore many factors that have brought and reinforced differentiation among a host of affected people—whether they are affected by dams, rubber plantations, or mining—including people's access to capital (both financial and social capital), their choices in using their labor, and changes in levels of market integration. I have unfolded the multiple layers of local villagers' struggles to cope with changes and improve their life chances as post-socialist subjects. In particular, the nature and intensity of market integration have played key roles in accelerating the differentiation process in the Northwest. Development alters social processes that (re)constitute the upland peasantry, which in turn has accelerated differentiation. The affected villagers have become stratified into different groups. In dam-resettled villages, the wealthier soon became owners, landlords, or investors, while the poor have had no other choice but to sell their labor. Villagers' relationship with the new forms of labor was not immediately fully capitalist; as we see in the case of the resettled village Muong Lanh, reciprocal relationships have, to some degree, influenced this new reality, even as reciprocity has eroded.

To carry on their traditions, villagers in the Northwest's mountains need access to land, but development projects such as dams, plantations, and mining take land away from villagers and dramatically change their lives. Ecological changes due to such mega-project development have caused constraints on livelihood choices, while agrarian changes have produced new forms of inequality, including spatial inequalities—resettled people simply receive less land.[9] There have been continuities and changes in terms of patterns of accumulation, appropriation, and dispossession for capitalist development as well as socialist construction all over the world.[10] Accumulation is not simply about the concentration and centralization of the power of capital but also about stripping alternative practices and shutting out options for alternative futures. In particular, as Philip McMichael highlights, "the ontology of capitalist modernity, rooted in economism, rules out a place for peasants, physically expelling them from the land and epistemologically removing them from history."[11]

This book has shown that development has engendered multilayered environmental conflicts in the Northwest. However, they are not as straightforward as conflicts between a state and its people, elite and poor, or outsiders and local communities. While elites are either part of the state or have intimate connections with state actors, the poor and their neighbors who have been able to take advantage of the development projects' benefits—as did the headman of Muong Ma or villagers in Muong Ta—can be locally positioned in one community.[12]

In the process of territorial subject formation, there have been constant negotiations, engagements, compromises, acts of resistance, and contradictions. The fact that there were northwesterners who resisted the changes and the rules that the development projects imposed reveals that this group doesn't hold single, homogeneous interests. Villagers have exercised their agency—destroying rubber trees or quitting their work as rubber workers or miners to find employment elsewhere—in ways that oppose the "benefits" that the government and developers assumed the villagers would embrace. At the same time, the ways that villagers exercised their agency are conditioned by unequal forces of domination and also by their cultural distinctions. Among ethnic minorities in the Northwest, it seems that more Thái people, the largest ethnic group in the region, took advantage of conditions created by development projects or worked out survival strategies thanks to their social connections and networks. People in the wealthy groups of Muong Muon, Muong Nhuong, or Muong Ma opened businesses and enjoyed success, a pattern that did not seem as strong among Dao, La Ha, Mảng, or Giáy people.

With the unequal consequences of development, upland people's responses, resistance, and coping strategies differ at various scales, from individuals to families to collectives. Upland peasants have not always been submissive to development-related changes, nor have they been afraid to express their opposition to unreasonable policies or to problems with policy implementation. Northwesterners have had to deal with constant pressure from the state and its development apparatus, and many have created their new livelihood trajectories in these alienated environments shaped by a number of factors. For example, resettlers connected to the Sơn La hydropower project may have started from a similar social position, but their futures were shaped by many factors, including ethnicity and gender. Sometimes disputes have been between villagers, rather than with state institutions or local authorities. (Similar issues occurred in affected areas of all three types of projects.) Collective actions to confront local governments have resulted from collective grievances and have occurred only when villagers felt that their interests were ignored and that government officers' promises were unreliable. Although specific actions varied in different situations and contexts, collective actions sometimes brought positive results after long fights.

In the Northwest, government development projects have created rural poverty, transformed and degraded the agrarian landscape, and accelerated differentiation. Differentiation is an ongoing process in agrarian transformation that occurs in all communities—host and resettled, upland and lowland, minority and majority ethnic people. In the introduction, I asked "How do the politics of everyday life associated with changes in resource extraction and access bring about differentiation within local communities?" This book has revealed how the contours of the displacement experience—both ex situ and in situ—shape the process of differentiated territorial subject formation, influenced by various factors that lead to differences in the dynamics of differentiation in upland communities, especially resettled ones. Among villagers affected by rubber plantations or mining, the majority became landless peasants with no choice but to sell their labor. More than twenty years of research in the region have confirmed for me that multiple factors influence villagers' choices, including social networks, availability of labor, access to capital, education, and even cunning (as in the case of the Muong Ma headman in chapter 5 who pushed his villagers to join the rubber plantations). Villager strategies have not always been effective but reflect an ability to adapt, draw upon available resources, and practice everyday politics.

The individual stories I have recounted illustrate the important role that changes in the nature and the intensity of market integration have played in accelerating the differentiation process. Instead of self-provisioning and partly engaging in the markets with their cash crops, many became dependent on the market, either because they had no land left, or the land that they worked so hard to hold on to was too small or not sufficient to sustain their lives. Despite these obstacles, most people that I talked to wanted to continue as peasants and be able to farm, either by choice or because they lacked alternatives.

Differentiation in the villages became more pronounced over the past decade. In resettled villages, some households, now quite wealthy when compared to their neighbors, have expanded their businesses; they earn more now than they may have imagined in the old village. Other households work hard to fend off hunger and sustain their lives. The resettlement process, the rubber plantations, and the mines have offered opportunities from which only some households have benefited, allowing them to also escape the constraints that changes in access to land and other resources have imposed on them. Most, however, became impoverished and have struggled to find alternative livelihoods, suffering from a food insecurity not known before the interventions of these projects.

The impact has been even greater on the region's ethnic minority peoples, who have long been politically marginalized in nation-building processes. In the past, their identity was expressed in the unity of the village community and defined by their clan, which included different generations inhabiting a particular physical space. They had their land, at least enough for them to live on, and held forests and other resources in common. The Black River supported their lives in many ways. For many generations, the ideology of reciprocity ruled the community. Households used their labor to clear land and farm that land for their subsistence. However, the construction of dams and establishment of rubber plantations or mines changed these practices radically. Poor families were pushed to further marginalized situations ecologically, economically, and politically.[13]

While many Northwest villagers long for their past lives, either their old villages or the old ways of accessing land and water, this does not mean that they want to return to a life without electricity, with poor (or absent) roads, a lack of schools, or no local hospitals. What they express a longing for is to have enough land, or effective support for alternative livelihoods, to sustain their lives without having to sell their labor on a daily basis.

This book has exposed development as an intertwined process of power relations that takes place not just at individual, family, or village levels but also reaching toward and caught up in unfolding processes at larger, regional, and national scales. The massive displacement and resettlement that resulted from political decisions far away from dam sites, the land dispossessions that are a by-product of rubber planta-tions, the pollution and loss of livelihoods that have accompanied min-ing activities have also imposed an unprecedented state control over the region. My last question in the introduction—about why villagers gave away their land and how they responded to the transformation of the uplands—is tightly connected to these issues of power relations and governmentality. Because development projects are often justified as both national symbols of modernization and the fastest means of improving the lives of ethnic minority people in upland regions (re-gardless of the devastating reality), villagers had almost no political or rhetorical recourse to oppose their dispossession, but they did not do so without resistance.

My focus on the politics of development has enabled me to simulta-neously draw attention to how development works as a force of domi-nation and to consider the ways in which the politics of hydropower, plantations, and mining are negotiated and contested. Ethnic minor-ity groups in the Northwest uplands have throughout history fought an unequal battle against outside oppressors—colonial rulers, the state and its development ideology, and the market. Although the governing power has changed over time, from French colonialists to Vietnamese nationalists to global capital, poor and marginalized ethnic minority people have experienced a steady erosion of their land, their livelihood, and their cultural autonomy. Constrained by their lack of access to and control over resources, in many cases the people have been forced to deplete the resources that they still had access to in ways contrary to their traditions. However, their continual resistance and forms of adaptation make clear that although they have been forced to accept the domination of the central state and the logics of development, they keep fighting in other important ways.

If you travel to the Northwest in March, you will see beautiful rhododendrons blooming in the mountains. To northwesterners, the flower is a symbol of balance, love, and loyalty. The plant loves the land where it takes root; it grows and blooms despite the quality of the soil. Once uprooted, though, it will never be as healthy, not even if replanted in rich and nurturing soil. As I write these closing words, I can't help but think about the woman on the bus whom we met at the start of the book. She and her family exercise everyday politics as part of their strategies to survive and to thrive, from supporting the government's proposed development in the Northwest, to compromising via their contribution of land for a rubber plantation, to "voting with their feet" by quitting their jobs as rubber workers and becoming migrant workers far from home. Development projects have driven villagers out of the Northwest, but those villagers still have faith that the government will find a way to offer people hope for and access to better livelihoods, for those who want to remain in the village as well as for those who are forced to make a life elsewhere. No matter where they go, the desire to return to their roots will endure, like the rhododendron.

# Notes

## Preface

1. While my research was mainly qualitative, I also conducted surveys on changes in resettlers' and rubber workers' lives before and after the dam or the rubber project came to their villages.
2. Scott 1976, 1985; Bernstein 2010; Turner and Michaud 2009.
3. Bryant and Bailey 1997; Castree and Braun 2001; Robbins 2004.
4. Blaikie 1985; Escobar 1995.
5. J. Scott 2009 highlights the power relations between uplands and the center/valley in his work.
6. In Turner 2013, authors discuss experience and challenges in doing fieldwork in Southeast Asia, especially in mountain regions of Vietnam, Laos, and China.
7. In Vietnam, the Women's Union (WU) is a sociopolitical organization that the Communist Party of Vietnam established. The WU operation spans from national to village levels.

## Introduction

1. Nguyễn Văn Chinh 2008; Salemink 1997, 2003; Lentz 2011; Turner, Bonnin, and Michaud 2015.
2. Sowerwine 2004a, 2004b.
3. Schwenkel and Leshkowich 2012, 384.
4. Moore 2005.
5. Kerkvliet 2009; Turner 2012.
6. Harwood 2013; McDuie-Ra 2012; Reeves 2014.
7. Vandergeest and Peluso 1995; Sack 1986.
8. Peluso and Vandergeest 2020.
9. Yeh 2013, 5.
10. Rasmussen and Lund 2018.
11. Rasmussen and Lund 2018.
12. Vandergeest and Peluso 1995; Das and Poole 2004; Yeh 2013; Sivaramakrishnan 1999; Rasmussen and Lund 2018.
13. Pile 2008.
14. D. Mitchell 2003, 787.
15. D. Mitchell 2003, 788.
16. Yeh 2013; D. Mitchell 2003.
17. Hardy 2000, 23–24; Hardy and Turner 2000; Hardy 2003; Turner, Pham, and Ngô 2020; Hà 2016a, 2016b.

18. N. Dao 2012.

19. Combined by author from Vietnam Rubber Group 2022; Huu 2021; Ngoc 2018; Bich 2020.

20. See Baviskar 2005; Siciliano and Urban 2017; White and White 2012; Klinger 2018.

21. Feldman, Geisler, and Silberling 2003, 9. Also see Feldman and Geisler 2012, 974 differentiate ex situ and in situ displacement associated with mega-development projects.

22. Thongchai 1997 argues that a nation's geobody is a territorial imaginary with its own practices and values; Anderson 1991, 6.

23. De Carvalho 2016, 58; Anderson 1991.

24. Thongchai in his book *Siam Mapped* (1997) analyzed a nation as geobody when deconstructing the nation as a natural entity.

25. J. Scott 2009, 63.

26. Hanoi, Vietnam's capital, is located in the Red River delta.

27. *Miền xuôi* refers to delta lowlands downstream, while *vùng thấp* refers to lowlands such as river valleys or areas at the foot of mountains.

28. General Statistics Office of Vietnam 2019.

29. McElwee 2004.

30. Hồ Chí Minh 1946.

31. Hồ Chí Minh 1955.

32. Trung tâm Lưu trữ Quốc gia Việt Nam IIII [National Archives of Vietnam Center 3], Hanoi 1958a. Báo cáo thành tích 3 năm khôi phục kinh tế xây dựng khu Tự Trị nhân kỷ niệm 3 năm thành lập khu Tự Trị Thái Mèo và chiến thắng Điện Biên Phủ (Tháng 4/1958). [Report on achievements of 3 years of economic recovery and construction of the Autonomous Region on the occasion of the 3rd anniversary of the establishment of the Thái Mèo Autonomous Region and the Dien Bien Phu victory (April 1958)].

33. Thái Đen is the ethnicity of Black Thái people, while Thái Trắng is the ethnicity of the White Thái. Thái Bình refers to the lowland Kinh people from Thái Bình Province in the Red River delta.

34. Lentz 2019; Cons and Eilenberg 2019; Cons 2016; McElwee 2016; Yeh 2013; Arnold 2006; Moore 2005; Sivaramakrishnan 1999; Peluso 1992.

35. Hà 2016a, 2016b.

36. The different phases include the people's democratic national revolution (1945–1959); the transition from the national democratic revolution to the socialist revolution in the North and national revolution in the South (1959–1975); the newly united country moving toward socialism (1976–1986); economic reforms (1986–2013); and the current stage after the country's constitution was revised in 2013. Since 1986, the National Assembly has been the highest representative body of the people, while the central government is the country's highest state administrative body and the decision maker. Lower levels of administration include governments at provincial, district, and commune levels. While the commune is the lowest administrative body, at village level there are headmen, the village's Communist Party secretary, and quasi-organizations such as elderly associations, youth unions, veteran associations, women's unions, and the Fatherland fronts.

37. Socialist Republic of Vietnam 2013a.

38. Gramsci 1971, 340.

39. Gramsci 1971, 340.

40. Gramsci 1971, 151.

41. Gramsci 1971

42. Gramsci 1971.

43. The saying in Vietnamese is "Người dân tộc lười lắm, lại lạc hậu. Chả chịu làm gì. Họ chỉ toàn chờ trợ cấp của chính phủ. Thế bao giờ mà khá lên được?"

44. Hà 2016a, 2016b.

45. Yeh 2013.

46. Jakobsen 2022; Cavanagh 2018.

47. Agrawal 2005; Moore 2005; Yeh 2013; Hoffmann 2014; McElwee 2016.

48. Foucault 1983, 221.

49. Miller and Rose 2008, 61.

50. Li 2007; Yeh 2013.

51. Foucault 2008, 313.

52. Valladares and Boelens 2019.

53. Cowen and Shenton 1995; Li 2007.

54. Li 2007, 2002.

55. Ferguson 1990,15.

56. Watts 2003.

57. Kerkvliet 2009, 232.

58. Kerkvliet 2009, 233.

59. Turner 2012, 407.

60. N. Dao 2016; Turner 2012.

61. Kerkvliet 1986, 108.

62. N. Dao 2016

63. Kerkvliet 2009, 235.

64. Kerkvliet 2005, 2009

65. Butler 1995, 1997; D. Smith 1987.

66. Bernstein 1977.

67. Hart, Turton, and White 1989.

68. Zoomers 1999.

69. Fraser 2014.

70. Rigg and Vandergeest 2012, 7.

71. Schneider and Niederle 2010.

72. Post-socialist subjects refer to Vietnamese people in general after the 1986 economic reforms.

73. Indeed, there has been a large volume of work on subject formation and subjectivity in geography (see Jakobsen 2022; also Moore 2005; Valentine 2007; Yeh 2013). The work by Yeh, for example, argues for complexity in Tibetan subject formation. She reveals how Tibetans played a crucial role in transforming material landscapes in Tibet, and while they resisted being associated with the PRC, their actions helped naturalize that association process.

## 1. The Cultural Politics of Development

1. For Thái people as well as other ethnic minority groups in the Northwest, bathroom and toilets traditionally are not part of the main living building.

The room for bathing does not include the toilet. They are located in separate spaces, and not every house has these extras.

2. Kerkvliet 2009.

3. Trung tâm Lưu trữ Quốc gia Việt Nam III, Hanoi, 1959.

4. *Đại Việt Sử ký toàn thư, Kỳ nhà Lý* 1993.

5. Lentz 2019.

6. Nguyễn Van Chinh 2008; Harms and Baird 2014.

7. Turner 2012; Turner, Bonnin, and Michaud 2015.

8. J. Scott 2009.

9. In 1959, to support the development of ethnic minority people in upland regions, the national government established a ministerial-level agency, the Committee for Ethnic Minority Affairs (CEMA), to perform state management functions related to ethnic minority affairs nationwide. CEMA's precursor was the Department of Ethnic Minorities (Nha Dân Tộc), set up in 1946 with the aim of training ethnic minority cadres and monitoring ethnic minority affairs. Since Đổi Mới, the government has issued a number of policies to emphasize priorities to upland people, including education, micro-credit, agricultural support, infrastructure, and health care, among others. In the late 1990s and early 2000s, Programs 134 and 135 were well-known support programs in Vietnam for ethnic minority people in the uplands. There are also other CEMA-produced documents that support the development of ethnic minorities, and on November 18, 2019, at its eighth session, the National Assembly passed a resolution approving a master plan on socioeconomic development in ethnic minority and mountainous areas for 2021 to 2030.

10. J. Scott 1998. With the establishment of the Thái-Mèo Autonomous Region on May 7, 1955, ethnic languages such as Thái and Hmông began to be taught in schools, and the government permitted their use in local administration offices. In 1962, the Thái-Mèo Autonomous Region (TMAR) was renamed as the Northwest Autonomous Region (TBAR, or Khu Tự trị Tây Bắc). It existed for thirteen years until the American War ended in 1975. From 1962 onward, however, ethnic minority languages were no longer taught in schools.

11. McElwee 2004.

12. Gerth and Mills 1946.

13. *Khau cút* is a decorative style found on traditional roofs, with many different designs, depending on the owner's status. For example, a commoner's house may have *khau cút* in the shape of a buffalo horn, while *phìa tạo* (rich families) may have *khau cút* in the shape of a lotus flower.

14. Prime Minister Võ Văn Kiệt issued a ban on logging in natural forests through Directive 462-TTg of September 11, 1993, which enforces the strict management of logging, transportation, and timber export. That was the first policy on forest closure. There were other related policies put in place in 2003 and 2014. The most recent was Notice No. 191 / TB-VPCP (July 22, 2016) to implement a policy to halt the exploitation of natural forest timber. Despite a several policies issued on this matter, deforestation and illegal logging have continued nationwide, largely by lowland Vietnamese, in an effort to meet the growing domestic demand for timber in urban areas.

15. Bonnin and Turner 2014.

16. Lentz 2019.

17. Bonnin and Turner 2012; Lentz 2019.

18. Salemink 2011 argues that despite the perception of perennial antagonism between lowlanders, who were organized in states, and highlanders, who remained marginal to lowland state centers, there has been a rich history in terms of long-distance trade connecting lowland and highland places and populations, with important political and cultural effects in both regions.

19. Michaud and Turner 2017.

20. Socialist Republic of Vietnam 1991.

21. The policy was updated in the Decree 57/2017/NĐ-CP of May 9, 2017.

22. Mr. Hin, personal communication with the author, Sơn La, July 10, 2009.

23. Traditionally, Black Thái women learned to sew and embroider from the age of five or six. They began at age twelve to prepare for their marriage by sewing mattresses for their future home and making headscarves (*khăn piêu*) to give to all of the groom's female family members and relatives on the wedding day.

24. *Tằng cẩu* is the way in which married Black Thái women arrange their hair into a big bun on the top of their head (see figure 1.2). A married woman always wears a dress and is never allowed to arrange her hair differently until after her husband's death.

25. Mr. Hin, personal communication with the author, Sơn La, July 10, 2009.

26. The Nậm Chiến hydropower dam is a 232-megawatt plant on the Nậm Chiến River, one of the main tributaries of the Black River.

27. Yeh 2013.

28. I focus on these two groups because I have spent much of my time in the Northwest with members of these groups.

29. Different Thái groups were named largely based on women's attire and hairstyle. Traditionally, White Thái women wear white shirts (now they can wear different color shirts but in the same style) with V-necks in the front. Their ornate headscarves are plain, either white or indigo. They do not have the custom that women must wear *tằng cẩu* after marriage. Black Thái women wear much shorter shirts, in a dark color (indigo or black) with a high, round neck, as well as *khăn piêu* (ornate scarves). Married Black Thái women have to *tằng cẩu* their hair. Red is the dominant color of Red Thái women's shirts and scarves. Their headscarves are ornate, with different designs (compared to *khăn piêu*), and they do not wear them in the same way as Black Thái women.

30. Viện Dân tộc học 1978.

31. General Statistics Office of Vietnam 2001.

32. Đặng 1993.

33. Davis 2011.

34. Le Failler 2011.

35. Le Failler 2011.

36. Le Failler 2011.

37. Nguyễn Tuân 1960.

38. Lentz 2019; Nguyễn Tuân 1960.

39. Lentz 2011, 91

40. Author's interviews with residents of the region between 2008 and 2019.

41. Đặng 1993.

42. Viện Dân tộc học 1978.

43. Đặng et al 1972.

44. Turner, Bonnin, and Michaud 2015.

45. "Người Thái ăn gừng không rửa, người La Ha ăn bẩn cả năm."

46. Villagers in Muong Ma and Muong Che later had to contribute land to the rubber plantations.

47. Taylor 2007.

48. Mrs. Thinh, personal communication with the author, Sơn La, May 10, 2009.

49. Mr. Tra, personal communication with the author, Sơn La, August 20, 2009.

50. Mr. Bin, personal communication with the author, Sơn La, May 19, 2018.

51. Mrs. Thu, personal communication with the author, Sơn La, November 10, 2009.

52. Baviskar 2005.

53. Mr. Te, personal communication with the author, Yên Bái, May 27, 2018.

## 2. State Power and the Conquest of Nature

1. During this period, the gathering of a group of almost forty people to talk about hydropower issues was a notable success.

2. N. Dao 2011.

3. Nguyễn Danh Oanh 2009.

4. Tuyengiao 2012.

5. Sneddon 2015.

6. Sneddon 2015, 4, frames river development: "Large dams offered the material capacity to profoundly alter rivers, while river basin development provided institutional and managerial scaffolding."

7. Kalinovsky 2018, 31.

8. Sneddon 2015; Biggs 2006.

9. Mitchell 2002, 21, also points out: "For many postcolonial governments, this ability to rearrange the natural and social environment became a means to demonstrate the strength of the modern state as a techno-economic power."

10. Phạm 2018. Circular 348-TTg dated August 30, 1961, defines a state farm as "production units of the State, managed according to the economic accounting regime, funded by the State to produce according to the State's plan. All products made by the farm (not including the part that the farm members can produce by themselves) belong to the State and product distribution is according to the plan of the State. The farm is responsible for delivering the product to the State in prescribed quantities, and for the agencies and units to

be distributed, at the internal mobilization prices and announced by the State Planning Committee. Relations between farms and consumption agencies are settled according to the Government's economic contract regime."

11. This concerns political training to support a socialist path and fight against capitalist ideology.

12. "Bài ca vỡ đất," a poem that Hoàng Trung Thông wrote in 1948, praises the role of human creative labor in taming nature to serve human life.

13. Nguyễn Khải 1960.

14. *How the Steel Was Tempered* was a novel translated from Russian that was very popular in North Vietnam in the 1960s and 1970s. High school students were required to study the book as a literature selection.

15. Mrs. Tuyet, personal communication with the author, Điện Biên, May 30, 2019.

16. Foucault 1991, 2008.

17. Valladares and Boelens 2019.

18. Electricity of Vietnam 2009, 2. On July 21, 1955, the minister of industry and trade signed Decision 169-BCT/ND/KB to establish the Electricity Agency, the first government organization responsible for managing electricity in the newly independent Vietnam.

19. Electricity of Vietnam 2018.

20. Electricity of Vietnam 2019; Phap Luat Newspapers 2020.

21. McElwee 2016, 21.

22. Vietnam Institute of Energy 2006. The prime minister approved the Adjusted PDP 7 on March 18, 2016, in Decision No. 428/QD-TTg.

23. "Potential" in this instance refers to what planners project to be Vietnam's total hydropower capacity.

24. Ministry of Industry and Trade 2018.

25. GWh (gigawatt hour) is a unit of energy representing one billion watt hours and is equivalent to one million kilowatt hours. GWh are used as a measure of the output of large electricity power stations; CEIC 2023.

26. According to Le Viet 2018, by November 20, 2018, installed capacity of hydropower was approximately 41 percent, coal power was 37 percent, oil and gas was 15 percent, and other forms were about 7 percent. In terms of production, coal power was the highest, accounting for 41 percent, while hydropower was 39 percent, oil and gas 19 percent, and other sources only 2 percent.

27. Ministry of Industry and Trade 2013.

28. N. Dao 2010.

29. T. Mitchell 2002; Sneddon 2015; Kalinovsky 2018.

30. Trang 1995; Sơn La 2006; Dao Xuan Hoc 2009.

31. N. Smith 1991.

32. O'Rourke 2004.

33. Harms 2016 examines land rights, injustice, and land dispossession for urbanization in Ho Chi Minh City.

34. Nguyễn Danh Oanh 2009; Dan 2009; Nguyễn Đức Đạt 2017. Hydropower plants contribute at least VNĐ 6.5 billion (US$3.25 million) annually to the treasury through various taxes. According to a 2017 report by an EVN branch company, the Central Hydropower Joint-Stock Company, in the dry

season Hòa Bình Dam provided water to irrigate about eight hundred thousand hectares of paddy rice in the Red River delta and northern midland area.

35. Nguyễn Như Phong 2018.

36. O'Connor 1989, 2, defined combined development as "the combination of economic, social and political forms characteristic of 'developed' regions with those found in 'underdeveloped' regions—a combination of new and older forms (where 'older forms' are understood as economic and social forms historically produced at some time in the past)."

37. Author's personal communication with resettlers in these areas during fieldwork in 2009 and 2012.

38. N. Dao 2010.

39. PanNature 2010.

40. Ministry of Industry and Trade 2010.

41. Ministry of Industry and Trade 2013.

42. N. Dao 2012.

43. These two projects (Đồng Nai 6 and 6A), fortunately, were later paused thanks to the hard work of the Vietnam Rivers Network and its allies, including Saving Cát Tiên.

44. Vietgiaitri 2009; Truong 2010.

45. BBC News Tieng Viet 2020a, 2020b; Nguyễn Xuân 2020.

46. Data from interviews with an official who served on the Hòa Bình hydropower plant's management board, November 2009.

47. N. Dao 2011.

48. VUSTA 2006; N. Dao 2011; Tran Van Ha 2011.

49. The Red (Sông Hồng) and Mekong Rivers are not included because they offer no hydropower potential within Vietnam's territory.

50. Lâm 2005.

51. Hung 2017.

52. Electricity of Vietnam officials, personal communication with the author, Hanoi, July 2 and 3, 2009.

53. Dao and Bui 2015.

54. Electricity of Vietnam 2019.

55. Electricity of Vietnam 2019.

56. Ministry of Industry and Trade 2019.

57. This was part of Decision No. 38/QD-TTg (January 10, 2018) and Decision No. 389/QD-TTg (April 11, 2018).

58. Vietnam has three versions of its Land Law, for 1993, 2003, and 2013, with an update in 2020; a few revisions of the Law on Environmental Protection in 1992, 2005, 2014, and 2020; and the 1998 Law on Water Resources was updated in 2012 and was under revision in 2022.

59. N. Dao 2010.

60. The Red River basin in the north, the Đồng Nai River basin in the southeast, and the Mekong River basin in the south.

61. The Đồng Nai, Cầu, and Nhuệ-Đáy Rivers.

62. Ministry of Industry and Trade 2013.

63. Ministry of Agriculture and Rural Development (MARD) officials, personal communication with the author. July 20, 2009.

64. Department of Project Appraisal officials, personal communication with the author, July 25, 2009.

65. Hoang 2010.

66. Tuoitrenews 2011.

67. Tuoitrenews 2011.

68. Van 2010.

69. Author's personal communication with a government official, Hanoi, June 10, 2012.

70. Hirsch et al. 1992.

71. The next studies on dam impact after Hirsch and colleagues' study on Hoà Bình Dam (1992) were conducted by the Center for Natural Resources and Environmental Studies (CRES) in 2001 and by Dao Trong Hung, Dao Nga, and Tran Tri Trung in 2004, respectively. The studies focused on impacts of the Yali Falls Dam in the Central Highlands of Vietnam.

72. Gaventa 2009.

73. Võ 2006; Dao Trong Hung 2006; Hoàng and Vo 2006; Đoàn and Đức Anh Nguyễn 2006; Hoàng 2006; Dương 2009; Le and Dao 2016. In Vietnam, unlike in other countries, a network cannot formally exist without an organization to host it. The host organization has to legally register with the government. Thus, colleagues and I worked together to establish the Center for Water Resources Conservation and Development (WARECOD) to host Vietnam Rivers Network. For fifteen years (2006–2021), WARECOD successfully coordinated VRN's work and helped to raise concerns about dam-related issues on a national level. Since 2021, stricter rules have been applied to NGOs that work on environmental issues and advocacy. Alongside a number of other environmental groups in Vietnam, WARECOD and VRN can no longer conduct research or engage in advocacy-related activities.

74. VTV2 (a national TV channel) often covers news on environmental issues, which include water and food security, river issues, hydropower, resettlement, etc. Tuoitrenews, *Thanh Nien*, and *Tien phong* are among the newspapers that often provide news related to hydropower and its associated problems, including resettlement, deforestation, etc.

75. PhapLuatTPHCM 2011a, 2011b, 2011c.

76. Adjusted Power Development Plan 7 posted on Vietnamnet 2016; Electricity of Vietnam 2019.

77. The 2019.

78. N. Dao 2010.

79. Le and Dao 2016.

80. Baviskar 2005.

## 3. Damming the Black River

1. Sơn La Province People's Committee 2006.

2. Gramsci 1971, 340.

3. Foucault 1983; Yeh 2013.

4. Kerkvliet 2009, 235.

5. Nhân Dân 2015.

6. Baird and Shoemaker 2007.

7. Baviskar 2005; Roy 2001; Richter et al. 2010; Jeuland 2010.

8. VBPL 2002. National Assembly Decision No. 44/2001-QH10.

9. Power Investigation, Design and Construction Company (PIDC) No. 1 1999.

10. Huong Nhung 2019.

11. Sơn La Province People's Committee 2006.

12. Resettlement officers in Sơn La, personal communication with the author, August 24, 2009. In the first year of construction of the Sơn La Dam, the river was narrowed to build diversion works. In the beginning of dry season of the second year, engineers implemented river closure work to rechannel the water to the diversion sluice. During the construction period, the water flowed through the diversion sluice in the dry season and through the unfinished spillway dam during the rainy season. When construction of the dam and related infrastructure—powerhouse, switchyard, transmission lines, etc.—was complete, engineers closed the diversion sluice to fill the reservoir for power generation.

13. Ministry of Industry and Trade 2013.

14. Sơn La Province People's Committee 2006.

15. The World Commission on Dam's (2000) seven recommendations for equitable and sustainable development of water and energy resources include (1) gaining public acceptance; (2) comprehensive options assessment; (3) addressing existing dams; (4) sustaining rivers and livelihoods; (5) recognizing entitlements and sharing benefits; (6) ensuring compliance; and (7) sharing rivers for peace, development, and security.

16. National Assembly members, interviews with the author, August 15 and 17, 2009.

17. Khuc 2007.

18. Two resettlement officers in Sơn La Province, personal communication with the author, December 10, 2005.

19. Moore 2005.

20. The headman was correct. These twelve village families were forced to move, and those who moved late often received lower-quality land for farming and less-than-ideal lots for housing, such as those at the edge of the village or without easy access to water. Police forcibly removed the villagers who held out until the bitter end.

21. Sơn La Province People's Committee 2006.

22. During dam construction, displacement was divided into three main periods: (1) preparation of the dam construction site (2003); (2) resettlement of people who lived below the dam's 140-meter water level (2005–2006); and (3) resettlement of those who lived above the 140-meter water level but below the 218-meter water level (2007–2009). In period 1, people were displaced from the area that would become the dam construction site to two pilot resettlement areas in Muong Ta (Sơn La) and Muong Phin (Lai Châu). For periods 2 and 3, according to Sơn La Province People's Committee 2006, there were five types of resettlement: (1) concentrated rural resettlement far from the reservoir; (2) concentrated rural resettlement surrounding the reservoir but at a

higher elevation; (3) mixed host communities and resettlers; (4) concentrated urban resettlement; and (5) voluntary resettlement, with the latter referring to people who purchased land in a location that they chose for themselves outside the project plan.

23. N. Dao 2011.

24. National Institute of Agriculture Planning and Projection 2005.

25. Sơn La Province People's Committee 2006.

26. Resettlers in Sơn La, interviews with the author, August and September 2009.

27. National Institute of Agriculture Planning and Projection 2005.

28. Mr. Tieu, personal communication with the author, Sơn La, April 17, 2008.

29. Villagers and resettlement officers in Sơn La and Lai Châu Provinces, interviews with the author, December 2005, January 2006, and April 2008.

30. Caouette and Turner 2009, 9.

31. Resettlement officers in Sơn La and Lai Châu Provinces, interviews with the author, 2008 and 2009.

32. Mr. Bao, personal communication with the author, Sơn La, August 10, 2009.

33. Brickell, Arrigoitio, and Vasudevan 2017; Scudder 2005; Cernea and McDowell 2000.

34. J. Scott 1985 highlights some tactics that villagers used as "weapons of the weak," including foot-dragging, sabotage, false compliance, pilfering, and slander.

35. Sơn La Province People's Committee 2006.

36. Author's observations in the late 1990s.

37. VUSTA 2006.

38. Roy 2001.

39. Phan Hien 2014.

40. Văn phòng Chính phủ 2018.

41. Government Decision 459/QD-TTg and Sơn La Province Decision 01/2005/QD-UB on how to implement resettlement for people displaced by the Sơn La Dam project. In Vietnam, people receive land-use rights only via a certificate for the land they have, not land ownership rights.

42. Decision 02/QD-TTg adjusts policies highlighted earlier in Decision 01.

43. National Institute of Agriculture Planning and Projection 2005.

44. Mr. Kha, personal communication with the author, Sơn La, August 12, 2009.

45. Blaikie and Brookfield 1987.

46. Mrs. Hoa, personal communication with the author, Sơn La, May 31, 2017.

47. By the time of the policy's issuance, VNĐ 5 billion was equivalent to about US$300,000 to US$350,000 (US$1 = VNĐ 15,000).

48. District-level resettlement officers, interviews with the author, 2009 (July 16, 17, 18; August 7, 8; September 10, 11, 12, 13).

49. Local authorities, interviews with the author, Sơn La, August 21, 22, 23, 2009.

50. Local authorities, interviews with the author, Sơn La, October 5, 6, 7, 2009.

51. Resettlement officers, interview with the author, August 2009. The authorities provided buses only at the beginning of the project, owing to the cost factor. For most of the resettlement planning period the affected had to travel to resettlement sites on their own.

52. Huong Nhung 2019. The average exchange rate during this period was US$1.00 = VNĐ 23,000.

53. Salemink 2011.

54. McMichael 2008, 213.

## 4. Subject Making, Market Integration, and Differentiation

1. Van der Ploeg 2009, 6.

2. Hua, Kono, and Zhang 2023; Nghiem, Kono, and Leisz 2020; Belton, Van Asseldonk, and Bush 2017; Li 2014; Wolford et al. 2013; Hall 2011; Hall, Hirsch, and Li 2011; Bernstein 2010.

3. Bernstein 2010.

4. Akram-Lodhi 2005, 107.

5. Bernstein 2010; Zhang and Donaldson 2010.

6. White 1989, 20.

7. Bernstein 1977, 2010.

8. Levien, Watts, and Hairong 2018.

9. Kerkvliet 2009; Turner 2012.

10. Mr. Quan, personal communication with the author, Sơn La, October 10, 2009.

11. Hazell et al. 2007.

12. Schneider and Niederle 2010.

13. Batterbury and Bebbington 1999.

14. Mr. Nhien, personal communication with the author, Sơn La, August 9, 2009; Mr. Bu, personal communication with the author, Sơn La, July 7, 2012.

15. Mr. Tu, personal communication with the author, Sơn La, August 13, 2009.

16. Mr. Hun, personal communication with the author, Sơn La, May 27, 2019.

17. Schneider and Niederle 2010.

18. Deere and de Janvry 1979, 602.

19. Watts 2013.

20. J. Scott 1976.

21. White 1989.

22. There were no formal ranking criteria for wealthy and medium groups. Based on Decision 09/2011/QD-TTg dated January 30, 2011, on poor criteria, a family with income less than VNĐ 400,000 per person per month was considered poor. The decision can be found in Socialist Republic of Vietnam 2011b.

23. Mrs. Tinh, personal communication with the author, Sơn La, July 19, 2009.

24. Mr. Nu, personal communication with the author, Sơn La, August 19, 2009.

25. Mr. Nu, personal communication with the author, Sơn La, April 29, 2022.

26. Mrs. Bin, personal communication with the author, Sơn La, July 22, 2011.

27. Mr. Tien, personal communication with the author, Sơn La, July 20, 2011.

28. Mr. Ghin, personal communication with the author, Sơn La, November 5, 2009.

29. Mr. Ong, Sơn La resettlement officer, personal communication with the author, May 25, 2012.

30. Mr. Ke, personal communication with the author, Sơn La, November 10, 2009.

31. Mr. Lam, personal communication with the author, Sơn La, November 20, 2009.

32. Mr. Thinh, personal communication with the author, Sơn La, November 5, 2009.

33. Mr. Thinh, personal communication with the author, Sơn La, May 28, 2019.

34. Socialist Republic of Vietnam 2008. See Vietnamese government Resolution 30a/2008/NQ-CP on rapid and sustainable poverty reduction for sixty-one poor districts nationwide since 2008. Under this program, each province would select districts that were considered the province's poorest to receive funding support.

35. Mrs. Tra, personal communication with the author, Sơn La, April 27, 2022.

36. Mr. Tin, personal communication with the author, Sơn La, November 19, 2009.

## 5. The Politics of Rubber Plantations

1. Ban Chỉ đạo Phát triển cây cao su 2007.

2. Mr. Hien, personal communication with the author, Điện Biên, May 31, 2019.

3. Mrs. Thanh, personal communication with the author, Điện Biên, May 31, 2019.

4. Borras et al. 2022; Fairhead, Leach, and Scoones 2012; Borras et al. 2011.

5. White et al. 2012, 620.

6. Fairhead, Leach, and Scoones 2012.

7. McMichael 2012; Zoomers 2010; De Schutter 2011; Lavers 2012; N. Dao 2015.

8. Hua, Kono, and Zhang 2023; Nghiem, Kono, and Leisz 2020; Belton, Van Asseldonk, and Bush 2017; Li 2014; Wolford et al. 2013; Hall 2011; Hall, Hirsch, and Li 2011; Barney 2008; Li 2002.

9. Sikor 2012; Hall 2011; Li 2002.

10. Wolford et al. 2013, 192.

11. Wolford et al. 2013, 194.

12. Rasmussen and Lund 2018.

13. Sowerwine 2004b.

14. Harms 2016 elaborates on the process of land categorization and acquisition in Ho Chi Minh City. A very similar process can be found in other development and urbanization projects throughout Vietnam.

15. Harms and Baird 2014.

16. McElwee 2016, 14.

17. J. Scott 1998.

18. Locke and Ward 2016.

19. Geisler 2012.

20. Trung tâm Lưu trữ quốc gia Việt Nam III, Hanoi 1958b.

21. Trung tâm Lưu trữ Quốc gia III, Hanoi, 1958d.

22. Harms 2016.

23. Figure 5.2./FgMen> shows the sign that hangs on the tree that General Secretary Nông Đức Mạnh planted on the occasion of visiting the Sơn La Rubber Joint-Stock Company on January 18, 2010. It reads: "Các đồng chí có cách làm mới, tôi rất cảm ơn và hoan nghênh. Tập đoàn cao su Việt Nam là một tập đoàn lớn của đất nước và đang muốn xây dựng thành một tập đoàn hùng mạnh không những ở trong nước mà còn vươn ra các nước bạn. Hôm nay đến đây thấy hình ảnh nông dân rất mới đập vào mắt tôi. Xây dựng các đội trồng cao su bằng đất góp của dân, đây là chủ trương đúng, là một trong những nội dung mà chúng tôi muốn nói trong nghị quyết TW 7 khoá X về nông nghiệp, nông dân, nông thôn. Tôi rất hoan nghênh và đánh giá cao mô hình này, mong rằng tập đoàn cao su kiên trì làm thế này. Đây là 1 chủ trương lớn, là vai trò chủ đạo của doanh nghiệp có vốn nhà nước" (Trích lời Đồng chí Tổng bí thư Nông Đức Mạnh trong lần về thăm công ty CP Cao su Sơn La 18/1/2010).

24. Chau 2019.

25. Officials from the Ministry of Agriculture and Rural Development, interviews by the author, July 26, 2009, and July 5, 2011; local officials, interviews with the author, Sơn La Province, November 19, 2009.

26. Mr. Son, personal communication with the author, Sơn La, July 20, 2009.

27. Sơn La Province People's Committee 2011.

28. Sơn La Province People's Committee 2011.

29. Mr. Ha, personal communication with the author, Sơn La, May 25, 2017.

30. Rasmussen and Lund 2018; Beban 2021.

31. In this section I partly draw on my 2015 paper published in the *Journal of Peasant Studies*.

32. Trần Đức Viên 2008.

33. Trần Đức Viên 2008, 2, 4.

34. Fox and Castella 2013, 159.

35. Vietcombank Security 2020.

36. Vietnamese National Assembly Decision No. 15/2003/QH11 (June 17, 2003) on tax exemptions for rubber plantations using agricultural land;

Government Decree 129/2003/ND-CP (November 3, 2003) to articulate Decision No. 15/2003/QH11.

37. Fox and Castella 2013; Sturgeon 2012, 2013.

38. Phan Thi Xuan Hue 2020.

39. Vietcombank Security 2020.

40. As Vietnam follows market-oriented economic socialism or a market economy socialist orientation (*nền kinh tế thị trường theo định hướng xã hội chủ nghĩa*), state-owned enterprises still play a key role in the economy, and all land is publicly owned, despite the diversified economy and forms of ownership. The state decides on key projects and directions for its economic development and promotes their implementation through state-owned enterprises. In cases where state-owned enterprises become joint-stock companies, they still operate under state direction. VRG has twenty member companies of 100 percent ownership of charter capital (the total value of assets contributed or committed to be contributed by members when establishing a limited liability company or partnership) and forty-five other member companies that hold more than 50 percent ownership.

41. N. Dao 2015.

42. Vietnam Rubber Group officials, interview with the author, December 9, 2011.

43. Manivong and Cramb 2008; Sturgeon 2013, 5.

44. Duc Long Gia Lai group is a private, joint-stock Vietnamese company. In 2012 the average exchange rate was US$1 = VNĐ 20,000.

45. Mr. Minh, VRG official, interview with the author, Sơn La Province, December 9, 2011.

46. Ministry of Agriculture and Rural Development officials, interviews with the author, July 24, 2009.

47. Ministry of Agriculture and Rural Development 2009.

48. Socialist Republic of Vietnam 2013b. The prime minister's Decision 899/QĐ-TTgv (June 10, 2013) on the restructuring of the agricultural sector, with an emphasis on rubber plantations.

49. N. Dao 2015.

50. Vietcombank Security 2020, 19.

51. Mr. Phuc, personal communication with the author, Sơn La, May 25, 2017.

52. "Love for rubber trees," in "Song Da memoirs" by Nguyễn Tuân (1960), tells the story about how the rubber trees were brought to the Northwest from Vĩnh Linh, Quảng Trị Province, in central Vietnam.

53. Sturgeon 2012.

54. Mr. Ha, personal communication with the author, Sơn La, November 21, 2009, and July 21, 2011; Mr. Vinh, personal communication with the author, Sơn La, May 27, 2012.

55. MARD officials, interviews with the author, Hanoi, July 24, 2009 (Mr. Tri) and July 5, 2011 (Mr. Hung); Mr. Chau and Mr. Ta, local officials, interviews with the author, Sơn La Province, November 15, 2009.

56. Foucault 2008, 132.

57. Sơn La Province People's Committee 2011.

58. The Sơn La Rubber Join-Stock Company is a member of the VRG, which holds controlling shares (over 50 percent of registered capital). Similar companies were established for Lai Châu and Điện Biên.

59. N. Dao 2015.

60. Sơn La Province People's Committee 2011.

61. AgroInfo 2011.

62. Sơn La Province People's Committee 2011. Decision No 363/2011/NQ-HĐND (March 18, 2011).

63. Báo Giao Thông Vận Tải 2013.

64. Excerpted from the speech of the general secretary of the Vietnam Communist Party's Central Committee Nguyễn Phú Trọng on the occasion of visiting the Sơn La Rubber Joint-Stock Company on January 8, 2014. This excerpt was engraved on a framed stone and placed in the original rubber tree garden in It Ong commune.

65. Ngoc 2018.

66. Subregion I: plan to plant 11,500 hectares in ten lowland communes of Sìn Hồ district, including Ma Quai, Nậm Tăm, Nậm Cha, Nậm Cuổi, Căn Co, Noong Héo, Nậm Hăn, Nậm Mạ, Pu Sam Cáp, and a part of Tả Ngảo commune. Rubber Subregion II: plan to plant 1,600 hectares in five communes of the Nậm Na River basin, Phong Thổ district, including Mường So, Nậm Xe, Khổng Lào, Hoang Thèn, and Huổi Luông. Subregion III: plan to plant 6,500 hectares of rubber in ten communes of the Nậm Na River basin of Sìn Hồ district, including Chăn Nưa, Lê Lợi, Pú Đao, Xà Dề Phìn, Pa Tần, Nậm Ban and Tủa Sín Chải, Làng Mô, Tả Phìn, and Hồng Thu. Subregion IV: plan to plant 7,000 hectares of rubber in six communes of the Mường Tè district, including Nậm Hàng, Nậm Manh, Mường Mô, Kan Hồ, Nậm Khao, and Mường Tè. There are an additional 3,400 hectares in five communes: Pắc Ta commune (Tân Uyên district), Phúc Than, Mường Than, and Mường Cang communes, and Than Uyên town of Than Uyên district; Vuong and Tran 2018.

67. Báo Tài Nguyên and Môi Trường 2018.

68. Two provincial government leaders, personal communication with the author, Lai Chau, May 17, 2019.

69. Bich 2020.

70. Chu 2019.

71. To conduct research at the village level in Vietnam, researchers have to send requests to the Province's People's Committee for approval. Once one's request is granted, the committee will issue a reference to the district level. From there, researchers can request a reference to use at the commune level.

72. Document No. 3492/BNN-NT (December 20, 2007), written by MARD officials and sent to the prime minister regarding direction and policies for rubber plantations in provinces in the Northwest region, page 1; Ministry of Agriculture and Rural Development 2007.

73. Opinion of a villager voiced during a meeting that local authorities organized with the aim of persuading people to participate in the project, November 11, 2009.

74. In Vietnam, if rural people have health insurance and need medical attention, they need to first go to the commune clinic. It is the commune clinic that issues documents to send the sick or injured to a district hospital. From the district-level hospital, they may be sent to a provincial-level hospital and then to a hospital in Hanoi, if necessary. If one goes directly to the hospital without first visiting the local clinic, the insurance company may refuse to cover the costs. In this case, villagers were told that if they refused to join the rubber project, they would not be considered part of the commune for health benefit purposes and would not have access to its clinic. This information comes from the author's interviews with villagers on November 10, 2009, and May 2, 2013. However, when asked, the local authorities' representatives did not confirm that this method was used to force villagers to join the project.

75. Mr. Nu, personal communication with the author, Sơn La, May 26, 2012; Mr. Trieu, personal communication with the author, Điện Biên, May 5, 2014.

76. Elden 2007; Valladares and Boelens 2017.

77. Lưu et al. 2009.

78. Tu La District People's Committee 2009, 5.

79. Mrs. Hoa, personal communication with the author, Sơn La, May 2, 2013.

80. Mr. Thi, local authority staff member, personal communication with the author, Sơn La, May 3, 2013.

81. Mr. Ta, personal communication with the author, Sơn La, May 27, 2019.

82. Mr. Ta, personal communication with the author, Sơn La, May 27, 2019.

83. Mr. Ta, personal communication with the author, Sơn La, May 27, 2019.

84. Mr. The, personal communication with the author, Sơn La, November 16, 2009.

85. Mr. Le, personal communication with the author, Sơn La, July 11, 2009.

## 6. Rubber Workers and the Making of Modern Subjects

1. Sikor 2011.

2. Wolford et al. 2013, 205.

3. Wolford et al. 2013, 205.

4. Author-led group discussions, Sơn La, May 4, 2009, May 24, 2012.

5. Mrs. Hoa, personal communication with the author, Điện Biên, May 16, 2018; Mr. Chu, personal communication with the author, Lai Chau, June 2, 2019.

6. The average exchange rate in 2009 was US$1 = VNĐ 17,800.

7. N. Dao 2015.

8. Mr. Son, personal communication with the author, Sơn La, November 19, 2009.

9. Author-directed survey, Sơn La, May 20–24, 2017.

10. Mr. Tra, personal communication with the author, Sơn La, June 7, 2014.

11. Mr. Son, personal communication with the author, Sơn La, November 19, 2009. Meanwhile the Sơn La Rubber Joint-Stock Company estimates that

maize production from intercropping among the young rubber trees was only five tons per hectare.

12. Li 2010.

13. Bernstein 2007, 6.

14. Mr. Son, personal communication with the author, Sơn La, July 20, 2009; Mr. Me, personal communication with the author, Sơn La, December 9, 2011.

15. Li 2017, 1252.

16. Sơn La Rubber Company 2012, 5.

17. Sơn La Joint-Stock Rubber Company staff member, interview with the author, May 2, 2013.

18. Sơn La Rubber Company 2012.

19. Sơn La Joint-Stock Rubber Company staff member, interview with the author, November 12, 2009.

20. Nhat 2019.

21. Mr. Tin, district official, personal communication with the author, Sơn La, May 23, 2019.

22. Nhat 2019.

23. Mr. Hien, personal communication with the author, Sơn La, May 26, 2019.

24. Mr. Hien, personal communication with the author, Sơn La, May 26, 2019.

25. Mr. Quanh, personal communication with the author, Sơn La, May 26, 2019.

26. VOV Tay Bac 2019.

27. Mr. Tin, district official, personal communication with the author, Sơn La, May 23, 2019.

28. Mrs. Chuyen, personal communication with the author, Sơn La, May 13, 2018.

29. Mrs. Le, personal communication with the author, Lai Chau, May 29, 2019.

30. Mr. Son, villager in Sơn La, personal communication with the author, June 1, 2018, and May 27, 2019.

31. There are a few restaurants in Sơn La City whose menus include crickets and/or goat meat.

32. Mrs. Tham, villager in Sơn La, personal communication with the author, May 27, 2019.

33. Muong Muon Commune People's Committee 2021.

34. In this section I partly draw on my 2018 paper published in *Gender, Place and Culture: A Journal of Feminist Geography*.

35. Nightingale 2006; Resurrección and Elmhirst 2008, 7.

36. Cleaver 2002; Price 2010; Connell 1995; Jackson 1998.

37. Silberschmidt 2001, 659.

38. Bonnin and Turner 2014, 2012.

39. Mrs. Ninh and Mrs. Luyen, villagers in Sơn La, personal communication with the author, May 12, 2016.

40. White and White 2012.

41. Mrs. Ninh, villager in Sơn La, personal communication with the author, May 12, 2016.

42. Locals often just purchased fake alcohol, which was made by dissolving illegally imported chemicals from China in pill form into a twenty-liter can.

43. Mr. Lo, villager in Sơn La, personal communication with the author, June 1, 2016.

44. Author-led group discussion, Sơn La, June 2, 2016.

45. Lyttleton 2004; Dupont 1999; UN News 2018.

46. Brickell and Chant 2010, 146.

47. Author-led group discussion, Sơn La, June 2, 2016.

48. Mrs. Hue, villager in Sơn La, personal communication with the author, June 1, 2016.

49. Mr. Hung, villager in Sơn La, personal communication with the author, June 1, 2016.

50. Lomas et al. 2016.

## 7. Materialities and Politics of Mining

1. Le Anh 2019. This quote was in the minister of MONRE's response to questions by National Assembly members at the seventh session of the 14th National Assembly on errors in mineral exploration management. See the Ministry of Natural Resources and Environment's formal Document No. 4545/BTNMT-DCKS (September 13, 2019). Ministry of Natural Resources and Environment 2019b.

2. Tran Huong 2021.

3. Tran Huong 2021.

4. Tran Huong 2021.

5. Rasmussen and Lund 2018, 391.

6. Rasmussen and Lund 2018, 393.

7. Rasmussen and Lund 2018, 391.

8. Peluso 2018, 401.

9. Similar problems occurred in the Bolivian Altiplano as described by Perrault 2013, in Burkina Faso as described in Côte and Korf's research in 2018, and in Peluso's (2018) work on Borneo.

10. Bridge 2004, 209.

11. Douglas and Lawson 2002; McNeill 2000.

12. SputnikVietnam 2022.

13. Moore and Luoma 1990; Bridge 2004.

14. Martinez-Alier et al. 2016; Scheidel et al. 2020.

15. Martinez Alier et al. 2014.

16. My 2018.

17. Nguyễn Đức Thành et al. 2023. Even before the French colonial period, the Northwest was known for its mineral richness.

18. Vinacomin 2013.

19. Humphreys 2018.

20. My 2018; Sputnik Vietnam 2022.

21. Le Van Huong 2015.

22. Ministry of Agriculture and Rural Development 2014.

23. Vimico 2020.

24. Le Van Huong 2015.

25. Socialist Republic of Vietnam 2018.

26. Mai 2021.

27. Socialist Republic of Vietnam 2011a.

28. Mai 2021.

29. Schiappacasse, Müller, and Le 2019, 138.

30. Socialist Republic of Vietnam 2011a.

31. Socialist Republic of Vietnam 2010.

32. VVCI-CODE 2011, 76.

33. Socialist Republic of Vietnam 1999.

34. United Nations Development Program 2015.

35. Tran Hai 2016.

36. Duane Morris LLP 2018.

37. Vimico 2017.

38. Huong Giang 2019.

39. Vinacomin 2016

40. Mr. Tuan, personal communication with the author, Yên Bái, May 10, 2019.

41. Mr. Giang, personal communication with the author, Yên Bái, May 11, 2019.

42. Gramsci 1971.

43. Đặng Giang 2013.

44. Tran Huong 2021.

45. Tran Huong 2021.

46. Sorting out the details about what each division, committee, or office does to meet the Department of Natural Resources and Environment directives remains impeded by understaffing.

47. Ministry of Natural Resources and Environment 2019a.

48. Ministry of Natural Resources and Environment 2019a.

49. Đặng Giang 2013; Tran Huong 2021. The average exchange rate in October 2021 was US$1 = VNĐ 22,750.

50. Hung 2014; Duc 2019; Hai 2020.

51. Mr. Hieu, Lào Cai, personal communication with the author, May 14, 2019.

52. Mr. Trung, villager in Yên Bái, personal communication with the author, May 10, 2019.

53. Dongsinquyen, n.d. https://dongsinquyen.vn/about/Gioi-thieu-chung.html, accessed July 7, 2022.

54. Minh 2013.

55. Lào Cai Provincial People's Committee 2022.

56. Dongsinquyen 2022.

57. Dongsinquyen 2022.

58. PetroTimes 2013.

59. Ty Ba District Government 2020.

60. Hung 2014.

61. Hung 2014.

62. Bridge 2004.

63. Mr. Tuan, personal communication with the author, Yên Bái, May 10, 2019.

64. Sở Công Thương Yên Bái 2012.

65. Sở Công Thương Yên Bái 2012.

66. Sở Công Thương Yên Bái 2012.

67. Nguyễn Quang and Pham 2022.

68. Yên Bái Province's People Committee 2006, 2008, 2011, 2017. They include Decision No. 82/QD-UBND (March 2, 2006) on zoning and planning of mineral activities in Yên Bái for the period 2006-2010; Decision No. 532/QD-UBND (April 7, 2008) on planning for exploration, mining, processing, and use of minerals as common construction materials and peat in Yên Bái for 2007-2015; Decision No. 1459/QD-UBND (September 30, 2011) on planning for exploration, mining, processing, and use of iron, copper, gold, lead-zinc, and other minerals (except minerals used as common construction materials and peat); and Decision No. 3520/QD-UBND (December 29, 2017) on the approval of the planning for exploration, mining, and use of minerals in Yên Bái Province, for the period 2016-2022, with a vision to 2030.

69. Nguyễn Mạnh Quân 2013.

70. Mr. Triet, villager in Yên Bái, personal communication with the author, May 10, 2019.

71. Mr. Ha, villager in Yên Bái, personal communication with the author, May 10, 2019.

72. Nguyễn Mạnh Quân 2013; Đặng Giang 2013.

73. Rasmussen and Lund 2018, 388-89.

## 8. Surviving the Mines, and the Everyday Politics of Marginalization

1. Bridge 2004.

2. Douglas and Lawson 2002.

3. Douglas and Lawson 2002.

4. Bebbington and Bury 2009.

5. Perreault 2013.

6. Thinh Tam Commune 2018.

7. Mr. Trieu, personal communication with the author, Yên Bái, May 10, 2019.

8. Mr. Thieng, personal communication with the author. Yên Bái, May 10, 2019.

9. Vinacomin 2016.

10. Vinacomin 2016.

11. Vinacomin 2016.

12. Mrs. Dang, personal communication with the author, Lào Cai, May 17, 2019.

13. Perreault 2013.

14. Kerkvliet 2009.

15. Bridge 2004; Hodges 1995.

16. Li 2010, 2014.

17. Li 2010.

18. Rasmussen and Lund 2018, 392.

19. Vinacomin 2016.

20. Author-directed focus group discussions, Lào Cai, July 13, 2021.

21. Mrs. Tam, personal communication with the author, Lào Cai, May 17, 2019.

22. Hung 2014.

23. Mr. Hu, personal communication with the author, Lào Cai, May 17, 2018.

24. Mr. Trung, personal communication with the author, Lào Cai, May 17, 2019.

25. Mr. Ha, personal communication with the author, Lào Cai, May 18, 2018.

26. Mr. Ba, personal communication with the author, Lào Cai. May 17, 2020.

27. Ministry of Natural Resources and Environment 2022.

28. Conde and Le Billon 2017; Kerkvliet 2009; Turner 2012.

29. Bebbington and Bury 2009.

30. Bebbington and Bury 2009, 17299.

31. Perreault and Valdivia 2010.

32. Elden 2007; Valladares and Boelens 2017.

33. Dinh 2014; Hung 2014.

34. The plight of those affected by mining in Vietnam was not well known until the late 2010s. Some mining activities are considered sensitive, such as bauxite mining in the Central Highlands. As a result, the impacts have been muted in the media and among the wider public, since permission to conduct research at such sites has not been granted.

35. Author-directed focus group discussions, Yên Bái, July 30, 2022.

36. Yen Bai Portal 2019.

37. Thanh 2020.

38. Yên Bái Province People's Committee 2020.

39. Thai 2020.

40. Author-directed group discussion, Yên Bái, July 30, 2022.

41. Author-directed group discussion, Lào Cai, July 31, 2022.

42. Ty Ba District Government 2020.

43. Laocaitv 2021.

44. Associated Press 2016. In early April 2016, toxic discharge from a Taiwanese-owned steel plant resulted in an estimated seventy tons of dead fish along more than two hundred kilometers of Vietnam's central coast, sparking rare protests across the country.

45. Kerkvliet 2009.

46. Dongsinquyen 2022.

47. Author-directed focus group discussions, Lào Cai, May 18, 2019, and July 31, 2022.

48. Ministry of Education and Training 2021.

49. Author-directed focus group discussions in 2018, 2019, 2022; government officials in Lào Cai and Yên Bái, interviews with the author, May 2019.

50. Author-directed group discussion, Lào Cai, July 31, 2022.

51. Author-directed group discussion, Yên Bái, July 30, 2022.

52. Ms. Yen, personal communication with the author, Lào Cai, May 18, 2019.

53. Mrs. Dang, virtual personal communication with the author, Lào Cai, May 5, 2020.

54. Ms. Hoai, virtual personal communication with the author, Lào Cai, May 6, 2020.

55. Mrs. Tram, personal communication with the author, Lào Cai, May 17, 2019.

56. Perreault 2013.

57. Nguyễn Đức Thành et al. 2023.

58. Martinez-Alier et al. 2014. Also see Barham and Coomes 2005.

## Conclusion

1. In the 1950s, the northern mountainous region of Vietnam was divided into Tây Bắc and Việt Bắc. During this period, Tây Bắc (Northwest) consisted of five northwestern provinces: Lào Cai, Lai Châu, Sơn La, Yên Bái, and Nghĩa Lộ. Việt Bắc consisted of six northeastern provinces: Cao Bằng, Bắc Kạn, Lạng Sơn, Thái Nguyên, Tuyên Quang, and Hà Giang.

2. Vandergeest and Peluso 1995; Das and Poole 2004; Yeh 2013; Sivaramakrishnan 1999; Rasmussen and Lund 2018.

3. Moore 2005, 5.

4. Rasmussen and Lund 2018.

5. Li 2014, 180.

6. Li 2014, 180.

7. Bui 2015, 86.

8. Agrawal 2005, 7.

9. Bernstein 1977.

10. Borras 2009.

11. McMichael 2008, 213.

12. Agrawal 2005, 215.

13. Blaikie and Brookfield 1987.

# References

Agrawal, Arun. 2005. *Environmentality: Technologies of Government and the Making of Subjects.* Durham, NC: Duke University Press. https://read. dukeupress.edu/books/book/936/EnvironmentalityTechnologies-of-Government-and-the.

*AgroInfo.* 2011. "Phát triển cao su ở phía Bắc không theo quy hoạch sẽ thất bại" [Rubber development in the North will be a failure if does not follow planning]. *AgroInfo,* August 18. http://agro.gov.vn/vn/tID21123_Phat-trien-cao-su-o-phia-Bac-Khong-theo-quy-hoach-se-that-bai.html.

Akram-Lodhi, A. Haroon. 2005. "Vietnam's Agriculture: Processes of Rich Peasant Accumulation and Mechanisms of Social Differentiation." *Journal of Agrarian Change* 5, no. 1: 73–116. https://doi.org/10.1111/j.1471-0366. 2004.00095.x.

Anderson, Benedict. 1991. *Imagined Communities: Reflections on the Origin and Spread of Nationalism.* New York: Verso. https://www.versobooks.com/en-ca/products/1126-imagined-communities.

Arnold, David. 2006. *The Tropics and the Traveling Gaze: India, Landscape, and Science, 1800–1856.* Seattle: University of Washington Press. https://www.jstor.org/stable/j.ctvct00hc.

Associated Press. 2016. "Vietnam Blames Toxic Waste Water from Steel Plant for Mass Fish Deaths." *Guardian,* July 1. https://www.theguardian.com/environment/2016/jul/01/vietnam-blames-toxic-waste-water-fom-steel-plant-for-mass-fish-deaths.

Baird, Ian G., and Bruce Shoemaker. 2007. "Unsettling Experiences: Internal Resettlement and International Aid Agencies in Laos." *Development and Change* 38, no. 5: 865–88. https://doi.org/10.1111/j.1467-7660.2007.00437.x.

Ban Chỉ đạo Phát triển cây cao su. 2007. *Tài liệu hướng dẫn Số 98-ĐC-BCD PTCCS* [Guiding Document No. 98-ĐC-BCD PTCCS]. Sơn La: Son La Ban Chỉ đạo Phát triển cây cao su.

Báo Giao Thông Vận Tải. 2013. "Trồng cao su ở miền Bắc chẳng khác nào đánh bạc" [Growing rubber trees in the North is like gambling]. *Báo Giao Thông Vận Tải,* December 12. http:// giaothongvantai.com.vn/thi-truong/lao-dong-viec-lam/201312/trong-cao-su-o-mien-bac-chang-khac-nao-danh-bac-427264/.

Báo Tài nguyên Môi Trường. 2018. "Lai Châu cho thuê trên 15.4 hecatres để xây dựng nhà máy chế biến mủ cao su" [Lai Chau leased more than 14.5 hectares for constructing rubber processing factory]. Báo Tài nguyên and Môi Trường, August 31. https://baotainguyenmoitruong.

vn/lai-chau-cho-thue-tren-15-4ha-de-xay-dung-nha-may-che-bien-mu-cao-su-230803.html.

Barham, Bradford L., and Oliver T. Coomes. 2005. "Sunk Costs, Resource Extractive Industries, and Development Outcomes." In *Nature, Raw Materials, and Political Economy*, Research in Rural Sociology and Development, vol. 10, edited by Paul S. Ciccantell, David A. Smith, and Gay Seidman, 159–86. Bingley, UK: Emerald Group. https://www.emerald.com/insight/publication/doi/10.1016/S1057-1922(2005)10.

Barney, Keith. 2008. "Local Vulnerability, Project Risk, and Intractable Debt: The Politics of Smallholder Eucalyptus Promotion in Salavane Province, Southern Laos." In *Smallholder Tree Growing for Rural Development and Environmental Services: Lessons from Asia*, edited by Denyse J. Snelder and Rodel D. Lasco, 263–86. New York: Springer. https://link.springer.com/book/10.1007/978-1-4020-8261-0.

Batterbury, Simon, and Anthony J. Bebbington. 1999. "Environmental Histories, Access to Resources and Landscape Change: An Introduction." *Land Degradation & Development* 10, no. 4: 279–89. https://doi.org/10.1002/(SICI)1099-145X(199907/08)10:4<279::AID-LDR364>3.0.CO;2-7.

Baviskar, Amita. 2005. *In the Belly of the River: Tribal Conflicts over Development in the Narmada Valley*. New York: Oxford University Press. https://global.oup.com/academic/product/in-the-belly-of-the-river-9780195671360?cc=ca&lang=en&.

BBC News Tiếng Việt. 2020a. "Mưa lũ miền Trung: Hàng trăm người chất, mất tích-Thiên tai hay nhân tai?" [Floods in the central region: Hundreds of people died and missing—natural or man-made disasters?]. BBC News Tiếng Việt, October 19. https://www.bbc.com/vietnamese/vietnam-54565141.

BBC News Tiếng Việt. 2020b. "Lũ lụt miền Trung: Hội chữ thập đỏ lo thảm hoạ nhân đạo" [Floods in central region of Vietnam: The Red Cross worries about humanitarian disasters]. BBC News Tiếng Việt, October 21. https://www.bbc.com/vietnamese/vietnam-54620472.

Beban, Alice. 2021. *Unwritten Rule: State-Making through Land Reform in Cambodia*. Ithaca, NY: Cornell University Press. http://www.jstor.org/stable/10.7591/j.ctv12sdwbz.

Bebbington, Anthony J., and Jeffrey T. Bury. 2009. "Institutional Challenges for Mining and Sustainability in Peru." *PNAS* 106, no. 41: 17296–301. https://doi.org/10.1073/pnas.0906057106.

Belton, Ben, Imke Josepha Matiana van Asseldonk, and Simon R. Bush. 2017. "Domestic Crop Booms, Livelihood Pathways and Nested Transitions: Charting the Implications of Bangladesh's Pangasius Boom." *Journal of Agrarian Change* 17, no. 4: 694–714. https://doi.org/10.1111/joac.12168.

Bernstein, Henry. 1977. "Notes on Capital and Peasantry." *Review of African Political Economy* 4, no. 10: 60–73. https://www.jstor.org/stable/3997920.

Bernstein, Henry. 2007. "Capital and Labour from Centre to Margins." Paper presented at the Living on the Margins Conference, Stellenbosch, South Africa, March 26–28.

Bernstein, Henry. 2010. *Class Dynamics of Agrarian Change*. Halifax, NS: Fernwood. https://fernwoodpublishing.ca/book/class-dynamics-of-agrarian-change.

Bich, Hong. 2020. "Sẽ có thêm 3 nhà máy chế biến cao su tại vùng núi phía bắc" [There will be three rubber latex processing factories in northern mountain region]. VietnamPlus, March 15. https://www.vietnamplus. vn/se-co-them-3-nha-may-che-bien-cao-su-tai-vung-mien-nui-phia-bac/628528.vnp.

Biggs, David. 2006. "Reclamation Nations: The U.S. Bureau of Reclamation's Role in Water Management and Nation Building in the Mekong Valley, 1945–1975." *Comparative Technology Transfer and Society* 4, no. 3 (December): 225–46. https://doi.org/10.1353/ctt.2007.0001.

Blaikie, Piers. 1985. *The Political Economy of Soil Erosion in Developing Countries*. London: Routledge. https://www.routledge.com/The-Political-Economy-of-Soil-Erosion-in-Developing-Countries/Blaikie/p/book/9781138638853.

Blaikie, Piers, and H. C. Brookfield. 1987. *Land Degradation and Society*. New York: Methuen. https://doi.org/10.4324/9781315685366.

Bonnin, Christine, and Sarah Turner. 2012. "At What Price Rice? Food Security, Livelihood Vulnerability, and State Interventions in Upland Northern Vietnam." *Geoforum* 43, no. 1: 95–105. https://doi.org/10.1016/j. geoforum.2011.07.006.

Bonnin, Christine, and Sarah Turner. 2014. "'A Good Wife Stays Home': Gendered Negotiations over State Agricultural Programmes, Upland Vietnam." *Gender, Place and Culture: A Journal of Feminist Geography* 21, no. 10: 1302–20. http://dx.doi.org/10.1080/0966369X.2013.832663.

Borras, Saturnino M., Jr. 2009. "Agrarian Change and Peasant Studies: Changes, Continuities and Challenges—an Introduction." *Journal of Peasant Studies* 36, no. 1: 5–31. https://doi.org/10.1080/03066150902820297.

Borras, Saturnino M., Jr., Jennifer C. Franco, Tsegaye Moreda, Yunan Xu, Natacha Bruna, and Binyam Afewerk Demena. 2022. "The Value of So-Called 'Failed' Large-Scale Land Acquisitions." *Land Use Policy* 119. https://doi. org/10.1016/j.landusepol.2022.106199.

Borras, Saturnino M., Jr., Ruth Hall, Ian Scoones, Benjamin White, and Wendy Wolford. 2011. "Towards a Better Understanding of Global Land Grabbing: An Editorial Introduction." *Journal of Peasant Studies* 38, no. 2: 209–16. https://doi.org/10.1080/03066150.2011.559005.

Brickell, Katherine, and Sylvia Chant. 2010. "'The Unbearable Heaviness of Being': Reflections on Female Altruism in Cambodia, Philippines, the Gambia and Costa Rica." *Progress in Development Studies* 10, no. 2 (April): 145–59. https://doi.org/10.1177/146499340901000204.

Brickell, Katherine, Melissa Fernández Arrigoitia, and Alexander Vasudevan. 2017. *Geographies of Forced Eviction*. London: Palgrave Macmillan. https:// link.springer.com/book/10.1057/978-1-137-51127-0.

Bridge, Gavin. 2004. "Contested Terrain: Mining and the Environment." *Annual Review of Environmental* Resources 29:205–59. https://doi.org/10.1146/annurev.energy.28.011503.163434.

Bryant, Raymond L., and Sinead Bailey. 1997. *Third World Political Ecology: An Introduction.* London: Routledge. https://www.routledge.com/Third-World-Political-Ecology-An-Introduction/Bailey-Bryant/p/book/9780415127448.

Bui, Hai Thiem. 2015. "In Search of a Post-socialist Mode of Governmentality: The Double Movement of Accommodating and Resisting Neo-liberalism in Vietnam." *Asian Journal of Social Science* 43, no. 1–2: 80–102. https://www.jstor.org/stable/i40138765.

Butler, Judith. 1995. "Contingent Foundations: Feminism and the Question of 'Postmodernism.'" In *Feminist Contentions: A Philosophical Exchange*, edited by S. Benhabib, J. Butler, D. Cornell, and N. Fraser, 35–57. New York: Routledge. https://doi.org/10.4324/9780203825242.

Butler, Judith. 1997. *The Psychic Life of Power.* Stanford, CA: Stanford University Press. http://www.sup.org/books/title/?id=819.

Caouette, Dominique, and Sarah Turner, eds. 2009. *Agrarian Angst and Rural Resistance in Contemporary Southeast Asia.* London: Routledge. https://www.routledge.com/Agrarian-Angst-and-Rural-Resistance-in-Contemporary-Southeast-Asia/Caouette-Turner/p/book/9780415681957.

Castree, Noel, and Bruce Braun. 2001. *Social Nature: Theory, Practices and Politics.* New York: Routledge. https://www.wiley.com/en-cn/Social+Nature:+Theory,+Practice+and+Politics-p-9780631215684.

Cavanagh, C. J. 2018. "Political Ecologies of Biopower: Diversity, Debates, and New Frontiers of Inquiry. *Journal of Political Ecology* 25, no. 1: 402–25.

CEIC. 2023. "Vietnam Electricity Production." https://www.ceicdata.com/en/indicator/vietnam/electricity-production.

Center for Natural Resources and Environmental Studies. 2001. "Study into Impact of Yali Falls Dam on Resettled and Downstream Communities." Working paper, Vietnam National University. https://www.irn.org/files/programs/vietnam/yali-e.pdf.

Cernea, Michael, and Christopher McDowell, eds. 2000. *Risks and Reconstruction: Experiences of Resettlers and Refugees.* Washington, DC: World Bank. https://documents1.worldbank.org/curated/en/947311468739277702/pdf/multi-page.pdf.

Chau, Giang. 2019. "10 năm chờ đợi, vạn hộ dân tan giấc mộng vàng trắng" [10 years of waiting, tens of thousands of households lost their dreams of gaining income from rubber plantation). *Vietnamnet*, May 4. https://vietnamnet.vn/10-nam-cho-doi-van-ho-dan-tan-giac-mong-vang-trang-528454.html.

Chu, Khoi. 2019. "Góc nhìn từ mô hình góp đất trồng cao su tại Tây Bắc" [Looking at the land contribution model for rubber plantation in the Northwest]. *VnEconomy*, May 7. http://vneconomy.vn/goc-nhin-tu-mo-hinh-gop-dat-trong-cao-su-tai-tay-bac-20190507091422328.htm.

Cleaver, Frances. 2002. *Masculinities Matter! Men, Gender and Development.* New York: Zed Books. https://www.bloomsbury.com/ca/masculinities-matter-9781842770658/.

Conde, Marta, and Philippe Le Billon. 2017. "Why Do Some Communities Resist Mining Projects While Others Do Not?" *Extractive Industries and Society* 4, no. 3: 681–97. https://doi.org/10.1016/j.exis.2017.04.009.

Connell, Raewyn. 1995. *Masculinities*. Berkeley: University of California Press. https://www.ucpress.edu/book/9780520246980/masculinities.

Cons, Jason. 2016. *Sensitive Space: Fragmented Territory at the India-Bangladesh Border*. Seattle: University of Washington Press. https://uwapress.uw.edu/book/9780295744247/sensitive-space/.

Cons, Jason, and Michael Eilenberg, eds. 2019. *Frontier Assemblages: The Emergent Politics of Resource Frontiers in Asia*. Oxford: John Wiley & Sons. https://onlinelibrary.wiley.com/doi/book/10.1002/9781119412090.

Côte, Muriel, and Benedikt Korf. 2018. "Making Concessions: Extractive Enclaves, Entangled Capitalism and Regulative Pluralism at the Gold Mining Frontier in Burkina Faso." *World Development* 101:466–76. https://ideas.repec.org/a/eee/wdevel/v101y2018icp466-476.html.

Cowen, Michael, and Robert Shenton. 1995. "The Invention of Development." In *Power of Development*, edited by Jonathan Crush, 25–41. London: Routledge. https://www.routledge.com/Power-of-Development/Crush/p/book/9780415111775.

*Đại Việt Sử ký toàn thư. Kỳ nhà Lý* [Viet historical chronical, Lý dynasty]. 1993. Translated by the Social Sciences Academy. Hanoi: Social Sciences Publishing House.

Dan, Tiep Phuc. 2009. "Study on the Impacts of Hoa Binh Hydropower Project on Resettlers Surrounding the Reservoir." Paper presented at a training workshop on the World Commission on Dams strategies hosted by the Vietnam Rivers Network, Hoa Binh, Vietnam, November 7–8.

Đặng, Nghiêm Vạn. 1993. *Quan hệ giữa các tộc người trong một quốc gia dân tộc* [Relationships among ethnic groups in a nation-state]. Hanoi: National Political Publisher.

Đặng, Nghiêm Vạn, Nguyễn Truc Binh, Nguyễn Văn Huy, and Thanh Thien. 1972. *Những nhóm dân tộc thuộc ngữ hệ Nam Á ở Tây Bắc Việt Nam* [Ethnic minority groups under South Asia language system in Northwest Vietnam]. Hanoi: Social Science Publisher.

Đặng Giang. 2013. "Tăng cường quản lý khoáng sản vùng Tây Bắc" [Strengthening mineral control in the Northwest]. *Nhan Dan*, January 25. https://nhandan.vn/tang-cuong-quan-ly-khoan-san-vung-tay-bac-post383524.html.

Dao, Nga. 2010. "Dam Development in Vietnam: The Evolution of Dam-Induced Resettlement Policy." *Water Alternatives* 3, no. 2: 324–40. http://www.wateralternatives.org/index.php/allabs/96-a3-2-19/file.

Dao, Nga. 2011. "Damming Rivers in Vietnam: A Lesson Learned in the Tây Bắc Region." *Journal of Vietnamese Studies* 6, no. 2: 106–40. https://doi.org/10.1525/vs.2011.6.2.106.

Dao, Nga. 2012. "Resettlement, Displacement and Agrarian Change in Northern Uplands of Vietnam." PhD diss., York University.

Dao, Nga. 2015. "Rubber Plantations in the Northwest: Rethinking the Concept of Land Grabs in Vietnam." *Journal of Peasant Studies* 42, no. 2: 347–69. https://doi.org/10.1080/03066150.2014.990445.

Dao, Nga. 2016. "Political Responses to Dam-Induced Resettlement in Northern Uplands Vietnam." *Journal of Agrarian Change* 16, no. 2: 291–317. https://doi.org/10.1111/joac.12106.

Dao, Nga. 2018. "Rubber Plantations and Their Implications on Gender Roles and Relations in Northern Uplands Vietnam." *Gender, Place and Culture: A Journal of Feminist Geography* 25, no. 11: 1579–1600. https://doi.org/10.1080/0966369X.2018.1553851.

Dao, Nga, and Bui Lien Phuong. 2015. "Rethinking Development Narratives of Hydropower in Vietnam." In *Hydropower Development in the Mekong Region: Political, Socio-economic and Environmental Perspectives*, edited by Nathanial Matthews and Kim Geheb, 173–97. London: Earthscan. https://www.routledge.com/Hydropower-Development-in-the-Mekong-Region-Political-Socio-economic-and/Matthews-Geheb/p/book/9781138377509.

Dao Trong Hung. 2006. "Nghiên cứu sinh kế và môi trường khu TĐC thuỷ điện KleiKrông, tỉnh Kon Tum" [The study on the livelihood and environment at resettlement area of KleiKrong hydropower project, Kon Tum Province]. Presentation at Vietnam Rivers Network's annual meeting, Hanoi, December 5.

Dao Trong Hung, Dao Nga, and Tran Chi Trung. 2004. "Study into Resettlement at the Yali Falls Dam, Kontum Province." Working paper, Institute of Ecology and Biological Resources and International Rivers Network. https://archive.internationalrivers.org/sites/default/files/attached-files/yalifalls2004_0.pdf.

Dao Xuan Hoc. 2009. "Tưới tiêu ở Việt Nam: Thành tựu và thách thức trong phát triển" [Irrigation in Vietnam: Achievements and challenges in development]. Opening speech at the 63rd Ceremony of the Traditional Day of Water Conservation in Hanoi, Water Resources University, Hanoi, August 28, 2009.

Das, Veena, and Deborah Poole, eds. 2004. *Anthropology in the Margins of the State.* Santa Fe, NM: School of American Research Press. https://sarweb.org/anthropology-in-the-margins-of-the-state/.

Davis, Bradley C. 2011. "Black Flag Rumors and the Black River Basin: Powerbrokers and the State in the Tonkin-China Borderlands." *Journal of Vietnamese Studies* 6, no. 2: 16–41. https://doi.org/10.1525/vs.2011.6.2.16.

de Carvalho, Benjamin. 2016. "The Making of the Political Subject: Subjects and Territory in the Formation of the State." *Theory and Society* 45:57–88. https://doi.org/10.1007/s11186-016-9264-0.

De Schutter, Olivier. 2011. "How Not to Think of Land-Grabbing: Three Critiques of Large-Scale Investments in Farmland." *Journal of Peasant Studies* 38, no. 2: 249–79. https://doi.org/10.1080/03066150.2011.559008.

Deere, Carmen Diana, and Alain de Janvry. 1979. "A Conceptual Framework for the Empirical Analysis of Peasants." *American Journal of Agricultural Economics* 61, no. 4: 601–11. https://doi.org/10.2307/1239907.

Dinh, Tuan. 2014. "Yên Bái dân kêu cứu vì ô nhiễm nguồn nước" [Villagers cried out for help in dealing with water pollution caused by mining]. Ministry of Natural Resources and Environment, Department of Water Resource Management, September 29, 2014. http://dwrm.gov.vn/index.php?language=vi&nv=news&op=Tin-thanh-tra/Yen-Bai-Dan-keu-cuu-vi-o-nhiem-nguon-nuoc-3722.

Đoàn, Bổng, and Đức Anh Nguyễn. 2006. "Đánh giá chất lượng cuộc sống của người dân vùng tái định cư dự án Hồ Tả Trạch- tỉnh Thừa Thiên- Huế. Báo cáo khoa học" [Assessment on life quality of resettlers in Ta Trach hydropower project, Thua Thien Hue Province]. Presentation at the Vietnam River Network's annual meeting, Hanoi, December 5.

Dongsinquyen. 2022. "Đồng Sin Quyền: Giới thiệu chung" [Overall introduction of the mine]. Accessed July 7, 2022. https://dongsinquyen.vn/about/Gioi-thieu-chung.html.

Douglas, Ian, and Nigel Lawson. 2002. "Material Flows Due to Mining and Urbanization." In *A Handbook of Industrial Ecology*, edited by Robert U. Ayres and Leslie W. Ayres, 351–64. Northampton, MA: Edward Elgar. https://www.e-elgar.com/shop/gbp/a-handbook-of-industrial-ecology-9781840645064.html.

Duane Morris LLP. 2018. *Vietnam—Mining Action Plan—Issues and Solutions—Impact of the Major Trade Agreements CPTPP, EUVNFTA and Investment Protection Agreement.* Hanoi: Duane Morris LLP. https://www.lexology.com/library/detail.aspx?g=cfd12324-fb6f-4fb2-b558-41054b9cc56f.

Duc, Tuong. 2019. "Công ty khai khoáng ở Yên Bái biến ruộng lúa thành đồng hoang" [Mining company in Yên Bái turns rice field into wastelands]. https://www.vietnamplus.vn/cong-ty-khai-khoang-o-yen-bai-bien-ruong-lua-thanh-dong-hoang/566235.vnp.

Dương, Anh Tuyên. 2009. "Tham vấn cộng đồng người dân địa phương bị ảnh hưởng của công trình thủy điện Bắc Hà" [Assessment of consultation process with affected people in Bac Ha hydropower project]. Presentation at the Vietnam Rivers Network's annual meeting, Hai Phong city, Vietnam, November 27–29.

Dupont, Alan. 1999. "Transnational Crime, Drugs, and Security in East Asia." *Asian Survey* 39, no. 3: 433–55. https://doi.org/10.2307/3021207.

Elden, Stuart. 2007. "Governmentality, Calculation, Territory." *Environment and Planning D: Society and Space* 25, no. 3: 562–80. https://doi.org/10.1068/d428t.

Electricity of Vietnam. 2009. *Điện lực Việt Nam đi lên cùng đất nước* [Electricity of Vietnam—growing up with the country]. Hanoi: Vietnam Electricity Group.

Electricity of Vietnam. 2018. *Tập đoàn điện lực Việt Nam* [2018 annual report]. Hanoi: Vietnam Electricity Group.

Electricity of Vietnam. 2019. "Công bố kết quả kiểm tra chi phí sản xuất kinh doanh điện năm 2018 của EVN" [Publicizing the results of examining EVN's 2018 production and business costs]. Electricity of Vietnam, December 18. https://www.evn.com.vn/d6/news/Cong-bo-ket-qua-kiem-tra-chi-phi-san-xuat-kinh-doanh-dien-nam-2018-cua-EVN-6-12-24826.aspx.

Escobar, Arturo. 1995. *Encountering Development: The Making and Unmaking of the Third World.* Princeton, NJ: Princeton University Press. https://

press.princeton.edu/books/paperback/9780691150451/encountering-development.

Fairhead, James, Melissa Leach, and Ian Scoones. 2012. "Green Grabbing: A New Appropriation of Nature?" *Journal of Peasant Studies* 39, no. 2: 237–61. https://doi.org/10.1080/03066150.2012.671770.

Feldman, Shelley, and Charles Geisler. 2012. "Land Expropriation and Displacement in Bangladesh." *Journal of Peasant Studies* 39, no. 3–4: 971–93. https://doi.org/10.1080/03066150.2012.661719.

Feldman, Shelley, Charles Geisler, and Louise Silberling. 2003. "Moving Targets: Displacement, Impoverishment, and Development." *International Social Science Journal* 55, no. 1: 7–13. https://doi.org/10.1111/1468-2451.5501001.

Ferguson, James. 1990. *The Anti-politics Machine: Development, Depoliticization, and Bureaucratic Power in Lesotho*. New York: Cambridge University Press.

Foucault, Michel. 1983. "Afterword: The Subject and Power." In *Michel Foucault: Beyond Structuralism and Hermeneutics*, edited by Hubert Dreyfus and Paul Rabinow, 208–39. Chicago: University of Chicago Press. https://press.uchicago.edu/ucp/books/book/chicago/M/bo3638224.html.

Foucault, Michel. 1991. "Governmentality." In *The Foucault Effect: Studies in Governmentality*, edited by Graham Burchell, Colin Gordon, and Peter Miller, 87–104. Chicago: University of Chicago Press. https://press.uchicago.edu/ucp/books/book/chicago/F/bo3684463.html.

Foucault, Michel. 2008. *The Birth of Biopolitics*. New York: Palgrave Macmillan. https://link.springer.com/book/10.1057/9780230594180.

Fox, Jefferson, and Jean-Christophe Castella. 2013. "Expansion of Rubber (*Hevea brasiliensis*) in Mainland Southeast Asia: What Are the Prospects for Smallholders?" *Journal of Peasant Studies* 40, no. 1: 155–70. https://doi.org/10.1080/03066150.2012.750605.

Fraser, Nancy. 2014. "Behind Marx's Hidden Abode." *New Left Review* 86 (March–April 2014). https://newleftreview.org/issues/ii86/articles/nancy-fraser-behind-marx-s-hidden-abode.

Gaventa, John. 2009. "Finding the Spaces for Change: A Power Analysis." *IDS Bulletin*, February 2. https://doi.org/10.1111/j.1759-5436.2006.tb00320.x.

Geisler, Charles. 2012. "New Terra Nullius Narratives and the Gentrification of Africa's 'Empty Lands.'" *Journal of World-Systems Research* 18, no. 1: 15–29. https://doi.org/10.5195/jwsr.2012.484.

General Statistics Office of Vietnam. 2001. "Tổng điều tra dân số và nhà ở Việt nam" [Vietnam statistical survey on housing and population]. In *Kết quả điều tra toàn bộ* [Results of the total survey]. Hanoi: Statistical Publishing House.

General Statistics Office of Vietnam. 2019. "Thông cáo báo chí kết quả tổng điều tra dân số và nhà ở năm 2019" [Press release on results of the population and housing census April 1, 2019]. https://www.gso.gov.vn/su-kien/2019/12/thong-cao-bao-chi-ket-qua-tong-dieu-tra-dan-so-va-nha-o-nam-2019/.

Gerth, H. H., and C. Wright Mills, eds. 1946. *From Max Weber: Essays in Sociology*. New York: Oxford University Press. https://www.routledge.com/From-Max-Weber-Essays-in-Sociology/Weber/p/book/9780415482691.

Gramsci, Antonio. 1971. *Selections from the Prison Notebooks of Antonio Gramsci.* Translated by Quintin Hoare and Geoffrey Nowell-Smith. New York: International. https://www.intpubnyc.com/browse/prison-notebooks-selections/.

Hà, Việt Quân. 2016a. "Brokering Power in Vietnam's Northwest: The Case of Ethnic Tai Cadres." PhD diss., Australian National University.

Hà, Việt Quân. 2016b. "Thai Entourage Politics in the Socialist State of Vietnam." In *Connected and Disconnected in Viet Nam: Remaking Social Relations in a Post-socialist Nation,* edited by Philip Taylor, 239–72. Canberra: Australian National University Press. https://www.jstor.org/stable/j.ctt1bw1h95.

Hai, Dang. 2020. "Mỏ đồng lớn nhất Đông Nam Á gây ô nhiễm" [Southeast Asia's largest copper mine causes pollution]. *Nongnghiep,* May 27. https://nongnghiep.vn/tinh-lao-cai-chi-dao-ra-soat-lam-ro-d265136.html.

Hall, Derek. 2011. "Land Grabs, Land Control, and Southeast Asian Crop Booms." *Journal of Peasant Studies* 38, no. 4: 837–57. https://doi.org/10.1080/03066150.2011.607706.

Hall, Derek, Philip Hirsch, and Tania Murray Li. 2011. *Powers of Exclusion: Land Dilemmas in Southeast Asia.* Singapore: National University of Singapore Press; Honolulu: University of Hawai'i Press. https://uhpress.hawaii.edu/title/powers-of-exclusion-land-dilemmas-in-southeast-asia/.

Hardy, Andrew. 2000. "Strategies of Migration to Upland Areas in Contemporary Vietnam." *Asia Pacific Viewpoint* 41, no. 1: 23–34. https://doi.org/10.1111/1467-8373.00104.

Hardy, Andrew. 2003. *Red Hills: Migrants and the State in the Highlands of Vietnam.* Singapore: Institute of Southeast Asian Studies; Copenhagen: Nordic Institute of Asian Studies Press. https://uhpress.hawaii.edu/title/red-hills-migrants-and-the-state-in-the-highlands-of-vietnam/.

Hardy, Andrew, and Sarah Turner. 2000. "Editorial: Migration, Markets and Social Change in the Highlands of Vietnam." *Asia Pacific Viewpoint* 41, no. 1: 1–6. https://doi.org/10.1111/1467-8373.00102.

Harms, Erik. 2016. *Luxury and Rubble: Civility and Dispossession in the New Saigon.* Oakland: University of California Press. https://doi.org/10.1525/luminos.20.

Harms, Erik, and Ian G. Baird. 2014. "Wastelands, Degraded Lands and Forests, and the Class(ification) Struggle: Three Critical Perspectives from Mainland Southeast Asia." *Singapore Journal of Tropical Geography* 35, no. 3: 289–94. https://doi.org/10.1111/sjtg.12074.

Hart, Gillian, Andrew Turton, and Benjamin White, eds. 1989. *Agrarian Transformations: Local Processes and the State in Southeast Asia.* Berkeley: University of California Press.

Harwood, Russell. 2013. *China's New Socialist Countryside: Modernity Arrives in the Nu River Valley.* Seattle: University of Washington Press. https://uwapress.uw.edu/book/9780295993386/chinas-new-socialist-countryside/.

Hazell, P. B. R., Colin Poulton, Steve Wiggins, and Andrew W. Dorward. 2007. "The Future of Small Farms for Poverty Reduction and Growth." Discussion paper, International Food Policy Research Institute. http://dx.doi.org/10.2499/9780896297647202.0vp42.

Hirsch, Philip, Tan Sinh Bach, Nguyen T. H. V., Do T. H., Nguyen Q. H., Tran N. N., Nguyen V. T., et al. 1992. "Social and Environmental Implications of Resource Development in Vietnam: The Case of Hoa Binh Reservoir." Occasional paper no. 17, Research Institute for Asia and the Pacific, University of Sydney, 1992. https://www.ngocentre.org.vn/print/16176.

Hồ, Chí Minh. 1946. "Thư Bác Hồ gửi đại hội các dân tộc thiểu số Miền Nam tại Pleiku ngày 19 tháng 4 năm 1946" [Letter to the Congress of Southern Ethnic Minorities at Pleiku, Vietnam, April 19, 1946]. Portal of the Committee for Ethnic Minority Affairs, Thai Nguyễn Province, Vietnam. https://bandantoc.thainguyen.gov.vn/bac-ho-voi-cac-dan-toc/-/asset_publisher/aswschm77NYQ/content/thu-gui-ai-hoi-cac-dan-toc-thieu-so-mien-nam-tai-play-cu?inheritRedirect=true.

Hồ, Chí Minh. 1955. "Thư gửi đồng bào khu tự trị Thái Mèo—7–5–1955" [Letter to the people in Thái Mèo Autonomous Zone, May 7, 1955]. Portal of the Committee for Ethnic Minority Affairs, Hanoi. http://www.cema.gov.vn/thu-gui-dong-bao-khu-tu-tri-thai-meo.htm.

Hoàng, Lan Anh. 2006. "Đánh giá chất lượng cuộc sống và triển vọng phục hồi sinh kế cho đồng bào tái định cư nhà máy thủy điện A Vương" [Assessing life quality and potential for rehabilitation of the resettlers in the A Vương hydropower project]. Presentation at the Vietnam River Network's annual meeting, Hanoi, December 5.

Hoàng, Nguyên Giáp, and Vo Huy Cường. 2006. "Nghiên cứu môi trường kinh tế xa hội khu tái định cư công tr.nh thuỷ điện Thác Bà, tỉnh Yên Bái sau 32 năm xây dựng đập" [Study on socioeconomic environment of resettlement area of Thác Bà Hydropower project, Yên Bái, 32 years after the dam's construction]. Presentation at the Vietnam River Network's annual meeting, Hanoi, December 5.

Hoang, Xuan. 2010. "Rừng quốc gia đáng giá bao nhiêu?" [How much do national forests cost?]. *Tuanvietnam*, May 5. http://www.tuanvietnam.net/2010-05-04-rung-quoc-gia-gia-bao-nhieu?

Hodges, Carroll Ann. 1995. "Mineral Resources, Environmental Issues, and Land Use." *Science* 268, no. 5215: 1305–12. https://doi.org/10.1126/science.268.5215.1305.

Hoffman, L. M. 2014. "The Urban, Politics and Subject Formation." *International Journal of Urban and Regional Research* 38, no. 5: 1576–1588.

Hua Xiaobo, Yasuyuki Kono, and Le Zhang. 2023. "Excavating Agrarian Transformation under 'Secure' Crop Boom: Insights from the China-Myanmar Borderland." *Journal of Peasant Studies* 50, no. 1: 339–68. https://doi.org/10.1080/03066150.2021.1926993.

Humphreys, David. 2018. "In Search of a New China: Mineral Demand in South and Southeast Asia." *Mineral Economics* 31:103–12. https://doi.org/10.1007/s13563-017-0118-7.

Hung, Vo. 2014. "Lào Cai: Dân vùng mỏ sống mòn trong khu tái định cư thiếu bền vững" [Lào Cai: Mining induced displaced communities are living in unsustainable resettlement sites]. *Vietnamplus*, September 19. https://www.vietnamplus.vn/lao-cai-dan-vung-mo-song-mon-trong-khu-tai-dinh-cu-thieu-ben-vung/281778.vnp.

Hung, Vo. 2017. ""Vỡ trận quy hoạch" thủy điện nhỏ ở các tỉnh miền núi phía Bắc" [Planning disaster for small hydropower in northern mountain region]. *Vietnamplus*, May 24. https://www.vietnamplus.vn/vo-tran-quy-hoach-thuy-dien-nho-o-cac-tinh-mien-nui-phia-bac/446287.vnp.

Huong Giang. 2019. "Năm 2018, lợi nhuận của TKV đạt trên 4,000 billion đồng" [In 2018, Vinacomin's profit reached over 4,000 billion VND]. *Vinacomin*, January 9. https://vinacomin.vn/tin-tuc-vinacomin/nam-2018-loi-nhuan-cua-tkv-dat-tren-4000-ty-dong-20190109161336591.htm.

Huong Nhung. 2019. "Công ty thuỷ điện Sơn La đóng góp lớn cho tỉnh Sơn La" [Sơn La Hydropower Company makes a major contribution to Sơn La Province]. *EVN*, February 27, 2019. https://www.evn.com.vn/d6/news/Cong-ty-Thuy-dien-Son-La-da-dong-gop-lon-cho-tinh-Son-La-6-12-23198.aspx.

Huu, Thang. 2021. "Hơn 10 năm đưa cây cao su lên Tây Bắc: Cần có cách nhìn toàn diện" [More than 10 years of bringing rubber trees to the Northwest: A comprehensive view on this matter is needed]. *Tạp chí Kinh tế nông thôn* [Rural economic magazine], July 5, 2021. https://kinhtenongthon.vn/hon-10-nam-dua-cay-cao-su-len-tay-bac-can-co-cach-nhin-toan-dien-post43692.html.

Jackson, David. 1998. "Breaking out of the Binary Trap: Boys' Underachievement, Schooling and Gender Relations." In *Failing Boys? Issues in Gender and Achievement*, edited by Debbie Epstein, Jannette Elwood, Valerie Hey, and Janet Maw, 77–102. Philadelphia: Open University Press.

Jakobsen, J. 2022. "Beyond Subject-Making: Conflicting Humanisms, Class Analysis, and the 'Dark Side' of Gramscian Political Ecology." *Progress in Human Geography* 46, no. 2: 575–89.

Jeuland, Marc. 2010. "Social Discounting of Large Dams with Climate Change Uncertainty." *Water Alternatives* 3, no. 2: 185–206. https://www.water-alternatives.org/index.php/allabs/89-a3-2-12/file.

Kalinovsky, Artemy. 2018. *Laboratory of Socialist Development: Cold War Politics and Decolonization in Soviet Tajikistan*. Ithaca, NY: Cornell University Press. https://www.cornellpress.cornell.edu/book/9781501715563/laboratory-of-socialist-development/#bookTabs=1.

Kerkvliet, Benedict J. Tria. 1986. "Everyday Resistance to Injustice in a Philippine Village." *Journal of Peasant Studies* 13, no. 2: 107–23.

Kerkvliet, Benedict J. Tria. 2005. *The Power of Everyday Politics: How Vietnamese Peasants Transformed National Policy*. Ithaca, NY: Cornell University Press. https://www.jstor.org/stable/10.7591/j.ctv2n7j9j.

Kerkvliet, Benedict J. Tria. 2009. "Everyday Politics in Peasant Societies (and Ours)." *Journal of Peasant Studies* 36, no. 1: 227–43. https://doi.org/10.1080/03066150902820487.

Khuc, Thị Thanh Vân. 2007. "Impacts of Resettlement Policy on People's Livelihoods after the Resettlement: A Case Study of Ban Ve Hydropower." MA thesis, Vietnam Institute of Sociology.

Klinger, Julie Mitchelle. 2018. *Rare Earth Frontiers: From Terrestrial Subsoils to Lunar Landscapes*. Ithaca, NY: Cornell University Press. https://www.jstor.org/stable/10.7591/j.ctt1w0dd6d.

Lâm, Du Sơn. 2005. "Hiện trạng và phát triển điện năng ở Việt Nam" [Current situation and electricity development in Vietnam]. Presentation at Dam and Sustainable Development: Challenges in Integration Period, Vietnam Union of Science and Technology Associations (VUSTA), Hanoi, March 24.

Lào Cai Province People's Committee. 2022. "Sở công thương. Văn bản số 1880/SCT-KT về việc thẩm định dự án" [Department of Industry and Trade, Document No. 1880/SCT-KT on appraising the project]. Lào Cai: Lào Cai Province People's Committee.

Laocaitv. 2021. "Huyện Uỷ làm việc với chi nhánh mỏ đồng Sin Quyền Lào Cai" [District committee meets with Sin Quyen, Lào Cai copper mine branch]. Laocaitv, December 14. http://laocaitv.vn/kinh-te-moi-truong/huyen-uy-bat-xat-lam-viec-voi-chi-nhanh-mo-dong-sin-quyen#:~:text=.

Lavers, Tom. 2012. "'Land Grab' as Development Strategy? The Political Economy of Agricultural Investment in Ethiopia." *Journal of Peasant Studies* 39, no. 1: 105–32. https://doi.org/10.1080/03066150.2011.652091.

Le Anh. 2019. "ĐBQH Huỳnh Thanh Phương: Chất vấn Bộ trưởng Bộ Tài Nguyên & Môi trường về sai phạm trong công tác quản lý, khai thác khoáng sản" [National Assembly member Huynh Thanh Phuong: Question the minister of natural resources and environment about violations in mineral management and mining]. *Quochoi*, October 11. http://quochoi. vn/hoatdongdbqh/pages/tin-hoat-dong-dai-bieu.aspx?ItemID=42307.

Le Anh Tuan and Dao Nga, eds. 2016. *Các thách thức trong Phát triển Thuỷ điện ở Việt Nam* [Vietnam hydropower and its challenges to sustainability]. Hanoi: Science and Technology Publisher.

Le Failler, Philippe. 2011. "The Đèo Family of Lai Châu: Traditional Power and Unconventional Practices." *Journal for Vietnamese Studies* 6, no. 2: 42–67. https://doi.org/10.1525/vs.2011.6.2.42.

Lehner, Bernhard, and Günther Grill. 2013. "Global River Hydrography and Network Routing: Baseline Data and New Approaches to Study the World's Large River Systems," *Hydrological Processes* 27, no. 15: 2171–2186. https://doi.org/10.1002/hyp.9740.

Le Van Huong. 2015. "Tác động của khai thác khoáng sản đến đời sống kinh tế xã hội cộng đồng dân cư tại các huyện miền Tây Nghệ An" [Impacts from mining to socioeconomic conditions of the population in western districts of Nghe An Province]. *Tạp chí các khoa học về trái đất* 37, no. 3: 213–21.

Le Viet. 2018. "Cung ứng điện năm 2019: Nhiều thách thức" [Energy supply in 2019: Many challenges]. EVN, November 21. https://www.evn.com.vn/d6/news/Cung-ung-dien-nam-2019-Nhieu-thach-thuc-6-12-22666.aspx.

Lentz, Christian C. 2011. "Making the Northwest Vietnamese." *Journal for Vietnamese Studies* 6, no. 2: 68–105. https://doi.org/10.1525/vs.2011.6. 2.68.

Lentz, Christian C. 2019. *Contested Territory: Dien Bien Phu and the Making of Northwest Vietnam*. New Haven, CT: Yale University Press. https://yale-books.yale.edu/book/9780300233957/contested-territory/.

Levien, Michael, Michael Watts, and Yan Hairong. 2018. "Agrarian Marxism." *Journal of Peasant Studies* 45, no. 5-6: 853-83. https://doi.org/10.1080/03 066150.2018.1534101.

Li, Tania Murray. 2002. "Local Histories, Global Markets: Cocoa and Class in Upland Sulawesi." *Development and Change* 33, no. 3: 415-37. https://doi. org/10.1111/1467-7660.00261.

Li, Tania Murray. 2007. *The Will to Improve: Governmentality, Development, and the Practice of Politics.* Durham, NC: Duke University Press. https://www. dukeupress.edu/the-will-to-improve/.

Li, Tania Murray. 2010. "To Make Live or Let Die? Rural Dispossession and the Protection of Surplus Populations." *Antipode* 41, no. s1: 66-93. https:// doi.org/10.1111/j.1467-8330.2009.00717.x.

Li, Tania Murray. 2014. *Land's End: Capitalist Relations on an Indigenous Frontier.* Durham, NC: Duke University Press. https://www.dukeupress.edu/ lands-end.

Li, Tania Murray. 2017. "After Development: Surplus Populations and the Politics of Entitlement." *Development and Change*, 48, no. 6: 1247-61. https:// doi.org/10.1111/dech.12344

Locke, John, and Lee Ward. 2016. *Two Treatises of Government.* Indianapolis: Focus.

Lomas, Tim, Tina Cartwright, Trudi Edginton, and Damien Ridge. 2016. "New Ways of Being a Man: 'Positive' Hegemonic Masculinity in Meditation-Based Communities of Practice." *Men and Masculinities* 19, no. 3: 289-310. https://doi.org/10.1177/1097184X15578531.

Lưu, Hồ Quang, Đào Nga, Nguyễn Thi Ngoc Lan, Nguyễn Vi Linh, and Nguyễn Đức Hiệp. 2009. "Cây cao su và chương trình phục hồi sinh kế tại các khu tái định cư thuỷ điện Sơn La" [Rubber plantation and livelihoods rehabilitation in resettlement sites of the Sơn La hydropower project]. Working paper, Center for Water Resources Conservation and Development, Hanoi.

Lyttleton, Chris. 2004. "Relative Pleasures: Drugs, Development and Modern Dependencies in Asia's Golden Triangle." *Development and Change* 35, no. 5: 909-35. https://doi.org/10.1111/j.1467-7660.2004.00386.x.

Mai, Dan. 2021. "10 năm thực hiện Luật Khoáng sản—những đóng góp cho nênd kinh tế: Thúc đẩy phát triển bền vững công nghiệp khai khoáng" [10 years of implementing the Mineral Law—contributions to the economy: Promoting sustainable development of the mining industry]. *Baotainguy-enmoitruong*, September 9. https://baotainguyenmoitruong.vn/10-nam-thuc-hien-luat-khoang-san-nhung-dong-gop-cho-nen-kinh-te-thuc-day-phat-trien-ben-vung-cong-nghiep-khai-khoang-330462.html.

Manivong, Vongpaphane, and R. A. Cramb. 2008. "Economics of Smallholder Rubber Expansion in Northern Laos." *Agroforestry Systems* 74:113-25. https://doi.org/10.1007/s10457-008-9136-3.

Martinez-Alier, J., I. Anguelovski, P. Bond, F. Del Bene, F. Demaria, J-F. Gerber, L. Grey, et al. 2014. "Between Activism and Science: Grassroots Concepts for Sustainability Coined by Environmental Justice Organizations."

*Journal of Political Ecology* 21, no. 1: 19–60. https://doi.org/10.2458/v21i1.21124.

Martinez-Alier, Joan, Leah Temper, Daniela Del Bene, and Arnim Scheidel. 2016. "Is There a Global Environmental Justice Movement?" *Journal of Peasant Studies* 43, no. 3: 731–55. https://doi.org/10.1080/03066150.2016.1141198.

McDuie-Ra, Duncan. 2012. *Northeast Migrants in Delhi: Race, Refuge, and Retail.* Amsterdam: Amsterdam University Press. https://www.aup.nl/en/book/9789089644220/northeast-migrants-in-delhi.

McElwee, Pamela D. 2004. "Becoming Socialist or Becoming Kinh: Government Policies for Ethnic Minorities in the Socialist Republic of Vietnam." In *Civilizing the Margins: Southeast Asian Government Policies for the Development of Minorities,* edited by Christopher R. Duncan, 182–213. Ithaca, NY: Cornell University Press.

McElwee, Pamela D. 2016. *Forests Are Gold: Trees, People, and Environmental Rule in Vietnam.* Seattle: University of Washington Press. https://uwapress.uw.edu/book/9780295995489/forests-are-gold/.

McMichael, Philip. 2008. "Peasants Make Their Own History, But Not Just as They Please...." *Journal of Agrarian Change* 8, no. 2–3: 205–28. https://doi.org/10.1111/j.1471-0366.2008.00168.x.

McMichael, Philip. 2012. "The Land Grab and Corporate Food Regime Restructuring." *Journal of Peasant Studies* 39, no. 3–4: 681–701. https://doi.org/10.1080/03066150.2012.661369.

McNeill, J. R. 2000. *Something New under the Sun: An Environmental History of the Twentieth-Century World.* New York: W. W. Norton.

Michaud, Jean, and Sarah Turner. 2017. "Reaching New Heights: State Legibility in Sa Pa, a Vietnam Hill Station." *Annals of Tourism Research* 66:37–48. https://doi.org/10.1016/j.annals.2017.05.014.

Miller, Peter, and Nikolas Rose. 2008. *Governing the Present: Administering Economic, Social and Personal Life.* London: Polity. https://www.wiley.com/en-cn/Governing+the+Present%3A+Administering+Economic,+Social+and+Personal+Life-p-9780745641010.

Minh, Tri. 2013. "Eximbank rót 1.500 tỷ đồng cho dự án khai thác đồng Sin Quyền" [Eximbank invested 1,500 billion VND in Sin Quyen copper mining project]. VNexpress, November 22. https://vnexpress.net/eximbank-rot-1-500-ty-dong-cho-du-an-khai-thac-dong-sin-quyen-2913012.html.

Ministry of Agriculture and Rural Development. 2009. "Nghị định 58/2009/TT-BNNPTNT về hướng dẫn trồng cây cao su trên đất rừng" [Circular 58/2009/TT-BNNPTNT. Circular for guiding rubber plantation on forestland (A guiding document for Document No. 3492/BNN-NT dated December 20, 2007)]. Hanoi: Ministry of Agriculture and Rural Development.

Ministry of Agriculture and Rural Development. 2014. *Báo cáo tổng quan* [Overview report 2014]. Hanoi: Ministry of Agriculture and Rural Development. https://doi.org/10.1016/j.annals.2017.05.014.

Ministry of Education and Training. 2021. "Bình đẳng giới ngành giáo dục phải thực chất, hiệu quả, tránh hình thức" [Gender equality in education must be substantive, effective and avoid formality]. Hanoi: Ministry of Education and Training. https://moet.gov.vn/tintuc/Pages/tin-tong-hop.aspx?ItemID=7295.

Ministry of Industry and Trade. 2010. *Báo cáo số 28/BC-BCT: Gửi Thủ tướng về hiện trạng thuỷ điện, Bộ Công Thương* [28/BC-BCT: Report to the prime minister regarding the hydropower situation]. Hanoi: Ministry of Industry and Trade.

Ministry of Industry and Trade. 2013. "Uỷ Ban Khoa học, kỹ thuật và Môi trường của Quốc hội: Rà soát quy hoạch, đầu tư, xây dựng và vận hành các nhà máy thuỷ điện trên toàn quốc" [National Assembly's Committee on Science, Technology and Environment's review on planning, investment, construction and operation of hydropower at nationwide level]. Hanoi: Ministry of Industry and Trade.

Ministry of Industry and Trade. 2018. "Công tác quy hoạch, xây dưng, quản lý và vận hành các công trình thuỷ điện" [Planning, build, manage and operate hydropower plants]. Hanoi: Ministry of Industry and Trade. https://moit.gov.vn/tin-chi-tiet/-/chi-tiet/cong-tac-quy-hoach-xay-dung-quan-ly-va-van-hanh-cac-cong-trinh-thuy-%C4%91ien-12729-22.html.

Ministry of Industry and Trade. 2019. *Khung giá phát điện 2019* [Power price frame for 2019]. Hanoi: Ministry of Industry and Trade. https://www.evn.com.vn/d6/news/Bo-Cong-Thuong-ban-hanh-khung-gia-phat-dien-nam-2019-2-10-23151.aspx.

Ministry of Natural Resources and Environment. 2019a. "Điều tra tổng thể về khoáng sản và hoàn thiện nền bản đồ địa chất tỷ lệ 1:50,000 vùng Tây Bắc" [Overall survey of mineral resources and finalizing the geological map of ratio 1:50,000 of the Northwest region]. Hanoi: Ministry of Natural Resources and Environment. http://www.monre.gov.vn/Pages/dieu-tra-tong-the-ve-khoang-san-va-hoan-thien-nen-ban-do-dia-chat-ty-le-150.000-vung-tay-bac.aspx.

Ministry of Natural Resources and Environment. 2019b. *Văn bản số 4545/BTNMT-DCKS ngày 13/9/2019 phản hồi chất vấn của các đại biểu Quốc hội về những sai phạm trong quản lý khai khoáng tại phiên họp thứ 7, kỳ họp 14* [Document No. 4545/BTNMT-DCKS (September 13) in response to questions by National Assembly members at the seventh session of the 14th National Assembly on erroneous situations in mineral exploration management]. Hanoi: Ministry of Natural Resources and Environment. http://quochoi.vn/hoatdongdbqh/pages/tin-hoat-dong-dai-bieu.aspx?ItemID=42307.

Ministry of Natural Resources and Environment. 2022. "Luật Bảo vệ môi trường" [Law on environmental protection]. Hanoi: Ministry of Natural Resources and Environment. https://thuvienphapluat.vn/van-ban/Tai-nguyen-Moi-truong/Van-ban-hop-nhat-21-VBHN-VPQH-2022-Luat-Bao-ve-moi-truong-559085.aspx.

Mitchell, Don. 2003. "Cultural Landscapes: Just Landscapes or Landscapes of Justice?" *Progress in Human Geography* 27, no. 6 (December): 787–96. https://doi.org/10.1191/0309132503ph464pr.

Mitchell, Timothy. 2002. *Rule of Experts: Egypt, Techno-politics, Modernity.* Berkeley: University of California Press. https://www.ucpress.edu/book/9780520232624/rule-of-experts.

Moore, Donald. 2005. *Suffering for Territory: Race, Place, and Power in Zimbabwe.* Durham, NC: Duke University Press. https://www.dukeupress.edu/suffering-for-territory.

Moore, Johnnie N., and Samuel N. Luoma. 1990. "Hazardous Wastes from Large-Scale Metal Extraction: A Case Study." *Environmental Science Technology* 24, no. 9: 1278–85. https://doi.org/10.1021/es00079a001.

Muong Muon Commune People's Committee. 2021. *Báo cáo xoá đói giảm nghèo* [Poverty alleviation report]. Muong Muon: Muong Muon Commune People's Committee.

My, Duyen. 2018. "Mining Vietnam 2018: Thúc đẩy ngành công nghiệp khai khoáng" [Mining Vietnam 2018: Promoting the mining industry]. Vietnam Energy Online. https://nangluongvietnam.vn/mining-vietnam-2018-thuc-day-nganh-cong-nghiep-khai-khoang-20132.html.

National Institute of Agriculture Planning and Projection. 2005. *Phương án điều chuyển dân cư dự án thuỷ điện Sơn La tỉnh Sơn La* [Project on people displacement of the Sơn La hydropower project in Sơn La Province]. Hanoi: National Institute of Agriculture Planning and Projection.

Nghiem, Tuyen, Yasuyuki Kono, and Stephen Leisz. 2020. "Crop Boom as a Trigger of Smallholder Livelihood and Land Use Transformations: The Case of Coffee Production in the Northern Mountain Region of Vietnam." *Land* 9, no. 2: 56. https://doi.org/10.3390/land9020056.

Ngoc, Thuan. 2018. "Khánh thành nhà máy chế biến cao su Sơn La" [Inauguration of the Sơn La rubber latex processing factory]. Báo Sơn La, December 26, 2018. http://www.baosonla.org.vn/vi/bai-viet/khanh-thanh-nha-may-che-bien-cao-su-son-la-2810-19539.

Nguyễn Danh Oanh. 2009. "Phát triển thuỷ điện ở Việt Nam: Hiện trạng và thách thức" [Hydropower development in Vietnam: Challenges and existing conditions]. Paper presented at a training workshop on the World Commission on Dams strategies hosted by the Vietnam Rivers Network, Hoa Binh, Vietnam, November 7–8.

Nguyễn Đức Đạt. 2017. "Nang luong Vietnam va tam quan trong cac du an thuy dien cua EVN" [Vietnam energy and the importance of EVN's hydropower projects]. Năng Lượng Việt Nam. https://nangluongvietnam.vn/vai-tro-va-tam-quan-trong-cac-du-an-thuy-dien-cua-evn-19600.html.

Nguyễn Đức Thành, Phạm Văn Long, Lê Hà Phương, Hoàng Long, and Đỗ Thị Lê. 2023. *Hướng tới một hệ thống quản trị tài nguyên tốt hơn cách tiếp cận kinh tế chính trị* [Toward a better resource management system than the political economy approach]. Study report, Nghiên cứu được thực hiện bởi

Liên minh công bằng thuế Việt Nam (VATJ) and và Trung tâm Nghiên cứu Kinh tế và Chiến lược Việt Nam (VESS), Hanoi.

Nguyễn Khải. 1960. *Mùa lạc* [Groundnut season]. Hanoi: Literature Publishing House.

Nguyễn Mạnh Quân. 2013. "Định hướng khai thác khoáng sản Việt Nam" [Orientation for mineral extraction in Vietnam]. *Vinachem*, May 14. https://www.vinachem.com.vn/nd/van-de-hom-nay-vnc/dinh_huong_khai_thac_khoang_san_viet_nam.html.

Nguyễn Như Phong. 2018. "Bí mật lá thư 'chôn' trong khối bê tông 10 tấn gửi hậu thế ở Thủy điện Hòa Bình" [The secret of the letter to future generation in 2100 in Hòa Bình hydropower plant]. Kenh14, August 1. https://kenh14.vn/bi-mat-la-thu-chon-trong-khoi-be-tong-10-tan-gui-hau-the-o-thuy-dien-hoa-binh-2018080108173303.chn.

Nguyễn Quang and Phạm Tiệp. 2022. "Yên Bái chấn chỉnh khai thác khoáng sản nhưng trên bảo dưới không nghe" [Yên Bái rectifies mineral extraction but decisions made from above are not followed]. *Công Thương* [Vietnam economic news], July 22, 2022. https://congthuong.vn/yen-bai-chan-chinh-khai-thac-khoang-san-nhung-tren-bao-duoi-khong-nghe-183668.html.

Nguyễn Tuân. 1960. *Sông Đà* [Song Da]. Nhà Xuất Bản Tác phẩm mới. Hanoi: New Book Publisher.

Nguyễn Văn Biểu 2009. "Nhà máy thuỷ điện Hoà Bình: Xây dựng và vận hành" [Hoa Binh hydropower plant: Construction and operation]. Paper presented at a training workshop on World Commission on Dams' strategies held by the Vietnam Rivers Network in Hoa Binh, November 7–8, 2009.

Nguyễn Văn Chinh. 2008. "From Swidden Cultivation to Fixed Farming and Settlement: Effects of Sedentarization Policies among the Kmhmu in Vietnam." *Journal of Vietnamese Studies* 3, no. 3: 44–80. https://doi.org/10.1525/vs.2008.3.3.44.

Nguyễn Xuân. 2020. "Vietnam Not Doing Enough to Protect Environment around Dams." *VnExpress*, October 15. https://e.vnexpress.net/news/news/vietnam-not-doing-enough-to-protect-environment-around-dams-experts-4177249.html.

Nhân Dân. 2015. "Thủ tướng Nguyễn Tấn Dũng dự lễ mừng phát điện tổ máy số 1 thuỷ điện Lai Châu" [Prime Minister Nguyễn Tan Dung attended the ceremony to celebrate the power generation of Unit 1 of Lai Chau hydropower plant]. Nhân Dân, December 23. https://nhandan.vn/tin-tuc-su-kien/thu-tuong-nguyen-tan-dung-du-le-mung-phat-dien-to-may-1-thuy-dien-lai-chau-251159/.

Nhat, Anh. 2019. "Tranh cãi gay gắt về hiệu quả cây cao su ở vùng Tây Bắc" [Fierce controversy over the effectiveness of rubber trees in the Northwest]. Bảo vệ môi trường, May 4. https://baovemoitruong.org.vn/tranh-cai-gay-gat-ve-hieu-qua-cay-cao-su-o-vung-tay-bac/.

Nightingale, Andrea. 2006. "The Nature of Gender: Work, Gender, and Environment." *Environment and Planning D: Society and Space* 24, no. 2 (April): 165–85. https://doi.org/10.1068/d01k.

O'Connor, James. 1989. "Uneven and Combined Development and Ecological Crisis: A Theoretical Introduction." *Race & Class* 30, no. 3: 1–11. https://doi.org/10.1177/030639688903000302.

O'Rourke, Dara. 2004. "Transition Environments: Ecological and Social Challenges to Post-socialist Industrial Development." In *Liberation Ecologies: Environment, Development and Social Movements*, 2nd ed., edited by Richard Peet and Michael Watts, 244–70. London: Routledge. https://www.routledge.com/Liberation-Ecologies-Peet-Watts/p/book/9780415312363.

PanNature. 2010. *Quy hoạch thủy điện và rừng đặc dụng ở Việt Nam* [Hydropower planning and special forest in Vietnam]. Báo cáo nghiên cứu, 29VQG/KBT. Hanoi: PanNature.

Peluso, Nancy Lee. 1992. *Rich Forests, Poor People*. Berkeley: University of California Press. https://www.ucpress.edu/book/9780520089310/rich-forests-poor-people.

Peluso, Nancy Lee. 2018. "Entangled Territories in Small-Scale Gold Mining Frontiers: Labor Practices, Property, and Secrets in Indonesian Gold Country." *World Development* 101:400–16. https://doi.org/10.1016/j.worlddev.2016.11.003.

Peluso, Nancy Lee, and Peter Vandergeest. 2020. "Writing Political Forests." *Antipode* 52, no. 4: 1083–1103.

Perreault, Tom. 2013. "Dispossession by Accumulation? Mining, Water and the Nature of Enclosure on the Bolivian Altiplano." *Antipode* 45, no. 5: 1050–69. https://doi.org/10.1111/anti.12005.

Perreault, Tom, and Gabriela Valdivia. 2010. "Hydrocarbons, Popular Protest and National Imaginaries: Ecuador and Bolivia in Comparative Context." *Geoforum* 41, no. 5: 689–99. https://doi.org/10.1016/j.geoforum.2010.04.004.

PetroTimes. 2013. "Tổ hợp đồng Sin Quyền: Không ai còn hoài nghi" [Sin Quyen copper mining complex: No one can doubt]. https://petrotimes.vn/to-hop-dong-sin-quyen-khong-ai-con-hoai-nghi-125289.html.

Phạm, Thị Vượng. 2018. "Vai trò của các nông tường Quân đội ở Miền Bắc Việt Nam, giai đoạn 1955–1960" [Role of army state farms in Northern Vietnam, period 1955–1960]. Tạp chí lịch sử Đảng. Hanoi.

Phan Hien. 2014. "Bổ sung vốn di dân tái định cư thuỷ điện Sơn La" [Additional funding is provided to Sơn La Dam induced resettlement]. Báo chính phủ, January 9. https://baochinhphu.vn/bo-sung-von-di-dan-tai-dinh-cu-thuy-dien-son-la-102157400.htm.

Phan Thi Xuan Hue. 2020. "Thực trạng ngành cao su sau khi Việt Nam ký kết hiệp định CPTPP" [Status of the rubber industry after Vietnam signed the TPP agreement]. *Công Thương* [Vietnam economic news], February 26. http://tapchicongthuong.vn/bai-viet/thuc-trang-nganh-cao-su-sau-khi-viet-nam-ky-ket-hiep-dinh-cptpp-69098.htm.

PhapLuatTPHCM. 2011a. "Thuỷ điện Tây Nguyên và hệ luỵ. Bài 1- Phá rừng làm thuỷ điện" [Hydropower in the Central Highlands and its consequences. Episode 1—deforestation for hydropower development]. PhapLuat TPHCM, November 28. www.baomoi.com/Thuy-dien-Tay-Nguyen-va-he-luy-Bai- 1-Pha-rung-lam-thuy-dien/148/7435635.epi.

PhapLuatTPHCM. 2011b. "Thuỷ điện Tây Nguyên và hệ luỵ. Bài 2- Sông khô dân khát" [Hydropower in the Central Highlands and its consequences. Episode 2—dry river and thirsty people]. PhapLuatTPHCM, November 29. http://phapluattp.vn/20111128111347387p0c1085/thuy- dien-tay-nguyen-va-he-luy-bai-2-song-kho-dan-khat.htm.

PhapLuatTPHCM. 2011c. "Thuỷ điện Tây Nguyên và hệ luỵ. Bài 3- nhường đất cho thuỷ điện rồi đói" [Hydropower in the Central Highlands and its consequences. Episode 3—giving up land to make way for hydropower and starving]. PhapLuatTPHCM, November 30. http://phapluattp. vn/2011112910101549p0c1085/thuy- dien-tay-nguyen-va-he-luy-bai-3-nhuong-dat-cho-thuy-dien-roi-doi.htm.

Phap Luat Newspapers. 2020. "Nhu cầu điện thương phẩm duy trì mức tăng 8.3% đến năm 2030" [Commercial electricity demand is at 8.3% increase until 2030]. *Phap Luat Newspapers*, November 18. https://plo.vn/nhu-cau-dien-thuong-pham-duy-tri-muc-tang-8-3-den-nam-2030-post602070. html.

Pile, Steve. 2008. "Where Is the Subject? Geographical Imagi-nations and Spatializing Subjectivity." *Subjectivity* 23, no. 1: 206–18.

Power Investigation, Design and Construction Company (PIDC) No. 1. 1999. "Dự án Thuỷ điện Sơn La—nghiên cứu khả thi, Báo cáo chính" [Feasibility study of the Sơn La hydropower project]. Hanoi: Power Investigation, Design and Construction Company No. 1.

Price, Linda. 2010. "'Doing It with Men': Feminist Research Practice and Patriarchal Inheritance Practices in Welsh Family Farming." *Gender, Place and Culture: A Journal of Feminist Geography* 17, no. 1: 81–97. https://doi. org/10.1080/09663690903522438.

Rasmussen, Mattias Borg, and Christian Lund. 2018. "Reconfiguring Frontier Spaces: The Territorialization of Resource Control." *World Development* 101:388–99. https://doi.org/10.1016/j.worlddev.2017.01.018.

Reeves, Madeleine. 2014. *Border Work: Spatial Lives of the State in Rural Central Asia*. Ithaca, NY: Cornell University Press. https://www.cornellpress. cornell.edu/book/9780801477065/border-work/#bookTabs=1.

Resurrección, Bernadette, and Rebecca Elmhirst. 2008. *Gender and Natural Resource Management: Livelihoods, Mobility and Interventions*. Ottawa: International Development Research Centre. https://idrc-crdi.ca/en/book/ gender-and-natural-resource-management-livelihoods-mobility-and-interventions.

Richter, Brian D., Sandra Postel, Carmen Revenga, Thayer Scudder, Bernhard Lehner, Allegra Churchill, and Morgan Chow. 2010. "Lost in Development's Shadow: The Downstream Human Consequences of Dams." *Water Alternatives* 3, no. 2: 14–42. https://www.water-alternatives.org/index. php/volume3/v3issue2/80-a3-2-3/file.

Rigg, Jonathan, and Peter Vandergeest, eds. 2012. *Revisiting Rural Places: Pathways to Poverty and Prosperity in Southeast Asia*. Honolulu: University of Hawai'i Press. https://uhpress.hawaii.edu/title/revisiting-rural-places-pathways-to-poverty-and-prosperity-in-southeast-asia/.

Robbins, Paul. 2004. *Political Ecology: A Critical Introduction*. Oxford: Blackwell. https://www.wiley.com/en-us/Political+Ecology%3A+A+Critical+Introduction,+3rd+Edition-p-9781119167440.

Roy, Arundhati. 2001. *Power Politics*. Cambridge: South End.

Sack, Robert D. 1986. *Human Territoriality: Its Theory and History*. Cambridge: Cambridge University Press. https://www.cambridge.org/us/universitypress/subjects/geography/historical-geography/human-territoriality-its-theory-and-history?format=PB&isbn=9780521311809.

Salemink, Oscar H. J. M. 1997. "The King of Fire and Vietnamese Ethnic Policy in the Central Highlands." In *Development or Domestication? Indigenous Peoples of Southeast Asia*, edited by Don N. McCaskill and Ken Kampe, 488–535. Bangkok: Silkworm Books.

Salemink, Oscar H. J. M. 2003. *The Ethnography of Vietnam's Central Highlanders: A Historical Contextualization, 1850–1990*. Honolulu: Routledge Cruzon / University of Hawai'i Press. https://uhpress.hawaii.edu/title/the-ethnography-of-vietnams-central-highlanders-a-historical-contextualization-1850-1990/.

Salemink, Oscar H. J. M. 2011. "A View from the Mountains: A Critical History of Lowlander-Highlander Relations in Vietnam." In *Upland Transformations in Vietnam*, edited by Thomas Sikor, Nghiêm Phương Tuyến, Jennifer Sowerwine, and Jeff Romm, 27–50. Singapore: National University of Singapore Press. https://nuspress.nus.edu.sg/products/upland-transformations-in-vietnam.

Scheidel, Arnim, Daniela Del Bene, Juan Liu, Grettel Navas, Sara Mingorría, Federico Demaria, Sofia Avila, et al. 2020. "Environmental Conflicts and Defenders: A Global Overview." *Global Environmental Change* 63:102104. https://doi.org/10.1016/j.gloenvcha.2020.102104.

Schiappacasse, Paulina, Bernhard Müller, and Le Thuy Linh. 2019. "Towards Responsible Aggregate Mining in Vietnam." *Resources* 8, no. 3: 138. https://doi.org/10.3390/resources8030138.

Schneider, Sergio, and Paulo André Niederle. 2010. "Resistance Strategies and Diversification of Rural Livelihoods: The Construction of Autonomy among Brazilian Family Farmers." *Journal of Peasant Studies* 37, no. 2: 379–405. https://doi.org/10.1080/03066151003595168.

Schwenkel, Christina, and Ann Marie Leshkowich. 2012. "How Is Neoliberalism Good to Think Vietnam? How Is Vietnam Good to Think Neoliberalism?" *positions* 20, no. 2: 379–401. https://doi.org/10.1215/10679847-1538461.

Scott, James C. 1976. *The Moral Economy of the Peasant: Rebellion and Subsistence in Southeast Asia*. New Haven, CT: Yale University Press. https://www.jstor.org/stable/j.ctt1bh4cdk.

Scott, James C. 1985. *Weapons of the Weak: Everyday Forms of Peasant Resistance*. New Haven, CT: Yale University Press. https://www.jstor.org/stable/j.ctt1nq836.

Scott, James C. 1998. *Seeing Like a State: How Certain Schemes to Improve the Human Condition Have Failed*. New Haven, CT: Yale University Press. https://www.jstor.org/stable/j.ctt1nq3vk.

Scott, James C. 2009. *The Art of Not Being Governed: An Anarchist History of Upland Southeast Asia*. New Haven, CT: Yale University Press. https://www.jstor.org/stable/j.ctt1njkkx.

Scott, Steffanie. 2000. "Changing Rules of the Game: Local Responses to De-collectivisation in Thai Nguyen, Vietnam." *Asia Pacific Viewpoint* 4, no. 1: 69–84. https://doi.org/10.1111/1467-8373.00107.

Scudder, Thayer. 2005. *The Future of Large Dams: Dealing with Social, Environmental, Institutional and Political Costs*. London: Earthscan. https://www.routledge.com/The-Future-of-Large-Dams-Dealing-with-Social-Environmental-Institutional/Scudder/p/book/9781844073382#.

Siciliano, Giuseppina, and Frauke Urban. 2017. "Equity-Based Natural Resource Allocation for Infrastructure Development: Evidence from Larger Hydropower Dams in Africa and Asia." *Ecological Economics* 134:130–39. https://doi.org/10.1016/j.ecolecon.2016.12.034.

Sikor, Thomas. 2011. "Land Allocation in Vietnamese Uplands: Negotiating Property and Authority." In *Upland Transformation in Vietnam*, edited by Thomas Sikor, Nghiem Phuong Tuyen, Jennifer Sowerwine, and Jeff Romm, 146–62. Singapore: National University of Singapore Press. https://www.jstor.org/stable/j.ctv1ntj0w.

Sikor, Thomas. 2012. "Tree Plantations, Politics of Possession and the Absence of Land Grabs in Vietnam." *Journal of Peasant Studies* 39, no. 3–4: 1077–1101. https://doi.org/10.1080/03066150.2012.674943.

Silberschmidt, Margrethe. 2001. "Disempowerment of Men in Rural and Urban East Africa: Implications for Male Identity and Sexual Behavior." *World Development* 29, no. 4: 657–71. https://doi.org/10.1016/S0305-750X(00)00122-4.

Sivaramakrishnan, K. 1999. *Modern Forests: Statemaking and Environmental Change in Colonial Eastern India*. Stanford, CA: Stanford University Press. https://www.sup.org/books/title/?id=424.

Smith, Dorothy. 1987. *The Everyday World as Problematic: A Feminist Sociology*. Ontario: University of Toronto Press.

Smith, Neil. 1991. *Uneven Development: Nature, Capitalism and the Production of Space*. Oxford: Blackwell.

Sneddon, Christopher. 2015. *Concrete Revolution: Large Dams, Cold War Geopolitics, and the US Bureau of Reclamation*. Chicago: University of Chicago Press. https://press.uchicago.edu/ucp/books/book/chicago/C/bo21028342.html.

Sở Công Thương Yên Bái (Sctyenbai). 2012. "Tình hình khai thác chế biến quặng sắt trên địa bàn tỉnh Yên Bái" [The situation of iron ore extracting and processing in Yên Bái Province]. Sở Công Thương Yên Bái, September 10. http://sctyenbai.gov.vn/vi/content/news/tinh-hinh-hoat-dong-khai-thac-che-bien-quang-sat-tren-dia-ban-tinh-yen-bai.

Sở Kế Hoạch và Đầu Tư Yên Bái. 2019. "Phụ lục số 1 kèm theo văn bản số 2091/SKHĐT-ĐTTĐ ngày 25/9/2019" [Annex no. 1 of the document number 2091/SKHĐT-ĐTTĐ dated September 25, 2019].

Socialist Republic of Vietnam. 1991. "Luật phổ cập giáo dục tiểu học" [Law on universal education in primary education]. https://luatvietnam.vn/linh-vuc-khac/luat-56-lct-hdnn8-quoc-hoi-2178-d1.html.

Socialist Republic of Vietnam. 1999. "Chính sách bảo vệ quyền lợi của người dân ở các khu vực khai thác và chế biến khoáng sản và bảo vệ các nguồn tài nguyên khoáng sản chưa khai thác" [Policy for the protection of the rights of people in localities where minerals are exploited and processed and the protection of untapped mineral resources]. Decision 219/1999/QD-TTg. Hanoi: Office of the Prime Minister.

Socialist Republic of Vietnam. 2008. "Nghị Quyết số 30a/2008/NQ-CP về chương trình hỗ trợ giảm nghèo nhanh và bền vững đối với 61 huyện nghèo" [Resolution 30a/2008/NQ-CP on a program to support rapid and sustainable poverty reduction for 61 poor districts]. https://thuvi enphapluat.vn/van-ban/Van-hoa-Xa-hoi/Quyet-dinh-09-2011-QD-TTg-chuan-ho-ngheo-can-ngheo-118397.aspx.

Socialist Republic of Vietnam. 2010. Luật khoáng sản [Mineral law]. 60/2010/QH12. Hanoi: National Assembly.

Socialist Republic of Vietnam. 2011a. Chiến lược khai thác khoáng sản đến năm 2020–2030 [Mineral resources strategy to 2020–2030]. Decision 2427/2011/QD-TTg. Hanoi: Office of the Prime Minister.

Socialist Republic of Vietnam. 2011b. "Thủ tướng Chính phủ Quyết định số 09/2011/QD-TTg về việc ban hành chuẩn hộ nghèo, hộ cận nghèo áp dụng cho giai đoạn 2011–2015" [Prime minister's Decision No. 09/2011/QD-TTg on issuing evaluation criteria standards for poor and near poor households applying for the period of 2011–2015]. https://thuvienphap luat.vn/van-ban/Van-hoa-Xa-hoi/Quyet-dinh-09-2011-QD-TTg-chuan-ho-ngheo-can-ngheo-118397.aspx. January 30.

Socialist Republic of Vietnam. 2013a. Hiến pháp nước công hoà xã hội chủ nghĩa Việt Nam [The Constitution of the Socialist Republic of Vietnam]. Hanoi: Socialist Republic of Vietnam. https://vbpl.vn/TW/Pages/vbpq-van-ban-goc.aspx?ItemID=32801.

Socialist Republic of Vietnam. 2013b. "Quyết định số 899/QD-TTg của Thủ tướng chính phủ: Phê duyệt Đề án tái cơ cấu ngành nông nghiệp theo hướng nâng cao giá trị gia tăng và phát triển bền vững, ngày 10 tháng 6 năm 2013." [The prime minister's Decision 899/QD-TTgv (June 10, 2013) on the restructuring of the agricultural sector]. Hanoi: Socialist Republic of Vietnam.

Socialist Republic of Vietnam. 2018. "Luật Khoáng sản điều chỉnh 2018" [Adjusted mineral law 2018]. Thuvienphapluat. https://thuvienphap luat.vn/van-ban/Tai-nguyen-Moi-truong/Van-ban-hop-nhat-20-VBHN-VPQH-2018-Luat-Khoang-san-410276.aspx.

Sơn La Province People's Committee. 2006. Tổng hợp chính sách tái định cư áp dụng cho dự án thuỷ điện Sơn La [Compiling of policies on resettlement for the Sơn La hydropower project]. Sơn La: Sơn La Province People's Committee.

Sơn La Province People's Committee. 2011. Ban chỉ đạo cây cao su. Một số tài liệu chính sách định hướng và hướng dẫn chương trình phast triển cây cao su của tỉnh Sơn La [Sơn La's rubber development steering committee. Some policy documents on directing and guiding on rubber development program in Sơn La Province (from 2009–2011)]. Sơn La: Sơn La Province People's Committee.

Sơn La Rubber Company. 2012. *Công ty cổ phần Cao su Sơn La, báo cáo cuối năm 2012* [Sơn La rubber joint-stock company year-end report 2012]. Sơn La: Sơn La Rubber Company.

Sowerwine, Jennifer C. 2004a. "The Political Ecology of Yao (Dzao) Landscape Transformations: Territory, Gender and Livelihood Politics in Highland Vietnam." PhD diss., University of California, Berkeley.

Sowerwine, Jennifer C. 2004b. "Territorialisation and the Politics of Highland Landscapes in Vietnam: Negotiating Property Relations in Policy, Meaning and Practice." *Conservation and Society* 2, no. 1: 97–136. http://www. conservationandsociety.org/article.asp?issn=0972-4923;year=2004;volume=2;issue=1;spage=97;epage=136;aulast=Sowerwine.

Sputnik Vietnam. 2022. "Việt Nam đang sở hữu nhiều mỏ khoáng sản trữ lượng tầm cỡ thế giới" [Vietnam owns many world-class mineral reserves]. Sputnik Vietnam, February 26. https://vn.sputniknews.com/20220226/ viet-nam-dang-so-huu-nhieu-mo-khoang-san-tru-luong-tam-co-the-gioi-13925346.html.

Sturgeon, Janet C. 2012. "The Cultural Politics of Ethnic Identity in Xishuangbanna, China: Tea and Rubber as 'Cash Crops' and 'Commodities.'" *Journal of Current Chinese Affairs* 41, no 4: 109–131. https://doi. org/10.1177/186810261204100404.

Sturgeon, Janet C. 2013. "Cross-Border Rubber Cultivation between China and Laos: Regionalization by Akha and Tai Rubber Farmers." *Singapore Journal of Tropical Geography* 34, no. 1: 70–85. https://doi.org/10.1111/ sjtg.12014.

Tài Nguyên and Môi Trường. 2018. "Lai Châu cho thuê trên 15.4 hecatres để xây dựng nhà máy chế biến mủ cao su" [Lai Chau leases over 15.4 hectares to build a rubber latex processing factory]. Báo tài nguyên môi trường, August 31. https://baotainguyenmoitruong.vn/lai-chau-cho-thue-tren-15-4ha-de-xay-dung-nha-may-che-bien-mu-cao-su-230803.html.

Taylor, Philip. 2007. "Poor Policies, Wealthy Peasants: Alternative Trajectories of Rural Development in Vietnam." *Journal of Vietnamese Studies* 2, no. 2: 3–56. https://doi.org/10.1525/vs.2007.2.2.3.

Thai, Sinh. 2020. "Công ty Tân Tiến coi trời bằng vung" [Tan Tien company ignores the rules]. Nongnghiep, April 13. https://nongnghiep.vn/cong-ty-tan-tien-coi-troi-bang-vung-d262292.html.

Thanh, Nga. 2020. "'Yên Bái' xử phạt công ty Tân Tiến 235 triệu đồng về lĩnh vực môi trường" [Yên Bái fined Tan Tien company 235 million VND for causing environmental problems]. Báo tài nguyên môi trường, April 8. https://baotainguyenmoitruong.vn/yen-bai-xu-phat-cong-ty-tan-tien-235-trieu-dong-ve-linh-vuc-moi-truong-302652.html.

The, Hai. 2019. "Loai hon 470 du an thuy dien nho khoi quy hoach" [Removing more than 470 small hydropower projects from the hydropower planning]. Báo Đầu tư, November 5. https://baodautu.vn/loai-hon-470-du-an-thuy-dien-nho-khoi-quy-hoach-d110348.html.

Thinh Tam Commune. 2018. *Báo cáo kinh tế xã hội 2018* [Thinh Tam Commune's socioeconomic report 2018]. Yên Bái: Thinh Tam Commune.

Thongchai, Winichakul. 1997. *Siam Mapped: A History of the Geo-body of a Nation.* Honolulu: University of Hawai'i Press. https://uhpress.hawaii.edu/title/siam-mapped-a-history-of-the-geo-body-of-a-nation/.

Trần Đức Viên. 2008. *"Phát triển bền vững ngành cao su Việt Nam trong việc hội nhập kinh tế thế giới"* [Sustainable development of Vietnam rubber sector in the integration of international economy]. Hanoi: Hanoi Agricultural University.

Tran Hai. 2016. "Một vài nét tổng quan về ngành công nghiệp khai khoáng Việt Nam" [Overview of the mining industry in Vietnam]. Open Development Vietnam, January 14. https://vietnam.opendevelopmentmekong.net/vi/topics/tieng-viet-mot-vai-net-tong-quan-ve-nganh-cong-nghiep-khai-khoang-viet-nam/.

Tran Huong. 2021. "Phát huy tiềm năng thế mạnh khoáng sản vùng Tây Bắc: Khoáng sản—trụ cột kinh tế của các tỉnh Tây Bắc" [Promoting the potential of mineral extraction in the Northwest: Mineral—the economic pillar of the northwestern provinces]. Báo tài nguyên môi trường, December 30. https://baotainguyenmoitruong.vn/phat-huy-tiem-nang-the-manh-khoang-san-vung-tay-bac-khoang-san-tru-cot-kinh-te-cua-cac-tinh-tay-bac-335453.html.

Tran Van Ha. 2011. "Local People's Participation in Involuntary Resettlement in Vietnam: A Case Study of the Sơn La Hydropower Project." In *Water Rights and Social Justice in the Mekong Region*, edited by Kate Lazarus, Bernadette P. Resurrección, Nga Dao, and Nathan Badenoch, 39–64. London: Earthscan. https://www.routledge.com/Water-Rights-and-Social-Justice-in-the-Mekong-Region/Lazarus-Resurreccion-Dao-Badenoch/p/book/9781138579064#.

Trang, Hieu Dung. 1995. *Cơ sở khoa học cho việc ổn định và phục hồi sinh kế cho người dân tái định cư: Nghiên cứu đề tài cấp Bộ* [Scientific basis for stabilizing and rehabilitating for resettlers: Scientific research at ministerial level]. Hanoi: Ministry of Agriculture and Rural Development.

Trung tâm Lưu trữ Quốc gia Việt Nam IIII [National Archives of Vietnam Center 3], Hanoi. 1958a. *Báo cáo thành tích 3 năm khôi phục kinh tế xây dựng khu Tự Trị nhân kỷ niệm 3 năm thành lập khu Tự Trị Thái Mèo và chiến thắng Điện Biên Phủ (Tháng 4/1958).* [Report on achievements of 3 years of economic recovery and construction of the Autonomous Region on the occasion of the 3rd anniversary of the establishment of the Thái Mèo Autonomous Region and the Dien Bien Phu victory (April 1958)].

Trung tâm Lưu trữ quốc gia Việt Nam III [National Archives of Vietnam Center 3], Hanoi. 1958b. Cục Nông trường Quân đội: *"Báo cáo tình hình đất đai Điện Biên"* [Report on land situation in Điện Biên].

Trung tâm Lưu trữ quốc gia Việt Nam III [National Archives of Vietnam Center 3], Hanoi. 1958c. Cục Nông trường Quân đội: *"Nông trường quân đội Điện Biên Phủ"* [Điện Biên Phủ army state farm].

Trung tâm Lưu trữ quốc gia Việt Nam III [National Archives of Vietnam Center 3], Hanoi. 1958d. Hồ sơ 103. Bộ Nông Trường, "Dự thảo báo cáo tổng kết 3 năm chuyển quân ra sản xuất" [Điện Biên state farm three-year report].

Trung tâm Lưu trữ Quốc gia Việt Nam III [National Archives of Vietnam Center 3], Hanoi. 1959. Võ Nguyên Giáp, "Bài nói chuyện trong chuyến thăm Tây Bắc 7/5/1959" [Speech on the trip to the Northwest in 1959].

Truong, Giang. 2010. "2009—Năm thiệt hại lớn nhất do bão lũ" [2009—the year with the biggest loss due to typhoons and floods]. Nongnghiep, January 3. https://nongnghiep.vn/2009---nam-thiet-hai-lon-nhat-do-bao-lu-d44483.html.

Tu La District People's Committee. 2009. *Báo cáo phát triển kinh tế xã hội 9 tháng đầu năm năm 2009 và báo cáo về các nhiệm vụ chính còn lại trong 3 tháng cuối năm* [Socioeconomic development report, the first nine months of 2009 and report of main tasks of the final three months of 2009]. Tu La, Sơn La: Tu La District People's Committee.

Tuoitrenews. 2011. "30% Environmental Reports Plagiarized: Official." Tuoitrenews, n.d. http://www.tuoitrenews.vn/cmlink/tuoitrenews/society/30-environmental-reports-plagiarized-official-1.50385.

Turner, Sarah. 2012. "Making a Living the Hmong Way: An Actor-Oriented Livelihoods Approach to Everyday Politics and Resistance in Upland Vietnam." *Annals of the Association of American Geographers* 102, no. 2: 403–22. https://doi.org/10.1080/00045608.2011.596392.

Turner, Sarah, ed. 2013. *Red Stamps and Gold Stars: Fieldwork Dilemmas in Upland Socialist Asia.* Vancouver: University of British Columbia Press. https://www.ubcpress.ca/red-stamps-and-gold-stars.

Turner, Sarah, Christine Bonnin, and Jean Michaud. 2015. *Frontier Livelihoods: Hmong in the Sino-Vietnamese Borderlands.* Seattle: University of Washington Press. https://uwapress.uw.edu/book/9780295994666/frontier-livelihoods/.

Turner, Sarah, and Jean Michaud. 2009. "'Weapons of the Week': Selective Resistance and Agency among the Hmong in Northern Vietnam." In *Agrarian Angst and Rural Resistance in Contemporary Southeast Asia*, edited by Dominique Caouette and Sarah Turner, 45–60. London: Routledge. https://www.routledge.com/Agrarian-Angst-and-Rural-Resistance-in-Contemporary-Southeast-Asia/Caouette-Turner/p/book/9780415681957#.

Turner, Sarah, Thi-Thanh-Hien Pham, and Ngô Thúy Hanh. 2020. "The Territorialization of Vietnam's Northern Upland Frontier: Migrant Motivations and Misgivings from World War II until Today." *Migration and Society: Advances in Research* 3, no. 1: 162–79. https://doi.org/10.3167/arms.2020.030113.

Tuyengiao. 2012. "Khánh thành công trình thuỷ điện Sơn La" [Inauguration of the Sơn La hydropower plant]. Tuyengiao, December 23. https://tuyengiao.vn/thoi-su/khanh-thanh-cong-trinh-thuy-dien-son-la-49003.

Ty Ba District Government. 2020. "Báo cáo số 373/BC-UBND trình tỉnh Lào Cai về việc chậm trễ của Chi nhánh mỏ đồng Sin Quyền trong xây dựng phương án bồi thường di chuyển cho người dân bị ảnh hưởng." [Document No. 373/BC-UBND to report to the province about the delay of Sin Quyen copper mine branch in having moving Văncompensation plan in place for affected people]. Ty Ba District Government, Lào Cai Province.

UN News. 2018. "'Alarming Levels' of Methamphetamine Trafficking in Asia's Mekong, UN Warns." *UN News*, May 21. https://news.un.org/en/story/2018/05/1010262.

United Nations Development Program. 2015. *Terms of Reference: Rights of Local People in Mining Areas Identified in Legal Documents*. Hanoi: United Nations Development Program.

Valentine, Gill. 2007. "Theorizing and Researching Inter-sectionality: A Challenge for Feminist Geography." *Professional Geographer* 59, no. 1: 10–21.

Valladares, Carolina, and Rutgerd Boelens. 2017. "Extractivism and the Rights of Nature: Governmentality, 'Convenient Communities' and Epistemic Pacts in Ecuador." *Environmental Politics* 26, no. 6: 1015–34. https://doi.org/10.1080/09644016.2017.1338384.

Valladares, Carolina, and Rutgerd Boelens. 2019. "Mining for Mother Earth. Governmentalities, Scared Water and Nature's Rights in Ecuador." *Geoforum* 100:68–79. https://doi.org/10.1016/j.geoforum.2019.02.009.

van der Ploeg, Jan Douwe. 2009. *The New Peasantries: Struggles for Autonomy and Sustainability in an Era of Empire and Globalization*. London: Earthscan. https://doi.org/10.4324/9781849773164.

Vandergeest, Peter, and Nancy Lee Peluso. 1995. "Territorialization and State Power in Thailand." *Theory and Society* 24, no. 3: 385–426. https://www.jstor.org/stable/658074.

Van, Nam. 2010. "Chấn chỉnh việc phát triển thủy điện" [Rectifying hydropower development]. *Saigon Times*, April 29. https://thesaigontimes.vn/chan-chinh-viec-phat-trien-thuy-dien/.

VBPL. 2002. "Nghị quyết về phương án xây dựng công trình thuỷ điện Sơn La" [Resolution regarding the construction plan for the Sơn La hydropower project]. Cơ sở dữ liệu quốc gia về văn bản pháp luật trung ương, December 16. https://vbpl.vn/TW/Pages/vbpq-toanvan.aspx?ItemID=24954.

Viện Dân tộc học. 1978. *Các dân tộc ít người ở Việt Nam (Các tỉnh phía Bắc)* [Ethnic minorities in Vietnam (Northern Provinces)]. Hanoi: Social Science Publisher.

Vietcombank Security. 2020. *Báo cáo ngành cao su* [A report on the rubber sector]. Hanoi: Vietcombank Security. http://images1.cafef.vn/Images/Uploaded/DuLieuDownload/PhanTichBaoCao/Nganhcaosu_060120_VCBS.pdf.

Vietgiaitri. 2009. "Hàng trăm người tranh nhau 'cướp' gỗ từ 'miệng Hà Bá'" [Hundreds of people fighting to get lumber from flood]. Vietgiaitri, October 5. http://www.vietgiaitri.com/xa-hoi/2009/10/hang-tram-nguoi-tranh-nhau-cuop-go-tu-mieng-ha-ba/.

Vietnam Chamber of Commerce and Industry, and Consultancy on Development (VVCI-CODE). 2011. *The Extractive Industries Transparency Initiative and the Implementation Perspective of Vietnam*. Hanoi: Vietnam Chamber of Commerce and Industry, and Consultancy on Development.

Vietnam Institute of Energy. 2006. *Quy hoạch tổng thể ngành điện IV* [Master plan VI on power development of Vietnam]. Hanoi: Vietnam Institute of Energy.

Vietnamnet. 2016. "Toàn văn Quy hoạch điện VII điều chỉnh" [Adjusted power development plan VII]. Vietnamnet, March 18. https://vietnamnet.vn/toan-van-quy-hoach-dien-vii-dieu-chinh-683795.html.

Vietnam Rubber Group. 2022. "Khúc tráng ca cao su Tây Bắc (Bài 2): Cuộc cách mạng ở cuối trời Lai Châu" [Northwest Rubber epic song (part 20): The revolution in Lai Chau]. https://vnrubbergroup.com/tin-tuc/Khuc-trang-ca-cao-su-Tay-Bac-Bai-2-Cuoc-cach-mang-o-cuoi-troi-Lai-Chau.

Vimico. 2017. "Vimico lịch sử hình thành và phát triển" [Vimico—history of its establishment and development]. http://vimico.vn/lich-su-hinh-thanh-va-phat-trien/.

Vimico. 2020. "Chi nhánh mỏ tuyển đồng Sin Quyền: Sản lượng khai thác và tuyển quặng" [Sin Quyen copper mine branch: Mining output and ore smelting]. https://vimico.vn/chi-nhanh-mo-tuyen-dong-sin-quyen-san-luong-khai-thac-va-tuyen-quang-tang/.

Vinacomin. 2013. "Định hướng khai thác khoáng sản Việt Nam" [Orientation for mineral extraction in Vietnam]. Vinacomin, May 14. https://vinaco-min.vn/vi/news/slug/Dinh-huong-khai-thac-khoang-san-Viet-Nam.

Vinacomin. 2016. "Quyết định số 2356-TKV ngày 15/6/2016" [Decision No. 2356-TKV dated June 15, 2016]. Hanoi.

Võ, Văn Hồng. 2006. "Nghiên cứu hiện trạng môi trường xa hội khu tái định cư công trinh thuỷ điện Bản Vẽ, Nghệ An" [Study on the environmental and social situation at resettled areas of Bản Vẽ hydropower project, Nghệ An]. Paper presented at the Vietnam River Network's annual meeting, Hanoi, December 5.

VOV Tay Bac. 2019. "10 năm trồng cao su ở Sơn La: Gỡ nút thắt cho dân bằng cách nào?" [Ten years of rubber growing in Sơn La: How to remove bottlenecks for the people?]. VOV Tay Bac, May 10. https://vov.vn/kinh-te/10-nam-trong-cao-su-o-son-la-go-nut-that-cho-dan-bang-cach-nao-907627.vov.

Văn phòng Chính phủ. 2018. "Bố trí 3600 tỷ đồng cho tái định cư thuỷ điện Sơn La" [Allocating 3,600 billion VND for Sơn La Dam induced resettlement]. Văn phòng Chính phủ, November 7. http://vpcp.chinhphu.vn/Home/Bo-tri-3600-ty-dong-cho-tai-dinh-cu-thuy-dien-Son-La-Tuyen-Quang/201811/24981.vgp.

Vuong, Canh, and Tran Hieu. 2018. "Lai Châu: 10 năm nỗ lực phủ xanh rừng cao su" [Lai Chau: 10 years of hard effort to green by rubber trees]. VRA, December 2. https://www.vra.com.vn/tin-tuc/tin-cao-su-ngoai-nuoc/tinh-lai-chau-10-nam-no-luc-phu-xanh-rung-cao-su.10450.html.

VUSTA (Vietnam Union of Science and Technology Associations). 2006. *Nghiên cứu tác động của dự án thuỷ điện Sơn La* [A work in progress: Study on the impacts of Vietnam's Sơn La hydropower project]. Hanoi: Vietnam Union of Science and Technology Associations. https://archive.interna

tionalrivers.org/th/resources/a-work-in-progress-study-on-the-impacts-of-vietnam's-son-la-hydropower-project-2607.

VVCI-CODE (Vietnam Chamber of Commerce and Industry, and Consultancy on Development). 2011. *The Extractive Industries Transparency Initiative and the Implementation Perspective of Vietnam*. Hanoi: Vietnam Chamber of Commerce and Industry and Consultancy on Development.

Watts, Michael J. 2003. "Development and Governmentality." *Singapore Journal of Tropical Geography* 24, no. 1: 6–34. https://doi.org/10.1111/1467-9493.00140.

Watts, Michael J. 2013. *Silent Violence: Food, Famine, and Peasantry in Northern Nigeria*. Athens: University of Georgia Press. https://ugapress.org/book/9780820344454/silent-violence/.

White, Benjamin. 1989. "Problems in the Empirical Analysis of Agrarian Differentiation." In *Agrarian Transformations: Local Processes and the State in Southeast Asia*, edited by Gillian Hart, Andrew Turton, and Benjamin White, 15–30. Berkeley: University of California Press.

White, Benjamin, Saturnino M. Borras Jr., Ruth Hall, Ian Scoones, and Wendy Wolford. 2012. "The New Enclosures: Critical Perspectives on Corporate Land Deals." *Journal of Peasant Studies* 39, no. 3–4: 619–47. https://doi.org/10.1080/03066150.2012.691879.

White, Julia, and Benjamin White. 2012. "Gendered Experiences of Dispossession: Oil Palm Expansion in a Dayak Hibun Community in West Kalimantan." *Journal of Peasant Studies* 39, no. 3–4: 995–1016. https://doi.org/10.1080/03066150.2012.676544.

Wolford, Wendy, Saturnino M. Borras Jr., Ruth Hall, Ian Scoones, and Benjamin White. 2013. "Governing Global Land Deals: The Role of the State in the Rush for Land." *Development and Change* 44, no. 2: 189–210. https://doi.org/10.1111/dech.12017.

World Commission on Dams (WCD). 2000. *Dams and Development: A New Framework for Decision Making*. London: Earthscan. https://archive.internationalrivers.org/resources/dams-and-development-a-new-framework-for-decision-making-3939.

Yeh, Emily. 2013. *Taming Tibet: Landscape Transformation and the Gift of Chinese Development*. Ithaca, NY: Cornell University Press. https://www.jstor.org/stable/10.7591/j.ctt32b5wn.

Yen Bai Portal. 2019. "Khẩn trương khắc phục ảnh hưởng tới môi trường, nguồn nước Ngòi Lâu" [Urgently deal with impacts on the environment and Ngoi Lau stream]. http://www.yenbai.gov.vn/noidung/tintuc/Pages/chi-tiet-tin-tuc.aspx?ItemID=20667&l=Tintrongtinh&lv=5.

Yên Bái Province People's Committee. 2006. "Quyết định số 82/QĐ-UBND ngày 2/3/2006 về việc khoanh vùng và quy hoạch các hoạt động khai khoáng tỉnh Yên Bái giai đoạn 2006–2010, định hướng đến năm 2030" [Decision No. 82/QD-UBND dated March 2, 2017, on zoning and planning of mineral activities in Yên Bái for the period of 2006–2010]. Yên Bái: Yên Bái Province People's Committee.

Yên Bái Province People's Committee. 2008. "Quyết định số 352/QĐ-UBND ngày 7/4/2008 về việc quy hoạch thăm dò, khai thác, chế biến, sử dụng khoáng sản vật liệu xây dựng thông thường và than bùn từ năm 2007–2015 tỉnh Yên Bái giai đoạn 2016–2020, định hướng đến năm 2030" [Decision No. 352/QD-UBND dated April 7, 2008, on planning for exploration, mining, processing, and use of minerals as common construction materials and peat in Yên Bái from 2007 to 2015]. Yên Bái: Yên Bái Province People's Committee.

Yên Bái Province People's Committee. 2011. "Quyết định số 1457/QĐ-UBND ngày 30/0/2011 về việc quy hoạch thăm dò, khai thác, chế biến và sử dụng khoáng sản sắt, đồng, vàng, chì-kẽm và các hoáng sản khác (trừ khoáng sản dùng vật liệu xây dựng thông thường và than bùn) tỉnh Yên Bái giai đoạn 2016–2020, định hướng đến năm 2030" [Decision No. 1459/QD-UBND dated September 30, 2011, on planning for exploration, mining, processing, and use of iron, copper, gold, lead-zinc, and other minerals (except minerals used as common construction materials and peat)]. Yên Bái: Yên Bái Province People's Committee.

Yên Bái Province People's Committee. 2017. "Quyết định số 3520/QĐ-UBND ngày 29/12/2017 về việc phê duyệt quy hoạch thăm dò, khai thác, sử dụng khoáng sản tỉnh Yên Bái giai đoạn 2016–2020, định hướng đến năm 2030" [Decision No. 3520/QD-UBND dated December 29, 2017, on the approval of the planning for exploration, mining and use of minerals in Yen Bai Province period 2016–2022 with a vision to 2030]. Yên Bái: Yên Bái Province People's Committee.

Yên Bái Province People's Committee. 2020. "Quyết định số 573/QĐ-XPVPHC ngày 26/3/2020 về việc xử phạt công ty Tân Tiến vi phạm hành chính về lĩnh vực bảo vệ môi trường" [Decision No. 573/QD-XPVPHC dated March 26, 2020, about penalizing Tan Tien company for violating environmental protection regulations]. Yên Bái: Yên Bái Province People's Committee.

Zhang, Q. Forrest, and John A. Donaldson. 2010. "From Peasants to Farmers: Peasant Differentiation, Labor Regimes, and Land-Rights Institutions in China's Agrarian Transition." *Politics & Society* 38, no. 4: 458–89. https://doi.org/10.1177/0032329210381236.

Zoomers, Annelies. 1999. *Linking Livelihood Strategies to Development: Experiences from the Bolivian Andes*. Amsterdam: Royal Tropical Institute / Center for Latin American Research.

Zoomers, Annelies. 2010. "Globalisation and the Foreignisation of Space: Seven Processes Driving the Current Global Land Grab." *Journal of Peasant Studies* 37, no. 2: 429–47. https://doi.org/10.1080/03066151003595325.

# INDEX